The Philosophical Computer

The Philosophical Computer

Exploratory Essays in Philosophical Computer Modeling

Patrick Grim, Gary Mar, and Paul St. Denis
with the Group for Logic and Formal Semantics

A Bradford Book
The MIT Press
Cambridge, Massachusetts
London, England

Set in Palatino by Techset Composition Ltd, Salisbury, England.
Printed and bound in the United States of America.

Library of Congress Cataloging-in-Publication Data

Grim, Patrick.
  The philosophical computer : exploratory essays in philosophical
  computer modeling / Patrick Grim, Gary Mar, and Paul St. Denis, with
  the Group for Logic and Formal Semantics.
      p.   cm.
  "A Bradford book."
  Includes bibliographical references (p.   ) and index.
  ISBN 0-262-07185-1 (hc : alk. paper)
  1. Philosophy—Computer simulation. 2. Logic—Computer
simulation. 3. Philosophy—Data processing. 4. Logic—Data
processing. I. Mar, Gary. II. St. Denis, Paul. III. Title.
B54.G75   1998
101'.13—dc21   97-39498
                                                                    CIP

Contents

Preface

The work that follows was born as a cooperative enterprise within the Logic Lab in the Department of Philosophy at SUNY Stony Brook. The first chapter represents what was historically the first batch of work, developed by Patrick Grim and Gary Mar with the essential programming help of Paul St. Denis. From that point on work has continued collaboratively in almost all cases, though with different primary researchers in different projects and with a constantly changing pool of associated undergraduate and graduate students. At various times and in various ways the work that follows has depended on the energy, skills, and ideas of Matt Neiger, Tobias Müller, Rob Rothenberg, Ali Bukhari, Christine Buffolino, David Gill, and Josh Schwartz. We have thought of ourselves throughout as an informal Group for Logic and Formal Semantics, and the work that follows is most properly thought of as the product of that group. Some of Gary Mar's work has been supported by a grant from the Pew foundation.

Some of the following essays have appeared in earlier and perhaps unrecognizable versions in a scattered variety of journals. The first chapter is a development of work that appeared as Gary Mar and Patrick Grim, "Pattern and Chaos: New Images in the Semantics of Paradox," *Noûs* XXV (1991), 659–695; Patrick Grim, Gary Mar, Matthew Neiger, and Paul St. Denis, "Self-Reference and Paradox in Two and Three Dimensions," *Computers and Graphics* 17 (1993), 609–612; and Patrick Grim, "Self-Reference and Chaos in Fuzzy Logic," *IEEE Transactions on Fuzzy Systems*, 1 (1993), 237–253. A report on parts of this project also appeared as "A Partially True Story" in Ian Stewart's Mathematical Recreations column for the February 1993 issue of *Scientific American*. A version of chapter 3 was published as Paul St. Denis and Patrick Grim, "Fractal Images of Formal Systems," *Journal of Philosophical Logic*, 26 (1997) 181–222. Chapter 4 includes work first outlined in Patrick Grim, "The Greater Generosity of the Spatialized Prisoner's Dilemma," *Journal of Theoretical Biology* 173 (1995), 353–359, and "Spatialization and Greater Generosity in the Stochastic Prisoner's Dilemma," *BioSystems* 37 (1996), 3–17. Chapter 5 incorporates material which appeared as Gary Mar and Paul St. Denis, "Chaos in Cooperation: Continuous-valued Prisoner's Dilemmas in

Infinite-valued Logic," *International Journal of Bifurcation and Chaos* 4 (1994), 943–958, and "Real Life," *International Journal of Bifurcation and Chaos*, 6 (1996), 2077–2086. An earlier version of some of the work of chapter 6 appeared as Patrick Grim, "The Undecidability of the Spatialized Prisoner's Dilemma," *Theory and Decision*, 42 (1997) 53–80. Earlier and partial drafts have occasionally been distributed as grey-covered research reports from the Group for Logic and Formal Semantics.

The Philosophical Computer

Introduction

The strategies for making mathematical models for observed phenomena have been evolving since ancient times. An organism—physical, biological, or social—is observed in different states. This observed system is the target of the modeling activity. Its states cannot really be described by only a few observable parameters, but we pretend that they can.

—Ralph Abraham and Christopher Shaw, *Dynamics: The Geometry of Behavior*[1]

Computers are useless. They can only give you answers.
—Pablo Picasso[2]

This book is an introduction, entirely by example, to the possibilities of using computer models as tools in philosophical research in general and in philosophical logic in particular. The accompanying software contains a variety of working examples, in color and often operating dynamically, embedded in a text which parallels that of the book. In order to facilitate further experimentation and further research, we have also included all basic source code in the software.

A picture is worth a thousand words, and what computer modeling might mean in philosophical research is best illustrated by example. We begin with an intuitive introduction to three very simple models. More sophisticated versions and richer variations are presented with greater philosophical care in the chapters that follow.

I.1 GRAPHING THE DYNAMICS OF PARADOX

I made a practice of wandering about the common every night from eleven till one, by which means I came to know the three different noises made by nightjars. (Most people only know one.) I was trying hard to solve the contradictions [of the set-theoretical paradoxes]. Every morning I would sit down before a blank sheet of paper. Throughout the day, with a brief interval for lunch, I would stare at the blank sheet. Often when evening came it was still empty.... It was clear to me that I could not get on without solving the contradictions, and I was determined that no difficulty should turn me aside from the completion of Principia

Mathematica, but it seemed quite likely that the whole of the rest of my life might be consumed in looking at that blank sheet of paper. What made it the more annoying was that the contradictions were trivial, and that my time was spent in considering matters that seemed unworthy of serious attention.
—Bertrand Russell, *Autobiography: The Early Years*[3]

Consider the Liar Paradox:

> The boxed sentence is false.

Is that sentence true, or is it false?

Let's start by supposing it is true. What it *says* is that it is false. So if we start by assuming it true, it appears we're forced to change our verdict: it must be false.

Our verdict now, then, is that the boxed sentence is false. But here again we run into the fact that what the sentence *says* is that it is false. If what it *says* is that it is false and it *is* false, it appears it must be true.

We're back again to supposing that the boxed sentence is true.

This kind of informal thinking about the Liar exhibits a clear and simple dynamics: a supposition of 'true' forces us to 'false', the supposition of 'false' forces us back to 'true', the supposition of 'true' forces us back to 'false', and so forth. We can model that intuitive dynamics very simply in terms of a graph.

As in figure 1, we will let **1** represent 'true' at the top of our graph, and let **0** represent 'false' at the bottom. The stages of our intuitive deliberation— 'now it looks like it's true...but now it looks like it's false...'—will be marked as if in moments of time proceeding from left to right. This kind of graph is known as a *time-series graph*. In this first simple philosophical application, a time series graph allows us to map the dynamic behavior of our intuitive reasoning for the Liar as in figure 2.[4]

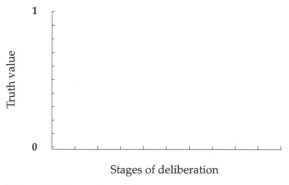

Figure 1 Time-series graph.

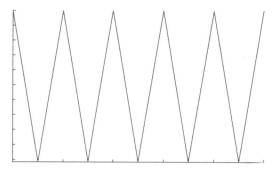

Figure 2 Time-series graph for intuitive reasoning in the Liar Paradox.

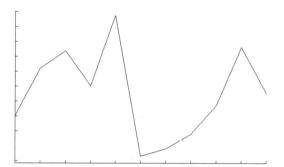

Figure 3 Time-series graph for the Chaotic Liar.

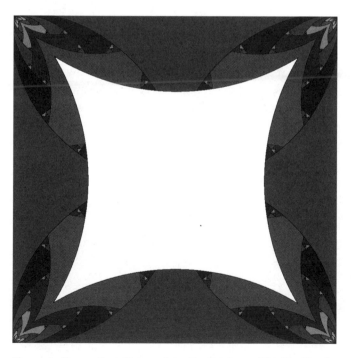

Figure 4 Escape-time diagram for a Dualist form of the Liar Paradox.

This simple model is the basic foundation of some of the work of chapter 1. There such a model is both carried into infinite-valued or fuzzy logics and applied to a wide range of self-referential sentences. One of these—the Chaotic Liar—has the dynamics portrayed in figure 3. The model itself suggests richer elaborations, offering images for mutually referential sentences such as that shown in figure 4. Similar modeling is extended to some intriguing kinds of epistemic instability in chapter 2.

I.2 FORMAL SYSTEMS AND FRACTAL IMAGES

The logician Jan Łukasiewicz speaks of his deepest intuitive feelings for logic in terms of a picture of an independent and unchangeable logical object:

> ...I should like to sketch a picture connected with the deepest intuitive feelings I always get about logistic. This picture perhaps throws more light than any discursive exposition would on the real foundations from which this science grows (at least so far as I am concerned). Whenever I am occupied even with the tiniest logistical problem, e.g. trying to find the shortest axiom of the implicational calculus, I have the impression that I am confronted with a mighty construction, of indescribable complexity and immeasurable rigidity. This construction has the effect upon me of a concrete tangible object, fashioned from the hardest of materials, a hundred times stronger than concrete and steel. I cannot change anything in it; by intense labour I merely find in it ever new details, and attain unshakeable and eternal truths.—Jan Łukasiewicz, 'W obronie Logistyki'[5]

Here we offer another simple model, one we develop further in chapter 3 in an attempt to capture something like a Łukasiewiczian picture of formal systems as a whole.

As any beginning student of formal logic knows, a sentence letter **p** is thought of as having two possible values, true or false:

p

T

F

It is in terms of these that we draw a simple truth table showing corresponding values for 'not **p**': if **p** happens to be true, 'not **p**' must be false; if **p** happens to be false, 'not **p**' must be true:

p ~**p**

T   F

F   T

What we have drawn for **p** and ~**p** are two two-line truth tables. But these are of course not the only two-line combinations possible. We get all four possibilities if we add combinations for tautologies (thought of as always true) and contradictions (thought of as always false):

⊥	**p**	~**p**	⊤
F	T	F	T
F	F	T	T

Now consider the possibility of assigning each of these combinations of truth and falsity a different color, or a contrasting shade of gray:

⊥	**p**	~**p**	⊤
F	T	F	T
F	F	T	T

With these colors for basic value combinations we can paint simple portraits of classical connectives such as conjunction ('and') and disjunction ('or'). Figure 5 is a portrait of conjunction: the value colors on its axes combine in conjunction to give the values at points of intersection. The conjunction of black with black in the upper left corner, for example, gives us black, indicating that the conjunction of two contradictions is a contradiction as well.

Figure 6 is a similar portrait of disjunction. When we put the two images side by side it becomes obvious that they have a certain symmetry: the symmetry standardly captured by speaking of disjunction and conjunction as dual operators.[6] What this offers is a very simple matrix model for logical operators. In chapter 3 we attempt to extend the model so as to depict formal systems as a whole, allowing us also to highlight some surprising formal relationships between quite different formal systems. One result is the appearance of classical fractal patterns within value portraits much like that outlined above. Figure 7 shows the pattern of tautologies in a more complicated value space, here for the operator NAND (or the Sheffer stroke) and for a system with three sentence letters

Figure 5 Value matrix for conjunction.

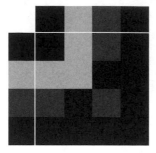

Figure 6 Value matrix for disjunction.

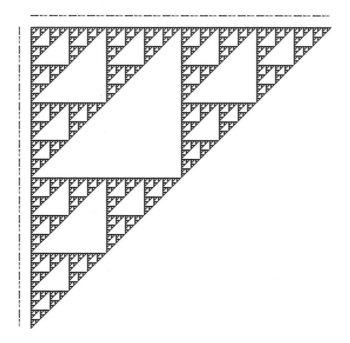

Figure 7 Tautologies in a value space for three sentence letters: the Sierpinski gasket.

and thus 256 possible truth-table columns. The image that appears is familiar within fractal geometry as the Sierpinski gasket.[7]

I.3 CELLULAR AUTOMATA AND THE 'EVOLUTION OF COOPERATION': MODELS IN SOCIAL AND POLITICAL PHILOSOPHY

Imagine a group of people beyond the powers of any government, all of whom are out for themselves alone: an anarchistic society of self-serving egoists. This is what Hobbes imagines as a state of war in which "every man is Enemy to every man" and life as a result is "solitary, poore, nasty, brutish, and short".[8]

How might social cooperation emerge in a society of egoists? This is Hobbes's central question, and one he answers in terms of two "general rules of Reason". Since there can be no security in a state of war, it will be clear to all rational agents "that every man, ought to endeavor peace, as farre as he has hope of obtaining it; and when he cannot obtain it, that he may seek, and use, all helps, and advantages of Warre". From this Hobbes claims to derive a second rational principle: "That a man be willing, when others are so too . . . to lay down this right to all things; and be contented with so much liberty against other men, as he would allow other men against himselfe."[9]

In later chapters we develop some very Hobbesian models of social interaction using game theory within cellular automata (akin to the 'Game of Life').[10] The basic question is the same: How might social cooperation emerge within a society of self-serving egoists? Interestingly, the model-theoretic answers that seem to emerge often echo Hobbes's second principle.

The most studied model of social interaction in game theory is undoubtedly the Prisoner's Dilemma. Here we envisage two players who must simultaneously make a 'move', choosing either to 'cooperate' with the other player or to 'defect' against the other player. What the standard Prisoner's Dilemma matrix dictates is how much each player will gain or lose on a given move, depending on the mutual pattern of cooperation and defection:

		Player A	
		Cooperate	Defect
Player B	Cooperate	3, 3	0, 5
	Defect	5, 0	1, 1

If both players cooperate on a single move, each gets 3 points. If both defect, each gets only 1 point. But if one player defects and the other cooperates, the defector gets a full 5 points and the cooperator gets nothing. Because it favors both mutual cooperation and individual defection, the Prisoner's Dilemma has been widely used to study options for cooperation in an egoistic society. In a model that we use extensively in later chapters, members of a society are envisaged in a spatial array, following particular strategies in repeated Prisoner's Dilemma exchanges with their neighbors. Figure 8, for example, shows a randomized array in which each cell represents a single individual and each color represents one of eight simple strategies for repeated play. Some of these are vicious strategies, in the sense of always defecting against their neighbors. Some are extremely generous, in the sense of cooperating no matter how often they are burned. A strategy of particular interest, called 'Tit for Tat', returns

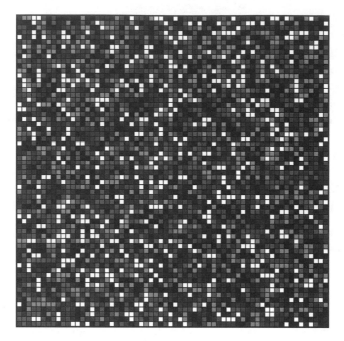

Figure 8 Randomized spatial array of eight Prisoner's Dilemma strategies.

like for like, cooperating with a cooperative partner but defecting against a defector. 'Tit for Tat' carries a clear echo of Hobbes's second 'rule of Reason': "Whatsoever you require that others should do to you, that do ye to them".[11]

Some strategies, in some environments, will be more successful than others in accumulating Prisoner's Dilemma points in games with their neighbors. How will a society evolve if we have cells convert to the strategy of their most successful neighbor? Will defection dominate, for example, or will generosity?

Figure 9 shows a typical evolution in a very simple case, in which Tit for Tat evolves as the standard strategy. In later chapters we explore more complicated variations on such a model, using ranges of more complicated meta-strategies and introducing forms of cooperation and defection that are 'imperfect' both probabilistically and in terms of degrees. An undecidability result for even a very simple Spatialized Prisoner's Dilemma appears in chapter 6.

I.4 PHILOSOPHICAL MODELING: FROM PLATONIC IMAGERY TO COMPUTER GRAPHICS

Here we've started with three simple examples of philosophical modeling—simple so as to start simple, but also representative of some basic kinds of models used in the real work of later chapters.

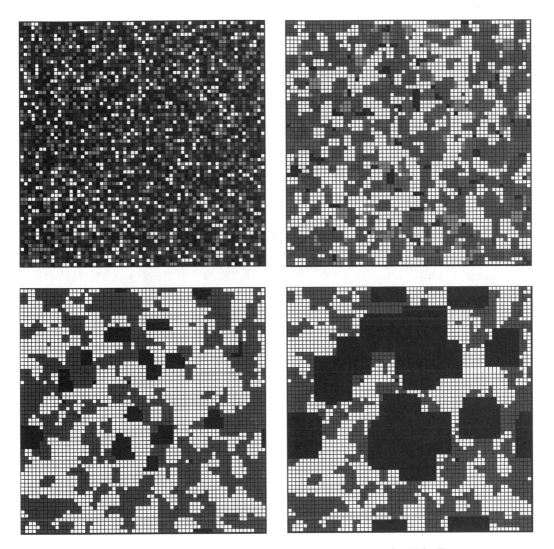

Figure 9 Evolution of randomized array toward dominance by Tit for Tat.

We are in fact heirs to a long tradition of philosophical modeling, extending from Plato's Cave and the Divided Line to models of social contracts and John Rawls's original position. If one is looking for philosophical models, one can find them in Heraclitus's river, in Plato's charioteer model of the tripartite soul, in Aristotle's squares of opposition, in the levels of Dante's *Inferno, Purgatorio,* and *Paradiso,* in Locke's impressions on the mind and in Descartes's captained soul in the sixth meditation. Logic as a whole, in fact, can be looked upon as a tradition of attempts to model patterns of inference. Philosophical modeling is nothing new.

In many cases, philosophical models might be thought of as thought experiments with particularly vivid and sometimes intricate structures. Just as thought experiments are more than expository devices, so models can be. The attempt to build intellectual models can itself enforce requirements of clarity and explicitness, and can make implications clear that might not be clear without an attempt at explicit modeling. The making of models can also suggest new hypotheses or new lines of approach, showing when an approach is unexpectedly fruitful or when it faces unexpected difficulties.

The examples of computer modeling we introduce here are conceived of in precisely this tradition of philosophical model building and thought experiments. All that is new are the astounding computational resources now available for philosophical modeling.

As our subtitle indicates, we conceive of the chapters that follow as *explorations* in philosophical computer modeling. In no case are they intended as the final word on the topics addressed; we hope rather that they offer some suggestive first words that may stimulate others to carry the research further. The topics we address, moreover—paradoxes and fuzzy logic, fractals and simple formal systems, egoism and altruism in game theory and cellular automata—are merely those topics to which our curiosities have happened to lead us. We don't intend them in any sense as a survey of ways in which computer modeling might be used; indeed our hope is that these exploratory essays will stimulate others to explorations of quite different philosophical questions as well.

In each of the following chapters the computer allows us to literally see things the complexity of which would otherwise be beyond our computational reach: fractal images showing the semantic behavior of a wide range of pairs of mutually referential sentences, vivid images of patterns of contradiction and tautology in formal systems, and evolving visual arrays demonstrating a wide social effect of local game-theoretic interactions. Whether these models answer questions which we might not have been able to answer without them is another matter. Often our logical results, such as the formal indefinability of chaos in chapter 1 or the undecidability of the Spatialized Prisoner's Dilemma in chapter 6, were suggested by our computer work but might also conceivably have been proven without it. We don't want to claim, then—at least not yet—that the computer is answering philosophical questions that would be in principle unanswerable without it. In no way do the astounding computational abilities of contemporary machines offer a substitute for philosophical research. But we do think that the computer offers an important new *environment* for philosophical research.

Our experience is that the environment of computer modeling often leads us to ask new questions, or to ask old questions in new ways—questions about chaos within patterns of paradoxical reasoning or epistemic crises, for example, or Hobbesian questions asked within a spatialization of game-theoretic strategies. Such an environment also enforces, unflinchingly and without compromise, the central philosophical desideratum of clarity: one is forced to construct theory in the form of fully explicit models, so detailed and complete that they can be *programmed*.

With the astounding computational resources of contemporary machines, moreover, hidden and unexpected consequences of simple theories can become glaringly obvious: "A computer will do what you tell it to do, but that may be much different from what you had in mind."[12]

Although difficult to characterize, it is also clear from experience that computer modeling offers a possibility for thoroughly conceptual work that is nonetheless undeniably *experimental* in character. Simple theories can be tested in a range of modeled counterfactual 'possible worlds'—Hobbesian models can be tested in worlds with and without perfect information or communication, for example, or with a greater or lesser Rawlsian 'veil of ignorance'. One can also, however, test theoretical variations essentially at will, feeling one's way through experimental manipulation toward a conceptual core: a hypothesis of precisely what it is about a theory that accounts for the appearance of certain results in certain possible worlds.

It must also be admitted with regard to computer modeling—as with regard to philosophical or intellectual modeling in general—that models can fail. All models are built with major limitations—indeed that is the very purpose of models. Models prove useful both in exposition and in exploration precisely *because* they're simpler, and therefore easier to handle and easier to track, than the bewildering richness of the full phenomena under study. But the possibility always remains that one's model captures too few aspects of the full phenomenon, or that it captures accidental rather than essential features. One purpose of labeling ours as *explorations* in computer modeling is to emphasize that they may fail in this way. When and where they fall short, however, it will be *better* models that we will have to strive for.

Computer modeling is new in philosophy and thus may be misunderstood. We should therefore make it clear from the beginning what the book is *not* about. What is at issue here is not merely the use of computers for teaching logic or philosophy. That has its place, and indeed the Logic Lab in which much of this work emerged was established as a computer lab for teaching logic. Here, however, our concentration is entirely on exploratory examples of the use of computer modeling in philosophical research. We will also have little to say that will qualify as philosophy *of* computation or philosophy *about* computers—philosophical discussions of the prospects for modeling intelligence or consciousness, for example, or about how computer technology may affect society. Those too are worthy topics, but they are not our topics here. Our concern is solely with philosophical research in the context of computer modeling.

Our ultimate hope is that others will find an environment of computer modeling as philosophically promising as we have. We offer a handful of sample explorations with operating software and accessible source code in the hope that some of our readers will not only enjoy some of these initial explorations but will find tools useful in carrying the exploration further.

SOME BACKGROUND SOURCES

We attempt throughout the book to make our explanations of the modeling elements we use as simple and self-contained as possible. Some readers, however, may wish for more background information on the elements themselves. For each of the topics listed below we've tried to suggest an easy popular introduction—the first book listed—as well as a more advanced but still accessible text.

Fuzzy and Infinite-Valued Logic

Bart Kosko, *Fuzzy Thinking: The New Science of Fuzzy Logic*, New York: Hyperion, 1993.

Graeme Forbes, *Modern Logic*, New York: Oxford University Press, 1994.

Nicholas Rescher, *Many-Valued Logic*, New York: McGraw-Hill, 1969; Hampshire, England: Gregg Revivals, 1993.

Chaos and Fractals

James Gleick, *Chaos: Making a New Science*, New York: Penguin Books, 1987.

Manfred Schroeder, *Fractals, Chaos, Power Laws: Minutes from an Infinite Paradise*, New York: W. H. Freeman and Co., 1991.

Cellular Automata

William Poundstone, *The Recursive Universe: Cosmic Complexity and the Limits of Scientific Knowledge*, Chicago: Contemporary Books, 1985.

Steven Wolfram, *Cellular Automata and Complexity*, Reading, Mass.: Addison-Wesley, 1994.

Game Theory

William Poundstone, *Prisoner's Dilemma*, New York: Anchor Books, 1992.

Robert Axelrod, *The Evolution of Cooperation*, New York: Basic Books, 1984.

1 Chaos, Fractals, and the Semantics of Paradox

Logicians, it is said, abhor ambiguity but love paradox.
—Barwise and Etchemendy, *The Liar*[1]

Semantic paradox has had a long and distinguished career in philosophical and mathematical logic. In the fourth century B.C., Eubulides used the paradox of the Liar to challenge Aristotle's seemingly unexceptional notion of truth, and this seemed to doom the hope of formulating the laws of logic in full generality.[2] The study of the paradoxes or *insolubilia* continued into the medieval period in work by Paul of Venice, Occam, Buridan, and others.

The Liar lies at the core of Cantor's diagonal argument and the "paradise" of transfinite infinities it gives us. Russell's paradox, discovered in 1901 as a simplification of Cantor's argument, was historically instrumental in motivating axiomatic set theory. Gödel himself notes in his semantic sketch of the undecidability result that "the analogy of this argument with the Richard antinomy leaps to the eye. It is closely related to the 'Liar' too . . .".[3] The limitative theorems of Tarski, Church, and Turing can all be seen as exploiting the reasoning within the Liar.[4] Gödel had explicitly noted that "any epistemological antinomy could be used for a similar proof of the existence of undecidable propositions." In the mid 1960s, by formalizing the Berry paradox, Gregory Chaitin demonstrated that an interpretation of Gödel's theorem in terms of algorithmic randomness appears not pathological but quite naturally in the context of information theory.[5]

In recent years philosophers have repeatedly attempted to find solutions to the semantic paradoxes by seeking patterns of semantic stability. The 1960s and the 1970s saw a proliferation of "truth-value gap solutions" to the Liar, including proposals by Bas van Fraassen, Robert L. Martin, and Saul Kripke.[6] Efforts in the direction of finding patterns of stability within the paradoxes continued with the work of Hans Herzberger and Anil Gupta.[7] More recent work in this tradition includes Jon Barwise and John Etchemendy's *The Liar*, in which Peter Aczel's set theory with an anti-foundation axiom is used to characterize liar-like cycles, and Haim Gaifman's "Pointers to Truth".[8]

In this chapter we take a novel approach to paradox, using computer modeling to explore dynamical patterns of self-reference. These computer models seem to show that the patterns of paradox that have been studied in the past have been deceptively simple, and that paradox in general has appeared far more predictable than it actually is. Within the semantics of self-referential sentences in an infinite-valued logic there appear a wide range of phenomena—including attractor and repeller points, strange attractors, and fractals—that are familiar in a mathematical guise in dynamical semantics or 'chaos' theory. We call the approach that reveals these wilder patterns of paradox *dynamical semantics* because it weds the techniques of dynamical systems theory with those of Tarskian semantics within the context of infinite-valued logic.

Philosophical interest in the concept of chaos is ancient, apparent already in Hesiod's *Theogeny* of the eighth century B.C. Chaos theory in the precise sense at issue here, however, is comparatively recent, dating back only to the work of the great nineteenth-century mathematician Henri Poincaré. The triumph of Newtonian mechanics had inspired Laplace's classic statement of determinism: "Assume an intelligence which at a given moment knows all the forces that animate nature as well as the situations of all the bodies that compose it, and further that it is vast enough to perform a calculation based on these data. . . . For it nothing would be uncertain, and the future, like the past, would be present before its eyes."[9] In 1887, perhaps intrigued by such possibilities, King Oscar II of Sweden offered the equivalent of a Nobel prize for an answer to the question "Is the universe stable?" Two years later, Poincaré was awarded the prize for his celebrated work on the "three-body problem." Poincaré showed that even a system comprising only the sun, the earth, and the moon, and governed simply by Newton's law of gravity, could generate dynamical behavior of such incalculable complexity that prediction would be impossible in any practical sense. Just as Einstein's theory of relativity later eliminated the Newtonian idea of absolute space, Poincaré's discovery of chaos even within the framework of classical Newtonian mechanics seemed to dispel any Laplacian dreams of real deterministic predictability.

We think that the results of dynamical semantics, made visible through computer modeling, should similarly dispel the logician's dream of taming the patterns of paradox by finding some overly simplistic and predictable patterns.

Perhaps the main reason why these areas of semantic complexity have gone undiscovered until now is that the style of exploration is entirely modern: it is a kind of "experimental mathematics" in which—as Douglas Hofstadter has put it—the computer plays the role of Magellan's ship, the astronomer's telescope, and the physicist's accelerator.[10] Computer graphic analysis reveals that deep within semantic chaos there are hidden patterns known as fractals—intriguing objects that exhibit infinitely complex self-affinity at increasing powers of magnification. This fractal world was previously inaccessible not because fractals were too small or too far away, but because they were too complex to be visualized by any human mind.

It should be emphasized that we are not attempting to 'solve' the paradoxes—in the last 2,000 years or so attempts at solution cannot be said to have met with conspicuous success.[11] Rather, in the spirit of Hans Herzberger's 'Naive Semantics' and Anil Gupta's 'Rule of Revision Semantics,'[12] we will attempt to open the semantical dynamics of self-reference and self-referential reasoning for investigation in their own right. Here we use computer modeling in order to extend the tradition into infinite-valued logic. Unlike many previous investigators, we will not be trying to find simple patterns of semantic stability. Our concern will rather be with the infinitely intricate patterns of semantic *instability* and chaos, hidden within the paradoxes, that have until now gone virtually unexplored.

1.1   FROM THE BIVALENT LIAR TO DYNAMICAL SEMANTICS

The medieval logician Jean Buridan presents the Liar Paradox as follows:

It is posited that I say nothing except this proposition 'I speak falsely.' Then, it is asked whether my proposition is true or false. If you say that it is true, then it is not as my proposition signifies. Thus, it follows that it is not true but false. And if you say that it is false, then it follows that it is as it signifies. Hence, it is true."[13]

Reduced to its essentials, the bivalent Liar paradox is about a sentence that asserts its own falsehood.[14]

> The boxed sentence is false.

Is the boxed sentence true, or is it false? Suppose it is true. But what it *says* is that it's false, so if we suppose it is true it follows that it's false. Suppose, on the other hand, that the boxed sentence is false. But what it *says* is that it's false, and so if it is false, it's true. So if we assume it's true, we're forced to say it is false; and if we say it is false, we're forced to say it is true, and so forth.

According to Tarski's analysis,[15] the paradox of the Liar depends on four components.

First, the paradox depends on self-reference. In this case, the self-reference is due to the empirical fact that the sentence 'the boxed sentence is false' *is* the boxed sentence:

'The boxed sentence is false' = the boxed sentence.

Secondly, we use the Tarskian principle that the truth value of a sentence stating that a given sentence is true is the same as the truth value of the given sentence. Tarski's principle is often formulated as a schema:

(T)   The sentence $\ulcorner p \urcorner$ is true if and only if **p**.[16]

Tarski's famous example is that 'snow is white' is true if and only if snow is white. In the case of the Liar paradox, this gives us

'The boxed sentence is false' is true if and only if the boxed sentence is false.

Third, by Leibniz's law of the substitutivity of identicals, we can infer from the first two steps that

The boxed sentence is true if and only if the boxed sentence is false.

Fourth, given the principle of bivalence—the principle that every declarative sentence is either true or false—we can derive an explicit contradiction. In the informal reasoning of the Liar, that contradiction appears as an endless oscillation in the truth values we try to assign to the Liar: true, false, true, false, true, false, ...

The transition to dynamical semantics from this presentation of the classical bivalent Liar can also be made in four steps, each of which generalizes to the infinite-valued case a principle upon which the classical Liar is based. We generalize the principles in reverse order.

The first step, which may be the hardest, is the step from classical bivalent logic to an infinite-valued logic—from two values to a continuum. The vast bulk of the literature even on many-valued logic adheres to the classical conception that there are only two truth values, 'true' and 'false', with occasional deviations allowing some propositions to have a third value or none at all. Here, however, we wish to countenance a full continuum of values. This infinite-valued logic can be interpreted in two very different ways. The first—more direct than the second but also most philosophically contentious—is to insist that the classical Aristotelian assumption of bivalence is simply wrong.

Consider, for example, the following sentences:

1. Kareem Abdul-Jabbar is rich.

2. In caricatures, Bertrand Russell looks like the Mad Hatter.

3. New York City is a lovely place to live.

Are these sentences true, or are they false? A natural and unprompted response might be that (1) is very true, that (2) is more or less true (see figure 1), but that (3) is almost completely false. Sentences like these seem

Figure 1 More or less true: In caricatures, Bertrand Russell looks like the Mad Hatter.

not to be simply true or simply false: their truth values seem rather to lie on some kind of continuum of relative degrees of truth. The basic philosophical intuition is that such statements are *more or less* true or false: that their truth and falsity is a matter of degree.

J. L. Austin speaks for such an intuition in his 1950 paper "Truth": "In cases like these it is pointless to insist on deciding in simple terms whether the statement is 'true or false'. Is it true or false that Belfast is north of London? That the galaxy is the shape of a fried egg? That Beethoven was a drunkard? That Wellington won the battle of Waterloo? There are various *degrees and dimensions* of success in making statements: the statements fit the facts more or less loosely . . . ".[17] George Lakoff asks: "In contemporary America, how tall do you have to be to be tall? 5'8"? 5'9"? 5'10"? 5'11"? 6'? 6'2"? Obviously there is no single fixed answer. How old do you have to be to be middle-aged? 35? 37? 39? 40? 42? 45? 50? Again the concept is fuzzy. Clearly any attempt to limit truth conditions for natural language sentences to true, false, and 'nonsense' will distort the natural language concepts by portraying them as having sharply defined rather than fuzzily defined boundaries."[18] If we take these basic philosophical intuitions seriously, it seems natural to model relative 'degrees of truth' using values on the [0, 1] interval. The move to a continuum of truth values is the first and perhaps hardest step in the move to infinite-valued logics, and is a move we will treat as fundamental in the model that follows.[19]

It should also be noted that there is a second possible interpretation for infinite-valued logics, however, which avoids at least some elements of philosophical controversy. Despite the authority of classical logic, some philosophers have held that sentences can be more or less true or false. Conservative logicians such as Quine, on the other hand, have stubbornly insisted that truth or falsity must be an all-or-nothing affair.[20] Yet even those who are most uncompromising in their bivalence with regard to truth and falsity are quite willing to admit that some propositions may be more *accurate* than others. It's clearly more accurate to say, for example, that Madagascar is part of Mozambique than to say that Madagascar is off the coast of Midway. If the swallows are returning to Capistrano from a point 20 degrees north-northeast, the claim that they are coming from a point 5 degrees off may qualify as fairly accurate. But a claim that they are coming directly from the south can be expected to be wildly and uselessly inaccurate.

If our basic values are interpreted not as truth values but as *accuracy* values, then, an important measure of philosophical controversy seems avoidable. Accuracy is quite generally agreed to be a matter of degree, and from there it seems a small step to envisaging accuracy measures in terms of values on the [0, 1] interval.

In the case of an accuracy interpretation, however, there are other questions that may arise regarding a modeling on the [0, 1] continuum. Even in cases in which accuracy clearly *is* a matter of degree, it may not be clear that there is a zero point corresponding to something like 'complete inaccuracy'. Consider, for example, the claim in sentence (4).

4. Kareem is seven feet tall.

If Kareem is precisely seven feet tall—by the closest measurement we can get, perhaps—then we might agree that the statement has an accuracy of 1, or at least close to it. But what would have to be the case in order for sentence (4) to have an accuracy of 0: that Kareem is 3 feet tall? 0 feet tall? 100 feet tall? In these cases we seem to have accuracy as a matter of degree, something it is at least very tempting to model with a real interval, and we also seem to have an intuitively clear point for full accuracy. We don't, however, seem to have a clear terminus for 'full inaccuracy'.[21]

One way to avoid such a difficulty is to explictly restrict our accuracy interpretation to the range of cases in which the problem doesn't arise. Consider, for example

5. The island lies due north of our present position.

The accuracy of (5) can be gauged in terms of the same compass used to indicate the true position of the island. If the island does indeed lie perfectly to the north, (5) can be assigned an accuracy of 1. If the island lies in precisely the opposite direction, however—if it is in fact due south— then the directional reading of (5) is as wrong as it can be. In such a case it seems quite natural to assign the sentence an accuracy of 0.

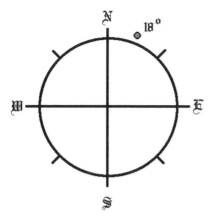

Figure 2 Compass model of accuracy.

Accuracy in the case of (5), unlike (4), does seem to have a natural terminus for both 'full accuracy' and 'full inaccuracy': here degrees of accuracy modeled on the [0, 1] interval seem fully appropriate. A similar compass or dial model will be possible for each of the following sentences:

The swallows arrive at Capistrano from the northwest.

The lines are perpendicular.

The roads run parallel.

Lunch is served precisely at noon.

A [0, 1] interval model for degrees of accuracy will also be appropriate in many cases in which there is no convenient compass or dial. In each of the following cases, for example, we also have a clear terminus for full accuracy and inaccuracy:

The story was carried by all the major networks.

fully inaccurate if carried by none

Radio waves occur across the full visible spectrum.

fully inaccurate if they don't occur within the visible spectrum at all

The eclipse was complete.

fully inaccurate if no eclipse occurred

There are thus at least two possible interpretations for the basic values of our infinite-valued logic: that they model degrees of truth, and that they model degrees of accuracy. The first interpretation, involving an explicit abandonment of bivalence for truth and falsity, is perhaps the philosophically more avant-garde. It is that interpretation we will use throughout this chapter: we will speak quite generally of sentences or propositions 'more or less true' than others. It should be remembered, however, that an alternative interpretation is possible for those whose philosophical scruples are offended at the thought of an infinite range of truth values: both philosophical and formal results remain much the same if we speak merely of propositions as more or less accurate than others. In chapter 2, with an eye to a variety of epistemic crises, we will develop the accuracy interpretation further.

The first step in the transition to dynamical semantics, then, is to abandon bivalence and to envisage sentences as taking a range of possible values on the [0, 1] continuum. A second step is to generalize the classical logical connectives to an infinite-valued context. Here we will use a core logic shared by the familiar Łukasiewicz system $Ł_{\aleph_1}$ and an infinite-valued generalization of the strong Kleene system.[22]

Let us begin with the logical connective 'not'. Just as a glass is as empty as it is *not* full, the negation of a sentence **p** is as true as **p** is *un*true. The negation of **p**, in other words, is true to the extent that **p** differs from 1 (i.e., from complete truth). If **p** has a truth value of 0.6, for example, **p**'s negation will have a truth value of 1 minus 0.6, or 0.4. Using slashes around a sentence to indicate the value of the proposition expressed by the sentence, the negation rule can be expressed as follows:

$$/\sim \mathbf{p}/ = 1 - /\mathbf{p}/.^{23}$$

In both Kleene and Łukasiewicz systems, a conjunction will be as false as its falsest conjunct. The value of a conjunction, in other words, is the minimum of the values of its conjuncts:

$$/(\mathbf{p} \ \& \ \mathbf{q})/ = \text{Min}\{/\mathbf{p}/, /\mathbf{q}/\}.$$

A disjunction will be as true as its truest disjunct, or as true as the maximum of the values of its disjuncts:

$$/(\mathbf{p} \vee \mathbf{q})/ = \text{Max}\{/\mathbf{p}/, /\mathbf{q}/\}.$$

Formal considerations cast a strong presumption in favor of treating conjunction and disjunction in terms of Min and Max, and cast an only slightly weaker presumption in favor of the treatment of negation above.[24] The same cannot be said, unfortunately, for implication: Kleene and Łukasiewicz part company on the conditional, and here it must simply be admitted that there are a number of alternatives. The Kleene conditional preserves the classical equivalence between $(\mathbf{p} \rightarrow \mathbf{q})$ and $(\sim \mathbf{p} \vee \mathbf{q})$:

$$/(\mathbf{p} \rightarrow \mathbf{q})/ = \text{Max}\{1 - /\mathbf{p}/, /\mathbf{q}/\}.$$

The Łukasiewicz conditional does not preserve that equivalence; however, it does preserve standard tautologies such as $(\mathbf{p} \rightarrow \mathbf{p})$:

$$/(\mathbf{p} \rightarrow \mathbf{q})/ = \text{Min}\{1, 1 - /\mathbf{p}/ + /\mathbf{q}/\},$$

or

$$/(\mathbf{p} \rightarrow \mathbf{q})/ = \begin{cases} 1 & \text{if} /\mathbf{p}/ \leq /\mathbf{q}/ \\ 1 - /\mathbf{p}/ + /\mathbf{q}/ & \text{if} /\mathbf{p}/ > /\mathbf{q}/ \end{cases}$$

In what follows we will not rely on the conditional and so will not in fact have to choose between Kleene and Łukasiewicz. We will use the Łukasiewicz biconditional, however, which can be independently motivated. The classical biconditional ($p \leftrightarrow q$) holds just in case there is no difference in truth value between p and q. The Łukasiewicz biconditional holds precisely *to the extent* that there is no difference in truth value between p and q: its value is 1 minus the absolute difference in value between p and q:

$$/(p \leftrightarrow q)/ = 1 - \text{Abs}(/p/ - /q/).$$

All the connectives outlined match the classical connectives when restricted to classical values of 0 and 1.

Having abandoned bivalence, and having generalized our classical bivalent logic to an infinite-valued logic, our third step is to generalize the classical two-valued Tarskian (T) schema to allow for degrees of truth.

Let us begin with an example. Consider the statement:

Patrick is a good golfer.

Consider also the 'second-order' statement asserting that the statement that Patrick is a good golfer is completely true—that it has the value 1:

It is *completely true* that **Patrick is a good golfer.**

Suppose for the moment that the actual value of the statement that Patrick is a good golfer is, say, 0.4:

Patrick is a good golfer.
<hr>
0.4

How true, then, is the second-order statement?

It is *completely true* that **Patrick is a good golfer.**
<hr>
0.4
<hr>
?

It's clear that the truth-value of this second-order statement will depend on two things: on the actual truth value (0.4) of 'Patrick is a good golfer', and on the attributed value of complete truth (1). Our second-order statement will be *un*true to the extent that the actual value and the attributed value differ. In this case the actual and the attributed value differ by $(1 - 0.4)$ or 0.6. Our second-order statement is 0.6 *un*true, and is therefore itself 0.4 true:

It is *completely true* that **Patrick is a good golfer.**
<hr>
0.4
<hr>
0.4

Notice that we would have been closer to the truth had we claimed that 'Patrick is a good golfer' was only half true, corresponding to an attributed value of 0.5:

It is *half true* that **Patrick is a good golfer.**

In that case our second-order statement would have been as *un*true as the difference between the actual value (0.4) and the attributed value (0.5). Our second-order statement would have been only 0.1 untrue and thus 0.9 true:

$$\frac{\text{It is } \textit{half true} \text{ that } \mathbf{Patrick\ is\ a\ good\ golfer.} \quad \overline{0.4}}{1 - \text{Abs}(0.5 - 0.4) = 0.9}$$

With this background we can generalize the Tarskian (T) schema to the infinite-valued case by allowing for degrees of truth. We'll use the notation 'V**tp**' to represent the assertion that the proposition **p** has the value true, or **t**. The Tarskian (T) schema can then be expressed in the form

V**tp** ↔ **p**.

Suppose we have some fixed statement **t** that is completely true. Saying that **p** is completely true will then amount to saying that it has the same value as **t**. The biconditional, as we have noted, can be read in both classical and infinite-valued logic as holding just in case its components have the same truth value. In terms of the biconditional, then, the statement that **p** is completely true will have the same value as a biconditional between **p** and the completely true statement **t**:

/V**tp**/ = /(**t** ↔ **p**)/.

Using the outline given for the biconditional above, we have

/V**tp**/ = 1 − Abs(**t** − /**p**/).

The value of a proposition V**tp** asserting that a proposition **p** has the value of **t** is 1 minus the absolute difference between **t** and the value of the proposition **p**.

If we now simply replace the Tarskian **t** throughout by a variable **v** ranging over truth values in the range [0, 1], we obtain Rescher's 1969 valuation schema for infinite-valued logic:

/V**vp**/ = 1 − Abs(**v** − /**p**/).

Intuitively, this V**vp** schema states that the proposition that **p** has the value **v** is untrue to the extent that the value of **p** differs from **v**.

According to one interpretation, the absolute difference between **v** and the value of **p** can be interpreted as the error of our estimate. In these terms, the V**vp** schema says that the truth value of a second-order sentence asserting that a sentence has the value **v** differs from complete truth (i.e., from the value 1) by the error of our estimate:

$$/V\mathbf{vp}/ \quad = \quad \mathbf{1} \quad - \quad Abs(\mathbf{v} - /\mathbf{p}/)$$

⇑ absolute truth   ⇑ error of estimate

To this point we have characterized our logic as 'infinite-valued' throughout, but there are also two modeling tools that we will borrow from 'fuzzy' logics. Although the two terms are often used interchangeably, 'fuzzy' logics standardly include not only the semantic predicates 'true' and 'false' but others generated by recursive application of linguistic modifiers, including 'very' and 'fairly'.[25] 'Very' is consistently treated in terms of squaring in the literature of fuzzy logic: if a statement is 0.6 true, the statement that it is 'very' true itself has the significantly smaller value of 0.6 squared, or 0.36. 'Fairly' is modeled in terms of square roots: if a statement is 0.6 true, the safer hedged statement that it is 'fairly' true is treated as having a higher value of $\sqrt{0.6}$ or approximately 0.77.[26] Here the general strategy seems quite plausible: stronger 'very' statements must pass more severe tests, with predictably lower truth values, weaker 'fairly' statements the contrary. No one, as far as we know, would try to give a philosophical defense of these convenient modelings as *precisely* those appropriate to ordinary uses of linguistic hedges.

So far we have abandoned bivalence, generalized our logic to an infinite-valued context, and generalized the Tarskian (T) schema to allow for degrees of truth. Our fourth and final step is to model self-reference using functional iteration.

We'll begin to model self-reference by replacing the actual value of the proposition **p** with estimated values x_n. We will then recycle these estimated values through the V**vp** schema to obtain new estimates. The general idea of functional iteration is that of feedback.[27] We start by inputting some initial value into a function and obtain some output, then recycle the output as a new input, and so forth.

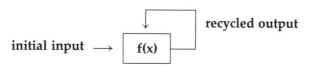

The subject of nonlinear dynamics or chaos theory is precisely the behavior of such iterated functional sequences. The fact that self-reference can be modeled as functional iteration thus affords us a a range of well-developed concepts and graphical techniques for understanding the semantics of paradox.

1.2 THE SIMPLE LIAR IN INFINITE-VALUED LOGIC

The classical Liar, limited to two truth values, forces a semantic oscillation: if true it must be false, so the intuitive reasoning goes, but if false it must then be true.... That semantic dynamics can be represented in what is called a *time-series graph*, though here we substitute for time an abstract series of points of deliberation. Figure 3 shows the intuitive dynamics of the classical Liar—an oscillation between 0 and 1—in terms of such a graph.[28]

We have now left bivalence far behind, however, expanding our logic to an infinite range of truth-values between 0 and 1, modifying our logical connectives and the Tarskian (T) schema to match, and modeling self-reference as functional iteration. We can certainly expect paradoxes to behave differently in this new logical realm. How will the Liar behave in an infinite-valued context?

The boxed sentence is false.

Let's call the boxed sentence '**b**'. Suppose that we start with an estimated value of, say, 1/4 for **b**. Given this estimate and taking the value of 'false' to be 0, we can use the V**vp** schema to calculate the value of the statement that **b** is false:

$$/V\mathbf{fb}/ = 1 - \mathrm{Abs}(0 - 1/4).$$

This gives a value of 3/4. The statement that **b** is false, however, is precisely what **b** itself asserts. Starting from our initial estimate, therefore, what the V**vp** schema gives us is a new or revised estimate for **b**. Starting with an estimate of 1/4, we are forced to a revised estimate of 3/4.

If **b** has a value of 3/4, however, the statement that **b** is false will have a value of:

$$/V\mathbf{fb}/ = 1 - \mathrm{Abs}(0 - 3/4).$$

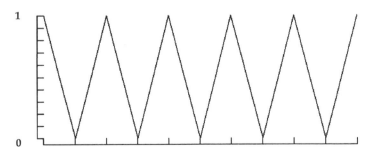

Figure 3 Time-series graph for intuitive reasoning in the classical Liar.

That **b** is false is precisely what **b** asserts, so from an estimate of 3/4 we are forced to a further revised estimate of 1/4....

We can think of the Liar as continuing in this way to generate a series of revised estimates, each calculated in terms of its predecessor. For any initial estimate x_0, the series of successively revised estimates is given by

$$x_{n+1} = 1 - \text{Abs}(0 - x_n).$$

For an initial value of 1/4, this gives us the oscillation between 1/4 and 3/4 shown in the first frame of figure 4. For an initial value of 2/3 we get the oscillation between 2/3 and 1/3 shown in the second frame. In the infinite-valued case, any initial value **v** generates a periodic alternation between the values **v** and $(1 - \mathbf{v})$. The one fixed point for the infinite-valued Liar is 1/2, which returns at each step an identical revised value of 1/2.

Were we to graph continued iteration using time-series graphs we would have to extend them indefinitely to the right. An alternative to this

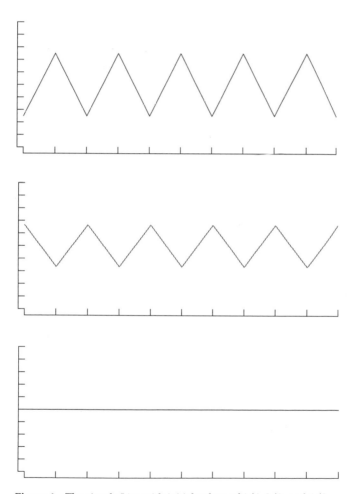

Figure 4   The simple Liar with initial values of 1/4, 2/3, and 1/2.

Chaos, Fractals, and the Semantics of Paradox

is a *web diagram*, in which repeated iteration of a function is represented by plotting ordered pairs of successive iterations in 'phase space'. We offer a schematic introduction to web diagrams in figure 5 by plotting the same information on a time-series graph and on the corresponding web diagram. Here we start with an initial estimated value x_0—0.1, in this case—indicated by the arrow in the time-series graph at the left. On the web diagram to the right we plot this value on the x-axis of the Cartesian plane, again using an arrow to indicate our starting point. In the web diagram we now move vertically until we reach the descending diagonal line. This line is the graph of our function, $x_{n+1} = 1 - \text{Abs}(0 - x_n)$ in iterated form, plotted here simply as $y = 1 - \text{Abs}(0 - x)$. Moving vertically from our starting point x_0, we hit this function line at a y-value corresponding to $1 - \text{Abs}(0 - x_0)$. The y value of the intersection point is thus x_1, the next value of our iterated series, and corresponds to the first peak in the time-series graph.

To continue iteration through our function, we want to convert the y-value of this first intersection point to a new x-value. That way we'll be able to recycle x_1 through the function to get x_2, then recycle x_2 through our function to get x_3, and so forth. In a web diagram we convert our first y-value to an x-value simply by reflecting that value off the $x = y$ line, which is the ascending diagonal in the web diagram. From our first point of intersection, we move horizontally to the right until we hit the $x = y$ line. The point of intersection here has an x-coordinate corresponding to what was our y-coordinate a minute ago—an x coordinate that therefore represents our value x_1. With that new x-coordinate in hand, we can move vertically to our function line again—down this time—intersecting our function line at a point with a y-value corresponding to x_2. This matches the valley in our time-series graph. We continue the process to plot the continuing series of revised estimates. At each step, we reflect our last value off the $x = y$ line to obtain a new value from the graph of our function.

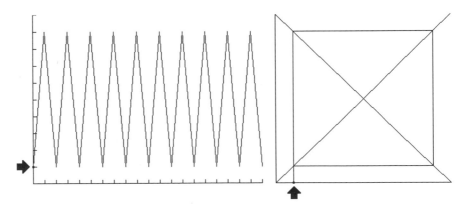

Figure 5 Time-series graph with corresponding web diagram.

The function we've mapped in figure 5 is that of the simple Liar. The closed box that appears in the web diagram reflects the fact that the Liar has a cycle of period 2: it simply alternates between two values. For any input **v**, the web diagram for the Liar is a simple box whose corners intersect the y = x line at the values **v** and (1 − **v**).

Figure 6 shows three cases in web diagrams. For the classical Liar, with an input of 0 or 1, the outermost limiting orbit is the unit box. An initial value of 1/4 gives a box intersecting at 1/4 and 3/4. The innermost limiting orbit is the single fixed point of 1/2.

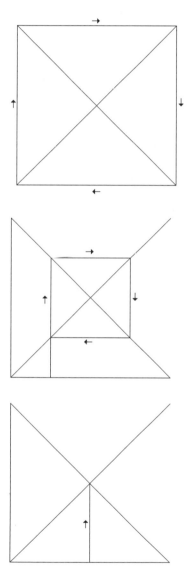

Figure 6 Web diagrams for the simple Liar with inputs, 1, 1/4, and 1/2.

1.3 SOME QUASI-PARADOXICAL SENTENCES

Now let us go beyond the simple Liar. In thinking of the semantic behavior of sentences on the model of iterated functions, it seems natural to entertain sentences that refer not merely to their own truth values but to their *estimated* truth-values.[29]

The V**vp** schema can be modified to capture self-referential sentences of this sort. As in the case of the simple Liar, the place allotted for the actual value of the proposition **p** in the V**vp** schema can be thought of as occupied by a series of estimated values x_n. But here we'll also replace the asserted value **v** with a function $S(x_n)$ that attributes a value to the sentence in terms of its previously estimated value. A canonical reading might be

This sentence is as true as $S(x_n)$.

With such an approach, we can explore for their own sake the dynamics of a range of self-referential sentences which are in some ways even wilder than the Liar. Consider for example a sentence we call the Half-Sayer:

This sentence is as true as *half* its estimated value.

In terms of our V**vp** schema, the successive values for the Half-Sayer will be given by the algorithm

$$x_{n+1} = 1 - \text{Abs}(1/2 \cdot x_n - x_n).$$

Consider also a second sentence, which we call the Minimalist:

This sentence is as true as whichever is smaller: its estimated value or the opposite of its estimated value.

Here we take the opposite of a value **v** to be $1 - \mathbf{v}$. An alternative reading for the Minimalist is

This sentence is as true as the estimated value of the conjunction of itself and its negation.

Successive values for the Minimalist will then be given by the algorithm

$$x_{n+1} = 1 - \text{Abs}(\text{Min}\{x_n, 1 - x_n\} - x_n).$$

Let us calculate some specific values for these sentences in order to get a feel for their self-referential dynamics.

Suppose you estimate the Half-Sayer to be 1/2 true. What that sentence asserts that it is as true as half our estimate—given an estimate of 1/2, what it asserts that it is 1/4 true. According to our V**vp** schema, the value of the Half-Sayer will then be

$$1 - \text{Abs}(1/4 - 1/2),$$

or 3/4. From an initial estimate of 1/4, the V**vp** schema thus forces us to a revised estimate of 3/4. But given an estimate of 3/4, what the Half-Sayer asserts is that its value is a mere 3/8. Continuing this pattern of reasoning through the V**vp** schema, the Half-Sayer leads us to a series of successive values 5/8, 11/16, 22/32, 42/64, ... In the limit the series converges to 2/3. The web diagram for the Half-Sayer (in figure 7) shows the cascade toward 2/3, an attractor fixed point.[30]

We can also graph the dynamic behavior of the Minimalist in a web diagram. An initial estimate of 0.6, as shown on the left in figure 8, gives us a series of values diverging outward to a Liar-like oscillation between 1 and 0. An initial estimate closer to 2/3—0.66, shown on the right—gives us a different series, which again moves to an infinite oscillation between 1 and 0. Here 2/3 serves as a unstable fixed point or a fixed point *repeller* in phase space.

Let us sum up a few points made visible in the investigation of these quasi-paradoxical sentences. The Half-Sayer and the Minimalist, in ways far from apparent from their surface structures alone, reveal precisely opposite dynamical behaviors in terms of attractor and repeller fixed points: the Half-Sayer exhibits an attractor fixed point precisely where the

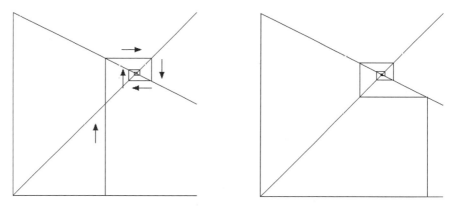

Figure 7   The Half-Sayer for inputs of 0.5 and 0.916.

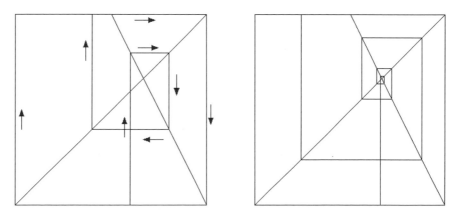

Figure 8   The Minimalist for initial values 0.6 and 0.66.

Minimalist exhibits a repeller fixed point. The semantic behaviors of the Minimalist and the simple Liar are identical within a classical logic: each gives an oscillation between 0 and 1. The behaviors of the two sentences diverge sharply in an infinite-valued context, however. Within a continuum of values, as we have seen, the Liar oscillates between any initial value x and $1 - x$. Perhaps unexpectedly, it is the Minimalist rather than the simple Liar that converges on the infinite classical oscillation between 0 and 1.

The Simple Liar, the Half-Sayer, and the Minimalist offer some striking examples of the kinds of formal lessons that dynamical semantics has to offer. The fact that each of these sentences exhibits fixed points might also be thought to offer a further lesson: that the 'solution' to the Liar is 1/2, for example, and that the 'true' value of the Half-Sayer and of the Minimalist correspond to their two (very different) fixed points of 2/3.

The appeal of such an approach, of course, is that within an infinite-valued logic a value of 1/2 *can* be assigned to the Liar without the contradiction of further dynamic revision. The same is true for 2/3 in the other cases. Here we want to express a bit of hesitation regarding the attempt to jump at fixed points as full *solutions* for phenomena of self-reference, however. One difficulty, which will appear in further examples, is that there are many cases with *multiple* fixed points; if a fixed point is identified with a 'true' value, precisely *which* of these will qualify as the 'true' value? There are in fact very simple cases, such as the Truth-teller, that have an *infinite* number of fixed points:

This sentence is true.

$$x_{n+1} = 1 - \text{Abs}(1 - x_n)$$

The infinite-valued Truth-teller is a perfect generalization of its classical relative, which can consistently be assigned a value of either true or false. The infinite-valued Truth-teller can be stably assigned any value whatsoever in the [0,1] interval: any estimate qualifies as a fixed point. Here, it seems, we simply have too many fixed points to count as a 'solution': are we to say that *each* of these infinite values is the sentence's 'true' truth value?

Another difficulty, familiar from the Strengthened Classical Liar but also present in an infinite-valued context, is that the search for fixed points will not offer a fully general solution to paradoxical or other self-referential phenomena. Consider for example a Strengthened Infinite-valued Liar:

6. This statement has a truth-value other than precisely 1.

If assumed to have a full 1 as its truth value, sentence (6) will have some lesser value: given what (6) says, it will in that case be *un*true to some extent. If the sentence is assumed to have any truth value other than precisely 1, on the other hand, it apparently will be simply and totally true.

We might also consider the following sentence:

7. This sentence has absolutely no fixed-point truth value other than 0.

Suppose (7) does have some fixed point other than 0. In that case, what (7) says appears to be simply false, with a value of 0. The assumption of a fixed point other than 0 is thus itself unstable: we are forced to revise such an assumption downward, apparently being driven to the conclusion that the 'solution' for (7) is that it has only one genuine fixed point: zero. In that case, however, what (7) says would seem to be simply true....[31] As indicated earlier, our concern throughout is less with a search for 'solutions' than with the attempt to model the semantical dynamics of a range of self-referential sentences as phenomena worthy of study in their own right.

Here we also want to offer two close relatives of the Half-Sayer and the Minimalist which employ linguistic 'hedges' borrowed from the literature of fuzzy logic. As was indicated in section 1.1, 'very' is standardly treated in fuzzy logic in terms of a squaring function, whereas 'fairly' is treated in terms of square roots. Given a value of 0.9 for 'Paul is tall', fuzzy logic assigns a value of $(0.9)^2 = 0.81$ for 'Paul is *very* tall'. Given a value of 0.25 for 'Paul is a good tennis player', fuzzy logic assigns a value of $\sqrt{0.25} = 0.5$ for 'Paul is a *fairly* good tennis player'. Treated as hedges on the entire sentence, 'fairly' and 'very' are calculated in general by squaring or square-rooting (respectively) the value the entire sentence would have without them.

Consider then two sentences that we might term the Modest Liar and the Emphatic Liar:

Modest Liar: This sentence is fairly false.

Emphatic Liar: This sentence is very false.

For 'this sentence is false' without a modifier—the simple Liar—the V**vp** schema gives us

$$x_{n+1} = 1 - \text{Abs}(0 - x_n).$$

For the Emphatic Liar, the right-hand side is squared in order to reflect the force of the added hedge 'very':

$$x_{n+1} = (1 - \text{Abs}(0 - x_n))^2$$

which reduces to simply

$$x_{n+1} = (1 - x_n)^2.$$

For the Modest Liar we will use a square root instead:

$$x_{n+1} = \sqrt{1 - \text{Abs}(0 - x_n)}.$$

The dynamics of the Modest Liar and the Emphatic Liar are shown in web diagrams in figure 9. The general behavior of the Modest Liar is like

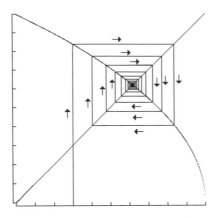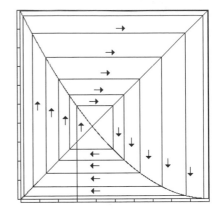

Figure 9 The Modest Liar and the Emphatic Liar for initial estimates of 0.3.

that of the Half-Sayer, though with a different fixed point. For any seed value, it turns out, the Modest Liar converges inexorably on a fixed-point attractor of $(-1 + \sqrt{5})/2$. The Emphatic Liar, on the other hand, parallels the Minimalist, but with an unstable repeller fixed point at $(3 - \sqrt{5})/2$. For any other values, it moves to the oscillation between 0 and 1 characteristic of the classical Liar.

Both fuzzy fixed points, interestingly enough, are related to the golden ratio, labeled ϕ by mathematicians because of its extensive work in the sculpture of the Greek artist Phidias. The golden ratio is widely used as an aesthetically perfect proportion, employed for example in the Parthenon, da Vinci's *Mona Lisa*, and Salvador Dali's *The Sacrament of the Last Supper*.[32] Here we find it in the semantics of fuzzy self-reference as well.

1.4   THE CHAOTIC AND LOGISTIC LIARS

With these quasi-paradoxical sentences as background, we are ready to construct a natural infinite-valued variant of the Liar which generates a particularly complex dynamical semantics. This sentence, like those considered above, self-attributes a value in terms of previously estimated value.

Consider a sentence that asserts not that it is simply *false*, but rather that it has the value of its *estimated falsehood*:

> This statement is as true as it is estimated to be false.

This sentence perversely asserts that it is as true as the value of its estimated falsehood. Since the estimated falsehood of a sentence turns out to be equivalent to 1 minus its estimated value, the successive values for this boxed sentence will be given by the algorithm

$$x_{n+1} = 1 - \text{Abs}((1 - x_n) - x_n).$$

We call this boxed sentence the 'Chaotic Liar' because its dynamical semantic behavior—in contrast to the metronomic predictability of the simple Liar—is genuinely chaotic in a precise, mathematically definable sense. It is interesting to note that the value this sentence attributes to itself—the value it says it has—is precisely that given by the full algorithm for the simple infinite-valued Liar:

Chaotic Liar : $\qquad x_{n+1} = 1 - \text{Abs}((1 - x_n) - x_n)$

$$\Uparrow$$

"This statement is as true as…" $\qquad (1 - x_n)$

$$\Uparrow$$

$$= 1 - \text{Abs}(0 - x_n)$$

Simple Liar: $\qquad x_{n+1} = 1 - \text{Abs}(0 - x_n).$

Plotting the iterated values for the Chaotic Liar in a time-series graph (here for an initial estimate of 0.314), we obtain the irregular, non-repeating chaotic pattern shown in figure 10. The dynamics of the Chaotic Liar is better portrayed, however, by the evolution of its web diagram (figure 11).

One point of interest is that the Chaotic Liar has not one fixed point but two: one at 0 and one at 2/3. Of greater interest for our purposes, however, is the fact that all the elements of chaos as mathematically defined are present in the dynamical semantics for the Chaotic Liar:

A function $f : J \to J$ is chaotic on J if

1. f has sensitive dependence on initial conditions;

2. f is topologically transitive;

3. the set of period points is dense in J.[33]

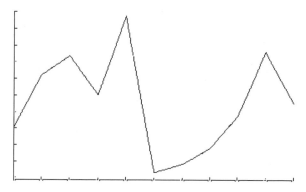

Figure 10   The Chaotic Liar for an initial estimate of 0.314.

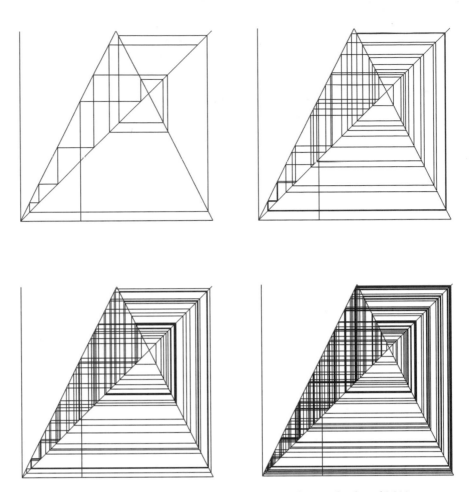

Figure 11 Progressive web diagram for the Chaotic Liar, for initial value of 0.314.

The requirement of density is that the closure of the period points—the periodic points together with limit points that series of periodic points approach—constitute the entire interval. A topologically transitive function is one points of which eventually move under iteration from one arbitrarily small neighborhood to any other. Though stronger and weaker characterizations of chaos appear in the literature, all agree that the quintessential element is sensitive dependence on initial conditions. Sensitive dependence has been picturesquely dubbed the "butterfly effect" to stand for the metaphorical idea that a butterfly flapping its wings in Brazil could set off a tornado in Texas a week later.[34] A better expression of the idea would be that two states of a deterministic system that differ at time t only in whether a butterfly is flapping its wings or not may differ at a later time in the presence or absence of a Texas tornado. A function is sensitive to initial conditions if, for any arbitrarily small neighborhood around any chosen point and for any arbitrarily large distance within the interval, there is some point in the immediate neighborhood which eventually diverges by that large distance from the chosen point.

This central idea of sensitive dependence is already quite clearly outlined in Poincaré's discussion of chance:

A very slight cause, which escapes us, determines a considerable effect which we can not help seeing, and then we say this effect is due to chance. If we could know exactly the laws of nature and the situation of the universe at the initial instant, we should be able to predict exactly the situation of this same universe at a subsequent instant. But even when the natural laws should have no further secret for us, we could know the initial situation only *approximately*. If that permits us to foresee the subsequent situation *with the same degree of approximation*, this is all we require, we say the phenomenon has been predicted, that it is ruled by laws. But this is not always the case; it may happen that slight differences in the initial conditions produce very great differences in the final phenomena; a slight error in the former would make an enormous error in the latter. Prediction becomes impossible and we have the fortuitous phenomenon.[35]

We can illustrate the sensitive dependence to initial conditions of the Chaotic Liar by observing the rapid spread of successive values when plotting a time-series overlay graph for initial values of 0.314 increasing by increments of 0.001 (figure 12).[36]

The basic algorithm for the Chaotic Liar is in fact a very simple and paradigmatically chaotic function, known as a 'tent map' because of the shape of its graph and more familiar in the mathematical guise

$x_{n+1} = 1 - \text{Abs}(2x_n - 1)$ or

$$x_{n+1} = \begin{cases} 2x_n & \text{for } 0 \le x < 1/2 \\ 2(1 - x_n) & \text{for } 1/2 \le x \le 1.^{37} \end{cases}$$

This characteristic algorithm is included in a group of mere 'mathematical curiosities' in Robert May's important paper applying chaos theory to ecology.[38] The work above indicates that this function is significantly more

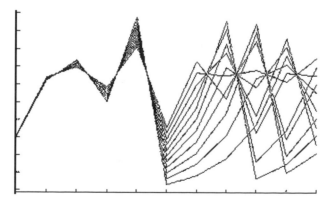

Figure 12   Time-series overlay, for an initial value of 0.314 increasing by increments of 0.001.

than a mere mathematical curiosity, however: it is in fact a natural generalization of the classical bivalent Liar paradox into the realm of infinite-valued logic. The Chaotic Liar is one of the simplest and most straightforward routes from dynamical semantics into semantic chaos.

As a final example in this section we want to introduce the Logistic Liar, a relative of the Chaotic Liar with a dynamics that corresponds to the logistic map, perhaps the most throughly studied function in nonlinear dynamics.

We can get the Logistic Liar from the Chaotic Liar in two steps. The Chaotic Liar asserts

This sentence is as true as it is estimated to be false.

Successive values are calculated in terms of the algorithm

$$x_{n+1} = 1 - \text{Abs}((1 - x_n) - x_n).$$

The first step toward the Logistic Liar is to add an initial negation, rendered either as 'it is not the case ...' or 'it is false that ...'. Our standard rule for negation, $/\sim \mathbf{p}/ = 1 - /\mathbf{p}/$, gives us the following sentence and algorithm:

It is false that this sentence is as true as it is estimated to be false.

$$x_{n+1} = 1 - (1 - \text{Abs}((1 - x_n) - x_n)).$$

For the Logistic Liar, however, we also take the second step of adding the fuzzy hedge 'very':

It is very false that this sentence is as true as it is estimated to be false,

or

It is very much not the case that this sentence is as true as it is estimated to be false.

As outlined, 'very' is standardly modeled in the fuzzy logic literature by squaring the value that the sentence would have without it. Revised values for the full Logistic Liar will thus be given by

$$x_{n+1} = (1 - (1 - \text{Abs}((1 - x_n) - x_n)))^2.$$

Figure 13 shows a developing web diagram for an initial value of 0.312.

It is clear from figure 13 that the dynamics of the Logistic Liar correspond to an inverted form of the Logistic or Quadratic equation, standardly rendered as $x_{n+1} = 4x_n(1 - x_n)$. For values in the [0,1] interval our algorithm for the Logistic Liar amounts to

$$x_{n+1} = (1 - (1 - \text{Abs}((1 - x_n) - x_n)))^2.$$
$$= 1 - 4x_n(1 - x_n).$$

We might also obtain a non-inverted form of the Logistic by adding a further negation outside of the scope of 'very':

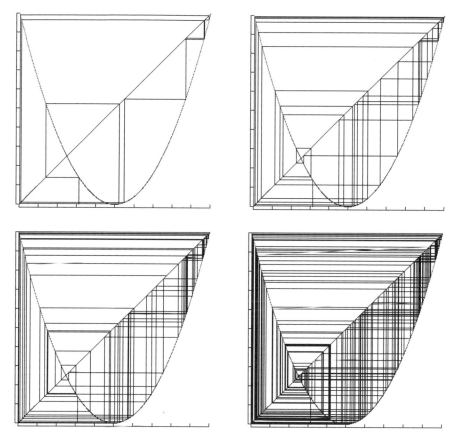

Figure 13 Progressive web diagram for the Logistic Liar.

It is not very false that this sentence is as true as it is estimated to be false.

Another route to a non-inverted Logistic is the following. One fairly literal reading of the Chaotic Liar is

There is no difference between the degree of truth and the degree of falsity of this sentence.

If we replace the notion of absolute difference with a notion of variance borrowed from statistics, where the variance between two values is the square of their difference, we get the following sentence and algorithm:

There is no *variance* between the degree of truth and the degree of falsity of this sentence.

$$x_{n+1} = 1 - ((1 - x_n) - x_n)^2$$

This algorithm is precisely equivalent to the Logistic $x_{n+1} = 4x_n(1 - x_n)$.[39]

With smaller values **k** used in place of the constant 4, the Logistic map yields a wide variety of dynamic behaviors. As shown in figure 14a, it has

Chaos, Fractals, and the Semantics of Paradox

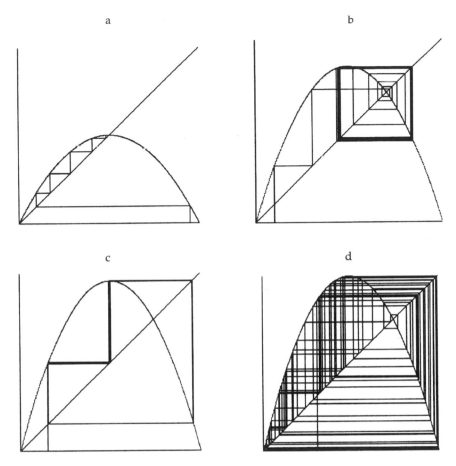

Figure 14 The Logistic equation with different parameters: (a) fixed points for values < 3; (b) a cycle of period 2; (c) a cycle of period 3; (d) full chaos corresponding to the Logistic Liar.

fixed-point attractors for values of **k** less than 3. Figure 14b shows an example of a cycle of period 2. Figure 14c shows an example of a cycle of period 3. According to a theorem by Sarkovskii any one-dimensional map which has a cycle of period 3 will also have periods of all other cycles. "Period three implies chaos."[40]

Increasing the value of **k** yields the well-known period doubling route to chaos.[41] (Simply increasing **k**, however, does not simply make things more complicated since there are still windows of periodic behavior.) With **k** = 4 we have the full chaotic behavior on the [0,1] interval corresponding to the dynamics of the Logistic Liar (figure 14d).

The Chaotic and Logistic Liars, we think, are prime examples of self-referential dynamics in infinite-valued logics more complex and more intricately unstable than previously studied patterns of paradox.

1.5 CHAOTIC DUALISTS AND STRANGE ATTRACTORS

Let us now turn to a somewhat more complicated class of examples, involving not a single self-referential sentence but two mutually referential sentences with interacting semantics.

As has been clear since at least the Middle Ages, beyond the Simple Liar lies an infinite series of Liar cycles in which indirect self-reference replaces the direct self-reference of the Liar. The simplest of these is the Dualist, which Buridan presents as follows: "The case may be posited that Socrates utters only this [proposition] 'Plato speaks falsely' and Plato, conversely, only this proposition 'Socrates speaks truly.' Then it is asked whether that proposition of Plato is true or false. And similarly also, it could be asked concerning Socrates' proposition."[42] Reduced to its essentials, we have one sentence which says a second sentence is true, and a second sentence which says the first is false:

X: Y is true.

Y: X is false.

The Liar-like pattern of reasoning should be clear: if X is true, then Y is true, but what Y claims is that X is false. So if X is true, X must be false. Suppose, on the other hand, that X is false. Since what Y *says* is that X is false, Y must then be true. But if Y is true, then X must be true, since that is precisely what X claims. If X is false, then, X must be true. The point, of course, in the Dualist as in the Liar, is that X is true if and only if it is false. (Indeed either statement is true if and only if it is false.)

Here we want to concentrate on some infinite-valued variations on the Dualist. Consider first two sentences that speak of each other in tones reminiscent not of the Simple Liar but of the Chaotic Liar:

X: X is as true as Y.

Y: Y is as true as X is false.

Sentence X claims it is as true as sentence Y. Sentence Y, on the other hand, claims that it is as true as X is false.

What X says is that its truth value is that of Y. Using the V**vp** schema, then, we can compute the value of X as 1 minus the absolute difference of the values of X and Y. Given initial estimates of x_n and y_n for X and Y, we will thus be forced to a revised estimate x_{n+1} for X in terms of the algorithm

$$x_{n+1} = 1 - \text{Abs}(y_n - x_n).$$

What Y says, on the other hand, is that it is true to the extent that X is false, or that its value is the opposite of that of X. With the same x_n and y_n, then, the value of Y at the next estimate will be given by a second algorithm:

$$y_{n+1} = 1 - \text{Abs}((1 - x_n) - y_n).$$

Suppose that we start with an initial estimated value of 1/8 for each of our two sentences. Like the Chaotic Liar, the Chaotic Dualist will then force us to a series of revised estimates. In the case of the Chaotic Dualist, however, we will have a series of revised estimates for each of our sentences—a series of revised estimate pairs.

Let us start by estimating that each sentence is 1/8 true. Step by step, recalculation through our two **Vvp** schemas will force us to the series of revised pairs of values numbered sequentially in figure 15. Graphically represented as Cartesian coordinates, these value pairs outline the triangular upper half of the unit square as they move toward a final fixed point of (0, 1).

Other pairs of initial values in the Chaotic Dualist give us periodic behavior: initial estimates of 0.4 and 0.6, for example, give us a repeating period of four points. Throughout the [0, 1] interval, however, the triangular upper half of the unit square remains as a persistent constraint.

Further variations of the Dualist lead us into the realm of strange attractors. We have already considered some simple examples of attractors. A fixed-point attractor, for example, is a point in phase space toward which the system converges. A limit cycle is a closed loop representing a periodic cycle. A strange attractor takes the form of a bounded region of chaotic orbits in phase space.

Here, for example, consider a slight variation on the Chaotic Dualist—one which uses the same two sentences as before but which employs a slightly different pattern of reasoning with regard to them.

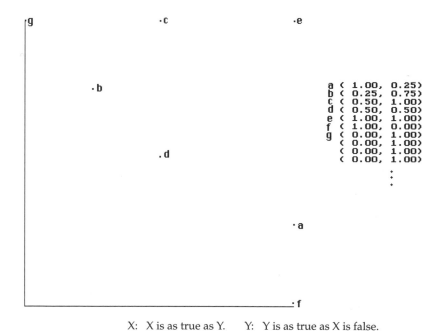

X: X is as true as Y.   Y: Y is as true as X is false.

Figure 15 Revised values for the Chaotic Dualist with initial estimates of (1/8, 1/8).

What the algorithms we've used for the Chaotic Dualist above actually capture is not merely our two sentences X and Y, however; they also capture a particular pattern of reasoning. Starting with a pair of estimates for X and Y, we have in effect calculated *simultaneously* a revised estimate for X in terms of those initial estimates and a revised estimate for Y in terms of those same initial estimates.

But one might think of the same two sentences in terms of a slightly different pattern of reasoning. When confronted with X and Y, one might first calculate a revised estimate for the first sentence in terms of our initial estimates, but then calculate a revised estimate for the second sentence in terms of the initial estimate for Y and the most recently *revised* estimate for X. In recalculating the value for Y, in other words, one might use not the initial estimate for X but the most recently revised estimate. Instead of calculating the values for X and Y simultaneously, in short, we might choose to calculate their values *successively*. This successive pattern of reasoning can be represented simply by replacing one occurrence of x_n with x_{n+1} in our previous algorithms:

$$x_{n+1} = 1 - \text{Abs}(y_n - x_n)$$

$$y_{n+1} = 1 - \text{Abs}((1 - x_{n+1}) - y_n).$$

For a wide range of initial values, this revision gives us a very persistent attractor that we call the 'origami attractor'. Initial values (0.1, 0.9), for example, give us the developing pattern of successive values shown in figure 16a.

The persistence of such an attractor is clearly evident if we superimpose graphs for a range of initial points. We can, for example, plot a graph for initial values (0, 0) and then overlay that with the graph for (0, 0.1), then with the graph for (0, 0.2), and so forth. Figure 16b shows the origami attractor as it appears in such an overlay diagram for initial points (x, y) where x and y range from 0 to 1 in intervals of 0.05. Here, for programming convenience, we have used a smaller number of iterations for each input, resulting in a degree of graininess. Nonetheless the general convergence of our points on trajectories within a single well-defined attractor is clear.

The third variation of the Dualist we want to consider is one in which the first member of our Dualist pair is replaced with a sentence reminiscent of the Half-Sayer:

X: X is true to half the extent that Y is true.

Y: Y is as true as X is false.

Here the second sentence, as before, says that it is true to the extent that the first sentence is false. The first sentence, however, now says that it is true to *half* the extent that the second sentence is. This gives us an entirely different attractor.

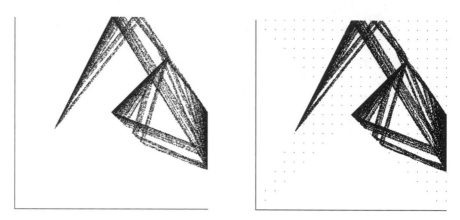

Figure 16 The origami attractor for successive computations of the Chaotic Dualist.

Following the pattern of successive reasoning outlined above, we get the following formulae for the Half-Dualist:

$$x_{n+1} = 1 - \text{Abs}(1/2 \cdot y_n - x_n),$$

$$y_{n+1} = 1 - \text{Abs}((1 - x_{n+1}) - y_n).$$

The attractor pattern for the Half-Dualist takes the general form of two ellipses. For initial values (0.8, 0.3) it emerges in the form shown in figure 17a. An overlay diagram using initial values in increments of 0.1 shows ellipses in much the same position but of differing sizes depending on initial values. For some values, only a fourfold scattering of dots or a central cross-pattern emerges (figure 17b).[43]

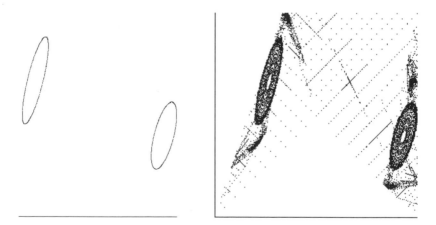

X: X is true to half the extent that Y is true.
Y: Y is as true as X is false.

Figure 17 Trajectories for the Half-Dualist.

1.6 FRACTALS IN THE SEMANTICS OF PARADOX

Our three variations—the Chaotic Dualist with a simultaneous calculation of values for X and Y, the Chaotic Dualist with successive calculation, and the Half-Dualist—exhibit three quite different patterns of attractors.

Here we can also introduce another way of graphically analyzing the semantic behavior of these three variations: a form of computer analysis, it turns out, that reveals fractal images within semantics. Technically, fractals are sets with a fractional or non-integer dimension, one measure of which is the Hausdorff dimension.[44] More intuitively, their essential property is simply that of self-affinity at descending scales: subsets or subsections of a fractal object bear a compelling though often complex affinity to the whole. The fact that fractal images appear within the semantics of paradox serves to emphasize the deep and intricate complexity of the logical phenomena at issue. One particularly intriguing form in which fractals emerge in the semantics of paradox is within escape-time diagrams.

The algorithms we have introduced above for variations on the Dualist give us revised values as series of ordered pairs. Now imagine those pairs of values as points in the Cartesian plane, and envisage each series of ordered pairs as tracing a path through the plane (figure 18).

Imagine also a chosen threshold of some kind. One quite natural threshold is that shown in figure 18 as an arc a given distance from the origin (0, 0). Since the origin represents 'double falsity' (a value of 0 for both sentences), such a threshold would correspond to a certain positive truth value for both of our sentences.

Different paths of points may require different numbers of iterations to move beyond our chosen threshold. An escape-time diagram plots initial points of paths accordingly, distinguishing them by color. Those points on the plane that generate paths reaching the chosen threshold in one iteration are given one color, those points that generate paths reaching the threshold in two iterations are given another color, and so on. The result is a static portrait which nonetheless captures some of the dynamic charcteristics of regions of points under iteration through the functions at issue.

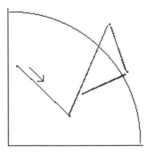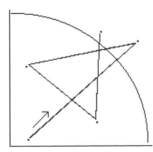

Figure 18 Escape-time diagrams: color coding for number of iterations to escape beyond a given threshold.

X: X is as true as Y.
Y: Y is as true as X is false.

Figure 19 Escape-time diagram for simultaneous computation in the Chaotic Dualist.

Figure 19 shows an escape-time diagram for our first version of the Chaotic Dualist, in which revised values for X and Y are calculated simultaneously. In this case we have picked a threshold of a little over 1 from the origin, or from 'double falsity'. What these intricately nesting colored areas reflect, then, are different numbers of iterations required for different points (i.e., pairs of values) to move beyond that semantic threshold. This figure shows only the unit square, reflecting the fact that semantic values for x and y within our logic are confined to the interval [0, 1]. Formally, however, this image is merely the central section of the larger one shown in figure 20. To produce this larger image we've simply expanded values for x and y a bit over a unit in each direction.

To make the structure of these escape-time diagrams even clearer, particularly in black and white, we can erase the colored areas so as to emphasize merely the interfaces between areas. Here we plot only those points at which the number of iterations required to reach our chosen threshold *changes*. In such a variation figures 19 and 20 become the fragile traceries shown in figure 21.

The clear fractal character of these images is of course visually compelling. Nonetheless what is being graphed within the unit square, it

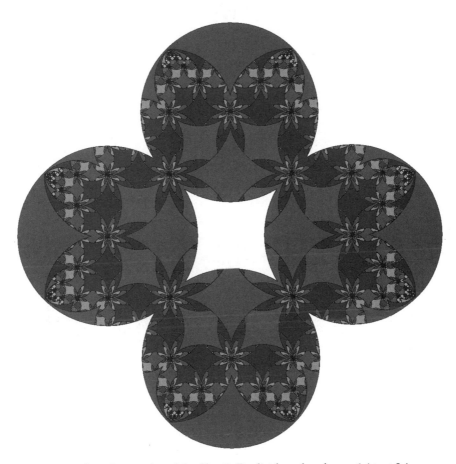

Figure 20 A formal expansion of the Chaotic Dualist for values from −1.4 to +2.4.

should be remembered, is simply information regarding the semantic behavior for different inputs of a pair of English sentences.

Figure 22 shows an escape-time diagram for our second version of the Chaotic Dualist, in which values for our two sentences are computed successively. This is the variation that gave us the 'origami' attractor above. (This diagram and the next are for values between −2 and +6.)

Our final variation, the Half-Dualist, gave us a double ellipse attractor. Its escape-time diagram is shown in figure 23.

Despite the fact that our attractors for the three variations on the Chaotic Dualist are so different (as different, for example, as the origami and double ellipse attractors) the general shape of their corresponding escape-time diagrams are quite clearly related. We can't claim to understand all features of these images, and further work is clearly needed. It is nonetheless tempting to speculate that what one is seeing in the similarities of these images is a visual representation of deep similarities in the self-referential semantics of these variants—similarities that might otherwise remain hidden in the complex details of their semantic behavior.

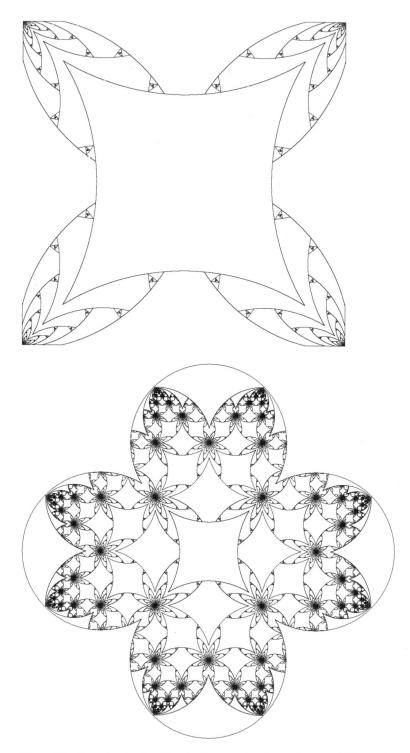

Figure 21 Traceries for the Chaotic Dualist, showing points at which numbers of escape iterations change.

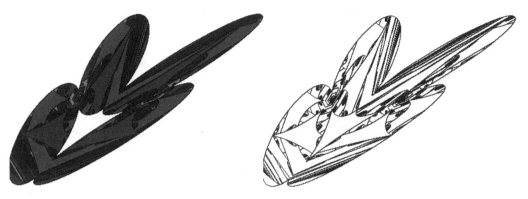

Figure 22 Sequential computation of the Chaotic Liar: escape-time diagrams corresponding to the origami attractor.

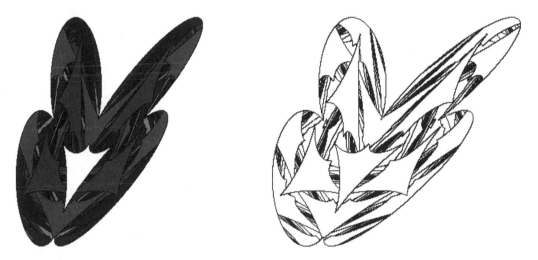

X: X is true to half the extent that Y is true.
Y: Y is as true as X is false.

Figure 23 The Half-Dualist.

There are, of course, an infinite range of further variations on the Dualist. One family of such variations—the Fuzzy Dualists—seems worthy of special note.

Consider a pair of statements obtained from the Chaotic Dualist by appending "It is very false that" to the first of our statements and "It is fairly false that" to the second. Treating 'it is false that' as a form of negation, and using fuzzy hedges as before to modify the value of the sentence as a whole, this gives us the following Fuzzy Dualist pair:

X: It is very false that X is as true as Y.

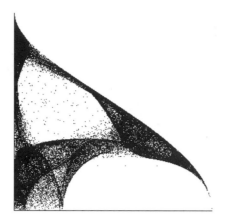 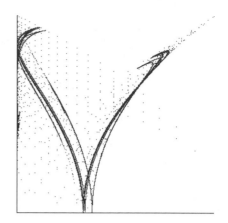

Figure 24 Attractors for the Fuzzy Dualist, calculated simultaneously (left) and sequentially (right).

Y: It is fairly false that Y is as true as X is false.

$$x_{n+1} = (1 - (1 - \text{Abs}(y_n - x_n)))^2$$
$$y_{n+1} = \sqrt{1 - (1 - \text{Abs}((1 - x_n) - y_n))}$$

For a simultaneous calculation of revised values, this gives us the persistent attractor shown in an overlay diagram in the first frame of figure 24. A sequential calculation will use these slightly different algorithms:

$$x_{n+1} = (1 - (1 - \text{Abs}(y_n - x_n)))^2$$
$$y_{n+1} = \sqrt{1 - (1 - \text{Abs}((1 - x_{n+1}) - y_n))}$$

This gives us the quite different overlay diagram shown in the second frame of figure 24. Figure 25 shows the corresponding escape-time diagrams for this Fuzzy Dualist in the two forms of computation, here using a threshold of 0.8 from the origin.

1.7   THE TRIPLIST AND THREE-DIMENSIONAL ATTRACTORS

Beyond the Dualist lie various Triplist variations, in which not two but three mutually referential sentences speak of one another's values. With three values in place of two, of course, our attractors leave the two-dimensional plane and take the form of three-dimensional logical objects. Here again we'll simply offer a few examples.

Consider, for example, a trio of sentences each of which says that its value is half the value of the difference between the other two. For a wide range of values, this gives us an attractor we call the 'Minerva'. Seen from the perspective of just two dimensions, it develops in the form shown in figure 26. Figure 27 shows a less fully iterated form of the Minerva rotated in three dimensions.

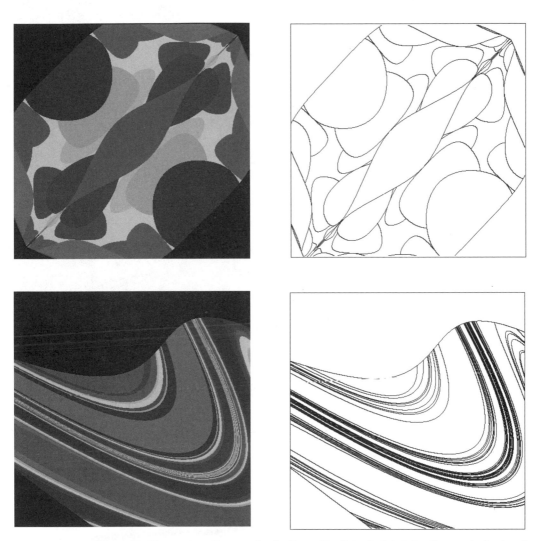

Figure 25 Escape-time diagrams for the Fuzzy Dualist, calculated simultaneously (top) and sequentially (bottom).

Consider a similar trio of sentences each of which says that its value is one-fourth the difference between the others. Here a braided attractor appears. Seen from the perspective of just two dimensions, it develops as shown in figure 28.

Figure 29 shows a simplified version, rotated in three dimensions.

Corresponding to the two-dimensional escape-time diagrams of the Chaotic and Logistic Dualists will be three-dimensional escape-time solids for Triplist variations. Here each point in a three-dimensional space is colored in terms of how many iterations are required for the initial set of values (x, y, z) represented by that point to reach a certain distance from (0, 0, 0) under iteration. Figures 30 and 31 show escape-time diagrams for the attractors above.[45]

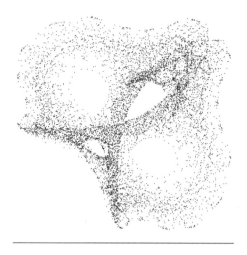

$$x_{n+1} = 1 - \text{Abs}(x_n - 1/2 \cdot \text{Abs}(y_n - z_n))$$
$$y_{n+1} = 1 - \text{Abs}(y_n - 1/2 \cdot \text{Abs}(x_n - z_n))$$
$$z_{n+1} = 1 - \text{Abs}(z_n - 1/2 \cdot \text{Abs}(x_n - y_n))$$

Figure 26   The Minerva.

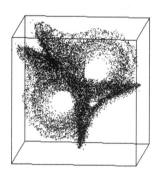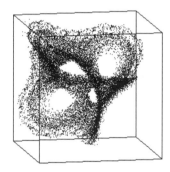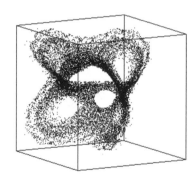

Figure 27   The Minerva rotated in three dimensions.

As a final image we offer a three-dimensional escape-time solid for a Fuzzy Triplist. Here each sentence says that its value is different from the claim that the other sentences have very much the same value. Expressed in terms of the biconditional:

X: $\sim (X \leftrightarrow$ it is very true that $Y \leftrightarrow Z)$

Y: $\sim (Y \leftrightarrow$ it is very true that $X \leftrightarrow Z)$

Z: $\sim (Z \leftrightarrow$ it is very true that $X \leftrightarrow Y)$

The escape-time solid for the Fuzzy Triplist is shown for two angles in figure 32.

In this chapter we have attempted to introduce, for the most part by example, a range of dynamical phenomena that appear in clear visual form with computer modeling of self-reference in infinite-valued and fuzzy

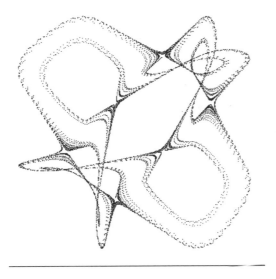

$$x_{n+1} = 1 - \text{Abs}(x_n - 1/4 \cdot \text{Abs}(y_n - z_n))$$
$$y_{n+1} = 1 - \text{Abs}(y_n - 1/4 \cdot \text{Abs}(x_n - z_n))$$
$$z_{n+1} = 1 - \text{Abs}(z_n - 1/4 \cdot \text{Abs}(x_n - y_n))$$

Figure 28   The Thunderbird.

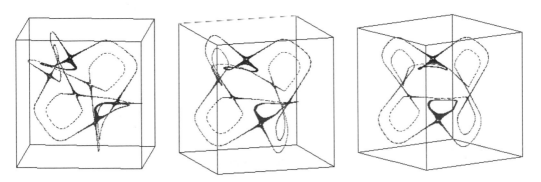

Figure 29   The Thunderbird rotated in three dimensions.

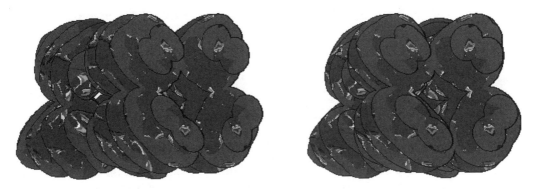

Figure 30   Escape-time solid for the Minerva.

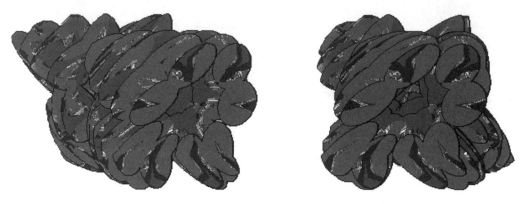

Figure 31 Escape-time solid for the Thunderbird.

Figure 32 Escape-time solid for a Fuzzy Triplist.

logics. This is intended, however, as merely an introduction; a great deal of further work remains to be done. There is much even in the images offered above that we can't yet claim to understand fully.

The promise of such an approach, of course, is that images such as these may have some important things to tell us: the fact that fractal images and strange attractors emerge so naturally from an infinite-valued semantic analysis of paradox, for example, seems not only to offer some strange beauty but also an intriguing promise of some deeper truths. Computer modeling of this sort affords a link—an immediate visual link—between logic and geometry. It is therefore tempting to speculate that what such an approach may promise in the long run is the possibility of a range of logical and metalogical results dreamt of in geometrical imagery and proven by geometrical means.

1.8 PHILOSOPHICAL AND METALOGICAL APPLICATIONS

In the next chapter we want to extend the application of some of the modeling tools introduced here beyond semantic dynamics to certain aspects of epistemic dynamics and certain sorts of epistemic crises.

The basic idea is this. Suppose that you receive information, of various shades of accuracy, from a number of sources with different track records of reliability. Some of the information you receive from these sources may be fairly straightforward. But some information received may itself be about the accuracy of other information or even about the general reliability of some of your other sources. This picture of conflicting information from conflicting sources, it can be argued, characterizes our epistemic lives quite generally. Information sets within such a model, we will want to show, can exhibit dynamic and chaotic phenomena quite similar to those introduced above.

In this final section we also want to note some metalogical applications related to the work above. We present these results in a standard form which makes it clear that they could, in principle, have been arrived at and proven without the work in computer modeling outlined above. Here we would emphasize 'in principle', however. We know full well that our own route to the results lay essentially through work in modeling; *we* would not have focused on these results in any other way.

Within a classically bivalent framework, the Strengthened Liar has long been the bane of attempts to solve the simple Liar. If one says that the Liar is neither true nor false but has some third semantic value C (neither-true-nor-false, for example), one is immediately confronted with a Strengthened Liar that seems to embody all the old problems anew:

This sentence is either false or has semantic value C.

If true, the sentence is untrue. If it has either of the alternative values, on the other hand, it appears it must be simply true. As we noted above, the Strengthened Liar can also be extended into infinite-valued logics in ways that seem to indicate that fixed-point 'solutions' will be similarly inadequate as general treatments of self-referential paradox.

Here we want to use the general structure of the Strengthened Liar together with some of the work above to motivate limitative theorems regarding the formal undefinability and effective undecidability of chaos. The deep structure of these results corresponds to that of a Strengthened Liar combined with the Chaotic Liar. We call the following sentence the Strengthened Chaotic Liar:

> Either the boxed sentence has a chaotic semantic behavior or it is as
> true as it estimated to be false.

Here we will assume that having a chaotic semantic behavior, as defined
strictly above, is itself a bivalent affair. But then does the Strengthened
Chaotic Liar have a chaotic semantic behavior or not? If it *does* have a
chaotic semantic behavior, it will be completely true in virtue of its first
disjunct. But the semantic behavior of a sentence that is completely true
will clearly not qualify as chaotic—it will have the constant value 1
regardless of previous estimates. If the Strengthened Chaotic Liar does *not*
have a chaotic semantic behavior, its truth-value will depend entirely on its
second disjunct. But the semantic behavior of that second disjunct will
mimic the behavior of the Chaotic Liar, which we know to be semantically
chaotic. We have derived a contradiction in either case.

This paradox can be used—much as Gödel used the Richard paradox, as
Tarski used the Liar, and as Chaitin used the Berry paradox—to motivate a
class of limitative theorems regarding chaos itself.

We offer a first form of the basic result using Gödel numbering and a
form of diagonalization. Here we will be concerned with formal systems
intended to deal with real arithmetic and adequate for number theory.
Systems of real arithmetic include, for example, Rogers's system **R**, taken
from Montague's formulation and equivalent to Tarski's theory of real
closed fields.[46] The condition 'adequate for number theory' requires
merely three additional axioms for 'is an integer'. We concentrate on
systems of real arithmetic because our target is limitative results regarding
chaos theory; chaotic functions are paradigmatically defined on the reals.

Formal systems of real arithmetic such as those at issue, however—
precisely because they remain formal systems—contain only denumerably
many expressions and thus cannot contain as many numerals as there
are reals.[47] One difficulty this creates is that the notion of *representation*
of a function that is standard within number theory cannot be carried
over to real arithmetic without qualification. Within number theory,
an n-place function $\mathbf{f}$ on natural numbers is said to be represented by
a formula $F(x_1, \ldots, x_n, x_{n+1})$ just in case, for any natural numbers
$p_1, \ldots, p_n, j$, if $\mathbf{f}(p_1, \ldots, p_n) = j$,

$$\vdash \forall x_{n+1}(F(\mathbf{p_1}, \ldots, \mathbf{p_n}, x_{n+1}) \leftrightarrow x_{n+1} = \mathbf{j})$$

where $\mathbf{p_1}, \ldots, \mathbf{p_n}$ and $\mathbf{j}$ are numerals within the system at issue for $p_1, \ldots, p_n$ and j respectively.[48] Within formal systems for the reals, on the other
hand, there simply won't be numerals $\mathbf{p_1}, \ldots, \mathbf{p_n}$ and $\mathbf{j}$ for all real numbers
$p_1, \ldots, p_n$ and j.

One way to accommodate this cardinality problem is to follow Tarski's
1931 work on the definability of sets of reals. We continue to address

functions genuinely on the reals, but we use the notion of functions *determined* within formal systems for real arithmetic instead of a notion of functions *represented* within such systems. Tarski outlines 'definable' sets of reals as follows: "A set X is a *definable set* (or a *definable set of order n*) if there is a sentential function (or a sentential function of order n at most) which contains some variable of order 1 as its only free variable, and which satisfies the condition that, for every real number x, $x \in X$ if and only if x satisfies this function."[49] Using 'determined' in place of Tarski's 'definable' for the sake of clarity, and treating one-place functions on the reals as sets of ordered pairs of reals, we can similarly speak of a function x on the reals as *determined* by a functional expression f^e just in case, for every pair of reals x, $x \in X$ if and only if x satisfies f^e.

With this background, we can offer a first form of limitative result regarding formal treatment of chaos: given any consistent formal system of real arithmetic **T** adequate for number theory, the set Γ of Gödel numbers of expressions that determine functions $\mathbf{f}(x)$ chaotic on the interval $[0, 1]$ is undefinable in **T**.

Theorem 1A on the formal undefinability of chaos: There is no function $\mathbf{c}$ representable in **t** such that

$$\mathbf{c}(\#\,\mathbf{f}(\mathbf{x})) = \begin{cases} 1 & \text{if } \#\mathbf{f}(\mathbf{x}) \subset \Gamma \\ 0 & \text{if } \#\mathbf{f}(\mathbf{x}) \notin \Gamma. \end{cases}$$

Proof Suppose, for a proof by contradiction, that such a function $\mathbf{c}$ *is* represented in **T**. There will then be a class of expressions that determine a class of functions $\mathbf{g}$ such that, for a fixed Gödel number $\#\mathbf{f_0}(\mathbf{x})$ of an expression determining a one-place function,

$$\mathbf{g}(y) = \begin{cases} 1 - (y - y) & \text{if } \mathbf{c}(\#\mathbf{f_0}(\mathbf{x})) = 1 \\ 1 - \mathrm{Abs}((1 - y) - y) & \text{otherwise.} \end{cases}$$

Different numbers $\#\mathbf{f_0}(\mathbf{x})$ in such a schema will give us different functions $\mathbf{g}$, of course. If $\#\mathbf{f_0}(\mathbf{x})$ is the Gödel number of an expression that determines a function that *is* chaotic on $[0, 1]$, assuming $\mathbf{c}$, we will have a $\mathbf{g}(y)$ that will simply give us a constant series of 1s for all iterations. If, on the other hand, $\#\mathbf{f_0}(\mathbf{x})$ is the Gödel number of an expression that determines a function *not* chaotic on $[0, 1]$, assuming $\mathbf{c}$, we will have a $\mathbf{g}(y)$ that gives us $1 - \mathrm{Abs}((1 - y) - y)$ as output. That formula, of course, is the formula of the Chaotic Liar, chosen here precisely because it is paradigmatically chaotic on the real interval $[0, 1]$.

On the assumptions above, by the diagonal lemma, there will be an expression that determines a function $\mathbf{g}$, where $\#\mathbf{G}(\mathbf{x})$ is the Gödel number of the expression at issue:

$$G(y) = \begin{cases} 1 - (y - y) & \text{if } c(\#G(x)) = 1 \\ 1 - \text{Abs}((1 - y) - y) & \text{otherwise.}^{50} \end{cases}$$

But will $G(y)$ be chaotic on the interval $[0, 1]$ or not?

Suppose that it is. In that case, on the assumption of a represented function c, and since $\#G(x)$ is the Gödel number of an expression that determines $G(x)$, it will be the case that $c(\#G(x)) = 1$. By the specifications of G, then, G will give us a constant output of 1s for any y. In that case G will clearly *not* be chaotic on the interval $[0, 1]$, and we have derived a contradiction.

Suppose instead that $G(y)$ is not chaotic on $[0, 1]$. Assuming function c represented, $c(\#G(x)) = 0$. By the specification of G, then, G gives us $1 - \text{Abs}((1 - y) - y)$. But G *will* then be chaotic on the interval $[0, 1]$; here again we have derived a contradiction.

Within any consistent system of real arithmetic adequate for number theory, then, there can be no function c represented. It follows that within any such system the set Γ of Gödel numbers of expressions that determine functions $f(x)$ chaotic on the interval $[0, 1]$ is undefinable in the formal sense. □

As related results, it should be noted, Γ will be nonrecursive and undecidable. Assuming Church's thesis, then, there can be no effective method for deciding whether an arbitrary expression of a system such as T determines a function chaotic on the interval $[0, 1]$.

We have offered this first approach to limitative results regarding chaos through Gödel numbering and diagonalization simply because these may be somewhat more familiar to philosophical logicians. A second approach, structurally similar but somewhat more elegant, can be sketched following Rice's Theorem in recursion theory.[51]

Theorem 1B on the non-calculability of chaos: Let C be the set of chaotic functions defined on the set of partially recursive functions F on the real interval $[0, 1]$. Assume that $\lambda x[1 - \text{Abs}((1 - x) - x)]$ is in C but that $\lambda x[1]$, the constant function identical to 1, is not in C. Then the index set $I(C) = \{i: f_i \in C\}$ is not effectively calculable.

Proof Assume, for proof by contradiction, that the index of chaotic functions is λ-definable. We have that $\lambda x[1 - \text{Abs}((1 - x) - x)]$ is some f_i in C and that $\lambda x[1]$ is some f_j not in C. Then we may define the diagonal function $d(x)$ to be j, if $f_x \in C$, and $d(x)$ to be i otherwise. By the fixed-point lemma, there will be a k such that $f_k = f_{d(k)}$. Hence, by the definition of $d(x)$, we have $f_k \in C$ if and only if $d(k) = j$; but since $f_j(x)$ is the non-chaotic constant function identical to 1, we have $f_k \in C$ if and only if $f_k \notin C$, which is a contradiction. Contrary to our assumption, therefore, I(C) is not λ-definable. It follows by Church's thesis that the index set of chaotic functions is not effectively calculable. □

In one tradition, the paradoxes are treated not as simple puzzles waiting for solution but as possible keys to a better understanding of incompleteness phenomena and semantics in general. Here, using the tools of computer modeling and dynamical systems theory, we have attempted to extend that tradition into the realm of infinite-valued logics.

Paradox is not illogicality, but it has been a trap for logicians: the semantic paradoxes look just a little simpler and more predictable than they actually are. Even in some of the most recent and logically sophisticated work on cyclical regularity in the semantic paradoxes, their deeper and more complex semantic patterns have remained hidden. Our attempt, rather than a search for semantic stability or simple patterns within the paradoxes, has been to offer some glimpses of the infinitely complex, chaotic, and fractal patterns of semantic *instability* that have gone virtually unexplored.

2 Notes on Epistemic Dynamics

We receive a variety of messages, all claiming to be genuine information, from a variety of sources. As a result, we have a range of different and often conflicting inputs. Some inputs give accurate information, or at least give accurate information under certain conditions or some of the time. Some do not. Our job as epistemic agents is to tell the difference: to figure out what information to accept as genuine, to what extent, and from what sources.

This general epistemic predicament appears in classical philosophical form in terms of questions regarding input from different senses. Montaigne, for example, has us

> ... think of the arguments, consequences, and conclusions which we infer by comparing one sense with another.... We can see from that how vital it would be for our knowledge of truth if we lacked another sense, or two or three senses. We have fashioned a truth by questioning our five senses working together; but perhaps we need to harmonize the contribution of eight or ten senses if we are ever to know, with certainty, what Truth is in essence.[1]

On March 2, 1693, William Molyneux sent Locke a question regarding inputs from different senses. Locke included Molyneux's question, with his answer, in the second edition of *An Essay Concerning Human Understanding*:

> ... I shall here insert a problem of that very ingenious and studious promoter of real knowledge, the learned and worthy Mr. Molineux, which he was pleased to send me in a letter some months since; and it is this:— "Suppose a man *born* blind, and now adult, and taught by his *touch* to distinguish between a cube and a sphere of the same metal, and nighly of the same bigness, so as to tell, when he felt one and the other, which is the cube, which the sphere. Suppose then the cube and sphere placed on a table, and the blind man be made to see: *quaere*, whether *by his sight, before he touched them*, he could now distinguish and tell which is the globe, which the cube? To which the acute and judicious proposer answers, Not. For, though he has obtained the experience of how a globe, how a cube affects his touch, yet he has not yet obtained the experience, that what affects his touch so or so, must affect his sight so or so; or that a protuberant angle in

the cube, that pressed his hand unequally, shall appear to his eye as it does in the cube." —I agree with this thinking gentleman, whom I am proud to call my friend, in his answer to this problem; and am of opinion that the blind man, at first sight, would not be able with certainty to say which was the globe, which the cube, whilst he only saw them; though he could unerringly name them by his touch, and certainly distinguish them by the difference of their figures felt.[2]

We can imagine an even more radical Molyneux-like situation in which the data from our senses *conflict*: in which something feels like a cube and yet looks like a sphere. A range of contemporary split-brain studies, on patients in which the corpus callosum has been cut, involves a technique in which conflicting information of this type is sent to the two hemispheres of the brain.[3] Because the hemispheres are communicatively isolated, two incompatible responses are elicited: a verbal response controlled by the left hemisphere, for example, contradicts a motor response controlled by the right. Of particular interest is the individual's often smooth incorporation of these incompatible responses, as if both had been intended, when asked to explain his behavior.[4]

The case of different messages from different senses is only an immediately perceptual instance of a quite general epistemic predicament, however. Our epistemic lives are filled with different and often conflicting inputs: inputs of conflicting experimental data, for example; of incompatible meter readings; of contradictory eyewitness testimony; of contradictory messages within human relationships; of rival claims or analyses or interpretations from rival texts or by rival theorists; of conflicting approaches from different disciplines; of warring religious, scientific, and political authorities. Conflicts appear between such levels as well as within them. Our job as epistemic agents is to make sense of it all: to sort the conflicting messages into the credible and the incredible, the more accurate and the less accurate, those messages that we act upon and those that we ignore.

The most extreme cases of informational conflict appear as motivations for Pyrrhonistic skepticism from Sextus Empiricus on. In the *Apology for Raymond Sebond*, for example, Montaigne repeatedly fuels the fires of skepticism with lists of contradictory authorities:

Thales was the first to inquire into such matters: he thought God was a spirit who made all things out of water; Anaximander said that the gods are born and die with the seasons and that there are worlds infinite in number; Anaximenes said God was Air, immense, extensive, ever moving; Anaxagoras was the first to hold that the delineation and fashioning of all things was directed by the might and reason of an infinite Spirit; Alcmaeon attributed godhead to the Sun, the Moon, the stars and the soul; Pythagoras made God into a Spirit diffused throughout all nature and from whom our souls are detached; for Parmenides God was a circle of light surrounding the heavens and sustaining the world with its heat. . . . Chrysippus made a chaotic mass of all these assertions and included among his thousand forms of gods men who had been immortalized. Diagoras and Theodorus bluntly denied that gods exist. . . .

So much din from so many philosophical brainboxes! Trust in your philosophy now! Boast that you are the one who has found the lucky bean in your festive pudding![5]

A skeptical passage from Hume in this regard reads as if written by Kafka:

The *intense* view of these manifold contradictions and imperfections in human reason has so wrought upon me, and so heated my brain, that I am ready to reject all belief and reasoning, and can look upon no opinion even as more probable or likely than another. Where am I, or what? From what causes do I derive my existence, and to what condition shall I return? Whose favour shall I court, and whose anger must I dread? What beings surround me? and on whom have I any influence?[6]

Such extreme cases of informational conflict and resultant epistemological crisis are not merely phenomena of philosophical skepticism. Alasdair MacIntyre notes the ubiquity of such crises in ordinary life:

What is an epistemological crisis? Consider, first, the situation of ordinary agents who are thrown into such crises. Someone who has believed that he was highly valued by his employers and colleagues is suddenly fired; someone proposed for membership of a club whose members were all, so he believed, close friends is blackballed. Or someone falls in love and needs to know what the loved one *really* feels; someone falls out of love and needs to know how he or she can possibly have been so mistaken in the other . . . . It is in such situations that ordinary agents who have never learned anything about academic philosophy are apt to rediscover for themselves versions of the other-minds problem and the problem of the justification of induction.[7]

In this chapter we will not deal with full skepticism or full epistemological crisis. But we will take seriously the idea that our general epistemic predicament is one in which we have to make sense of conflicting information from various inputs. One characteristic of our general predicament which makes the task particularly difficult—a characteristic emphasized by both Hume and MacIntyre—is that some of the messages received from different sources are themselves directly or indirectly *about* either the accuracy of other messages or the general reliability of other sources. One of our experiments may indicate that an important variable was not in fact held constant in an earlier test, for example; if one of our meters is right, another of our meters is only roughly and intermittently reliable; two of our friends are unanimous in telling us that another of our friends is no true friend at all; against the background of one statistical measure the data from another is highly misleading; one of our investigators in the field claims that the report shortly to be filed by another field investigator is inaccurate; one of our secret agents reports that another has defected and his reports are not to be trusted, though it may in fact be that first agent who has defected and the second who is sending reliable reports; each of a handful of respected authorities warns us that trust in the others is misplaced. One of our aims in what follows is to try to model this type of mutual reference within conflicting sources of information. Clearly some of the tools used in chapter 1 for modeling tangled reference in the semantic case will be applicable in the epistemic case as well.

In the simplest cases of informational conflict, we may finally decide that one input is simply to be discounted. We decide that one batch of data must have been tainted, for example, or that the scientists are right: you can never trust politicians. But there is also an enormous range of more complicated ways that we use to deal with informational conflict. We may decide that batches of data that initially appeared to be contradictory are not—what they indicate instead, we decide, are real differences that depend on subtle changes in experimental conditions. We may decide that rival interpretations are both partially true, or capture something of the truth, that conflicting authorities are addressing different and incommensurable questions, and the like. Deliberation as to how to deal with a particular case of informational conflict, moreover, may not be instantaneous. Epistemic deliberation may rather display a complex dynamics: we may change our minds repeatedly but systematically, going through a series of revised 'takes' on the situation. Nice attempts at axiomatizing some of the simpler concepts in the dynamics of belief change, including expansion of belief sets, contraction, and a form of revision in which minimal changes are made to make way for expansion, appear in a chain of recent work stemming from van Benthem and Gärdenfors.[8] Veltman makes the intriguing further proposal in his 'updating semantics' that the meaning of a sentence should be construed not in terms of its truth-conditions but its epistemic dynamics: "you know the meaning of a sentence if you know the changes it brings about in the information state conveyed by the sentence."[9] The work discussed here, though motivated by the same basic convictions about the philosophical importance of epistemic dynamics, starts from an independent base and offers an importantly different approach. Our attempt, in which shades of accuracy and tangled reference play a much more fundamental role, is to offer at least a starting model for some of the wilder and more complex dynamical phenomena of informational conflict.

Finally, it should be noted that there are some cases in which we may decide that informational conflict is not something that is going to be resolved at all: that it is something we're going to have to live with. One can imagine extreme cases of informational conflict that are genuinely unlivable, approaching the abstract philosophical world of the skeptic or the all-too-immediate world of the institutionalized paranoiac. In less extreme cases, however, informational conflict may be recognized to be irresolvable and yet nonetheless manageable. We certainly do evolve strategies of containment and control for dealing with some varieties of epistemic chaos, and this too should be reflected in the model.

2.1   TOWARD A SIMPLE MODEL: SOME BASIC CONCEPTS

The model we have to offer, designed to deal primarily with cases of tangled epistemic reference, is ultimately a very simple one. Here we want to outline it carefully, piece by piece, in order to make clear both its core motivation and some of its artificialities.

Our model will ultimately be written in terms of a continuum of degrees of estimated accuracy for different reports from different epistemic sources. It helps to start with a simple sketch of our epistemic predicament, however, drawn in terms of simple bivalent truth and falsity.

At times, we can tell the truth-value of what someone has told us from internal evidence alone. If what he's told us is the following, for example, we can be sure that what he's said is false:

This statement is both true and false.[10]

At other times we can tell from internal evidence that what someone has told us is true:

This statement is not both true and false.[11]

There are also stranger cases, of course. In some cases, it seems clear that internal evidence is the only evidence that will be relevant—that issues of truth and falsity won't be settled by additional information from outside— and yet it is also clear that internal evidence is insufficient to decide the matter. One such case is the Truth-teller, outlined in the previous chapter:

This sentence is true.

In the strangest cases of all, internal evidence seems adequate to convince us that *neither* of our standard values can be consistently assigned: such is the case of the classical Liar.

Self-reference as simple and explicit as these extreme cases, however, is epistemically rare.[12] The great bulk of our knowledge concerns situations in which it is clear that internal evidence is not all that counts:

1. The solid crust of Venus is less than 100 meters thick.

To establish the truth or falsity of (1) we clearly need more than internal evidence. What we rely on, of course, is information gathered directly or gleaned by inference from further sources. Patterns of inference involved can be very complicated and are in many cases poorly understood— inference to the best explanation, for example, or inference guided by the simplest available theory.

What we want to emphasize here is that the larger patterns of inference even for cases such as (1) will often involve questions of consistency and internal coherence—questions of *internal* evidence. Though rarely self-referential in any simple sense, these larger patterns of inference also quite generally involve larger sets of claims with tangled patterns of challenge and support. The further information from which we infer (1), for example, may consist of a blurred image through a telescope, mechanical pen marks on paper reflecting spectroscopic analyses, transmitted impulses decoded as video photographs from satellites, or a weighted combination of all these and more. It may be information that we ourselves gather, or that we accept from others. For any case like (1), however, it seems inevitable that the pattern of epistemic support will involve an epistemic predicament of competing information. Woven into that web of epistemic support will be data regarding other data and claims regarding the validity of other claims—claims as simple as the observation that we should not be swayed by the fact that the whole of Venus appears smaller than a millimeter to the naked eye, for example, or as complex as corrections for red shift. In any such case we will also be relying on information regarding the reliability of general sources of information—information as simple as the claim that what purport to be photographs from a satellite have not been faked, or as complex as the theoretical support for spectrographic analysis. The great bulk of our knowledge has the look of (1), non-self-referential and for which internal evidence alone is insufficient. But even that knowledge relies on larger patterns of epistemic support which *are* referentially tangled, essentially incorporating information regarding the accuracy of other information, and of source claims regarding the general reliability of other sources of information.

This picture of our epistemic predicament is reminiscent of Quine's web of belief, "impinging on experience at its edges," though here phrased in terms of lines of epistemic support rather than logical connections and with an emphasis on the patterns of tangled reference within such a web:

The totality of our so-called knowledge or beliefs, from the most casual matters of geography and history to the profoundest laws of atomic physics or even pure mathematics and logic, is a man-made fabric which impinges on experience only along the edges. Or, to change the figure, total science is like a field of force whose boundary conditions are experience. A conflict with experience at the periphery occasions readjustments in the interior of the field. Truth values have to be redistributed over some of our statements. Reëvaluation of some statements entails reëvaluation of others, because of their logical interconnections—the logical laws being in turn simply certain further statements of the system, certain further elements of the field. Having reëvaluated one statement we must reëvaluate some others, which may be the statements logically connected with the first or may be the statements of logical connections themselves.[13]

The epistemic picture we've offered here, however, is also deliberately less contentious than Quine's: one can see the appropriateness of the web metaphor without claiming that there can be no analytic connections or points of pure epistemic foundation within the web.

Before leaving bivalence behind we should note examples in which it is not single self-referential sentences but mutually referential sets of sentences that allow us to establish truth values internally. Consider for example a case from Anil Gupta in which two people, A and B, make the following claims:

A1:   Venus is not a planet but a star.

A2:   All of the claims made by B are true.

A3:   At least one of the claims made by B is false.

B1:   Venus is not a star but a planet.

B2:   At most one of the claims made by A is true.

Which of A's claims are true? As Gupta points out, we reason quite naturally in the following way: Since A2 and A3 contradict each other, they cannot both be true. We know on independent grounds that A1 is false. Thus at most one of A's claims can be true, and therefore B2 is true. We know on independent grounds that B1 is true, and thus know that all of B's claims are true. It must therefore be A2 that is true and A3 that is false.[14]

Such cases, though still restricted to questions of internal evidence and still clearly artificial, come one step closer to the tangled patterns of epistemic support and denial that we have sketched as defining the general human predicament. Patterns of mutual reference, both to the accuracy of claims and the general reliability of information sources, will be one of the phenomena that we want our model to capture.

In this chapter we present an epistemic model in terms of degrees of accuracy. As indicated in chapter 1, the assumption of bivalence can be challenged even for truth. Accuracy, on the other hand, seems on the face of it a matter of degree: we ordinarily think of one piece of information as more accurate than another, of a measurement or a piece of data as highly accurate, of some statement or claim as hopelessly and uselessly inaccurate. A natural first step, then, is to model degrees of accuracy using values in the [0, 1] interval. For purposes of epistemic modeling we can think of claims as having a very respectable accuracy of 0.9, for example, or a pitifully low accuracy of 0.1. Again as in chapter 1, even this first modeling assumption limits us to cases in which we can speak of both complete accuracy and complete inaccuracy. Although not all cases satisfy that assumption, it's not hard to find a wide range of cases that do—cases of accuracy in compass orientation, in time of day, in angles of alignment, in percentage or proportion, and the like. A further question for modeling appears even in simple compass cases, however. Consider

The island lies due north of our present position.

If the island does indeed lie due north, we can happily accord the statement an accuracy of 1. If the island lies due south, the statement couldn't be farther off—and thus gets an accuracy of 0. If the island is somewhere in between—18° east of north, for example—then the statement is clearly inaccurate to some degree. But how much?

The simplest answer is to mark off the compass at regular intervals. If the island is 18° east of true north, our statement is assigned an accuracy of 0.9. If the island is directly west, the statement that it lies due north would be considered half accurate—precisely as inaccurate, intuitively enough, as it would have been were the island due east. In even this simple compass model there are clearly more complicated ways of treating relative accuracy. We might for example square proportions, so that a statement that is 18° off would be treated not as 0.9 accurate but $((180 - 18)/180)^2 = 0.81$ accurate. On that measure, a report 90° off in either direction would be assigned an accuracy of only $1/4$. For our purposes, however, we need not decide between such alternatives; it will be enough to assume that some consistent way of speaking of relative accuracies is in place.

Further complications should be noted. Measures of accuracy quite plausibly depend upon context: we may treat a statement about the direction from which the swallows arrive as incredibly accurate if it is off a mere five degrees, for example, although we would reject as unacceptably inaccurate a report, off by precisely the same five degrees, of a torpedo approaching. This is one of the features that makes comparison between different cases problematic. It may be only fairly accurate to say that lunch is served as noon, just as it may be only fairly accurate to say that a story was carried by all the major networks. But suppose the story was in fact carried by six of seven major networks. Just when would lunch have to be served for the first statement to be as accurate as the second in such a case?[15] All that can be said here is that our approach in modeling will be to

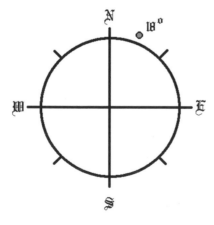

Figure 1   A compass model of accuracy.

abstract from problems of contextual sensitivity and cross-context comparison. This limitation can be enforced in examples if we think of all the statements within in a given set as being of the same type (degrees of island-location, for example) and considered in the same context.

All models involve limitations; that is what makes them models. There is therefore no shame in admitting that ours is a deliberately simplified picture of degrees of accuracy for a carefully restricted class of statements. What is of interest is whether even such a simple model is adequate to capture important aspects, including dynamic aspects, of situations involving conflicting and referentially tangled information.

Within both a compass model of accuracy and an interval model more generally it seems natural to model the inaccuracy of a statement $\mathbf{p}$ as $1 - /\mathbf{p}/$, where $/\mathbf{p}/$ is taken as its degree of accuracy. Within such a model we can moreover think of predicates as coming in matched pairs of opposites: 'north' and 'south', '18°' and '198°', 'noon' and 'midnight', 'parallel' and 'perpendicular'. Negation within such a model can then be treated as an 'opposite-operator': to add a negation to a sentence is to change its basic predicate to its paired opposite. Where $\mathbf{p}$ is

The swallows arrive at Capistrano from the northwest,

for example, the claim that the swallows do *not* arrive from the northwest can be taken as

The swallows arrive at Capistrano from the southeast.

Our claim is not, of course, that negation only functions in this way. Within the modeling constraints specified above, however, such a reading of negation allows a formal treatment of accuracy parallel to that outlined for truth in the previous chapter and familiar from multivalued logics and probability theory. Construing negation as an opposite-operator, we can treat the accuracy of a claim's negation as 1 minus the accuracy of the original claim. Using $/\mathbf{p}/$ here to indicate not a truth-value but an accuracy-value for $\mathbf{p}$,

$$/\sim \mathbf{p}/ = 1 - /\mathbf{p}/$$

A conjunction will only be as accurate as its least accurate conjunct, and a disjunction as accurate as its most accurate disjunct:

$$/(\mathbf{p}\ \&\ \mathbf{q})/ = \text{Min}\{/\mathbf{p}/, /\mathbf{q}/\}$$

$$/(\mathbf{p} \vee \mathbf{q})/ = \text{Max}\{/\mathbf{p}/, /\mathbf{q}/\}$$

Another important tool which we will borrow from the previous chapter and adapt to the concept of accuracy rather than truth is the V$\mathbf{vp}$ schema. Suppose a statement $\mathbf{p}$ is accurate to degree 0.8. How accurate then is a second-order accuracy claim to the effect that $\mathbf{p}$ is only half accurate? In what follows we use 'V$\mathbf{vp}$' to represent the proposition that a statement $\mathbf{p}$ has an *accuracy* of $\mathbf{v}$. Intuitively, a V$\mathbf{vp}$ statement about the accuracy of another statement **p** will be as inaccurate as it is off the target—as inaccurate as the real accuracy of **p** differs from the attributed accuracy **v**. Our V**vp** schema from chapter 1 can thus be reinterpreted in terms of accuracies:

$$/\text{V}\mathbf{vp}/ = 1 - \text{Abs}(\mathbf{v} - /\mathbf{p}/)$$

The final elements we will carry over to the epistemic context are the algorithmic treatments of linguistic hedges found in the literature of fuzzy logic. 'Very' we will treat in terms of a squaring function; 'fairly' in terms of square roots. In the case of accuracies, as in the case of truth, all that we want to claim is that such a model does seem to capture roughly the right features of such linguistic hedges—stronger 'very' statements must pass more severe tests, weaker 'fairly' statements the contrary.

With these components of a simple model of accuracy in hand, let us return to the sketch of our epistemic world with which we began. What does our epistemic predicament look like when characterized in terms not of bivalent truth and falsity but rather of a continuum of degrees of accuracy?

Much that was said for the bivalent case still holds. Our job as epistemic agents is still to gauge the accuracy of information from a variety of incoming sources—though perhaps to gauge it in terms of relative degree of accuracy—and we will in general have to do so in terms of competing claims regarding both the accuracy of particular pieces of information and the general reliability of particular sources of information. As in the bivalent case there will be statements capable of evaluation on internal evidence alone, though the dynamics of evaluation may be importantly different. Consider for example an analogue of the Half-Sayer of chapter 1:

This statement is half as accurate as it is estimated to be.

Though written here in terms of accuracy rather than truth, the formal behavior of the Half-Sayer will be the same. *Any* initial accuracy x_0 assumed for such a sentence will force a series of revisions in accord with the V**vp** schema and modeled by the following formula:

$$x_{n+1} = 1 - \text{Abs}((1/2 \cdot x_n) - x_n)$$

The result is a series of revised estimates of accuracy driving toward a fixed point of $2/3$ (figure 2). An accuracy evaluation of $2/3$ is thus the only one consistently assignable to such a sentence—a value assignable on internal grounds alone.[16]

Some sentences regarding degrees of accuracy behave better than their close cousins regarding bivalent truth and falsity. The classical Liar is of course notorious for its ill-behaved periodicity. Corresponding to the classical Liar, however, is a self-referential claim of total inaccuracy akin to the Infinite-valued Liar:

This statement is entirely inaccurate.

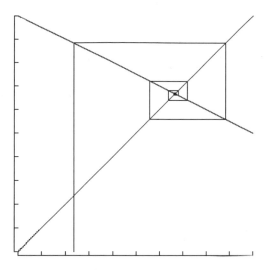

'This statement is half as accurate as it is estimated to be.'

Figure 2   An accuracy form of the Half-Sayer with initial estimate of 0.234.

Like the Infinite-valued Liar, this accuracy variation will take 1/2 as its fixed point. We can in fact solve for such a fixed point algebraically by starting with the V**vp** schema itself:

$$/V\mathbf{vp}/ = 1 - \text{Abs}(\mathbf{v} - /\mathbf{p}/)$$

Since in this case **p** *is* the V**vp** sentence,

$$/\mathbf{p}/ = 1 - \text{Abs}(\mathbf{v} - /\mathbf{p}/)$$

Our accuracy Liar claims it is *entirely* inaccurate. The attributed value **v** is therefore 0:

$$/\mathbf{p}/ = 1 - \text{Abs}(0 - /\mathbf{p}/)$$

For $0 \leq \mathbf{p} \leq 1$, then,

$$/\mathbf{p}/ = 1 - /\mathbf{p}/$$

$$2 \cdot /\mathbf{p}/ = 1$$

$$/\mathbf{p}/ = 1/2^{17}$$

Despite the fact that 1/2 is a fixed point for which algebraic solution is possible, however, it is not an attractor fixed point—there is no series of progressive approximations, as in the case of the Half-Sayer, drawing us inexorably toward that point.

There are also many sentences regarding degrees of accuracy which are not so well-behaved, of course. One example is an accuracy analogue of the Minimalist of chapter 1:

The true accuracy of this sentence is whichever is smaller: its estimated accuracy or its estimated inaccuracy.

Such a sentence behaves like the Liar when restricted to classical values of 0 and 1. For cases other than 0 and 1, however, it is the accuracy Minimalist rather than an accuracy Liar that converges on the behavior of the classical Liar.

Within an epistemic predicament drawn in terms of degrees of accuracy, then, as in one drawn in terms of bivalent truth and falsity, there will be statements for which internal evidence alone seems relevant. Here too, however, these would seem to be limiting cases. The standard message for which we will need to gauge accuracy will rather be something like

A torpedo approaches from 18°,

or

The enemy attacks at sunrise.

In either case an estimation of accuracy demands additional information, and here as before that information can be expected to be tangled in a web of competing claims about the relative accuracy of particular pieces of information or the relative reliability of various sources. A great part of the epistemic predicament takes the character of 'Who do you trust?', though in the case of degrees of accuracy the question becomes 'Who do you trust, and how much?'[18]

Here as before we should note that there will be wider puzzle cases involving not strict self-reference but tangles of mutually referential claims.

2. This statement has an accuracy of 1/2.   Accuracy: _____

3. Statement (2) is 1/2 accurate.   Accuracy: _____

4. Statements (2) and (3) have the same value. Accuracy: _____

5. This statement has the same value as (4).   Accuracy: _____

Is there any consistent set of accuracy assignments—any 4-dimensional fixed point, as it were—that can be given to the sentences of this set? Indeed there is. Statement (2), for reasons outlined regarding the Half-Sayer above, can only be given an accuracy of 2/3. Statement (3) is therefore 1/3 off—and itself gets an assignment of 2/3. Statement (4) is then fully accurate. Statement (5) will have a value of $1 - \text{Abs}(1 - /(5)/)$, and can therefore consistently be assigned any value within the [0,1] interval.

Here we have made self-referential and mutually referential sentences regarding accuracy both explicit and direct. Most of the patterns of self- and mutual-reference that appear within standard epistemic situations are neither: a message that applies to a class of messages including itself may rest on considerations of external evidence and may even call for empirical investigation.[19] The same holds true for messages that turn out on investigation to apply to each other. Patterns of reference become more tangled and more complex when it is not merely the accuracy of particular messages but the general reliability of certain sources of information that is at stake. We think one should not be deceived, then, by the puzzle-like character of explicit examples. Similar tangles of mutual reference may be buried under epistemic and deliberative situations as common as the following—a fictional example, but only barely so:

Imported major-ticket items, including high-end computers over $5,000 and automobiles, tend to have very similar sales curves.

IBM has found that its sales are inversely related to those of the major American car manufacturers: when people buy cars, they don't buy computers (or at least IBM computers). They decide to gear their production scheduling to well-known annual trends in automobile sales.

General Motors has noted a decline their share of the market over the last few years, directly related to an increase in the sales of imports.

Hitachi intends to introduce the first of its fifth-generation computers at Christmas.

The prospect for such tangles seems greater, rather than less, given the now massive use of computerized trading algorithms. It has been claimed that a computer-assisted slide of the stock market of precisely this type occurred in September of 1986 due to a positive feedback loop in the buy-sell programs of major investment and brokerage houses, which introduced an instability in the system.[20]

In the outline above we have emphasized fixed points in cases of self- and mutual-reference, characterizing fixed-point solutions as the only accuracy values consistently assignable to particular sentences or pieces of information. Here as in chapter 1, however, we remain suspicious of the notion that such fixed points should be taken without question as *solutions* for phenomena of self-reference. Again, such an approach would seem to face embarrassing questions in the case of sentences with multiple or even infinitely many fixed points and would seem incapable of the full generality required to deal with Strengthened Infinite-valued Liars and the like. Our interest in this chapter lies less in seeking simple solutions to epistemic instability than in providing a model that captures some of the complex dynamics of epistemic predicaments.

There is one final modeling tool that we wish to add, mentioned in informal discussion throughout. This is the notion of background reliability or epistemic reputation—a measure of trust applied not to individual claims but to general sources of information. In the absence of independent confirmation or disconfirmation regarding a particular piece of information, or even in supplement to external information, we commonly gauge a statement's reliability in terms of the general reliability of its source: "Consider the source." Ceteris paribus, a source of unexceptionally accurate information in the past will be believed this time around as well. Information from a source with a checkered history of inaccuracy will be treated with suspicion and epistemic reserve.

It is clear, then, that the reliability of a source is a function of its past accuracy. But precisely how? One modeling option is to take the reliability of a source to be simply the average of past statement accuracies. For some purposes, however, such a policy might be far too conservative. Secret agents in the British secret service of *Smiley's People*[21] have an unhappy tendency to defect to the other side. The use of a simple average would force us to treat as prima facie reliable a whole series of lies from a recently defected double agent, simply because that source had given accurate information for a long period in the distant past. Simple averaging generally fails to warn us of progressive *patterns* in inaccuracy: a dangerous inaccuracy that developed quite suddenly in the last ten reports would be treated as no more serious in terms of estimated reliability than would ten juvenile inaccuracies committed years ago or a scattered pattern of random error noise throughout a record of service. At the other extreme, it is clear that a reliability measure that represented only the accuracy of the last five statements that could be checked, regardless of the source's previous history, would have major shortcomings as well.

In what follows, we'll think of reliability, like accuracy, as on a scale between 0 and 1, and we'll use a recursive model for updating. Given a past reliability R_n for a source and a measurement of $/p/$ for the accuracy of a current statement p, our new reliability R_{n+1} will be calculated as:

$$R_{n+1} = ((2 \cdot R_n) + /p/)/3$$

The reputation for a source at any time, on such a model, is a weighted average of its past reputation and the accuracy of the most recent piece of information received. Such a formula has the advantage of combining recent accuracy and background reputation in a way that avoids both a simple averaging formula and one that neglects some element of the past entirely. But it is of course only one of an infinite number of formulae, even of this general type, that do so: we might have considered a heavier weighting for R_n, for example, or a formula that considers the average of the last five statements rather than simply the value of p.[22] We don't claim that this formula offers the only or even the most plausible measure of reliability. What it does offer is a simple model with which to start to envisage some of the more complicated aspects of epistemic dynamics.

Among those more complicated aspects are messages regarding not the accuracy of other statements but the reliability of general sources. Given a background reliability of 0.7 for a source, how accurate are we to gauge a message that its reliability is 0.6? For questions like this we will use a slight variation on the V**vp** schema. Where V**rs** is a statement attributing a reliability **r** to a source **s** with true reliability [**s**], we calculate the accuracy of V**rs** as

$$/V\mathbf{rs}/ = 1 - \text{Abs}(\mathbf{r} - [\mathbf{s}])$$

The claim that a source has a reliability of 0.6, for example, when its reliability is actually 0.7, is to underestimate it by 0.1; that claim of reliability itself we will therefore assign an accuracy rating of only 0.9.

It is clear on such a model that estimates of reliability for a source can be sensitive to judgments of accuracy regarding recent pronouncements, which may themselves be statements about—and hence be judged in terms of—estimates for the reliability of other sources. "You can't trust stratigraphic dating," say the radiocarbon people. "Radiocarbon isn't entirely reliable," say the molecular geneticists. "The molecular genetics model remains largely speculative," say the excavators. Interestingly enough, the notion of reliability of a source is closer to the substance of the original Epimenides paradox than is either truth or accuracy of a particular utterance. For decades philosophical logicians have introduced Epimenides the Cretan, who says:

All Cretans are Liars

and have then taken great pains to 'purify' the paradox into a single self-referential sentence asserting its own falsehood. In this original form of the paradox, however, it is clearly the reliability of Cretans in general as an informational source that Epimenides impugns, rather than the truth or accuracy of a particular claim.

In this section we've tried to sketch the background motivation for a small handful of conceptual tools. In what follows, we indicate some features of epistemic dynamics that appear in models employing these tools. It is worth emphasizing that the phenomena that follow are phenomena observable within this *model* of epistemic predicaments. It is an entirely appropriate question at a number of stages whether these are aspects of epistemic phenomena themselves, genuinely captured and revealed in the chosen model, or are in some way merely artifactual, limited to this particular model and doomed to disappear in a more sophisticated or more intuitive alternative. Such a question is not always easy to answer. Philosophical modeling of this type offers, we think, some surprising new tools for conceptual imaging. That is its promise. But that is also why we think it proper to handle all such modeling with a significant measure of methodological caution.

2.2 SELF-REFERENCE AND REPUTATION: THE SIMPLEST CASES

Agent 007 has been giving us accurate information for years, on the basis of which he has a sterling background reputation of 0.96. His most recent message, however, leaves us puzzled:

6. This piece of information is only half as accurate as you think it is.

What 007 has sent us is an accuracy version of the Half-Sayer. By this point we are familiar with the dynamics of accuracy estimates for such a message. But how will it affect our estimate of 007's reliability?

Our gauge of an agent's reliability is important not only for its own sake but because that reliability estimate will be used essentially as a default accuracy value regarding further statements for which we do not have, or do not yet have, independent confirmation or disconfirmation. If 007's next message is that there is a mole highly placed in the organization, for example, or that the enemy's nuclear warheads have been rendered harmless, or that they have not, how much credence we give that next message will depend ceteris paribus on our estimate of 007's general reliability. What hangs on reliability estimates is thus not merely the merit of our agent but the believability of the next message that we receive from him—a message that may be of quite immediate importance.

The reliability formula introduced on intuitive grounds above calls for updating background reliability in terms of the accuracy of the most recent piece of information $\mathbf{p}$:

$$R_{n+1} = ((2 \cdot R_n) + /\mathbf{p}/)/3$$

In updating 007's reputation, then, we need some estimate of the accuracy of this most recent message. Let us start with a simple guess: that message (6) has an accuracy of $1/2$. In light of that rating, 007's reliability would have to be updated as $((2 \cdot 0.96) + 0.5)/3$, or approximately 0.81. (Moneypenny is of the opinion that it serves James right for sending such an explicitly self-referential message.) On reflection, however, it is clear that we cannot assign a value of $1/2$ to the message received. That message is itself a $V\mathbf{vp}$ statement, claiming that a particular sentence $\mathbf{p}$—itself, as it happens—has an accuracy half of what it is estimated to have. If it is estimated to be half-accurate, the value that (6) self-ascribes will be half of *that*. Using the $V\mathbf{vp}$ schema we are thus forced to revise our estimate as follows:

$$/V\mathbf{vp}/ = 1 - \text{Abs}(\mathbf{v} - /\mathbf{p}/)$$

$$/(6)/ = 1 - \text{Abs}((0.5 \cdot 0.5) - 0.5)$$

$$/(6)/ = 1 - 0.25$$

$$/(6)/ = 0.75$$

It appears we have done 007 an injustice by our first calculation. We're forced on second thought to revise our initial estimate for (6) upwards to 0.75. Using 0.75 in place of 0.5, 007's reputation should be updated not to 0.81 but rather to $((2 \cdot 0.96) + 0.75)/3$, or 0.89. That is significantly better. Sorry, James.

On further reflection, however, it is clear that we still don't have an appropriate assignment for the accuracy of this most recent message. If we estimate its accuracy at 0.75, since it says it has an accuracy of only half of that, the **Vvp** schema will force us to recalibrate its accuracy as $((0.5 \cdot 0.75) - 0.75)$, or 0.625. 007's reputation would then be updated as $((2 \cdot 0.96) + 0.625)/3$, or approximately 0.85. With continued deliberation, our estimates for the accuracy of (6) and our corresponding gauge of 007's general reputation converge to single values:

Accuracy of Message	General Reputation
0.5	0.96
0.75	0.89
0.625	0.8483333
0.6875	0.8691667
0.62625	0.85875
0.671875	0.8639583
0.6640625	0.8613542
0.6679688	0.8626562
00.6660156	0.8620052
0.6669922	0.8623307
0.6665039	0.862168
0.666748	0.8622493
0.66626	0.8622087
0.666687	0.862229
0.6666565	0.8622188
0.6666718	0.8622239
0.6666641	0.8622214
0.6666679	0.8622226
0.666666	0.862222
0.666667	0.8622223
0.6666665	0.8622221
0.6666667	0.8622223
0.6666666	0.8622222
0.6666667	0.8622222
0.6666667	0.8622222

Given an initial guess of $1/2$, the estimated accuracy for message (6) converges on 0.6666667. Against an initial background reputation of 0.96, 007's reputation converges correspondingly on 0.8622222. Had our initial guess regarding the accuracy of the message been 0.234, and had 007's initial reputation been 0.8, estimated accuracy would again have converged on 0.6666667 and 007's updated reputation would have converged on 0.7555556. Had 007 started with an abysmal reputation of 0.3, message accuracy would have converged on 0.6666667 and his reputation would have risen to 0.422222.

In all cases the value of (6) will converge on $2/3$, regardless of our initial accuracy estimate, with the updated reputation changing from any initial R to $((2 \cdot R) + 2/3)/3$. In this first simple case, in other words, updated reputation shadows the dynamics of the self-referential piece of information at issue. This pattern is perhaps clearer in time-series graphs, shown for three examples in figure 3. Here one line indicates revisions in accuracy estimates, starting at different values; the other indicates the effect of such revisions on reputation updates.

A more revealing way of illustrating the pattern is in terms of web diagrams, outlined in chapter 1. In figure 4, the collapsing spiral shows the evolution of accuracy estimates for message (6)—a convergence in all cases

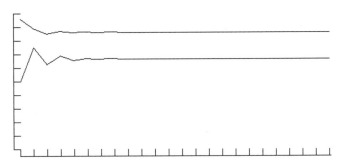

Initial background reliability = 0.96   Initial accuracy estimate for Half-Sayer = 0.5

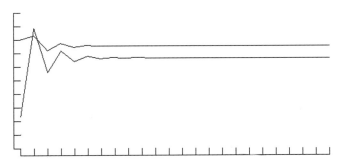

Initial background reliability = 0.8   Initial accuracy estimate for Half-Sayer = 0.234

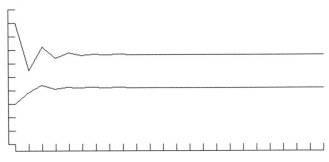

Initial background reliability = 0.3   Initial accuracy estimate for Half-Sayer = 0.9

Figure 3 Time-series graph for the Half-Sayer with influence on background reputation.

on an attractor fixed point of 2/3. The line descending from the upper left corner in each case is our graph for the Half-Sayer function; the solid line ascending from the lower left corner is the $x = y$ line used in graphing the web. The third line graphed in each of the frames in figure 4 represents the effect on the background reputation of the agent. Lines at different heights reflect the different background reputations in our three cases. For any point in the evolution of accuracy estimates for message (6), indicated by

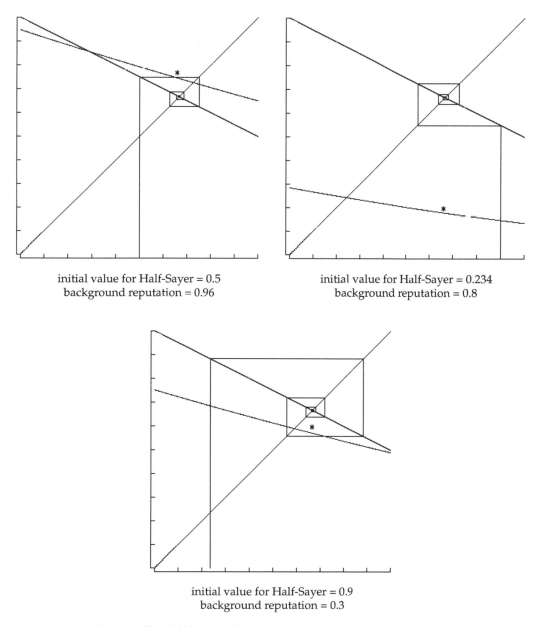

initial value for Half-Sayer = 0.5
background reputation = 0.96

initial value for Half-Sayer = 0.234
background reputation = 0.8

initial value for Half-Sayer = 0.9
background reputation = 0.3

Figure 4 The Half-Sayer with shadowed reputation.

the y-value for a point of intersection with the graph of the Half-Sayer function, the corresponding value for reputation will be the y-value of a point on the reputation line directly below or above that point of intersection. As accuracy values for (6) evolve, in other words, they cast a vertical 'shadow' on a reputation line. Accuracy estimates for (6) converge on 2/3 in all cases; different initial reputation values converge on the y-values of points marked roughly with asterisks.

For our first example, however, we have chosen a peculiarly well-behaved self-referential sentence. What if our agent—still with a sterling background reputation of 0.96—sends us a version of the Minimalist instead?

7. This piece of information is as accurate as whichever is smaller: your estimate of its accuracy or of its inaccuracy.

For any initial estimate other than 2/3, the evaluation of (7) will converge on a periodic oscillation between 0 and 1. What this means intuitively is that deliberation regarding the accuracy of (7) starting from almost any initial estimate—for which there might be various grounds, including the background reputation of the agent—will fail to reach any tidy conclusion. If reputation is updated using accuracy estimates for the most recent information from a source, we will be unable to reach a final point for updated evaluation of reliability as well. Unable to decide the accuracy of (7) on the simple model at issue, we will also be unable to decide on the general reliability of its source.

The behavior of progressive accuracy estimates for (7), shadowed by corresponding estimates for reliability, is shown for a background reliability of 0.96 in the time-series graph of figure 5. A corresponding web diagram appears as figure 6. Both make it clear why our reliability estimates for an agent uttering (7) will themselves become periodic. For a background reputation of 0.96, the period established for reputation estimates will be between 0.64 and 0.973333, the y-values of the points marked with asterisks on the reputation line in figure 6. For a background

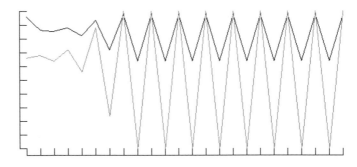

Initial background reliability = 0.96   Initial accuracy estimate for minimalist = 0.66

Figure 5 Time-series graph for the Minimalist.

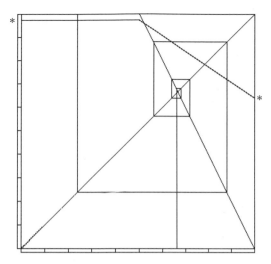

Figure 6 Web diagram for the Minimalist. Background reputation = 0.96, initial accuracy estimate = 0.66.

reputation of 0.6, on the other hand, reputation estimates will oscillate between 0.4 and 0.733333. For a background reputation of 0.2 the period will be between 0.466667 and 0.133333. We can also solve for final results algebraically: if our value for (7) cycles periodically between 0 and 1, our update R of a reliability estimate starting from an initial background reliability of Z will cycle correspondingly between 2Z/3 and (2Z + 1)/3.[23]

The simple lesson is that the unsettled epistemic behavior of some pieces of information produces unsettled estimates of reliability regarding their source. On the intuitive formulae built into our simple model, at least, background reliability estimates carry no guarantee of stability: estimates of reliability for a source can prove unstable by contagion from the instability of the accuracy of pieces of information received from that source. The instability of a reliability estimate is important not only in its own right, of course, but also because it signals a lack of any stable accuracy estimate usable as a default regarding the next message from our source. If reliability for our agent is to some extent undecidable, the initial credibility of his next message will be as well.

An extreme case of reputation-contagious instability is that of full chaos. Let us suppose, against a background reputation of 0.7, say, that Agent 007 transmits the following piece of information:

8. This is as inaccurate as your accuracy estimate for it.

Such a message is of course an accuracy version of the Chaotic Liar, a sentence fully chaotic on the [0, 1] interval. The chaotic evolution of (8) for an initial value of 0.234 is shown in the lighter line of the time-series graph of figure 7. Corresponding revisions in update estimates for an initial background estimate of 0.96 are shown in the darker line. A web diagram of the same information appears in figure 8. The evolution of accuracy estimates for our chaotic message forms the tangled inner web, spanning the [0, 1] interval. Corresponding revisions to an initial background reputation of 0.96 will be the y-values of those points projected onto the wide tent drawn as a dark line at the top. Figure 9 shows both forms of graph for the same message, but with an initial accuracy estimate of 0.678 against a background reliability of 0.3.

It is clear that an epistemically chaotic piece of information from a source can force the background reliability estimate for that source to become chaotic as well. Unlike the chaos of *message* (8), however, the chaos of background *reliability* will not be chaos on the full [0, 1] interval. The reliability shadow of informational chaos will be bracketed chaos, confined

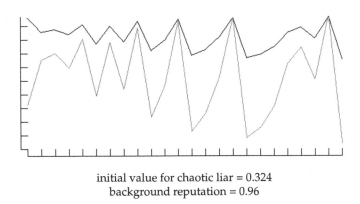

initial value for chaotic liar = 0.324
background reputation = 0.96

Figure 7   The Chaotic Liar with reputation shadow.

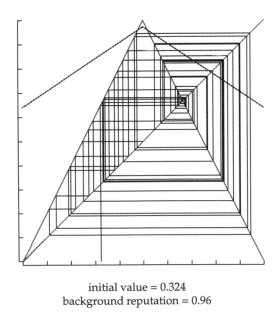

initial value = 0.324
background reputation = 0.96

Figure 8   The Chaotic Liar with reputation shadow (top black tent).

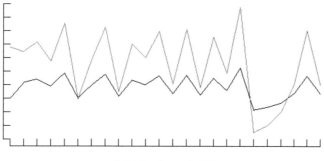

initial value = 0.678
background reliability = 0.3

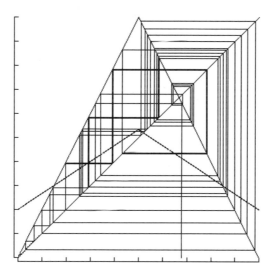

Figure 9 The Chaotic Liar with reputation shadow.

to a smaller range of values. For a background reputation of 0.96, for example, reputational chaos will be confined to the interval [0.64, 0.97333 . . .], corresponding to [((2 · 0.96) + 0)/3, ((2 · 0.96) + 1)/3]. For a background reputation of 0.3 the window of chaos will be [0.2, 0.53333 . . .]. In each case chaos is confined to a third of the unit interval.

Confined chaos is in some sense controlled chaos. Even if our computations cannot lead us to a final reputational value for a source that sends a message such as (8), we can know that our revised estimates will remain within a certain range. If we start with a background reputation of 0.96, for example, our reliability estimates are sure to remain above 0.64. Message (8) in effect forces us to replace a representation of background reliability in terms of a point with an image of reliability as chaos within a particular segment interval. Further complications arise if we envisage an agent sending not just one piece of self-referential information but several. Consider the interesting case of an agent in high standing—carrying a background reputation of 0.96, say—who first sends us an accuracy variant of the Minimalist:

7. This piece of information is as accurate as whichever is smaller: your estimate of its accuracy or of its inaccuracy,

followed by an accuracy version of the Chaotic Liar:

8. This is as inaccurate as your accuracy estimate for it.

Given a background reputation of 0.96, used also perhaps as an initial accuracy estimate, (7) will force an eventual oscillation in reliability estimates between 0.97333 and 0.64. For the first of these—a reliability estimate of 0.97333—message (8) would generate an interval of reputational chaos between 0.648 and 0.99222. For the second of these—a reliability estimate of 0.64—(8) would generate an interval of reputational chaos between 0.42666 and 0.76. In other words, if our epistemic situation is first one of periodically unstable indecision with regard to reputation based on receipt of message (7), it will become a situation of periodic indecision with regard to the two chaotic intervals generated on the basis of each period point by message (8). Putting these together, receipt of both messages will leave us with a range of computational uncertainty extending from 0.42666 and 0.97333, significantly greater than the 1/3 spread incumbent on (7) alone.

Chaos and indecision need not always get worse, however: on the model at issue, self-reference appears capable of dampening or lessening epistemic instability as well as producing it. Consider a case, for example, in which our rogue agent starts with a background reliability of 0.96, sends us the bizarre messages (7) and (8), but then sends (6) as well:

6. This piece of information is only half as accurate as you think it is.

Deliberation regarding (7) and (8), as outlined above, leaves us with an interval of computational uncertainty regarding reliability that extends from 0.42666 and 0.97333; (6), as we know, seeks a final fixed accuracy estimate of 2/3. For the low end of our reliability interval, then—0.4266—(6) will force a revised reliability estimate of 0.50644. For the high end of the interval—0.97333—the additional message will force a revision to 0.86422. Values within the original window of chaos will similarly be revised to values within this smaller interval. Though computational chaos remains, the receipt of self-referential message (6) has narrowed the range of that chaos significantly: from almost 0.55 to 0.36.

One last point to note about series of self-referential messages is that their ultimate effect on reputation can depend quite crucially on the order in which they are sent. This perhaps should not be surprising, since it holds for pieces of non-self-referential information as well. The background reliability formula employed in the current model puts greatest emphasis on the accuracy measure for the most recent piece of information, giving it a weight of 1/3 relative to a weight of 2/3 for previous background reputation. Thus a source with a background reliability of 0.96 from which we receive a series of statements with independently established accuracies 0.5, 0.5, and 1 will end up with a reliability of 0.8029. A source with a background reliability of 0.96 from which the same statements are received in a different order—1, 0.5, 0.5—will end up with a revised reliability estimate of 0.7104 instead.[24] In the self-referential case, a source with background reliability 0.96 from which we receive the three messages above, but in a different order—(6), (7), and then (8)—will end up with an overlapping chaos spread from 0.38266 to 0.93888: a spread of slightly greater than 0.55 rather than 0.36.

The epistemic undecidability these examples display is, we think, of an important but little noticed type. Ignorance and uncertainty in fact form a range of related phenomena, of various types and from various sources, for which it is instructive to at least try to construct a rough taxonomy. Such an attempt, we think, shows this type of computational instability to occupy an interesting but little noticed place in the general structure.

On the bottom of a hierarchy of ignorance we might posit a class of indeterminacy that is in the world itself, or at least that appears in the world at its first characterization in terms of basic categories. Whatever its real character, base level indeterminacy appears to be of at least two types: the applicational indeterminacy of vague categories, for which fuzzy logic has been offered as a model, and the indeterminacy of events for which there are merely probabilities, including most notably purely statistical phenomena for which a probabilistic description would be the only one possible.

On a second rung of ignorance appear those aspects of uncertainty that arise during the process of gathering evidence. Here also there are at least two types: epistemic indeterminacy due to incomplete evidence, and indeterminacy due to more complete but conflicting evidence. In the first case epistemic indeterminacy is due to gaps in the evidence; in the second case it is due to conflicting gluts. The differences between this second rung and the first are emphasized by Robert Klir, who characterizes modeling attempts for this level as 'fuzzy measures', of which probability theory is only the most familiar option.[25]

On a third rung of ignorance appears epistemic indeterminacy not in the phenomena or basic categories themselves, not in underdetermination or overdetermination of evidence, but arising from computational difficulties beyond the evidence-gathering stage: uncertainty due to difficulties of information processing. All the data is in, but our computers are down.

One familiar form of third-rung ignorance is computational complexity. Here we include classes of problems involving some variable v (the number of towns a salesman visits, for example) or Turing-encodable in a string of length l, but in which the resources required for computation increase faster than any polynomial on v or l: the realm of the NP-hard. We lack information in the general case because it lies beyond computational reach—corresponding to second-rung questions for which we have inadequate evidential support.[26]

A second type of epistemic indeterminacy on this third rung, however, appears to be the computational instability we have emphasized throughout the examples above and which appears in richer variety in the work below. In these cases we face computational complexity of a different kind: instability and chaos incumbent not on too little computing power, in a sense, but on too much. It is not that we lack a computable answer to a particular problem, but that computation refuses to yield a unique answer: patterns of self- and mutual-reference generate series of too *many* computable answers. This new type of computational indeterminacy thus corresponds on the computational level to those questions on the second level for which there is not a lack of evidential support but a glut of conflicting and contradictory evidence.

The fourth rung of ignorance—one we will not pursue here, but which does appear in both the first and last chapters of the book—is that of full formal undecidability. Here lies a range of problems algorithmically unapproachable altogether—questions for which computation by any algorithm is not merely NP-hard but logically impossible.

2.3   EPISTEMIC DYNAMICS WITH MULTIPLE INPUTS

Our epistemic model is easily extended, with some beautiful results, to the case of multiple and mutually referential epistemic sources, starting with epistemic Dualists.[27]

Here as in the case of single inputs there is a range of fairly well behaved cases. Consider for example messages received from Agents 001 and 002, who have background reputations of 0.9 and 0.2. Agent 001 sends a message reading as follows:

9. The next message received from 002 will be 0.8 accurate.

Agent 002 sends the following message:

10. The last message received from 001 has a accuracy of 0.1.

If we assume initial accuracy estimates of, say, 0.9 and 0.2 for these two messages, a computation would proceed as follows. Since what the first says is that the second has an accuracy of 0.8, the accuracy of that second-order V**vp** sentence will be recalculated through the V**vp** schema as $1 - \text{Abs}(0.8 - 0.2) = 1 - 0.6$, or 0.4. By a similar computation, 'simultaneous' in that it is blind to the deliberation we've just gone through, we find our second sentence's accuracy claim regarding the first will be 0.8 off and will thus itself be recalculated as having an accuracy of 0.2.

On a simultaneous computation we therefore revise our initial estimates for our two messages from (0.9, 0.2) to (0.4, 0.2). But now let us consider the sentences again. If message (10) has a value of 0.2, the claim in (9) that (10) has a value of 0.8 will be 0.6 off, which as it happens is entirely consistent with (9)'s currently assigned value of 0.4. If (9) has a value of 0.4, however, the claim in (1) that (9) has a value of 0.1 must be 0.3 off—giving (10) a value of 0.7 rather than 0.2. At this iteration accuracy estimates have been revised to (0.4, 0.7). On further reflection, these values will lead us to (0.9, 0.7) and then to (0.9, 0.2). We have therefore completed a periodic re-evaluation of accuracies from (0.9, 0.2) through (0.4, 0.2), (0.4, 0.7), (0.9, 0.7), and back to (0.9, 0.2).

Given simultaneous computation, most initial accuracy estimates for these two messages will give us a similarly fourfold periodicity. A sequential computation, on the other hand, gives us a two-fold periodicity—in this case between (0.9, 0.2) and (0.4, 0.7). The fixed point for both computations, however, is the same: accuracy estimates of (0.65, 0.45) can be assigned without epistemic instability.

Not all cases of mutual reference will be as well behaved as this first example. Consider the following two messages, for example, received from 001 and 002 respectively:

11. This is as accurate as 002's next message is inaccurate.

12. This is as accurate as 001's last message.

Here we can use the following V**vp** schemas:

$$x_{n+1} = 1 - \text{Abs}((1 - y_n) - x_n)$$

$$y_{n+1} = 1 - \text{Abs}(y_n - x_{n+1}).$$

Initial accuracy estimates of 0.9 and 0.2—read off our agents' background reliabilities, perhaps—and sequential calculation give us the pattern of recomputed accuracy value pairs (x, y) plotted as Cartesian coordinates in figure 10. This is, in fact, a very robust attractor: other pairs of initial estimates are attracted to precisely the same twisted path. Figure 11 makes this persistence clear in terms of an overlay, as before, for initial accuracy estimates at 0.05 intervals between (0, 0) and (1, 1). Chaotic behavior, rather than attraction to a persistent period, appears across the range of possible initial estimates.

Confined chaos, we've noted, is in some sense controlled chaos, and the computational chaos in such a case is quite predictably bounded. The attractor in figure 10 does not cover the entire unit interval on either dimension, and thus we know that in the depths of repeated computation certain values beyond the edges—the pair of values (0.1, 0.1), for example— will *not* appear. We in fact know quite a bit more than that: given the shape of the attractor we also know that (0.5, 0.6), for example, will not appear in

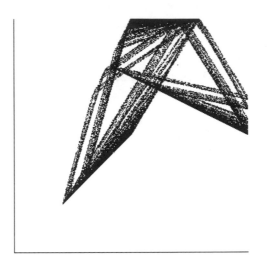

Figure 10   Accuracy estimates for messages (11) and (12) starting with 0.9, 0.2.

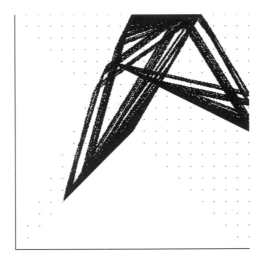

Figure 11   Overlay diagram: accuracy estimates for (11) and (12) for all initial estimates between (0, 0) and (1, 1) in 0.05 intervals.

the depths of computation. For the present, however, we will concentrate merely on the outer limits of chaotic spread within each dimension.

If computations for the accuracy of (11) and (12) refuse to stabilize, of course, the same will be true of our updates for background reliability. In this case we can think of the revised reliability estimates for Agent 001 as 'shadows' of our chaotic attractor projected vertically onto the reliability line marked 001 in figure 12—a line that plots

$$y = ((2 \cdot 0.9) + x)/3$$

and that therefore models the effect of an accuracy value x on a background reliability of 0.9. Projection onto the reputation line works

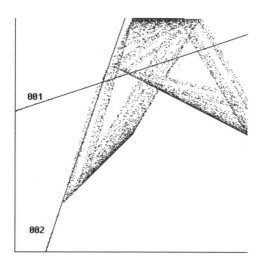

Figure 12 Attractor of accuracy points with reputation shadow lines for Agent 001 and Agent 002.

as follows. Every accuracy revision pair for (12) and (13) is represented by a point on our twisted attractor. Its shadow on 001's reliability line will be a point with the same x-coordinate, and the y-coordinate of *that* point represents our update for Agent 001's reliability at that stage in the computation. Line 002 in figure 12 graphs a similar reputation line for a background reputation of 0.2:

$$x = ((2 \cdot 0.2) + y)/3.$$

A shadow for any point in the accuracy attractor, projected horizontally to the 002 line, will therefore give an x-value corresponding to our estimate for Agent 002's reliability at that stage in the computation.

Such an image makes graphically clear how reliability computations dampen the wild behavior of accuracy estimates: the range of y-values for shadows on line 001, and the range of x-values for shadows on line 002, are significantly smaller than the range of x and y values in the full attractor. If we now graph points for revision pairs not of accuracy estimates but of reliability updates we will therefore get a miniature of the original attractor, shown in figure 13 for background reliabilities of 0.9 and 0.2 and corresponding accuracy estimates for our two messages. Here chaos, though of precisely the same form as in previous figures, is more severely confined. The position of this miniature attractor within the unit square depends on which background reliabilities we start with. Its size, interestingly enough, does not: for any background reliability and any initial estimate of accuracies, the reputational chaos wreaked by the referential tangle of (11) and (12) will be confined to a range of slightly more than 0.26 on each axis.

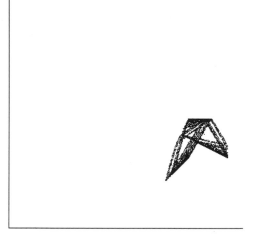

Figure 13 Reputational chaos for Agents 001 and 002 with background reputations 0.9, 0.2.

One of the lessons here is that reputational chaos may remain within tolerable limits for some purposes despite a much wider range of chaos regarding estimates of accuracy. In a variety of cases it may be enough to know that the reliability of our informational sources lies within a manageably small interval; the fact that computational chaos appears within that interval, inherited from a greater computational chaos of mutually referential messages, may be of less practical significance. That may allow us a tolerable range of accuracy estimates for the next message down the line, for example, even if it does not deliver us a point-value.

Not all Dualist predicaments generate attractors as robust as this. Consider another pair of messages received from agents 001 and 002, once again computed sequentially:

13. This is half as accurate as the next message received from Agent 002.

14. This is as accurate as the last message from Agent 001.

$$x_{n+1} = 1 - \text{Abs}((5 \cdot y_n) - x_n)$$

$$y_{n+1} = 1 - \text{Abs}(x_{n+1} - y_n)$$

If we start with an assumption of full inaccuracy for both sentences—a value of 0 in each case—the trajectory that maps our revised estimates takes the form of the oval in the first frame of figure 14, formed progressively by an apparently chaotic dance of points around the perimeter. If we choose initial estimates of 0 and 0.3 the trajectory takes the same shape, but this time forms the significantly smaller oval shown in the second frame of figure 14. The same oval but with radically different sizes, indicating a radically different range for computational instability, appears across the range of possible estimates. Figure 15 shows an overlay

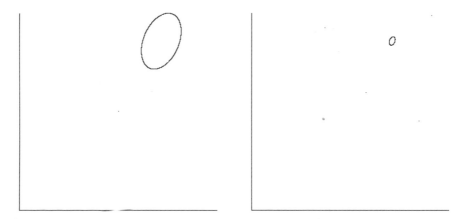

Figure 14 Trajectories for (13) and (14) with initial estimates (0, 0.3) (left) and (0, 0) (right).

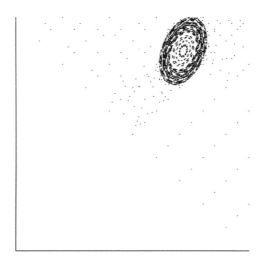

Figure 15 Overlay diagram for initial estimates for (13) and (14) between 0 and 1 in 0.1 intervals

of patterns of attraction for estimates between (0, 0) and (1, 1) in intervals of 0.1. Here as above it is clear that computational chaos will be strictly confined. This case differs from that of the robust attractors above, however, in that the range of computational instability is itself sensitive to our initial accuracy estimates. For initial accuracy estimates of 0 and 0.3, messages (13) and (14) generate a range of computational chaos of only 0.0308 in the computed accuracy of the first message and 0.0436 in the computed accuracy of the second. For an initial assumption of total inaccuracy for each message, on the other hand, the range of computational chaos is a much more significant 0.2020 in the first case and 0.2857 in the second.

An even greater variety of patterns of attraction appears for different accuracy estimates in the case of the following pair of messages, very similar to the Half Dualist of chapter 1:

15. This is as accurate as Agent 002's next message is inaccurate.

16. This is half as accurate as the last message received from Agent 001.

$$x_{n+1} = 1 - \text{Abs}((1 - y_n) - x_n)$$
$$y_{n+1} = 1 - \text{Abs}((1/2 \cdot x_{n+1}) - y_n)$$

For some initial estimates, sequential computation of these two messages generates trajectories in the form of four tiny ovals, shown in the central frame of figure 16. For other initial estimates only two ovals form, small in some cases and large in others, as shown in the first and third frames. Figure 17, an overlay showing trajectories for values between (0, 0) and (1, 1) in 0.1 intervals, shows some of the variety of patterns of attraction formed for different values.

Figure 16 Trajectories for messages (15) and (16) with initial estimates of (0.78, 0.23), (0.95, 0.5), and (0.9, 0.9).

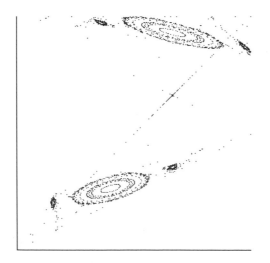

Figure 17 Overlay diagram for messages (15) and (16) in 0.1 intervals.

For initial estimates 0.95 and 0.5 (as in the second frame of figure 16) our accuracy values for our first statement are radically unstable between 0.1449 and 0.9999, with accuracy values for our second statement unstable in a similarly extensive range between 0.1819 and 0.9863. For initial estimates 0.78 and 0.23, on the other hand, computational instability for our second message is still between 0.2569 and 0.9431, but uncertainty with regard to the first statement is confined to a much smaller range between 0.3759 and 0.6977. For some cases, moreover, it may not be simply the absolute range of epistemic instability but its particular shape that is important—the fact that instability in each case is distributed in such a way that central areas are left clear, for example.

Background reputation is part of this picture in two ways. If we use background reputation as our guide in making first estimates for accuracies—an intuitive procedure quite consistent with the general use of background reputations—it is clear that the range of computational instability for accuracy estimates will be contingent on our background reliabilities. But of course reputation is also updated in terms of recent accuracy estimates. If we are unable to establish any final estimate of accuracy in a case of tangled reference, we will have to accept a corresponding range of computational chaos with regard to reputation.

For some sets of referentially tangled messages, differences in background reliability and/or accuracy estimates make a great deal of difference in ultimate epistemic instability—a great deal of difference with regard to the amount of computational chaos we will have to live with. For some initial estimates, read off some background reliabilities, computational instability may remain small and relatively manageable, a source of ignorance but not a serious threat. For other reliability and accuracy estimates, computational instability for those same sets of messages can be expected to be considerable. In some cases, moreover, small *differences* in background reliabilities and initial estimates make only small differences in the amount of computational chaos at stake. In other cases, however, things may be much more seriously dependent on initial informational conditions: small differences or small uncertainties with regard to our initial reliability and/or accuracy estimates can result in major differences in the amount of computational chaos.

One vivid way of mapping these characteristics of epistemic predicaments of these sorts is in terms of epistemic hazard maps. Consider messages (13) and (14) again. Each pair of initial accuracy estimates for our two messages can be plotted as a point in the unit square using our values (x, y) as Cartesian coordinates. Different initial accuracy estimate pairs will generate different degrees of computational chaos, and we can map the interval of computational chaos produced by a particular point in terms of color. If the spread of chaos for a particular point is less than 0.1, that point can be colored a safe dark blue. If it is somewhat greater—between 0.1 and

0.2—it can be colored a somewhat less safe green. Chaos between 0.2 and 0.3 can be signaled by light blue, chaos between 0.4 and 0.5 carrying a warning red, between 0.5 and 0.6 carrying a shocking magenta, and so forth. The result is a map showing epistemic 'danger areas'. Those areas with colors corresponding to higher spreads of computational chaos will be areas of accuracy or reliability estimate in which the utterance of a pair of mutually referential sentences signals an area of major computational chaos. Those areas with colors corresponding to lower spreads of computational instability, on the other hand, can be treated as relatively safe: for background reputations in these areas, for example, receipt of mutually referential reports like those above may be much less significant.

An epistemic hazard map of this type is shown for sentences (13) and (14) in figure 18. Here we've used shades of color to graph the interval of computational chaos for our first message. In black and white, as shown here, a spider-webbing of dark grey in areas of white indicates a high hazard area of greater than 0.2. Major portions of white indicate computational chaos spreads between 0.15 and 0.2. From there colors progress toward the center of target and heart-shapes with degrees of decreasing hazard safety. The outer grey indicates a hazard between 1 and 1.5, the next darker band a hazard between 0.075 and 1, the darkest grey in the target areas a hazard between 0.05 and 0.075, with a lighter band indicating a hazard between 0.025 and 0.5 and a central grey indicating a very safe area between 0 and 0.025. Safe areas form targets floating in a

This message is half as accurate as the next one received from Agent 002.
This is as accurate as the last message from Agent 001.

Figure 18 Epistemic hazard map.

general sea of higher hazard, forming a complex pattern not easily predictable from merely the form of our mutually referential messages. A similar hazard map appears if we graph the interval of computational chaos for our second agent instead.

Figure 19 graphs the same information topographically. Here height in a third dimension is used, rather than color, to indicate danger with regard to computational chaos. The higher ranges represent ridges of danger, marking contiguous patterns of coordinates, which can be expected to lead to wide computational instability in this case when taken as accuracy estimates or as background reliabilities on which such estimates are made. The valleys are by contrast relatively safe.

Reputational updates, we know, shadow computational patterns for accuracy. Figure 20 makes this graphic by portraying the range of reputational chaos for our first agent incumbent on receipt of messages (13) and (14), using coordinates to represent background reliabilities for our

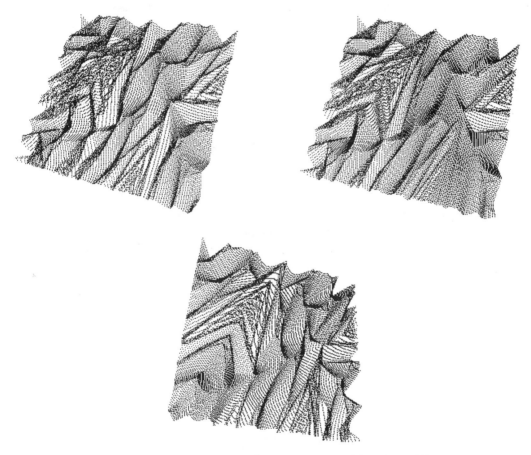

This message is half as accurate as the next one received from Agent 002.
This is as accurate as the last message from Agent 001.

Figure 19 Topographical epistemic hazard map.

This message is half as accurate as the next one received from Agent 002.
This is as accurate as the last message from Agent 001.

Figure 20 Reputational hazard map.

two agents and assuming initial accuracy estimates to be read off those background reliabilities. In black and white, we've used white to indicate an instability interval in reputational computations between 0.05 and 0.075, grey to indicate a hazard between 0.025 and 0.5, and black a safe area between 0 and 0.025. What is visually obvious is that the pattern of computational chaos for reputation shadows the pattern for accuracy outlined above. The same basic pattern, though for somewhat different values, appears in the reputational hazard map for our second agent. In both cases, of course, degrees of reputational instability dictate degrees of uncertainty regarding the degree of accuracy to accord the next message received from an agent. This reputational hazard map might thus also be read as a map of background reputations for which future accuracy projections will be uncertain.

A hazard map for another set of messages—(15) and (16) above—is shown in figure 21. This is a more dangerous epistemic territory altogether. One clear indication of greater danger is the wider spread of computational instability, calling for a different color scale. For purposes of black and white illustration, we indicate hazard intervals greater than 0.8 in white. Hazards between 0.6 and 0.7 are indicated with a dark grey, those between 0.5 and 0.6 by a very light grey, followed by three more greys of increasing darkness in the centers of the targets. These indicate hazard intervals between 0.4 and 0.5, between 0.3 and 0.4, and below 0.3. All values are for intervals of instability in the computation of accuracy for our second

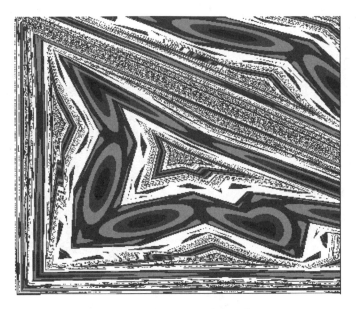

This is as accurate as the next message is inaccurate.
This is half as accurate as the last message received.

Figure 21   Epistemic hazard map.

message. Figure 22 shows the same hazard map in topographical form. Because of the depth of field in this case, however, we've attempted an alternative topographic mapping, which plots a sampling of points as small spheres. Here degree of hazard is indicated by both spatial orientation and distinct coloration. There is also a second sense, beyond mere size of intervals, in which the maps in figures 21 and 22 portray more dangerous epistemic territory than those above. Clear in these maps are areas in which no one color or level predominates, in which one has instead a blizzard of different hazard measures. These areas are dangerous not because they are areas of uniformly wide computational instability, which is at any rate predictable and fairly insensitive to slight changes in initial values, but because they are areas in which infinitesimal differences in initial estimates or background reputation can cause radically divergent results in degree of computational instability. In such areas any margin of error might be fatal. Here in fact our hazard maps seem to indicate importantly *unpredictable* amounts of hazard: computational intractability regarding computational intractability itself.

Here as before it is important to remember that we are working within a particular model—a particularly simple model—of epistemic dynamics. Within the basic assumptions of that model, however, the graphs above offer not merely intriguing fractal images but real information: information as to when background reliabilities or background accuracy estimates generate different degrees of computational instability in the context of

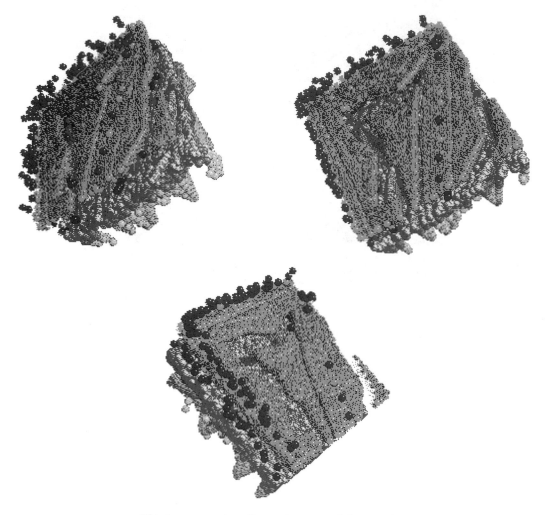

This is as accurate as the next message is inaccurate.
This is half as accurate as the last message received.

Figure 22 Topographical epistemic hazard map.

mutually referential pieces of information. In more realistic cases, in which tangled reference might appear indirectly or implicitly, maps of this type might in principle provide an important guide for navigating the shoals of at least one type of epistemic indeterminacy.

Here we offer another fractal image, which we find intriguing but significantly less informative in the long run. Consider messages (15) and (16) again, but in this case computed simultaneously rather than sequentially. In such a case we get a robust attractor rather than a range of different attractors for different initial values: the pentagonal attractor shown in figure 23. Using the same tools as those above, we can graph intervals of computational instability for different pairs of initial estimates

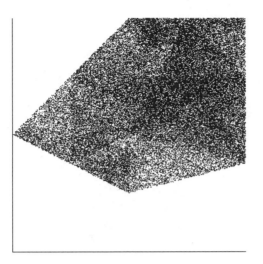

Figure 23 Attractor for simultaneous computation of (15) and (16).

or background reliabilities. If we do this for a simultaneous computation of (15) and (16), though only for iterated revisions 10 through 20, we get the marvelous array of fractal insects shown in the first frame of figure 24. In black and white, hazard areas between 0.3 and 0.35 are shown in white and intervals between 0.25 and 0.3 are shown in black, using shades of grey for values above and below these. Unlike the hazard maps above, however, the image of figure 24a is very much an artifact of limited iterations. By 40 iterations the insects have been eaten by fractal images into the scattered values of figure 24b, well on their way to a two-dimensional form of Cantor dust.[28] By the hundredth generation, shown in figure 24c, the image is dominated by only two values, indicating intervals between 0.3 and 0.35 and 0.25 and 0.3. By the five-hundredth generation almost all values have converged on the interval between 0.25 and 0.3.

What is happening in this case, it appears, is that over increased iterations bordering points traverse more and more similar areas within the attractor of figure 23, reflected in more and more similar intervals of instability. Since we are dealing with a persistent attractor for a wide range of values, we can expect the convergence to a single color demonstrated in the iterative evolution of figure 24. In the hazard maps above, by contrast, different values generate quite different attractors—as different as the various patterns and sizes of scattered ovals noted for an intuitively sequential rather than simultaneous computation for (15) and (16). Deeper iteration remains trapped in these different attractors, and thus the information offered in the above hazard maps remains constant: what these show us are robust differences in intervals of computational instability that are not remediable simply by deeper computation.

Here we have confined ourselves to simple cases of two agents and two mutually referential messages. That seems appropriate in a first modeling.

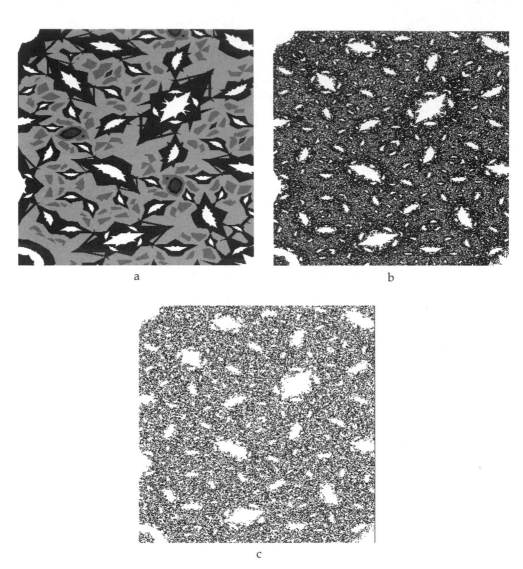

Figure 24 Stages in computational spread for a simultaneous treatment of (15) and (16), shown for (a) iterations 10–20; (b) iterations 10–40; and (c) iterations 10–100.

More complex results can be expected for cases of tangled reference involving both accuracy and updated reputation for three agents or more. (Some hint of those complexities appears already in the three-dimensional images drawn for the Triplist variations in chapter 1.)

2.4 TANGLED REFERENCE TO REPUTATION

In the cases considered so far our messages have concerned accuracy, amounting either to statements regarding their own accuracy or concerning the accuracy of some other piece of information. An important feature of the philosophical sketch of epistemic predicaments with which we began, however, is that information received as input may concern not only the accuracy of some other piece of information but the general reliability of some epistemic source. One thing texts may tell us is to distrust particular texts; one thing we may learn from sensory experience is to distrust particular sensory experiences. David Lewis invokes a reputational dilemma of this type for inductive methods, defined as systematic ways of letting available evidence govern one's degree of belief in hypotheses:

The trouble is that you need an inductive method to estimate anything, even to estimate the accuracy of various inductive methods. And your selection of a method with the highest estimated accuracy will come out differently depending on which method you use to make the estimate. It is as if *Consumer Reports, Consumer Bulletin*, etc., each published rankings of the consumers' magazines, as they do of other products. You would have to know which one to read in order to find out which one to read.[29]

In this final section we want to introduce some implications of our simple reputational model for this aspect of epistemic predicaments.

Let us suppose that Agent 007, with a sterling background reputation of 0.96, sends us the following message:

17. You're wrong about my reliability: I'm only half as reliable as I'm reputed to be.

Using x for the accuracy of message (17) and r for reputation, we can frame a basic **Vrs** schema for (17)—the **Vvp**-like schema for reputations outlined in section 2.1—as

$$x = 1 - \text{Abs}((1/2 \cdot r) - r).$$

Allowing for computational sequence and our formula for reputation, computations might more completely be represented in terms of the pair of formulae

$$x_{n+1} = 1 - \text{Abs}((1/2 \cdot r_n) - r_n).$$

$$r_{n+1} = ((2 \cdot r_i) + x_{n+1})/3.$$

where r_n is a series of revised reputation updates and r_i remains our initial background reputation.

In such a case our first concern, of course, is with the accuracy of (17). The only information we have in terms of which its accuracy can be gauged, however, is our independent estimate of 007's reliability, compounded over years of messages received and verified. That background reputation stands at 0.96, and thus—at first estimate, at least—we will take (17) to have an accuracy of $1 - \text{Abs}((0.5 \cdot 0.96) - 0.96)$, or 0.52. 007 has sent us a message of middling accuracy.

The second computational step is to update agent reputation. Using our standard updating formula of $R_{n+1} = ((2 \cdot R_n) + p)/3$, then, we revise our reliability estimate for 007 to 0.81333 .... 007's reliability, once thought to be a full 0.96, now appears on the books as a mere 0.81 or so.

But what then of the accuracy of (17)? Here it is important to note that there are in fact two ways this message can be read. On one reading, 'I'm only half as reliable as I'm reputed to be' involves reference to a particular reliability rating at a particular time: 'as reliable as I'm reputed to be' is functioning as a rigid designator for our initial reliability estimate of 0.96.[30] As a rigid designator, it might be intended to tag that numerical value, whatever it is, even if 007 himself doesn't know precisely what his background reputation happens to be. Here, however, we want to track the behavior of (17) on another reading, in which 'as I'm reputed to be' functions as a floating or flaccid designator, indicating different reputations in different contexts. On such a reading, (17) will refer to shifting values in the course of shifting reputational calculations. For normal contexts this might be a less realistic way of reading a message like (17), but messages demanding such an interpretation certainly *can* be sent. Our concern is with their dynamics.

On this second reading, the revised estimate for 007's reliability which we reached above will force a further re-evaluation of the accuracy of (17). We now think that our agent's reliability is 0.81. But 007's message is that his true reliability is half of what it is estimated to be. How accurate then is (17)? Against the background of our revised estimate, the Vrs schema sets its accuracy at $1 - \text{Abs}(0.81/2 - 0.81)$, or 0.595. Given our revised take on his reliability, 007's statement is more accurate than we thought it was. But here again we will have to revise our reliability estimate, to $((2 \cdot 0.96) + 0.595)/3$, giving us a reliability of 0.838. Note that here we continue to use 0.96 as the background reliability R_i in our formula.

The evolution of revisions for accuracy estimates for (17), reflected in reliability estimates for 007, is shown in a time series graph in the first part of figure 25. Final convergence is to an accuracy estimate of approximately 0.5828 and a reliability estimate of approximately 0.8343. These values can be solved for algebraically using a Vrs schema written directly in terms of our reputational formula:

$$p = 1 - \text{Abs}((0.5 \cdot r) - r)$$

$$p = 1 - \text{Abs}([0.5 \cdot ((2 \cdot 0.96 + p)/3)] - [(2 \cdot 0.96 + p)/3])$$

for $((2 \cdot 0.96) + p)/3$ positive,

$$p = 1 - [0.5 \cdot ((2 \cdot 0.96 + p)/3)]$$

$$p = 1 - [0.96/3 + 0.5p/3]$$

$$p = 1 - 0.32 - p/6$$

$$7/6p = 0.68$$

$$p = \sim 0.5828$$

Initial R = 0.96   Initial P= 0.52

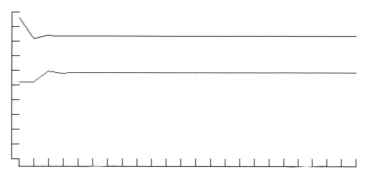

"I'm half as reliable as I'm reputed to be"

Final Acc. = 0.5828571
Final Rep. = 0.8342857

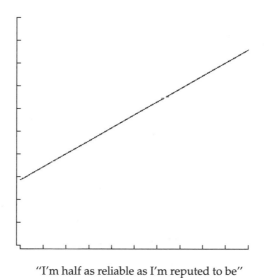

"I'm half as reliable as I'm reputed to be"

Figure 25 Time series graph for an initial reliability of 0.96 (top), and sloping graph of final fixed points for all initial reliabilities on the x-axis.

Our fixed point for R can then be solved for using the above value for p in our original reputational formula.

In the informal reasoning above we started with an accuracy estimate for (17) read off our background reliability: If 007's reputation is 0.96, and he says it is half that, his statement must have an accuracy of 0.52. One lesson of the algebraic treatment, however, is that it doesn't in fact matter whether we start with a different initial estimate for the value of (17) or not: given *any* initial estimate, the deliberation above will bring us to the same fixed point for the reputation of our agent. Somewhat surprisingly, both the final accuracy for a statement such as (17) and the final reliability estimate of our agent depend only on our initial reliability estimate. We can therefore construct the simple graph for (17) shown in the second part of figure 25. Here final reputation for a case in which message (17) is received is shown as a direct function of initial reputation.

A similar convergence to fixed points, variable with regard to initial reputation but blind to choice of initial accuracy estimates, appears for the following messages regarding reputation:

18. My true reliability is terribly unappreciated: I'm twice as reliable as I'm reputed to be.

$$x = 1 - \text{Abs}((2 \cdot r) - r)$$

19. My true reliability is precisely the opposite of my reputation.

$$x = 1 - \text{Abs}((1 - r) - r)$$

20. My real reputation is zero.

$$x = 1 - \text{Abs}(0 - r)$$

21. My real reputation is whichever is smaller: my reputation or its opposite.

$$x = 1 - \text{Abs}(\text{Min}(r, 1 - r) - r)$$

Messages (17) through (21) are clearly related to self-referential statements concerning accuracy or truth considered earlier: (17) is a reliability variation on the Half-Sayer, (19) an analogue of the Chaotic Liar, (20) a reputational variant on the infinite-valued Liar, and (21) an analogue of the Minimalist. In their earlier instantiations regarding truth or accuracy, such messages generated semantic behavior ranging from periodic, for the infinite-valued Liar, to a repellor point in the case of the Minimalist and chaos in the case of the Chaotic Liar. Where it is background reputation rather than immediate message accuracy that is referred to, however, all of these analogues give us a well-behaved convergence on fixed points, dependent only on the background reputation with which we begin.[31] Time-series graphs for (18) through (21), each using an initial reputation of 0.9 and an initial accuracy estimate of 0.2, appear in figure 26.

There will also of course be two-agent cases of tangled reference involving reputation. Consider for example agents 003 and 004, each of whom sends a single message regarding the other's reliability:

22. Agent 003 is overrated: his reliability is only half what it is estimated to be.

23. Agent 004's reputation is exactly the opposite of what it should be.

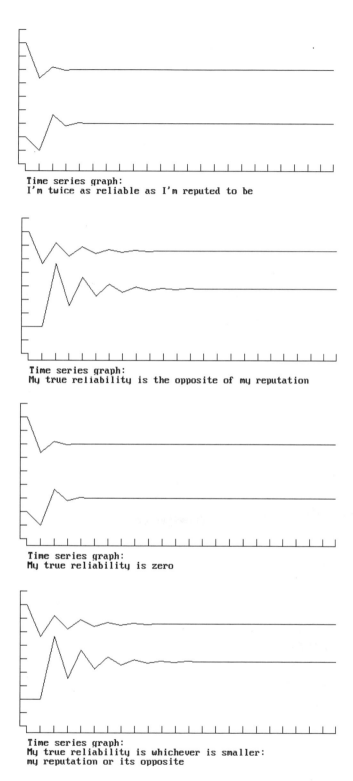

Time series graph:
I'm twice as reliable as I'm reputed to be

Time series graph:
My true reliability is the opposite of my reputation

Time series graph:
My true reliability is zero

Time series graph:
My true reliability is whichever is smaller:
my reputation or its opposite

Figure 26 Time series graphs for sentences (18) through (21), showing convergence on fixed points.

Using $r3_n$ for the updated reputation of our first agent and $r4_n$ for the updated reputation of our second, we can envisage (22) and (23) in terms of the basic Vrs schemas:

$$x = 1 - \text{Abs}((0.5 \cdot r3_n) - r3_n)$$
$$y = 1 - \text{Abs}((1 - r4_n) - r4_n),$$

although complicated by sequential updating of reputations in terms of accuracy estimates for x and y.

Let us assume a background reliability for each—0.3 for Agent 003, perhaps, and 0.4 for Agent 004. On a sequential procedure of revision, but without repeated statements, we would then evaluate (22) for accuracy in terms of our background estimate for Agent 004 and would update our estimate for 003 accordingly. We would then evaluate (23) for accuracy in terms of our updated reliability for 003 and go on to update 003's reliability in turn. Repeating the process, we in fact reach a fixed point. Accuracies for (22) and (23) converge on 0.72 and 0.88, respectively, with agents 003's and 004's reliabilities converging on 0.44 and 0.56.

How differences in initial reliabilities affect our final values is shown in figure 27. Initial reliabilities for 003 are plotted between 0 and 1 on the x-axis, and those for 004 on the y-axis, so that the coordinates (x, y) of any point indicate initial reliabilities (r003, r004). In black and white, white and the bottom three greys represent areas in which 003's final reliability is higher; black and the top three greys represent areas in which 004 achieves a higher final reputation.

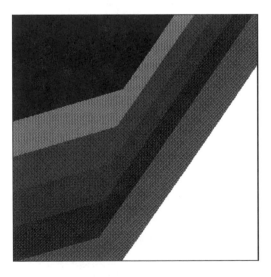

Figure 27 The effect of background reliabilities for 003 (x-axis) and 004 (y-axis) in the case of messages (22) and (23). Black and the top three greys indicate areas of initial reliabilities for which 004's final reliability exceeds 003's, by decreasing intervals of 0.01. White and the bottom three greys indicate areas in which 003's final reliability trumps 004's.

The reputation-referential claims we've considered have been extraordinarily well-behaved, converging conveniently on fixed points throughout. Consider finally a mixed category, however, in which a message may concern *both* accuracy and reputation. Here we might begin with

This message has an accuracy inverse to my reliability.

Or, somewhat more colloquially:

This message is as inaccurate as I am generally reliable.

$$x_{n+1} = 1 - \text{Abs}((1 - r) - x_n)$$

Here 'I' and 'my' are used in reference not to these messages, of course, but to the agent or source that sent them. The basic **Vrs** schema for such a message we can represent as

$$x = 1 - \text{Abs}((1 - x) - r)$$

where x is the accuracy of our message and r represents the background reliability of the agent. In principle, evaluation of such a statement and updating of background reliability requires two initial values: an estimate for x and an estimate for r. When pressed for an initial estimate for x, however, it seems quite natural to pull a value from background reputation r, so that x = r. Our modeling below relies on this simplifying assumption. In figure 28 we have plotted initial r and x values (r = x) between 0 and 1 on the x-axis, with y points plotted for computations through 100 iterations. A few initial iterations have been ignored in order to allow points to settle to an attractor in each case. The area shown in grey represents plots for accuracy through 100 iterations for our message above. The area shown in

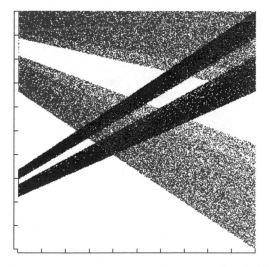

This message is as inaccurate as I am generally reliable

Figure 28 Values for 100 iterations, with r = x along the x-axis. Grey = accuracy values, black = revised reputation.

black represents the corresponding reflection on computations of updated reputation. As a whole the graph shows bands of computational instability, with a middle window, for all reputation-accuracy values between 0 and 1, though both the position and extent of the computational instability varies with background values. Here instability itself seems to follow a clear and gradual course.

Consider also an emphatic form of our message, in which we add a 'very', standardly modeled in fuzzy logic in terms of squaring:

It is very true that this statement is as inaccurate as I am reliable.

$$x_{n+1} = (1 - Abs((1 - x_n) - r))^2$$

This gives us, once again calculated for $x = r$ on the x-axis, the range of values shown in figure 29. Here it is clear that background reliability can make a great deal of difference. Up to the crisis point of approximately 0.25, our sentence is extremely well-behaved: for reputations below that threshold it gives us a manageable fixed point for both accuracy and reliability. From that crucial point on, however, we have computational chaos of varying degrees and patterns, including a clear window above 0.8 at which point we return to a period of 3. For reputations greater than 0.25 in general, however, such a message is a very real computational hazard.

A similar case appears if we use the square-root hedge applied for 'fairly':

It is fairly true that this statement is as inaccurate as I am reliable.

$$x_{n+1} = \sqrt{(1 - Abs((1 - x_n) - r))}$$

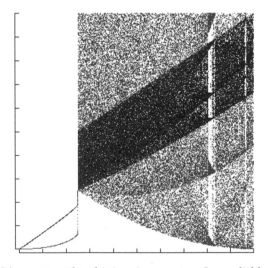

It's very true that this is as inaccurate as I am reliable.

Figure 29 Values for 100 iterations, with $r = x$ along the x-axis. Grey = accuracy values, black = revised reputation.

The result is shown in figure 30. What is clear is that for most background reliabilities this is a much safer piece of information to receive in terms of computational complexity. For almost any background reliability it gives us a well-managed fixed point or a manageably small interval. The exceptions are background reliabilities above roughly 0.8 and especially above 0.9. If this generally 'safe' message is received from an agent with very high reliability the cost in computational instability may be considerable.

The form that some of these graphs seem to approach is reminiscent of certain graphs for the period-doubling route to chaos. This impression is strengthened if we consider a mixed-referential sentence slightly farther afield:

It is very true that this is twice as inaccurate as I am generally reliable.

$$x_{n+1} = (1 - Abs((2 \cdot (1 - x_n)) - r))^2$$

The graph for this sentence, which appears as figure 31, can be seen as a distorted mirror image of figure 32, which shows the route to chaos for the Logistic or Quadratic equation $x_{n+1} = 4x_n(1 - x_n)$, perhaps the most studied formula in non-linear dynamics. As indicated in chapter 1, smaller values **k** in place of 4 in the Logistic yield a variety of dynamic behavior. For values of **k** less than 3 the Logistic map exhibits fixed point attractors; for slightly higher values it has periods of 2, 4, and so forth, to full chaos: the 'period-doubling route to chaos'.[32] In figure 32, however, our pattern graphs more than just changes in the parameter of a formal equation. Within the limits of our model, it reflects a real phenomenon of epistemic

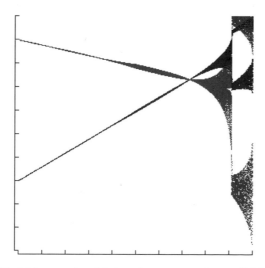

It's fairly true that this is as inaccurate as I am reliable.

Figure 30 Values for 100 iterations, with r = x along the x-axis. Grey = accuracy values, black = revised reputation.

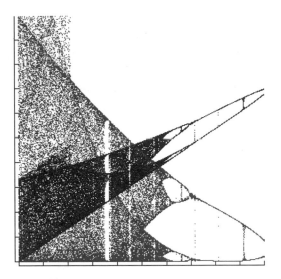

It is very true that this is twice as inaccurate as I am generally reliable.

Figure 31 Values for 100 iterations: message (64) with r = x along the x-axis. Grey = accuracy values, black = revised reputation.

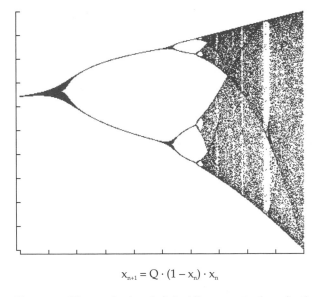

$$x_{n+1} = Q \cdot (1 - x_n) \cdot x_n$$

Figure 32 The standard period-doubling route to chaos for the Quadratic equation, shown with Q from 2.8 to 4.

chaos. What plays the role of an artificial parameter in this case is the role of an agent's background reputation and initial accuracy estimate based on that reputation. Starting from the right, for some reputations close to 1, it is clear that receipt of a message such as above would cause a relatively small problem of a closely confined period-two oscillation. With a background reputation in the range of 0.75 that period will be doubled to four, then will increase into chaos. Within the chaotic realm, however, 'windows' do appear, with for example a visible period of 3 against a background reputation of approximately 0.36.

2.5 CONCLUSION

Our epistemic situation generally is one in which we receive varying pieces of information—or what purports to be information—from a variety of sources. Our job as epistemic agents is to make sense of that information. John Stuart Mill makes the point eloquently in *A System of Logic*:

To draw inferences has been said to be the great business of life. Every one has daily, hourly, and momentary need of ascertaining facts which he has not directly observed, not from any general purpose of adding to his stock of knowledge but because the facts themselves are of importance to his interests or to his occupations. The business of the magistrate, of the military commander, of the navigator, of the physician, of the agriculturist is merely to judge of evidence and to act accordingly . . . as they do this well or ill, so they discharge well or ill the duties of their several callings. It is the only occupation in which the mind never ceases to be engaged and is the subject, not of logic, but of knowledge in general.[33]

One of the inevitable complications of this 'great business of life' is that it often includes judging in terms of information about information—information reflecting on the accuracy of itself, or on the accuracy of other information—and information about general sources of information. To live without ignorance is beyond us—the most we can hope for is to manage our inevitable ignorance with some degree of success. The same, we think, holds true for the ignorance incumbent on computational complexity that has been our focus here. What we have tried to offer in this chapter are some modeling tools for epistemic dynamics, designed to capture and display some of the intricate, complex characteristics of our epistemic predicaments. That, we hope, is a first step toward a deeper understanding.

3 Fractal Images of Formal Systems

While at Princeton, I came to know Einstein fairly well. I used to go to his house once a week to discuss with him and Gödel and Pauli. . . . Gödel turned out to be an unadulterated Platonist, and apparently believed that an eternal 'not' was laid up in heaven, where virtuous logicians might hope to meet it hereafter.
—Bertrand Russell, *Autobiography*[1]

Concerning my 'unadulterated' Platonism, it is no more 'unadulterated' than Russell's own in 1921. . . . At that time Russell had met the 'not' even in this world, but later on under the influence of Wittgenstein he chose to overlook it.
—Kurt Gödel, quoted in Hao Wang, *Reflections on Kurt Gödel*[2]

[Russell had written "Logic is concerned with the real world just as truly as zoology, though with its more abstract and general features."]

Familiar formal systems include propositional calculus, predicate calculus, higher-order logic and systems of number theory and arithmetic. As standardly outlined, these consist of a grammar specifying well-formed formulae, together with a set of axioms and rules. Derivations are series of formulae, each of which is either an axiom or is generated from earlier items by means of the rules of the system; the theorems of the system are simply those formulae for which there are derivations.

Given this standard approach to formal systems, however, attempts to envisage formal systems as a whole seem of necessity remotely abstract and incomplete. As a psychological matter, if one is asked to imagine predicate calculus in its entirety, one seems at best able to conjure up an image of the axioms and the (psychologically) empty category of 'whatever follows from them'. The incompleteness of such a psychological picture accords perfectly with constructivist or intuitionist approaches to formal systems. It may even seem to confirm them.

One classical statement of constructivism is Heyting's:

...I must still make one remark which is essential for a correct understanding of our intuitionist position: we do not attribute an existence independent of our thought, i.e., a transcendental existence, to the integers or to any other mathematical objects. Even though it might be true that every thought refers to an object conceived to exist independently of it, we can nevertheless let this remain an open question. In any event, such an object need not be completely independent of human thought. Even if they should be independent of individual acts of thought, mathematical objects are by their very nature dependent on human thought. Their existence is guaranteed only insofar as they can be determined by thought. They have properties only insofar as these can be discerned in them by thought. But this possibility of knowledge is revealed to us only by the act of knowing itself. Faith in transcendental existence, unsupported by concepts, must be rejected . . .[3]

It is clear that there are alternatives to constructivism, however, and we are certainly not endorsing an approach such as Heyting's. On the contrary, the work of this chapter can be seen as an attempt to motivate realistic and non-constructivist interpretations of formal systems by giving them a visual presence. In what follows we will outline some importantly different and immediately visual ways of envisaging formal systems, including a modeling of systems in terms of fractals. The progressively deeper dimensions of fractal images can be used to map increasingly complex well-formed formulae (wffs) or what we will term 'value spaces', which correspond directly to columns of traditional truth tables. Within such an image, theorems, contradictions, and various forms of contingency can be coded in terms of color or shading, resulting in a visually immediate and geometrically suggestive representation of systems as infinite wholes. One promise of such an approach, it is hoped, is the possibility of asking and answering questions about formal systems in terms of fractal geometry. As a psychological matter, complete fractal images of formal systems seem to correspond to a realist and non-constructivist approach to formal systems.

Paul Bernays emphasizes the contrast between these two approaches, using Euclid as a constructivist and David Hilbert as a realist or Platonist:

If we compare Hilbert's axiom system to Euclid's . . . we notice that Euclid speaks of figures to be *constructed,* whereas, for Hilbert, systems of points, straight lines, and planes exist from the outset. Euclid postulates: One can join two points by a straight line; Hilbert states the axiom: Given any two points, there exists a straight line on which both are situated. 'Exists' refers here to existence in the system of straight lines. . . . [T]he value of platonistically inspired mathematical conceptions is that they furnish models of abstract imagination. These stand out by their simplicity and logical strength. They form representations which extrapolate from certain regions of experience and intuition.[4]

In this chapter we want to use the computer to portray visually, and in progressively deeper and more revealing ways, the formal systems that Bernays refers to as "models of abstract imagination."

We begin with the example of tic-tac-toe, a simple game rather than a simple formal system, in order to introduce both the general approach and a number of the tools to be used at later stages. We then offer some first maps of familiar formal systems in terms of enumerations of formulae, starting with 'rug' images and moving on to a more complete portrayal in terms of fractal embedding. An alternative semantic portrayal of formal systems in terms of 'value spaces' and 'value solids', however, turns out to be significantly more revealing. The semantic approach offers a number of surprises. The first of these is the appearance of the Sierpinski triangle, a familiar fractal, as the pattern of tautologies in standard value spaces. A second surprise is an intriguing correspondence between the value solids for classical logic and sets of competing connectives for infinite-valued logics. A final surprise, which we don't yet understand in full depth, is a clear connection between fractal images of formal systems and cellular automata: the value spaces of standard logics, it turns out, can be generated step-by-step using elementary two-dimensional cellular automata.

3.1 THE EXAMPLE OF TIC-TAC-TOE

Although our primary concern is with fractal images for formal theories rather than for games, many of the techniques can be made clear by constructing a fractal image for the simple game of tic-tac-toe.

The first player in tic-tac-toe, conventionally labeled X, has a choice of one of nine squares in which to place his marker. The opposing player O then has a choice of one of the remaining eight squares. On X's next turn he has a choice of seven squares, and so forth. There are thus a total of $9 \times 8 \times 7 \times \ldots 3 \times 2 \times 1$ possible series of moves, giving us 362,880 possible tic-tac-toe games. Some of these are wins for X, some for O, and some draws (wins for neither player). The fractal image shown in figure 1 offers an analytic presentation of all possible tic-tac-toe games.

In figure 1 we've emphasized the divisions corresponding to the nine basic squares of the tic-tac-toe game. Figure 2 shows progressive enlargements, which track the course of a particular game. Here X's first move is to the upper left-hand corner of figure 1, which is then enlarged as 2A. The upper left square is now occupied, having already been played by X, but O can choose any of the remaining eight squares for the second move of the game. In the series of moves shown, player O chooses the upper right corner, which is then enlarged as 2B. In the color version, patterns of yellow and blue can be used to indicate wins for O and X, respectively. In the complete view of the fractal in figure 1, however, the yellow wins in particular are small enough—meaning deep enough in the game—so as to be practically invisible. Were the resolution of our illustration great enough, and our eyes sharp enough, we would be able to see all such wins embedded in the image. Winning strategies, as a matter of fact, could be thought of as routes through the fractal toward those winning games.

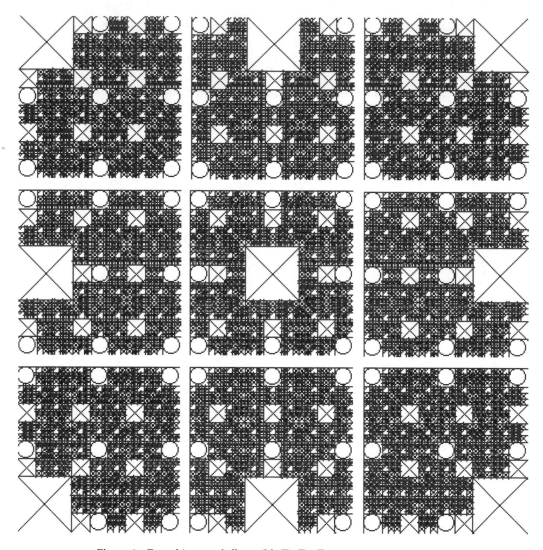

Figure 1   Fractal image of all possible Tic-Tac-Toe games.

Tic-tac-toe is convenient as an illustration because we have only two players and only three final outcomes of concern (a win for X, a win for O, or a draw), and because the game has a definite terminus after nine plays. The principles of a game fractal could in principle be extended to checkers and even chess, though it's also clear that these would become explosively complex in short order.[5]

In what follows we apply some of the same graphic techniques to simple formal systems, first with simpler 'rug' images but moving eventually to full fractal images of formal systems. In such an application wffs or equivalence classes of wffs will replace moves or series of moves in the example of tic-tac-toe, colors for wins and draws will be replaced with

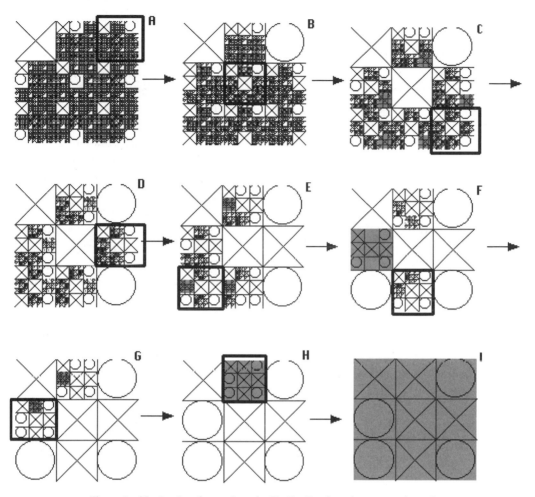

Figure 2 Navigating deeper into the Tic-Tac-Toe fractal: one sample path.

colors coded to theorems, contradictions, and various contingencies, and the fractal images used will be infinitely rather than merely finitely deep.

3.2 'RUG' ENUMERATION IMAGES

We begin with an extremely simple formal system, for which we will construct several different forms of images. The system at issue is propositional logic, made even simpler by restricting it to a single sentence letter **p**. In order to make things simpler still, we use a single connective: either the Sheffer stroke |, which can be read as NAND, or the dagger ↓, which can be read as NOR. As is well known, either NAND or NOR suffices as a complete base for all Boolean connectives.

Our goal, then, is to construct an image of truth-values for all formulae expressible in terms only of **p** and | or ↓. The values at issue are merely four, equivalent to **p**, ~**p** (**p** | **p** or **p**↓**p**), tautology ⊤, or contradiction ⊥. In figures 4 through 8 we use light grey for **p**, dark grey for ~**p**, white for tautologies, and black for contradictions.

Let us start with a simple 'rug' pattern with an enumeration of all formulae expressible in terms of our single sentence letter and single connective. For a first enumeration the plan of the rug is laid out schematically, as in figure 3. Here formula 1 is **p** | **p**, formed by a single stroke between the formula heading its row and the formula at the top of its column. That formula, now simply labeled '1', is then placed in the second position along each axis. Formula 2 is formed as a 'slash product' of the formula heading its row and its column—in the form (row | column)— in the same way. Formula 2 is thus (**p** | 1) or (**p** | (**p** | **p**)). Formula 2 is added as the third formula on each axis. Formula 3 is ((**p** | **p**) | **p**), formula 4 is (**p** | (**p** | (**p** | **p**))), formula 5 is ((**p** | **p**) | (**p** | **p**)), formula 6 is ((**p** | (**p** | **p**)) | **p**), and so forth. The pattern continues to generate progressively longer formulae, constituting in the abstract an infinite partial plane extending to the bottom and right and containing all formulae of our simple single-sentence-letter form of propositional calculus.

In figure 4 the schema is shown in shades of color. Squares correspond directly to the formulae indicated in the schematic sketch above, including formulae along the axes, and are colored in terms of their values: as noted, light grey = **p** or equivalent formulae, dark grey = **p** | **p** or ~**p**, white represents tautologies ⊤, and black represents contradictions ⊥. The first graph in figure 4 is a smaller fragment of the upper left corner of the rug, with the values of formulae indicated on axes as well. The second image in figure 4 shows a larger section, incorporating the first. Here a number of

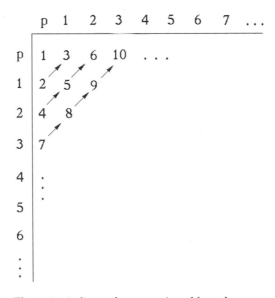

Figure 3   A diagonal enumeration of formulae.

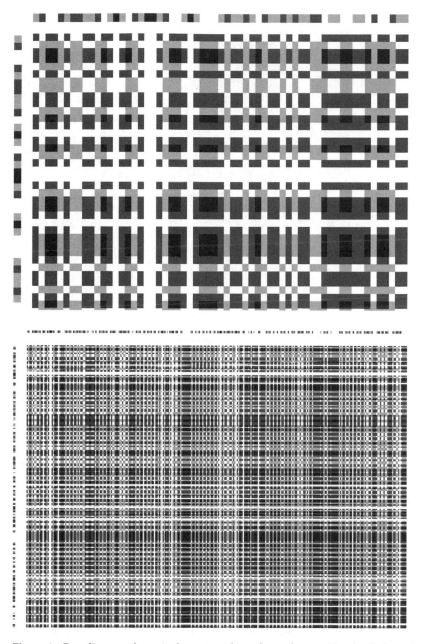

Figure 4 Rug diagrams for a single sentence-letter form of propositional calculus using the Sheffer stroke NAND, diagonal enumeration.

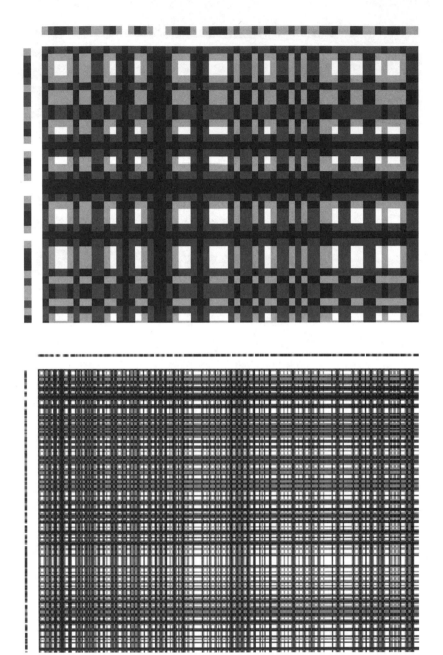

Figure 5 Rug diagrams for a single sentence-letter form of propositional calculus using the dagger NOR, diagonal enumeration.

systematic features are immediately evident. The first is that the images in figure 4 are symmetric, reflecting the fact that $x \mid y$ has the same value as $y \mid x$ for any formulae x and y. The 'stripes' in the rug are also obvious, reflecting the fact that both $x \mid \perp$ and $\perp \mid x$ will be tautologous for any x: once any formula on either axis has the value $\perp$, any formula composed of it with a single stroke will have the value $\top$. Closer attention shows that rows in which the value of the formula at the top is $\top$ will simply reflect the value of the formulae on the column axis, with the same being true for columns with the value $\top$ and the formulae listed along the top.

Figure 5 shows the rug pattern created from the same enumeration of formulae but in which the Sheffer stroke $\mid$ is replaced with the NOR connective $\downarrow$. Side by side, figures 4 and 5 also serve to make obvious certain relationships between these two connectives: a contradiction on either side of the stroke gives us a tautology, for example, whereas a tautology on either side of the dagger gives us a contradiction. It is clear that dagger tautologies mirror Sheffer stroke contradictions, and dagger contradictions correspond to Sheffer tautologies: a graphic expression of the familiar duality of the stroke and dagger. For systems with only one sentence letter, moreover, it is clear that the colors for areas other than contradictions and tautologies are identical. In these simple systems, any formula equivalent to **p** or to $\sim$ **p** written in terms of the Sheffer stroke retains that value if written in terms of the dagger. In none of these cases do our images offer genuinely new information regarding the stroke and dagger, of course—all the facts indicated are well known—though these patterns do make such features vividly evident.

Figures 7 and 8 show a rug pattern using a different enumeration of formulae, following the alternative schematic in figure 6. Nothing, it should be noted, dictates any particular form for enumeration in such a display; nothing dictates the diagonal enumeration of figure 3 over the square enumeration of figure 6, for example, nor either of these over any of the infinite alternatives. There is therefore an ineliminable arbitrariness to the choice of any particular rug pattern for a formal system. It is also clear, however, that certain properties of patterns—including those noted above—will appear regardless of the pattern of enumeration chosen. Pattern-properties invariant under enumeration can be expected to correspond to deep or basic properties of the system.

The rug patterns sketched here are for an extremely simple form of propositional calculus, explicitly restricted to just one sentence letter. Can such an approach be extended to include systems with additional sentence letters as well? One way of extending the enumeration schemata to include two sentence letters rather than one is simply to begin with the two sentence letters on each axis. In all other regards enumeration can proceed as before (see figure 9). With two sentence letters, of course, four colors no longer suffice for values of tautologies, contradictions, and all possible

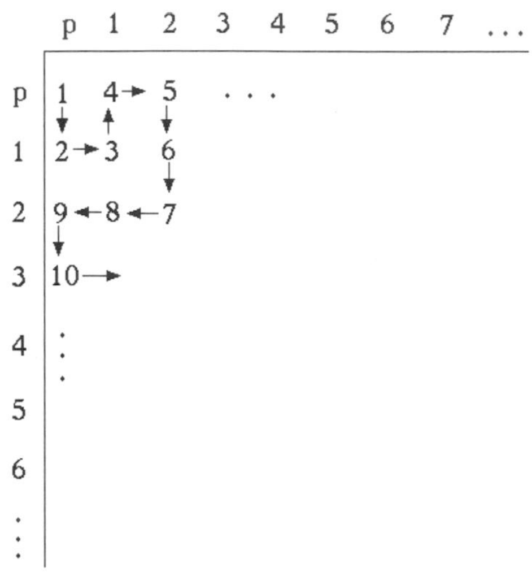

```
        p  1   2   3   4   5   6   7  . . .

p  │  1   4→  5    . . .
   │  ↓   ↑   ↓
1  │  2→ 3   6
   │            ↓
2  │  9← 8← 7
   │  ↓
3  │ 10→

4  │  ⋮

5  │

6  │

⋮  │
```

Figure 6   A square enumeration of formulae.

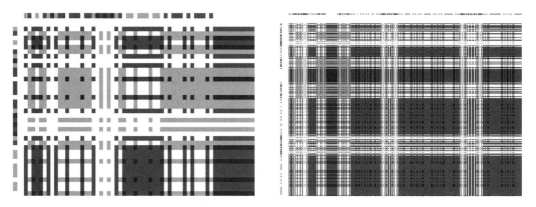

Figure 7   NAND using square enumeration.

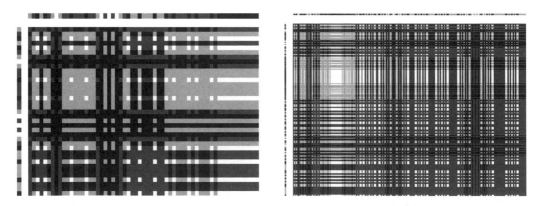

Figure 8   NOR using square enumeration.

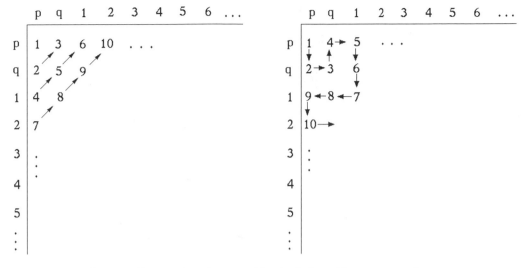

Figure 9 Enumerations for propositional calculus with two sentence letters.

shades of contingency. For a system with both **p** and **q** we will require sixteen colors in all, corresponding to the sixteen possible truth tables composed of four lines, or equivalently the sixteen binaries composed of four digits.

Complete color shade patterns for propositional calculus with **p** and **q**—employing a complete palette of contingencies—are shown in figure 10. These represent NAND and NOR with our initial diagonal enumeration scheme. Although a number of the characteristics noted above with respect to propositional calculus involving a single sentence letter still hold, one does not: it is no longer true that contingent values match between NAND and NOR versions. That property, though provable for propositional calculus with a single sentence letter, disappears in richer systems.

In both figures 10 and 11 the number of colors at issue becomes even more bewildering in larger sections of the display. In figure 11 we have compensated for this difficulty by eliminating all colors for various contingencies in a larger array, leaving only black for tautologies and grey for contradictions.[6] Figure 11 shows an extended view of tautologies and contradictions for NAND and NOR in our first pattern of enumeration.

In theory, any finite number of sentence letters can be added at the beginning of an array in the manner of the enumerations in figure 9. For n sentence letters, however, the number of colors required to cover all contingencies is 2 raised to 2^n colors. At three variables, therefore, we have already hit 2^8 or 256 contingency colors. At four variables we hit 65,536.

In theory the full countable set of sentence letters required for standard propositional calculus might also be introduced along the axes, by simply adding an additional sentence letter at some regular interval (figure 12).

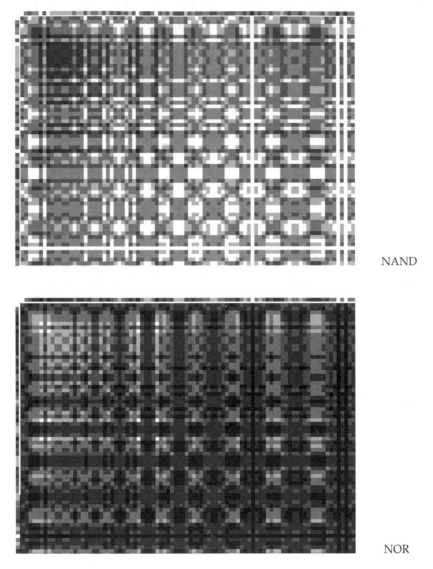

NAND

NOR

Figure 10 Propositional calculus with two sentence letters, diagonal enumerations.

Because the standard propositional calculus is limited to finite connectives, we would here require countably many contingency colors as well.

Similar representations of formal systems beyond propositional calculus are undoubtedly possible for forms of predicate calculus as well. One way to start mapping a form of predicate calculus that has multiple quantifiers but is limited to monadic predicates applied to variables, for example, is the following. In a first grid we enumerate all combinations of n-place predicates and variables, giving us Fx, Fy, Fz, . . . Gx, Gy, Gz, ... These we can think of as a series of propositional functions P1, P2, P3, . . . , which can be introduced into a grid for full propositional logic by simply placing

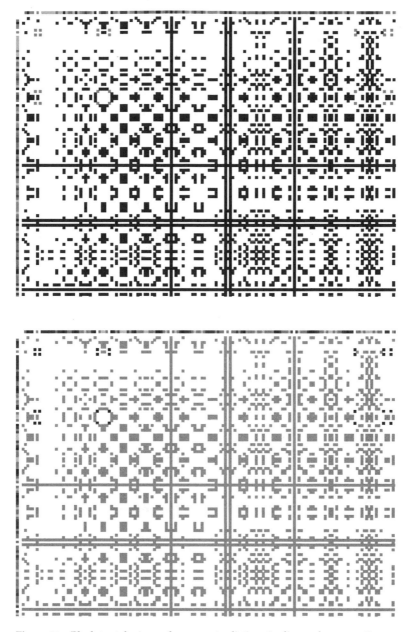

Figure 11 Black tautologies and grey contradictions in diagonal enumeration.

them between our progressively introduced sentence letters—**p**, P1, **q**, P2, **r**, P3 . . . —in an expansion of an enumeration pattern such as that outlined in figure 12. Quantification over formulae in variables x, y, z . . . might then be introduced by adding spaced occurrences for ∀x, ∀y, ∀z along just one axis. Here the application of a lone quantifier to formulae in its row could be interpreted as a universal quantification in that variable over that

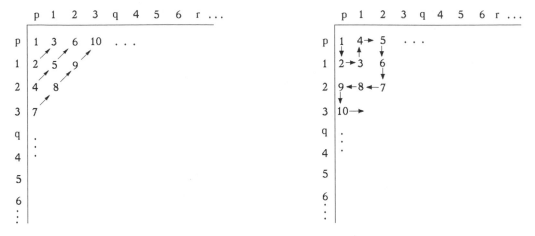

Figure 12   Enumerations for a full propositional calculus.

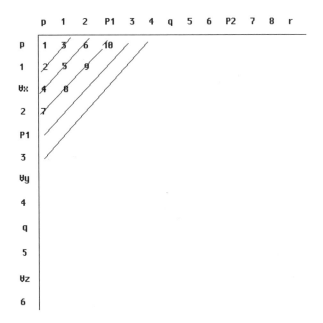

Figure 13   An enumeration scheme for quantification.

formula.[7] All other intersections would be interpreted as before, in terms
for example of the Sheffer stroke (figure 13). Existential quantification can
be expressed in terms of universal quantification and negation, and the
latter can be expressed by the Sheffer stroke in familiar ways.[8]

Figure 13 is limited to monadic predicates applied to variables simply
because the scheme becomes complicated so quickly even in that case. A
representation of polyadic predicates limited to variables would demand
only the further complication that we include all n-valued predicate letters
paired with n-tuplets of our variables. These can be generated in separate

grids first so as to form a single enumeration, then introduced into the main grid in the position of P1, P2, P3 . . . .

The purpose of outlining such a schema is to show that rug images of formal systems can be extended to forms of predicate calculus. On seeing a dog walk on two legs, Abraham Lincoln is reputed to have said, "The amazing thing is not that he does it well but that the thing can be done at all." In even the simple case of propositional logic with a single sentence letter, artificiality was introduced by arbitrary choices of enumeration for wffs. In the schema outlined for predicate calculus this artificiality is magnified many times over—by repeated arbitrary choices regarding forms of enumeration within a grid, by choices of how to incorporate different infinite classes of formulae on the axes, and by choices of how to incorporate quantification into the grid. The end product succeeds in showing that the thing can be done; but it should not be expected, we think, to give any particularly perspicuous view of the theorems of the calculus.

If we return for a moment to the simple form of propositional calculus restricted to a single sentence letter, it should be clear that either of the

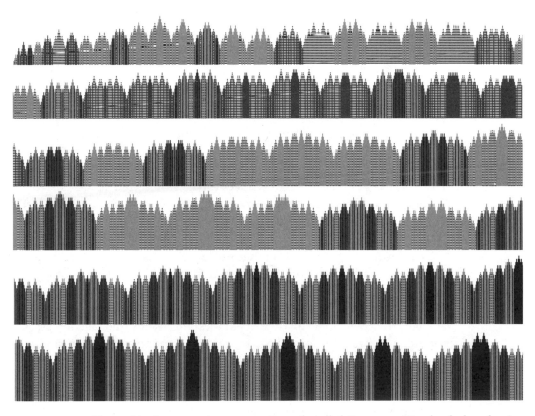

Figure 14 A progressive enumeration of single-letter propositional calculus showing formula length and value.

enumerations offered above will generate progressively longer wffs. It is not true, of course, that the length of wffs within such an enumeration increases monotonically; formula 10 in our original enumeration is shorter than formula 9, for example. Along the diagonal of either schema, however, formulae do increase in size with each step. How does such an enumeration look if we graph the formulae sequentially in terms of length with colors assigned for value? The beginning of such a result, using NAND and our first enumeration, is shown in figure 14. We have chopped this up for illustration purposes only: the series should be thought of as a seamless series continuing from the right side of each row to the left side of that beneath it. Shading used is the same as in the rug patterns above except that tautologies are indicated in white with horizontal cross-hatching so that height will be visible. In the program used for generating this image, one can continue to flip through progressively longer wffs with no apparent repeat of color patterns.

3.3   TAUTOLOGY FRACTALS

The rug enumeration patterns offered above are perhaps the most direct way to attempt to model a complete formal system in terms of the values of its wffs. There is one large respect in which these patterns do *not* correspond to the fractal outlined for tic-tac-toe, however. That fractal exhibits all possible tic-tac-toe games in a finite area: all tic-tac-toe games are contained within the large initial square, though progressive moves are exhibited more 'deeply' at decreasing scales. The rug patterns offered above, on the other hand, are not in principle exhibitable in a finite space: all occupy an infinite plane extending without limit to the right and bottom. It is also possible, however, to outline fractals for at least simple systems of propositional calculus which *do* embed information in a finite space in the way the tic-tac-toe fractal does. In the case of systems with infinite wffs, of course, the corresponding fractal must be infinitely deep. For a simple form of propositional calculus with one sentence letter and a single connective | such a fractal is shown in figure 15.

The form of the fractal in figure 15 can most easily be outlined developmentally (see figure 16). We start from a single triangle occupying the whole space, representing the formula **p** and assigned light grey as the contingent value of **p**. We then take half of this space and divide it into two smaller triangles. One of these triangles represents the Sheffer stroke formulae (a | b) for the formula a of the divided triangle over all formulae b exhibited in the whole graph before division—including formula a itself, of course. The other small triangle represents the symmetrical Sheffer stroke formulae (b | a) for all formulae b previously exhibited over the present formula a. At the first step both of these amount to simply (**p** | **p**), colored dark grey as a representation of the contingent value ~**p**. At the next step

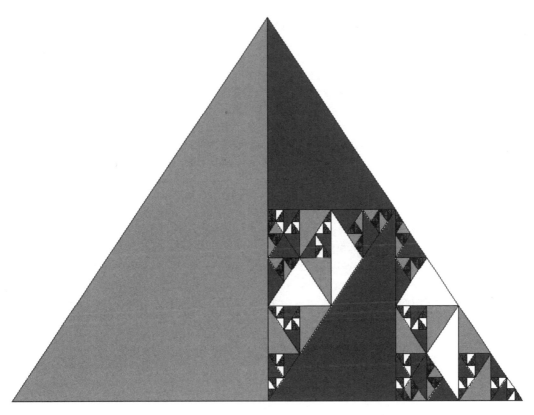

Figure 15 Fractal image of propositional calculus with one sentence letter and NAND.

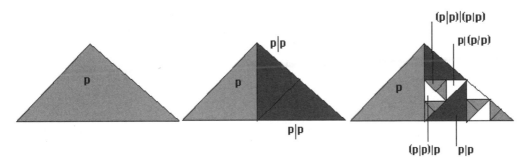

Figure 16 A developmental outline of the fractal.

we take each of the new triangles thus created, divide them into two, and embed in each of these smaller triangles an appropriately colored image of the whole—representing Sheffer stroke formulae (a|b) of the present formulae over all formulae previously exhibited and Sheffer stroke formulae (b|a) of all formulae previously exhibited over the present formula.

At each step a new set of more complex formulae is created, and at each step all Sheffer stroke combinations of elements of this new set with all formulae previously exhibited, including itself, are embedded in the total image. Tautologies are colored white and contradictions black. All formulae of our simple formal system are thus represented with their value colors somewhere in the infinite depths of the fractal. Indeed all formulae except **p** are represented redundantly—(**p** | **p**) appears twice at the first step, for example (representing the present formula **p** over the previous formula **p** and vice versa), and later complexes with (**p** | **p**) on either side will carry the redundancy further. The complete fractal represents the entire propositional calculus formulated in terms of the Sheffer stroke for a single sentence letter, infinitely embedded on the model of the tic-tac-toe fractal with which we began.

Modeling in terms of tautology fractals can be extended to more than a single sentence letter by starting with a larger number of initial areas: an initial triangle with two major divisions for **p** and **q**, for example, with three for **p**, **q**, and **r**, and so forth. Any of these could then be subdivided precisely as before, once again embedding the whole image into each subdivision. If we wish, we can even envisage an initial triangle with room for infinitely many sentence letters arranged Zeno-style in infinitely smaller areas. The embedding procedure would proceed as before, though of course each embedding would involve the mirroring of infinitely many areas into infinitely many. We haven't yet tried to extend such a pattern to quantification.

3.4   THE SIERPINSKI TRIANGLE: A PARADOXICAL INTRODUCTION

In the following section we want to outline another way of visualizing simple formal systems. An important fractal image that appears there, however—and which surprised us when it did—deserves a brief introduction of its own. Here we want to introduce that fractal in terms of paradox, in ways reminiscent of some of the work of chapter 1.

Zeno's paradox of the Stadium comes in two forms. In the progressive form, the argument is that Achilles will never be able to run across the Stadium. For him to do so, he would first have to reach the halfway point. Once there, he would have to reach the halfway point of the remaining distance, then the halfway point of the remaining distance, and so on *ad infinitum*. If space and time are infinitely divisible, so the argument goes, Achilles could never reach the other side; to do so would require traversing an infinite number of points in a finite amount of time.

In the regressive form of the paradox, Achilles can't even get started. Before he could reach the halfway point, Achilles would first have to reach a point halfway to the half way point. In order to reach that, he would first have to reach the point halfway to it, and so on *ad infinitum*. If space and time are infinitely divisible, the argument goes, motion could never be initiated. For Achilles to get started at all would require him to traverse an

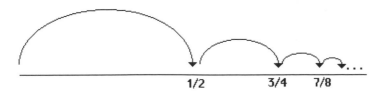

Figure 17 A geometric representation of the infinite regresses in the progressive and regressive forms of Zeno's Stadium paradox.

infinite number of points in a finite amount of time. Both forms of Zeno's paradox are represented geometrically in figure 17.

Having looked at the path of Achilles geometrically, let's examine his path arithmetically. Since the argument proceeds in terms of halving distances throughout, a binary decimal notation proves particularly perspicuous. In such notation, 0.1 represents $1/2$, 0.01 represents $1/4$, 0.001 represents $1/8$, and so forth: a 1 in the nth decimal place represents a value of $1/2^n$.

In the progressive form of the paradox, Achilles must first reach the half-way point $1/2$, then the further point $3/4$, then the further point $7/8$, and so forth:

Fraction	Binary Representation
1/2	0.1
3/4	0.11
7/8	0.111
9/16	0.1111
⋮	

In the regressive form of the paradox, before he reaches the half-way point he must reach the $1/4$ point, but before that he must reach the $1/8$ point, before that the $1/16$th point, and so forth:

Fraction	Binary Representation
1/2	0.1
1/4	0.01
1/8	0.001
1/16	0.0001
⋮	

From the arithmetic point of view, then, the positions in the progressive form of Achilles' route are generated by appending a '1' after the binary point. The positions in the regressive form—positions of repeated halving—are generated by appending a '0' after the binary point.[9]

The classical Zeno paradox is expressed throughout in terms of one dimension: the one-dimensional line of Achilles' route across the stadium. But consider also a variation in which Achilles is traveling between three points arranged in a triangle. We can envisage him placed randomly within this triangular stadium, and so confused as to follow the rule:

The Trivalent Achilles: I run halfway to one of the three points chosen at random.

We can imagine marking the points on which Achilles' route might converge. This two-dimensional version of Zeno's Achilles, dubbed the Chaos Game by Michael Barnsley,[10] generates the fractal Sierpinski triangle or gasket shown in figure 18.

There is another way of obtaining the Sierpinski fractal, important for some of our results regarding formal systems in the following section. In this variation, which we might call the Escapist Achilles, we again begin by choosing any point inside the triangle. Here, however, we envisage Achilles running in straight lines *from* the points of the triangle, following a deterministic rather than a randomized rule:

The Escapist Achilles: I run twice the distance away from the nearest point.

If we plot those initial points from which Achilles can never break out of the triangle—those points from which there will be no escape—we once again obtain the Sierpinski triangle of figure 18.[11]

Figure 18 The Sierpinski triangle.

A Zeno-like paradox with three points may seem reminiscent of Liar-like paradoxes with three speakers—the Triplist variations of chapter 1. And indeed there is an intriguing connection. Consider a Triplist in the tradition of Buridan, discussed by Tyler Burge and Brian Skyrms:[12]

Socrates: What Plato says is true.

Plato: What Socrates says is false.

Chrysippus: Neither Socrates nor Plato speak truly.

Assuming a bivalent evaluation scheme, let us suppose that what Socrates says is true. Then what Plato says is false, since we assumed Socrates to speak truly and Plato says that he does not. On this assumption what Chrysippus says is also false, since what Socrates says is assumed to be true. If Socrates is assumed to speak truly, in other words, the other two speakers must be speaking falsely. Indeed the lesson holds for any of the speakers: if any of them speak truly, the others do not.

But of course the Triplist also has a Liar-like dynamics. We started out assuming that what Socrates says is true. But what Socrates says is that what Plato says is true. If what Plato says is true, then what Socrates (and Chrysippus) say must be false . . . . If we represent bivalent truth and falsity by 1 and 0, respectively, our progressive evaluations for the three statements above might look as follows:

Socrates: 1 0 0 1 0 1 . . .

Plato: 0 1 0 0 0 0 . . .

Chrysippus: 0 0 1 0 1 0 . . .

At every place in the series, precisely one statement will have a value of 1; the others will have a value of 0. Different patterns of evaluation, in fact—starting with the assumption that Socrates speaks truly, or Plato instead, or Chrysippus instead, and moving from that point to the implications for one rather than the other speaker—will give us different patterns of this basic form. For each progressive pattern of evaluation, there is such a series of triples in 1 and 0, and for each such pattern of triples there is an infinite pattern of reasoning regarding the three sentences above. This pattern too, it turns out, maps directly on to the Sierpinski triangle. Here let us think of the vertices of our triangle as axes x, y, and z, plotting the position of a point within the triangle in terms of a binary decimals and these axes. Vertex x will have the coordinates $(1, 0, 0)$, representing a full '1' for the x-value and 0 for the other two. Vertices y and z will have coordinates $(0, 1, 0)$ and $(0, 0, 1)$, respectively. Using binary notion, a midpoint on the side across from the x-vertex will have a value $(0, 0.1, 0.1)$, and so forth. Consider now the possibility of transferring our progressive values for the Triplist above into decimals in this axis system. The first value for each of our three speakers will be the first value to the right of the decimal in the three coordinates of such a system, the second value the second place, and so forth. The pattern above, for example, thus becomes the triplet $(0.100101\ldots, 0.011000\ldots, 0.001010\ldots)$. Manfred Schroeder has shown that the set of all such values is precisely the set of points of the Sierpinski triangle.[13]

The Sierpinski triangle thus seems to emerge in surprising ways from two-dimensional generalizations of the Zeno paradoxes and from a Triplist version of the Liar. These connections, however, we did not recognize immediately. The first surprise was the appearance of the Sierpinski within a fractal representation of standard logical connectives.

3.5   A SIERPINSKI TAUTOLOGY MAP

In the rug patterns of section 3.3 we graphed an enumeration of formulae for simple forms of propositional calculi, coloring the grid locations of formulae in terms of their values. For forms of propositional calculus with n sentence letters, we noted, there are 2 raised to 2^n such colors or values— essentially, a color for each possible truth table of length 2^n. Here we consider a different type of display for such systems, constructed using those values themselves on the axes rather than enumerated wffs. This frees us from particular enumerations of formulae since it frees us from the formulae themselves; the value space is constructed not in terms of particular formulae but in terms of the values of equivalence classes of formulae.

Consider two sentence letters **p** and **q** in standard truth-table form:

p	q		p	q
T	T		1	1
T	F		1	0
F	T		0	1
F	F		0	0

For the four-line truth tables appropriate to two sentence letters there are sixteen possible combinations of T and F, or 1 and 0. These include solid 0s, corresponding to a contradiction or necessary falsehood; solid 1s, corresponding to a tautology; the pattern 1100, corresponding to the value of **p**; and the pattern 1010, corresponding to **q**. The sixteen values for two sentence letters can be thought of simply as all four-digit binaries. These can be arranged in ascending order along the two axes of a two-dimensional display. Following the approach above we can think of these values as distinguished by color as well (figure 19).

Combinatorial values for any chosen binary connective can now be mapped in the interior value space. If our value map is that of the Sheffer stroke, for example, the value of $(\perp \mid \perp)$ will appear at the intersection of 0000 and 0000, the value of $(\top \mid p)$ at the intersection of 1111 and 1100, etc. In terms of the colors on our axes the complete graph for the Sheffer stroke

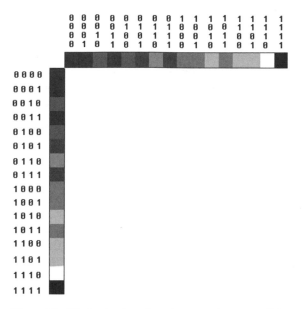

Figure 19 The basic plan of a value space in terms of binary representations and colors.

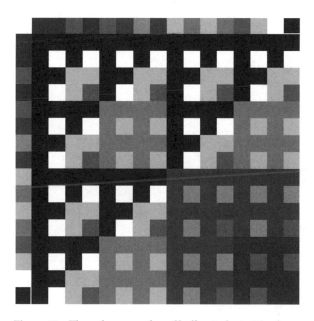

Figure 20 The value space for a Sheffer stroke in 16 values.

Fractal Images of Formal Systems

appears in figure 20. A Sheffer stroke between ⊥ and 0000 or any other value, of course, amounts to a tautology. In figure 20, 0000 is represented using the darkest grey, tautologies are shown in black, and this fact is represented by black values representing tautologies in all cases along the left column and along the top row—all cases in which a value of 0000 appears on either side of the stroke. A Sheffer stroke between two tautologies, on the other hand, amounts to a contradiction, indicated by the dark grey square at the intersection of two black axis values in the lower right corner. As a whole the graph represents the value space for all Sheffer stroke combinations of our sixteen values.[14]

A particularly intriguing feature of the value space appears more dramatically if we emphasize tautologies by whiting out all other values (figure 21). The fractal pattern formed here in black is of course that of the Sierpinski triangle. If we expand our value space to that of three variables, with 256 values corresponding to all eight-digit binaries, an even finer representation of the Sierpinski triangle appears (figure 22). At any number of variables, given a standard listing of binaries corresponding to truth table values, the tautologous Sheffer combinations will form a Sierpinski triangle. As indicated below, we can in fact think of diagrams with increasing numbers of sentence letters as increasingly finer approximations to a full system, with infinitely many sentence letters and infinitely many values. For that diagram, the tautologies of the system form an infinitely fine Sierpinski dust.

The main connective of figures 20 through 22 is NAND or the Sheffer stroke. A similar display for NOR, or the dagger, appears in figure 23. Here

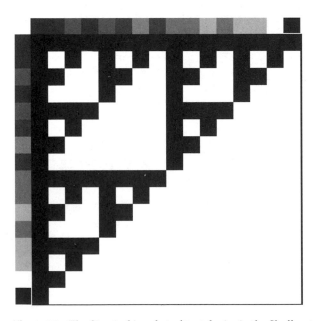

Figure 21 The Sierpinski gasket of tautologies in the Sheffer stroke.

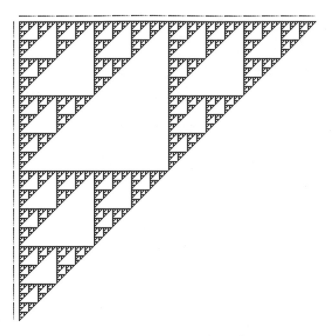

Figure 22 The Sierpinski gasket of tautologies for NAND in 256 values.

there is only one tautology, at the intersection of 0000 and 0000. The Sierpinski triangle does show up again, however, as a graph of contradictions in the lower right-hand corner. Other connectives generate other patterns in value space. 'And' and 'or', for example, are shown in figure 24. In the case of 'and' the persistent image of the Sierpinski triangle appears in the upper left as a value pattern for contradiction; in the case of 'or' it appears in the lower right as a value pattern for tautology. In material implication the Sierpinski triangle shifts to the lower left as a value pattern for tautology.

In the course of our research the appearance of the Sierpinski triangle within the value space of propositional logic came as a surprise. But its appearance can easily be understood after the fact, as we will see below.

We can think of value space displays for forms of propositional calculus with increasing numbers of sentence letters as approximations to a fuller system. As long as we have some finite number of sentence letters n we will have finitely many value spaces, corresponding to all possible truth tables of length 2^n. The full propositional calculus toward which our approximations seem to build, however, is *not* limited to any finite number of sentence letters: it includes a countably *infinite* number instead. What then would the complete value space for the full system look like?

Here we will continue to think of value spaces as corresponding to possible truth tables, encodable in terms of binaries. Truth tables of any given length 2^n, however, can offer value spaces appropriate only to a system limited to n sentence letters. For a full system with a countably

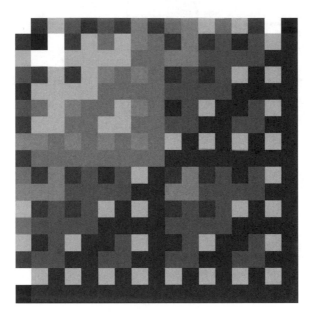

Figure 23 NOR.

infinite number of sentence letters the basic strategy will have to be extended to what are in effect truth tables of *infinite* length. This is less difficult than it may at first appear. In constructing finite truth tables for n variables the standard procedure is to start with a sentence letter represented as 0101 ... to length 2^n, to represent the next sentence letter with 00110011 ... to that length, the third with 00001111 ..., and so forth. For infinite truth tables adequate to finite complexes of countably many sentence letters, our first sentence letter **p** can be thought of as having an infinite truth table that starts with 01010101 .... Our second sentence letter **q** can be thought of as having the infinite truth table that starts 00110011 ..., our third sentence letter **r** as having the infinite truth table 000011111 ..., and so forth. Each of our sentence letters, in other words, can be thought of as having infinitely periodic truth tables that otherwise follow the standard scheme used for constructing truth tables of finite length. There will always be room for 'one more' sentence letter since it will always be possible to introduce a larger period of 0s and 1s for the next sentence letter needed. Sentence letters of a full form of propositional calculus can thus be thought of as corresponding to a subset of the periodic binary decimals: those that alternate series of 0s and 1s of length 2^n for some n.

Any set of values for any finite set of sentence letters will have an appropriate line in this infinite extension of truth tables, and in fact will have a line that will itself reappear an infinite number of times. Since the infinite truth tables for our sentence letters are periodic in this way, complex sentences formed of finitely many connectives between finitely

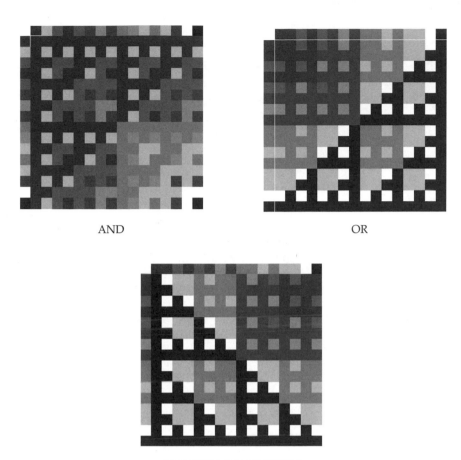

AND

OR

MATERIAL IMPLICATION

Figure 24

many sentence letters will be periodic as well. The largest period possible for a complex sentence of this sort will in fact be the longest period of its sentence-letter components. All values for the full propositional calculus will thus be represented by periodic binary decimals. It is important to note, however, that not all periodic binary decimals will have corresponding formulae; those periodic in multiples of 3, for example, will not be producible by finite combination from sentence letters periodic in powers of 2.[15]

The important point here is simply that any value space for finitely many sentence letters can be thought of as an approximation to this richer system, adequate to propositional calculus as a whole. In the richer system, of course, the squares of the value spaces illustrated above shrink to mere points in value space, just as values on the axes shrink to mere points on the continuum. Although these points do not by any means exhaust the full [0, 1] interval—they constitute merely a subset of the periodic decimals—they can be envisaged as embedded within it. It is easy to show that these value points are "dense" in the continuum, in the sense that given any interval within the continuum there will be a formula with a value within that interval.[16] The argument below regarding the appearance of the Sierpinski triangle applies to a full continuum as well as to the envisaged subsets, and is valid both for the full propositional calculus and for the envisaged approximations to it.

In terms of NAND or the Sheffer stroke the appearance of the Sierpinski triangle can be outlined as follows. Similar explanations will apply for the other connectives. Let us emphasize that the binary representations of values on each axis of our value spaces, whether finite or infinite, correspond to columns of a truth table. The value assigned to any value space or point v is a function of the truth-table values from which it is perpendicular on each axis. In asking whether a point in the value space represents a tautology in a graph for NAND, for example, what we're really asking is whether the truth tables of these two axis values share any line in which both show a '1'. If there is such a line, their combination by way of NAND is not a tautology. The value point v will have the value of a tautology if and only if its axis values at no point show a '1' on the same line.

Consider now the Escapist Achilles route to the Sierpinski triangle, which generates the fractal in terms of a rule for doubling distance from the nearest vertex. For any given triangle, there is a set of points which, when distance is doubled from the nearest vertex, will be 'thrown' outside of the triangle itself—more precisely, which will map under doubling from the nearest vertex to points outside the triangle itself. These points in fact form an inverted triangle in the center (figure 25). There is a further set of points which, when distance is doubled from the nearest vertex, will be thrown into this central region—and thus which will be thrown out of the triangle upon *two* iterations of the 'doubling from nearest vertex' procedure. The Sierpinski triangle is composed of all those points that remain within the triangle despite unlimited iteration of such a procedure.[17] The Escapist Achilles route to the Sierpinski triangle, it turns out, corresponds quite neatly to its appearance as a map of tautologies in the value space for NAND.

Consider the diagram of a unit square in figure 26, and the upper triangle marked between A (0, 1), B (0, 0), and C (1, 0). This 'inverted' form of the unit square corresponds to our axes for value spaces above. Were we to characterize the Escapist Achilles rule of doubling the distance from the closest vertex in terms of x and y values for particular points within this triangle, our rules could be rendered as follows:

If B is closest, $(x_n, y_n) = (2x, 2y)$

If A is closest, $(x_n, y_n) = (2x, 1 - 2(1 - y))$

If C is closest, $(x_n, y_n) = (1 - 2(1 - x), 2y)$

These will give us the Sierpinski triangle by the Achilles rule of doubling the distance from the nearest vertex.

Figure 25 The Achilles doubling-the-distance route to the Sierpinski gasket.

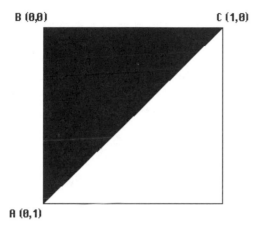

Figure 26 Converting doubling-the-distance to numerical transforms.

Here it's clear that doubling the distance is in all cases a matter of either multiplying an axis value by 2 or subtracting 1 from a multiplication by 2. But now let us envisage the axes of our unit square as marked in terms of binary decimals. For binary decimals multiplication by 2 involves simply moving a decimal point one place to the right: 2 times 0.001 is 0.01; 2 times 0.01 is 0.1. $1 - 2(1 - x)$ equals $2x - 1$, which moves the decimal point one place to the right and 'lops off' any ones that thereby migrate to the left of the decimal point. The crucial point is that for binary decimal expression of axis values, both forms of transformation preserve the order of digits which remain beyond the decimal point. Iterated application of such transformations to pairs of values (x, y) thus effectively moves down each series of binary digits one at a time, checking for whether a 1 occurs in both places. If it does, our iterated transformations have resulted in two values both of which are greater than 1/2 as expressed in binary, and the point will therefore have migrated under iteration outside the region of the dark triangle.

The points of the triangle ABC which will not migrate out under an iterated Achilles procedure of doubling the distance from the nearest vertex—the 'non-escaping' points of a Sierpinski triangle in that upper region—are therefore those points (x, y) such that the binary representation of x and y do not both have a 1 in the same decimal place. Given our representation of values in terms of binary decimals, those points that generate tautologies under NAND are precisely those same points: points with axis values with no 1s in corresponding truth-table lines, or equivalently with no 1s in corresponding decimal places of their binary representation. The initially startling appearance of the Sierpinski triangle as a map of tautologies under the Sheffer stroke can thus be understood in terms of (i) what a binary representation of values means and (ii) a corresponding rendering of the Escapist Achilles route to the Sierpinski in terms of binaries. An outline for the appearance of the Sierpinski in the value space of other connectives can be drawn along the same lines.[18]

The Escapist Achilles route to the Sierpinski does involve a full-continuum unit square. As indicated above, even the full propositional calculus has a value space short of that full continuum; although each sentence letter and each connective corresponds to an infinite decimal, these form a subset of even the merely periodic decimals. None of that, however, affects the basic mechanism of the argument above, which turns merely on the question of whether two decimals share a particular value at any place. Multiplication by 2 from the closest vertex simply 'checks' them place by place. Thus the fact that our value space for propositional calculus comprises a mere subset of the full unit square tells us simply that tautologies in the case of NAND, for example, will constitute an infinitely fine Sierpinski dust within that grainy unit square.

One of the promises of a graphic approach to formal systems of this sort is that there may be results of fractal geometry that can be understood as facts about the logical systems at issue. Here the appearance of the Sierpinski triangle as a map of theorems in value space offers a few minor but tantalizing examples. It is well known that the points constitutive of the Sierpinski triangle within a continuous unit square are infinitely many, but nonetheless 'very few' in the sense that a random selection of points has a probability approaching zero of hitting such a point. The same is true of the full propositional calculus and its infinitary extension; there will be infinitely many complexes with the value of tautology in such a value space, but the probability will approach zero of hitting a tautology in terms of a Sheffer combination of random axis values.

A similar point can be expressed in terms of area. Within any finite approximation to an infinitely fine-grained unit square, the Sierpinski triangle retains a definite area. Within any value space limited to n sentence letters, tautologies retain a similar area of value space. In the case of an infinitely-grained unit square, on the other hand—whether fully continuous or not—the Sierpinski triangle has an area approaching 0. Within the full propositional calculus the relative area of tautologies will similarly amount to zero. In terms of the Sheffer stroke, tautologies end up distributed as unconnected points within value space on the model of three-dimensional Cantor dust.[19]

One measure commonly used in fractal geometry—the origin, in fact, of the term 'fractal'—is the notion of *fractional dimension*. One definition of such a notion is the Hausdorff dimension: For smooth curves, an approximate length L(r) can be given as the product N · r of the number N of straight-line segments of length r required to 'cover' the curve from one end to the other. As r goes to zero, L(r) approaches the length of the curve as a finite limit. For fractal curves, on the other hand, it is standard for L(r) to go to infinity as r goes to zero, since what are being 'covered' are increasingly fine parts of the curve. The Hausdorff dimension d of the intricacy of fractal curves is that exponent d such that the product N · r^d stays finite. The Hausdorff dimension of the Sierpinski triangle is known to be log 3/log 2 ≈ 1.58. Given the work above, it's clear that we will be able to sign the same fractal measure to tautologies within the value space of the Sheffer stroke.

3.6   VALUE SOLIDS AND MULTI-VALUED LOGICS

A slight variation in the representation of the value spaces outlined above offers an intriguing comparison with a way of envisaging connectives in multi-valued logics, including infinite-valued or fuzzy logics.

Rather than graphing values in our value space in terms of color, the use of binary decimals makes it easy to graph them in terms of height in a third dimension. A value of 0.0000 will graph as 0, a value of 0.1000 as the decimal equivalent 0.5, 0.1100 as 0.75, and so forth. A fairly rough graph of this sort for NAND, seen from a particular angle, appears in figure 27. This corresponds directly to figure 20, though here the origin is in the right rear corner. Smoother forms of the value solid for NAND, from two angles, appear in figure 28. Because the rough solids are often more revealing of basic structure, however, we will continue with these throughout. Value solids for conjunction, disjunction, and material implication appear in figure 29. In each case the origin is shown in the left figure at the front left, and in the right figure at the rear right. These value solids make obvious the relationships between NAND and OR, the dual character of conjunction and disjunction, and the rotation properties of negation. Perhaps more significantly, however, these value solids for simple classical systems also show a striking resemblance to a very different type of solid that can be drawn for connectives within multi-valued or infinite-valued logics.

In this second type of solid, values on the axes represent not truth-table columns but degrees of truth. Within this value solid, height at a certain point represents the degree of truth of a complex of two sentences with the axis values of that point. In one standard treatment of infinite-valued connectives, for example, the value of a conjunction of sentences **p** and **q** is the minimum value of the two, represented as:

$$/\mathbf{p} \,\&\, \mathbf{q}/ = \mathbf{Min}(/\mathbf{p}/, /\mathbf{q}/).$$

Figure 27   A value solid for NAND.

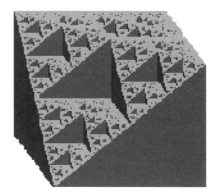

Figure 28   Smoother forms of the value solid for NAND.

The value solid of this type for conjunction will thus at each point have a height corresponding to the minimum of its axis values.

There are, however, rival sets of connectives that have been proposed for multi-valued and infinite-valued or fuzzy logics. One such set, perhaps most common within multi-valued and fuzzy logics, is shown in the left column of figure 30. Another set, grounded more directly in the original multi-valued logic of Łukasiewicz,[20] is shown in the right column. It should be emphasized that the value solids appropriate to connectives in infinite-valued logic are radically different from the value solids for systems outlined above. In system value solids, for example, 0.1000 might represent a truth table in which the first line has a 'T' and the others do not. In that regard it is perfectly symmetrical to 0.0001, which simply has a 'T' on a different line. Using similar binary decimals for the values of sentences in an infinite-valued logic, on the other hand, a statement with the value 0.1000 would be half true. One with a value of 0.0001 would be almost completely false. Given this radical difference, the value solids

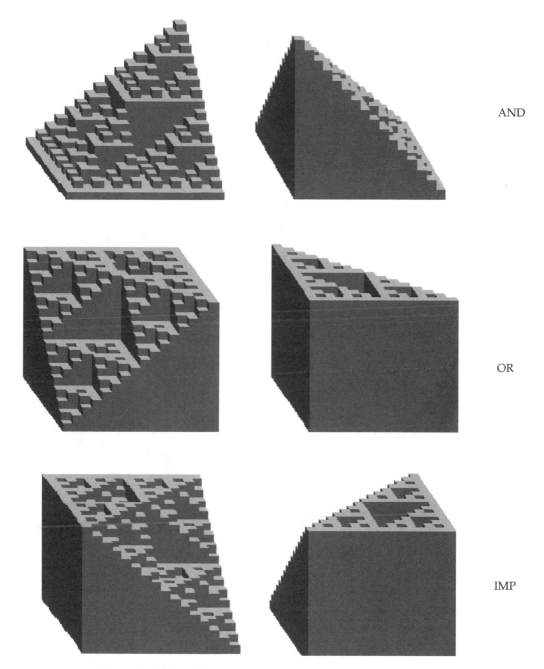

AND

OR

IMP

Figure 29　Value solids.

　Fractal Images of Formal Systems

outlined here for classical systems and those sketched below for infinite-valued logics seem much more alike than they have any right to be. Intriguingly, the system solid for each connective seems to embody a compromise between the corresponding infinite-valued connective solids. The system-solid for 'or', for example, amounts neither to 'Max' nor to the Łukasiewicz 'or'. It rather appears to be a compromise, in which some values correspond to one treatment of the infinite-valued connective and some to another.

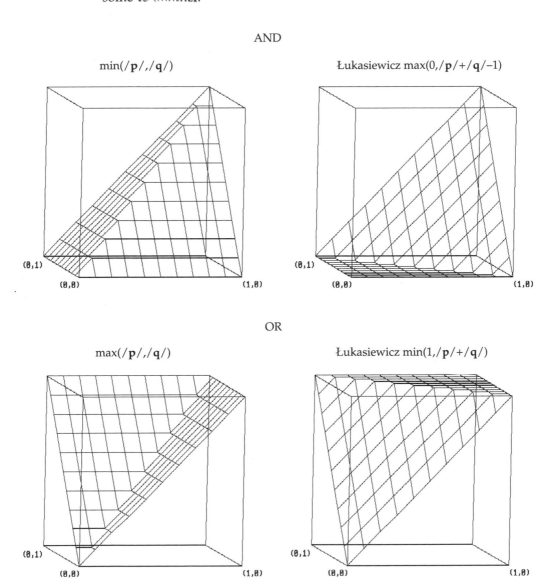

Figure 30 Rival infinite-valued connectives.

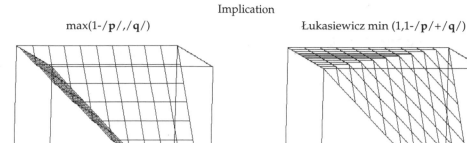

Implication

max(1-/**p**/,/**q**/)   Łukasiewicz min (1,1-/**p**/+/**q**/)

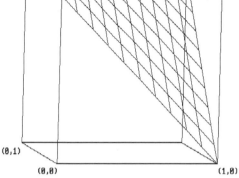

(0,1)

(0,0)   (1,0)

(0,1)

(0,0)   (1,0)

Figure 30   (*continued*).

Indeed this is precisely what is happening. How it occurs—and why there is such a resemblance between these two radically different kinds of value solid—becomes clear if we return to two dimensions and consider a simple form of our basic value grid. In a system grid for 'or', in which we are calculating the truth-table values for an 'or' between truth-table values on the axes, the value assigned to any intersection point is what might be called a 'bitwise or' of the values on the corresponding axes. A '1' occurs in any row in the value of that intersection point just in case a '1' occurs in that row in one or the other of the corresponding axis values. In bitwise 'or' the 1s cannot of course add together and carry to another row:

0   0   0
1   1   1
1   0   bitwise or =   1
0   1   1

The values assigned in a system grid for 'or', then, correspond to a bitwise 'or'. The values assigned to intersection points in an infinite-valued grid will be more complicated, amounting to either the maximum of the axis values **p** and **q** or, in the case of the Łukasiewicz 'or', to Min(1, **p** + **q**). Nonetheless these three values for intersection points occasionally overlap.

In the simple case of three-digit binary decimals, in fact, where we take 111 as the closest approximation to 1 in the Łukasiewicz formula, every bitwise 'or' is equal to either Max, the Łukasiewicz 'or', or both. This is reflected in the grids shown in figure 31. On the left are mapped those intersection points in which a bitwise 'or' corresponds to 'Max'. On the right are mapped those intersection points in the grid in which bitwise 'or' corresponds to the Łukasiewicz 'or'. (Where either contradiction or

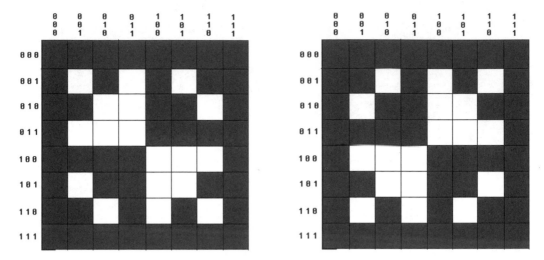

Figure 31 Convergence of bitwise 'or' with 'max' (left) and the Lukasiewicz 'or' (right) in 8 values.

tautology is involved—000 or 111—'Max' and the Łukasiewicz 'or' coincide, accounting for agreement in the two diagrams around the outside border.) Here it is clear that (a) the middle areas, exclusive of the edges, are the negatives of each other, (b) together these two graphs will therefore cover the entire area of the grid, and (c) each middle area represents a simple Sierpinski triangle, rotated 90 degrees from its position in the other graph. A value solid for bitwise 'or' geared to just three-digit binaries, then, corresponds at each intersection point to one or the other of the two infinite-valued connectives outlined above: the eight-valued system solid constitutes a perfect Sierpinski compromise between the two infinite-valued solids.

The result does not generalize in this pure form to system- and infinite-valued solids of more than eight units on a side, however. In more complex cases the Sierpinski patterns persist, but their overlap fails to cover the entire area. For a grid of 256 values on each side, figure 32 shows in black those intersection points in which bitwise 'or' equals one or the other of our two infinite-valued connectives. The holes left are the holes formed by one Sierpinski triangle overlying another rotated at 90 degrees. Even in more complex systems a sort of compromise remains, however. For in all cases the bitwise 'or' for an intersection point will equal either one of the two infinite-valued 'or's above or will have a value between them, less than the Łukasiewicz 'or' but greater than simply 'Max'. Similar compromises hold in the case of the other connectives. Thus in an intriguing way value solids for simple systems map a compromise among the quite different value solids appropriate to rival connectives within infinite-valued or fuzzy logic.

Figure 32 Points in 256 values at which bitwise 'or' equals one of the infinite-valued connectives.

3.7 CELLULAR AUTOMATA IN VALUE SPACE

One of the connections that came as a major surprise in our work was the link between fractal images for formal systems and the evolution of simple cellular automata.

Cellular automata consist of a lattice of discrete sites, each of which may take on values from a finite set. In classical (synchronous) automata the values of sites evolve over discrete time steps from an initial configuration s_0 in accord with deterministic rules that specify the value of each site in terms of the values of sites in a chosen neighborhood n. The two-dimensional value graphs outlined for systems above might also be thought of on the model of two-dimensional automata arrays of this type. What we were surprised to find was that the distribution of values under particular connectives within such arrays can also be generated by simple automata rules.

Consider, for example, an array corresponding to a system value space with sixteen units along each axis, such as that shown in figure 19. Here, however, we are concerned only with the lattice of spaces itself. Each cell in such a lattice, with the exception of those at the edges, is surrounded by eight neighbors. We are concerned in particular with just three of these neighbors, which we will term 'southeastern' neighbors and which are marked with Xs in the sketch below.

☐ ☐ ☐
☐   ☒
☐ ☒ ☒

Let us start with a 'seed' in the lower right-hand corner of our sixteen-by-sixteen grid, consisting of one darkened square. Consider now the following cellular automata rule:

A square will be darkened on the next round if and only if exactly one southeastern neighbor is darkened on the current round.

The series of steps in the evolution of a sixteen-sided array under this simple rule is shown in figure 33. The surprising fact is that the squares occupied by black in each step in this evolution correspond precisely and in order to the values occupied by 0000, 0001, 0010, ... in our original value space for the Sheffer stroke. Careful comparison with figure 20, for example, shows that the single cell 'alive' in the first step of the evolution in figure 33 corresponds to that cell in our value space with a truth-table value of 0000, the daughter cells alive in the second step correspond to those cells with a value of 0001, those alive in the third step correspond to those cells with a semantic value of 0010, and so forth. What this simple cellular automaton is doing, in other words, is 'ticking off' progressive values for NAND plotted in value space. By the sixteenth step—the array for the value 1111—the display evolves into the Sierpinski pattern for tautologies noted in section 3.4. An exactly similar progression through all values represented appears if we begin with 256 values on each side instead of 16. This same simple automata rule, in fact, generates progressive values in the proper places for a value space corresponding to NAND regardless of the number of cells in our value space: for any finite approximation such an automaton is in effect constructing a value space for a limited form of propositional calculus.

Other equally simple automata will generate value spaces for the other connectives outlined above. With precisely the same rule and starting point, but thinking of our values in reverse—from 1111 to 0000 in the case of a sixteen-sided value space, for example—the value space generated step by step is that of conjunction. The value space for disjunction is generated by beginning in the upper left hand corner with the value 0000 following a second rule, symmetrical to that above:

☒ ☒ ☐
☒   ☐
☐ ☐ ☐

Figure 33 A cellular automata generation of the Sierpinski tautology gasket.

A square will be darkened on the next round if and only if exactly one northwest neighbor is darkened on the current round.

This second rule and starting place, thought of as enumerating values in order from 1111 through 0000, generates the value space for NOR or the dagger. Further changes in rule and beginning position give us a cellular automaton adequate to implication.

A bit of thought shows that indeed these rules must generate the progressive values noted within the lattice of any value space. The following twelve paragraphs offer some of the details; those who wish to skip over these may want to go directly to the last paragraph of the section.

Consider as an example the case of 'or', evolution for which will begin from the upper left corner with the second rule above. The 'or' of the system-value grid, it will be remembered, is what we have termed a 'bitwise or', giving a '1' in any row just in case at least one of its disjuncts has a 1 in that row. Regardless of the number of binary digits in our value representation, it should also be noted, each step along the axis amounts to addition by 1: our values are listed in binary sequence ...000, ...001, ...010, and so forth. What we want to show for the general case, therefore, given axes numbered in binaries of any given number of digits, is that the central cell marked D below will take a binary value of $n + 1$ if and only if precisely one of the cells marked x takes a value of n.

We first show, left to right, that if just one of the squares marked x has a value n, y must have the value $n + 1$. Consider to begin with the case in which it is A that is the square with value n, using x and y to represent the axis values which combine in a bitwise 'or' to give us A. Axis values for D are then of course $x + 1$ and $y + 1$.

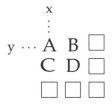

In this case, since B does not have the value n, the bitwise compound 'y or $x + 1$' must have a different value from bitwise 'y or x'. (For ease of exposition we will simply use 'or' for 'bitwise or' throughout.) Since C has a value other than n, 'x or $y + 1$' must similarly differ from 'y or x'. If either x or y ends in 0, then, both must end in 0: were only one to end in 0, addition to that one would not change the value of their bitwise 'or', and thus either B or C would equal A, contrary to hypothesis. The same argument applies not only to a 0 in the last digit position but in any first position counting from the right: x has a first 0 in a given position counting from the right if and only if y also has a first 0 in that position. Otherwise either B or C would equal A, contrary to hypothesis.

Either x and y will contain no zeros, therefore, or they will share a 0 in the same first position from the right. If neither contains zeros, A occupies the lower right-hand corner of the lattice and there is no place for D; the position exhibited does not form a part of our lattice. In all other cases x and y share a 0 in the same first position from the right. Adding 1 to each—moving along the axes from x to $x + 1$ and from y to $y + 1$—will close that 0 with a 1, changing all 1s to its right to 0s in each case. The series of digits represented by x and y will stay the same in all other regards. A bitwise 'or' between $x + 1$ and $y + 1$ will therefore give us an increase of precisely 1 over the value of the bitwise 'or' between x and y: given a value of n for A, D will take a value of $n + 1$.

Consider secondly the case in which it is B that carries the value n, once again using x and y to represent A's axis values:

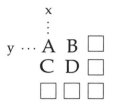

Since $B \neq C$, x and y cannot share either a final 0 or a rightmost 0 in the same place. If they did, addition of 1 to either would produce the same change from A in a bitwise 'or', giving us $B = C$, contrary to hypothesis. One of x and y, then, has a rightmost 0 farther to the right than the other. Since $B \neq A$, it must be y that has a 0 furthest to the right: otherwise x's furthest right 0 would be 'masked' by 1s in y, and thus the bitwise $(x + 1$ or y) would equal that of (x or y), contrary to our hypothesis that $B \neq A$.

In this case x and y therefore have the form:

x: ...111

y: ...011

for some number of 1s (perhaps none) to the right of y's 0. It is clear, therefore, that $x + 1$ and y side by side will have the form:

x + 1:   ...000

y: ...011

since addition of 1 to x will have changed some zero to the left of y's to a 1 with all 1s to its right changed to 0s. B's value is that of a bitwise 'or' between these two. But then it is clear that adding 1 to y will result in an increase of precisely 1 for the bitwise compound $(x + 1$ or $y + 1)$. Thus if B is the cell with a value of n, D must again take a value of $n + 1$. A symmetrical argument shows that if it is C that is the single northwest neighbor with value n, D must again take a value of $n + 1$.

For the case of 'or' we have shown that if precisely one of the neighbors northwest of any D has a value of n, D must itself take a value of $n + 1$. It suffices for the rest of our justification to show that if a cell D has a value $n + 1$, one and only one of its northwest cells must have a value n.

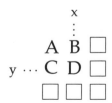

We specify that D has a value $n + 1$, generated as the bitwise compound (x or y). Subtraction of 1 from either x or y amounts to changing its rightmost 1 to a 0 and all 0s from there to the right to 1s.

Suppose now that x and y have a rightmost 1 in the same position. In that case subtracting 1 from each will result in a subtraction of 1 from bitwise (x or y), and thus A—representing ($x - 1$ or $y - 1$)—will have the value n. Subtraction of 1 from just one of these, however, cannot result in n. In that case a rightmost 1 in either x or y will change to a 0, but the other will have a rightmost 1 which masks that change in terms of the bitwise 'or'. What will change in the bitwise 'or' is that all digits to the right of that place (if any) will change from 0 to 1. Since this can only represent a figure equal to or greater than $n + 1$, however, it cannot equal n.

Suppose secondly that x has the furthest 1 to the right: that y has a 0 in that position and at all places to the right. Subtracting 1 from x will then change its rightmost 1 to a 0 and all 0s to its right to 1s. Because y has only 0s from that position to the right, the change from bitwise (x or y) to ($x - 1$ or y) will be precisely the same, representing a subtraction of 1, and thus it will be C that has a value of n.

In this case subtracting 1 from only y or from both x and y could not result in n. Subtraction of 1 from $n + 1$ demands that the rightmost 1 in $n + 1$ be changed to a 0, with all 0s to its right (if any) changed to 1s. Given our hypothesis, however, the rightmost 1 in $n + 1$ must correspond to x's rightmost 1. Because y has 0s from that point to the right, subtraction of 1 from y must result in 1s from that point to the right, which will of course also appear in those positions in any bitwise 'or' involving $y - 1$. Thus neither (x or $y - 1$) nor ($x - 1$ nor $y - 1$) will have a 0 in the position of x's rightmost 1; $y - 1$ will mask anything in that position and to the right with 1s. Since a 0 in that position is what a value of n would demand, neither A nor B can have a value of n.

A similar argument can be constructed for the case in which it is y that is assumed to have the furthest 1 to the right.

To sum up: if a single northwest neighbor has a value of n, a cell will take a value of $n + 1$, and if a cell has a value of $n + 1$ one and only one of its northwest neighbors will have a value of n. Thus a cell will take a value of $n + 1$ if and only if precisely one of its northwest neighbors carries a value of n.

Similar arguments can clearly be constructed in the case of other connectives. What they demonstrate is the inevitability of the cellular rules outlined for value spaces of any chosen dimension. It must be confessed, however, that despite such an explanation we continue to find something magical in the fact that such simple automata rules can generate a value space appropriate to propositional calculus for any chosen approximation.

We offer the cellular automata generation of value spaces as a phenomenon well worthy of further study. Here we're also tempted to engage in a bit of wild speculation, however, noting a link to the fictional substance 'computronium', introduced in another context and for another purpose by Norman Margolus and Tommaso Toffoli.[21] As envisaged by Margolus and Toffoli, 'computronium' would be a 'computing crystal': a mineral substance capable of functioning as a ready-made CPU. We can envisage ourselves building computers with shining chunks of computronium at their core. The speculation which the work of this chapter invites is that there may be natural processes that follow something akin to the simple cellular automata rules above and that thereby 'grow' units instantiating value spaces appropriate to forms of propositional calculus. If so, might there not be natural processes capable of 'growing' something like computronium? The lattice positions of computronium might be occupied by particular molecules or by molecules in particular states, for example, with the directionality of our rules above corresponding perhaps to magnetic orientation.

3.8 CONCLUSION

Our attempt here has been to open for consideration some new ways of envisaging and analyzing simple formal systems. What these approaches have in common is a clear emphasis on visual and spatial instantiations of systems, with perhaps an inevitable affinity to fractal images. Our hope, however, is that in the long run such approaches can offer more than a visual glimpse of systems as infinite wholes; that new perspectives of this type might suggest genuinely new results. In the manner of the three simple examples offered in our final sections—the Sierpinski map of tautologies in value space, formal parallels between value solids for systems of propositional logic and the quite different value solids appropriate to infinite-valued connectives, and an approach to the values of propositional calculus in terms of cellular automata—our hope is that visual and spatial approaches to formal systems may introduce the possibility of approaching some logical and meta-logical questions in terms of geometry. Number-theoretical analysis of logical systems forms a familiar and powerful part of the work of Gödel and others. Analysis in terms of geometry and fractal geometry, we want to suggest, may be a promising further step.

4 The Evolution of Generosity in a Hobbesian Model

What, then, is the conduct that ought to be adopted, the reasonable course of conduct, for this egoistic, naturally unsocial being, living side by side with similar beings?
—Henry Sidgwick, *Outlines of the History of Ethics*[1]

Under what conditions will cooperation emerge in a world of egoists without central authority?
—Robert Axelrod, *The Evolution of Cooperation*[2]

The portrait Thomas Hobbes paints of social organization is one in which cooperation arises from an initial state of purely egoistic competition among isolated individuals. Hobbes's claim is that this can indeed occur; his philosophical project is an attempt to show how.

The state of nature with which Hobbes begins is one of unfettered individualistic egoism:

...during the time men live without a common Power to keep them all in awe, they are in that condition which is called Warre; and such a warre, as is of every man, against every man.... Whatsoever therefore is consequent to a time of Warre, where every man is Enemy to every man; the same is consequent to the time, wherein men live without other security, than what their own strength, and their own invention shall furnish them withall. In such condition, there is no place for Industry; because the fruit thereof is uncertain; and consequently no Culture of the Earth; no Navigation, nor use of the commodities that may be imported by Sea; no commodious building; no Instruments of moving, and removing such thing as require much force; no Knowledge of the face of the Earth; no account of Time; no Arts; no Letters; no Society, and which is worst of all, continuall feare, and danger of violent death; And the life of man, solitary, poore, nasty, brutish, and short. (*Leviathan*, Chapter XIII)[3]

With such individualistic egoism as a starting point, how might genuine social cooperation—with all its benefits—arise? Hobbes's answer, to which we will return, is that the emergence of cooperation is dictated by a Law of Nature, "a Precept, or generall Rule found out by Reason":

And because the condition of Man ... is a condition of Warre of every one against every one; in which case every one is governed by his own Reason; and there is nothing he can make use of, that may not be a help unto him, in preserving his life against his enemyes ... there can be no security to any man (how strong or wise soever he be,) of living out the time, which Nature ordinarily alloweth men to live. And consequently it is a precept, or generall rule of Reason, *That every man, ought to endeavor Peace, as farre as he has hope of obtaining it; and when he cannot obtain it, that he may seek, and use, all helps, and advantages of Warre. The first branch of which Rule, containing the first, and Fundamentall Law of Nature; which is, to seek Peace, and follow it.* The second, the summe of the Right of Nature; which is, *By all means we can, to defend our selves.* (*Leviathan*, Chapter XIV)

This first Fundamental Law of Nature might seem merely to reinforce egoism. But from this first principle, Hobbes proposes, follows another:

From this Fundamentall Law of Nature ... is derived this second Law; *That a man be willing, when others are so too, as farre-forth, as for Peace, and defence of himself he shall think it necessary, to lay down this right to all things; and be contented with so much liberty against other men, as he would allow other men against himself.* For as long as every man holdeth this Right, of doing any thing he liketh; so long are all men in the condition of Warre. But if other men will not lay down their Right, as well as he; then there is no Reason for any one, to devest himselfe of his; For that were to expose himself to Prey, (which no man is bound to) rather than to dispose himselfe to Peace. This is that Law of the Gospell; *Whatsoever you require that others should do to you, that do ye to them.* And that Law of all men, *Quod tibi fieri non vis, alteri ne feceris.*[4] (*Leviathan*, Chapter XIV)

In this chapter we will follow Hobbes in attempting to model conditions under which cooperation might evolve within what appears to be—indeed, what is constructed to be—a society of self-serving egoists. Our model will in many ways be even starker than Hobbes's: our individuals will be merely the cells of a spatialized grid, behaving entirely in terms of simple game-theoretic strategies and motivations specifiable in terms of simple matrices. Despite this formalization, however, the basic purpose of the model remains entirely Hobbesian in tone: our interest is how something resembling cooperation and even generosity can arise as a dominant pattern of interaction in even a simple computer model constructed fundamentally in terms of individual self-interest.

Here several warnings are appropriate. The first should by now be familiar: that what we have to offer is a model, and that all modeling has limitations. As Robert Axelrod notes regarding precisely the kinds of models we want to pursue here,

The value of any formal model, including game theory, is that you can see some of the principles that are operating more clearly than you could without the model. But it's only some of the principles. You have to leave off a lot of things, some of which are bound to be important.[5]

A more specific warning is also appropriate. Ultimately our philosophical concern is with questions of self-interest, cooperation, and generosity—questions clearly in the general domain of ethics. Our models, on the other hand, are merely abstract mathematical constructions. Parts of those constructions represent agents with particular interests and particular interactive strategies, but what this means is that the behavior and dynamics of those parts of the construction are intended to be analogous in some sense to the behavior of genuine agents, with real interests in real social interaction. If our models are successful ones, the analogy will hold and we will indeed have captured formally some aspects of phenomena that are of more than merely formal interest.

Although there are some who might argue the point, we think it is clear that true generosity and cooperation do not literally appear within our mathematical models—the formal individuals of our algorithms or the pixel-displayed cells of our cellular automata are simply not the kinds of things that can be literally generous or cooperative. The same can be said, in fact, for self-interest and egoism: the elements of our formal models are not entities that have genuine interests or can act egoistically to maximize them. In the same way that our models of social individuals are not of real social individuals, the dynamics intended to model cooperative or generous behavior do not constitute instances of real cooperation or generosity.

In other areas such a warning would probably be unnecessary: no one is tempted to think that the numbers used to tally farm produce are themselves a form of numerical farm produce. In the tradition of modeling we want to build on here, however, it *is* quite standard to speak of the dynamics used to model cooperative or generous behavior as itself 'cooperative' or 'generous'. As we think will be clear from some of the examples that follow, in practice it is almost impossible to avoid thinking of certain dynamics of these models as the 'spread of cooperation' or the 'triumph of generosity'. For the most part we will simply follow general practice, without fighting this informal tendency. In sober introduction, however, we think it important to bracket this as a mere way of speaking.

There are two philosophically important reasons to be wary of this informal tendency. The first is that the formal dynamics are in fact dynamics intended to *model* genuine cooperation or generosity by real agents. They are intended as in some way *analogous* to the real thing. Whether our formal dynamics model that behavior successfully, however—whether the analogy actually holds—is a separate question. One danger of the tendency to refer to modeling dynamics as 'cooperative' or 'generous' is that one may forget that the separate question remains open.

Another philosophical danger is that this kind of modeling might be improperly viewed as supporting various kinds of reductionism in ethics. At their base, what our models show is that certain parameters favor the spread, in a clearly defined sense, of certain formal game-theoretic strategies. If we are right in thinking that such parameters may in some sense model real situations, and that those strategies are importantly analogous to real cooperative or generous behavior, we perhaps get conclusions relevant to theoretical sociology, economics, and social and political philosophy regarding the social dynamics of certain patterns of cooperative and generous behavior. This is the optimistic hope. But even a glorious satisfaction of that hope would not yet tell us that the social dynamics we have uncovered are what 'justify' cooperation, generosity, or some other aspect of ordinary ethics. No such result alone would show that cooperation, generosity, or other aspects of ordinary ethics 'reduce to' or 'are merely' behaviors that display successful social dynamics. Both of these are strong philosophical claims that have appeared occasionally in the sociobiology literature and in some philosophical treatments of game-theoretic models.[6] We regard such claims as requiring a great deal of argument above and beyond the kind of modeling results at issue here.

Hobbes, interestingly enough, offers a theory of how certain forms of social cooperation might arise but does not seem to offer unambiguous answers as to what extent his work either supports or amounts to an ethical theory. Commentators disagree: Michael Oakeshott claims that civil philosophy, the subject of the *Leviathan*, is concerned purely with causes and effects: "Civil philosophy is settling the generation or constitutive cause of civil association."[7] In much the same spirit, Johann P. Sommerville claims that "it is doubtful whether it makes sense to describe Hobbes as having any genuine moral system at all."[8] Our models will be "Hobbesian" in only this minimal sense. There are also traditions in which Hobbes is interpreted as a moral reductivist or eliminativist in a much stronger sense, as maintaining that morality is to be either explained or explained away in terms of a basic model of social dynamics. Again, this issue we regard as an area that demands philosophical work well beyond the reach of the models themselves.

4.1 THE PRISONER'S DILEMMA

[A problem of isolation] arises whenever the outcome of the many individuals' decisions made in isolation is worse for everyone than some other course of action, even though, taking the conduct of the others as given, each person's decision is perfectly rational. This is simply the general case of the prisoner's dilemma of which Hobbes's state of nature is the classical example. (John Rawls, *A Theory of Justice*)[9]

The most studied model in game theory is undoubtedly the Prisoner's Dilemma. The formal structure of the game was developed in the work of Merrill Flood and Melvin Drescher at the Rand Corporation around 1950. The popular story that gives the Prisoner's Dilemma its name is credited to Rand consultant Albert W. Tucker.[10]

Lefty and Scarface, arrested for bank robbery, are kept in separate cells to prevent any communication between them. The District Attorney has enough evidence to convict each of a lesser charge—breaking and entering, perhaps—but will need a confession to convict either of them for the more serious charge of bank robbery. The D.A. therefore approaches Lefty and says:

"Lefty, I've got to admit that the evidence against you guys is pretty thin. If you both stonewall, you'll probably get off with two years each.

"If Scarface confesses to the bank robbery and you try to stonewall, on the other hand, I promise you we'll let him walk and we'll nail you for five years for the robbery. I'll make you the same deal: If you confess and Scarface stonewalls, we'll let *you* walk and nail *him* for the five years.

"If you both confess, well, then we'll get you both. With a little benefit for a guilty plea you guys will be looking at four years each."

Here there is no deception; the D.A. makes the same offer to each prisoner, and each knows that the same offer has been made on the other side. Lefty faces a clear dilemma: whether to try to cooperate with Scarface by stonewalling, in the hope that Scarface will stonewall as well, or to defect on Scarface by turning state's evidence. Scarface, of course, is faced with the same dilemma, of whether to cooperate with his accomplice or to defect against him. Such is the Prisoner's Dilemma.

In a slightly more formal sketch of the situation, each of two players can either cooperate C or defect D. There are four possible payoffs for a player: a reward R, contingent on mutual cooperation, a punishment P, in the case of mutual defection, a temptation T for the player who defects against cooperation on the other side, and a sucker's payoff S for the player who cooperates only to be faced with defection. Technically, a Prisoner's Dilemma requires that payoffs be ordered such that the best a player can hope for is the temptation of defection against cooperation on the other side, the worst a player can achieve is the sucker's payoff, and mutual cooperation is preferable to mutual defection: $T > R > P > S$. Mutual cooperation is also to be more highly rewarded than any simply repeated pattern of alternating exploitations: $2 \cdot R > T + S$. The specific payoff matrix used throughout the literature is the following, where numbers to the left are read as gains for player B and those on the right are read as gains for player A.

| | | Player A | |
		Cooperate	Defect
Player B	Cooperate	3, 3	0, 5
	Defect	5, 0	1, 1

The story of Lefty and Scarface uses precisely this matrix, though in the story we've expressed outcomes negatively in terms of years in prison. When recast in terms of years of freedom out of the next five we get the standard payoff grid above.

The philosophical force of the Prisoner's Dilemma, of course, is a stark contrast between egoistic rationality and collective benefit. If Player B chooses to cooperate, it is to Player A's advantage to defect: A then gets five points in place of a mere three for mutual cooperation. If Player B chooses to defect, it is still in Player A's interest to defect: in that case A salvages at least the one point from mutual defection rather than the zero of the sucker's payoff. Thus whatever Player B chooses to do, the rational thing for A to do is to defect: defection is *dominant* in the Prisoner's Dilemma.

The situation is a symmetrical one, in which all information regarding payoffs is common knowledge; what is rational for one player is rational for the other. Two rational players in the Prisoner's Dilemma can thus be expected to defect against each other, economic rationality on each side resulting in the payoff situation that is clearly worse than mutual cooperation for each player and is collectively the *least* desirable of all. The rational attempt to maximize gains on each side seems inevitably, predictably, to fail.

Even in this simple form the analogy between the Prisoner's Dilemma and Hobbes's state of nature should be clear. In each case the pursuit of individual advantage results in a situation worse for all parties; the game-theoretic result of mutual defection corresponds to something like Hobbes's state of war, "where every man is Enemy to every man." The payoff for mutual defection—particularly repeated mutual defection, or defection on all sides—might well be read as that of a life inevitably "solitary, poore, nasty, brutish, and short."

The Prisoner's Dilemma would be fascinating even if it were merely a formal problem. But it does not appear that it is: the conditions of the Prisoner's Dilemma seem to arise quite spontaneously in a range of bargaining situations. David Gauthier offers a thinly disguised example:

Consider two nations, which for convenience (and disclaiming any apparent reference to real nations as purely coincidental) we shall call the US and the SU. They are both engaged in an arms race, the dangers of which are appreciated by both, for neither wants all-out war with the other. Mutual disarmament would remove the threat of war, and would not, let us suppose, have other disadvantages (such as depressing the economy), so that both strongly prefer mutual disarmament to continuation of the arms race. However, there is no way to ensure compliance with an agreement to disarm, and each knows that, were it alone to disarm, it would be at the other's mercy, whereas if it alone were to remain armed, it would be the world's dominant power. Each prefers the arms race, despite the risk of all-out war, to being at the mercy of the other, and each prefers the prospect of being top nation to mutual disarmament. Hence, before concluding an agreement to disarm, each represents the aftermath to itself thus:

SU

		Comply	Violate
US	Comply	2nd, 2nd	1st, 4th
	Violate	4th, 1st	3rd, 3rd

The structure of this situation precisely parallels that faced by [Lefty and Scarface]. Hence the reasoning is also parallel. Whatever the other does, violation maximizes one's own utility. The only outcome in equilibrium is mutual violation. Needless to say, the US and the SU do not conclude an agreement which would not be worth the paper on which it was written....[11]

The dominance of defection in Prisoner's Dilemma situations is in fact used in a story by Edgar Allan Poe written more than a hundred years before Flood and Drescher's formal work. Poe's "The Mystery of Marie Roget: A Sequel to 'The Murders in the Rue Morgue'" centers on the mysterious disappearance of a girl, later found murdered. In the story, as in the real case on which it is based, a reward is offered together with a promise of pardon:

...The Prefect took it upon himself to offer the sum of twenty thousand francs for the conviction of the assassin, or, if more than one should prove to have been implicated, for the conviction of any one of the assassins. In the proclamation setting forth this reward, a full pardon was promised to any accomplice who should come forward in evidence against his fellow....[12]

General speculation in the story is that the kidnap and murder was the work of a gang. Poe's detective C. Auguste Dupin argues the contrary, using reasoning based essentially on the dominance of defection in the Prisoner's Dilemma:

I shall add but one to the arguments against a gang, but this one has, to my own understanding at least, a weight altogether irresistible. Under the circumstances of large reward offered, and full pardon to any king's evidence, it is not to be imagined, for a moment, that some member of a gang of low ruffians, or of any body of men would not long ago have betrayed his accomplices. Each one of a gang, so placed, is not so much greedy of reward, or anxious for escape, as fearful of betrayal. He betrays eagerly and early that he may not himself be betrayed.[13]

The reasoning that leads to defection in a single round of the Prisoner's Dilemma leads also to defection on the last round of any known finite series of plays. If you and I know we are to play exactly one-hundred rounds, whatever cooperation we may have developed in the meantime, it seems predictable that we will defect against each other on the one-hundredth round. The situation on the last round, after all, is precisely that of a single round. Defection is dominant: whatever you do, I will be better off if I defect.

It can be argued that this reasoning extends to the ninety-ninth round as well. The one-hundredth, after all, is a write-off: both of us, knowing that the other is rational, can predict that the other will defect on the one-hundredth round. Nothing we do on the ninety-ninth round will change the outcome of the one-hundredth, and thus the ninety-ninth round is essentially the last round in which cooperation is in question. But then it seems that defection will be dominant on the ninety-ninth round as well: no matter what you do on that round, I will be better off if I defect. Knowing that the other player is rational, then, both players can predict mutual defection on the ninety-ninth round. But then the ninety-eighth round is essentially the last round in which cooperation is in question. . . .

By similar reasoning, it can be argued that on *any* round within a known finite series the rational play will be defection: the dominance of defection seems to infect any finite series of known length inductively from the 'back end'. If that reasoning is sound, the general lesson of the Prisoner's Dilemma would be the same in both single and predictably finite rounds: in either case players individualistically rational in terms of the dominance of defection will quite predictably end up with scores lower over all than players 'irrational' in opting for cooperation.[14]

Although this line of reasoning extending the dominance of defection in a single round to the dominance of defection in every round of a series of known finite length is often outlined in the theoretical literature, it does not seem to be generally believed. In the classic *Games and Decisions*, R. Duncan Luce and Howard Raiffa recognize the force of the argument but exclaim "If we were to play this game we would *not* take the second [defect] strategy at every move!"[15] Robert Axelrod treats the result as something of a theorem, but seems happy to leave it behind with the claim that it will not apply in the more realistic case in which players interact an indefinite number of times.[16] Anatol Rapoport and Albert M. Chammah claim that "Confronted with this paradox, game theoreticians have no answer. Ordinary mortals, however, when playing Prisoner's Dilemma many times in succession hardly ever play DD one hundred percent of the time."[17] William Poundstone treats the reasoning as a backward induction paradox, but notes that "Game theorists' feelings about the backward induction paradox have been equivocal. The prevailing opinion has long been that it is 'valid' in some abstract sense but not practical advice."[18]

Suspicion regarding the argument can be strengthened by noting its similarity to the reasoning of the Surprise Examination Paradox. An instructor announces to his students that they will have a surprise exam in one of the next five days, where 'surprise' means that they will not know the day before it occurs that the exam will occur on the following day. The students argue that he cannot truthfully make such an announcement. Their reasoning is as follows:

The exam cannot be on Friday. If it were, Monday through Thursday would have passed without an exam. We would thus know it must be on Friday, and it wouldn't then be a surprise.

Friday is therefore out. But then the exam cannot be on Thursday. If it were, Monday through Wednesday would have passed without an exam. We would know by the reasoning above that it couldn't be on Friday, leaving Thursday as the only possibility. So we would know on Wednesday night that the exam would be given on Thursday, and it wouldn't be a surprise. Thursday and Friday are out. But then the exam cannot be on Wednesday. . . .

Sometimes the paradox is presented with a punch line. Having convinced themselves that the exam cannot be given at all, the students are completely surprised when the instructor keeps his word and hands it out on Tuesday.

The similarity of this reasoning to that of the argument for dominant defection throughout a series of known finite length is worth noting because of course the Surprise Examination is treated standardly in the philosophical literature as a *paradox*, thought to hide some fallacious piece of logical legerdemain. That the same form of reasoning is thought of as valid in the theoretical economics literature, though perhaps inapplicable in some practical sense, indicates that important work remains to be done in bridging the two bodies of work.

The Prisoner's Dilemma is not the only two-person game that might be significant in modeling particular bargaining situations. Another game is that of Chicken, in which the cost of mutual defection falls below that of being defected against. Using the same numbers as before, Chicken can be outlined in terms of a matrix as follows:

		Player A	
		Cooperate	Defect
Player B	Cooperate	3, 3	1, 5
	Defect	5, 1	0, 0

Consider also the game of Stag Hunt, sometimes called a 'trust dilemma', 'assurance game', or 'coordination' game. Here mutual cooperation takes on the highest value for each player; everything is fine as long as the other player does not defect. Cooperation against defection, however, remains far inferior to defection against either cooperation or defection:

		Player A	
		Cooperate	Defect
Player B	Cooperate	5, 5	0, 3
	Defect	3, 0	1, 1

Stag Hunt takes its name, interestingly enough, from a passage in Rousseau emphasizing that each individual involved in a collective hunt for a deer may abandon his post in pursuit of a rabbit adequate merely for his individual needs:[19]

When it came to tracking down a deer, everyone realized that he should remain dependably at his post; but if a hare happened to pass within reach of one of them, he undoubtedly would not have hesitated to run off after it and, after catching his prey, he would have troubled himself little about causing his companions to lose theirs. (Rousseau, *Discourse on the Origin of Inequality*)[20]

Our present attempt is to use the Prisoner's Dilemma matrix as the basis for studying Hobbesian models of cooperation. The Stag Hunt matrix might prove appropriate for the study of models of cooperation in the tradition of Rousseau instead. All of these are symmetric and non-zero-sum games: no player is advantaged in the bargaining situation, and losses on one side need not equal gains on the other—it is possible for both players to lose. No other game, however, has captured the attention that the Prisoner's Dilemma has, either in formal terms or in application. What the Prisoner's Dilemma seems to capture, in a particularly pointed way, is the conflict between the best situation for all concerned and a rational individualistic pursuit of egoistic ends. As such the model embodies the essential assumptions of Hobbes, and it can be taken as a vindication of Hobbes's basic vision that this simple model has become "the *e. coli* of social psychology," applied extensively in theoretical sociology, economics, and theoretical biology over the past thirty years.

In what follows we will explore some new and richer variations of Hobbesian models, which yield some positive results regarding the evolution of cooperation and generosity that we think would have surprised even Hobbes himself.

4.2 CLASSICAL STRATEGIES IN ITERATION

The Prisoner's Dilemma becomes both more interesting and more realistic as a model of biological and social interaction when it is made open-ended: when players are envisaged as engaging in repeated games, never knowing when or whether they might meet again. In the indefinitely iterated Prisoner's Dilemma players must take into account the effects of their current choices on future interactions, with no clear terminus in sight.

Here competing strategies for unlimited play emerge, including for example a 'vicious' strategy of universal defection (AllD), or a come-on initial cooperation followed thereafter by vicious defection (Deceptive Defector). The strategy called Tit for Tat (TFT) cooperates on the first round and thereafter simply repeats its opponent's play from the previous round. Each of these simple examples is a 'reactive' or 'one-dimensional' strategy in the sense that it depends only on the opponent's play in the previous round. Reactive strategies can be characterized in general by triples $\langle i, c, d \rangle$, where i indicates the starting play, c the response to cooperation, and d the response to defection on the other side. The eight simple reactive or one-dimensional strategies can thus be set out in binary fashion as follows, with 1 standing for cooperation and 0 for defection:[21]

i	c	d	reactive strategy
0	0	0	Always Defect (AllD)
0	0	1	Suspicious Doormat
0	1	0	Suspicious Tit for Tat
0	1	1	Suspicious Quaker
1	0	0	Deceptive Defector
1	0	1	Gullible Doormat
1	1	0	Tit for Tat (TFT)
1	1	1	Quaker (AllC)

In 1980, Robert Axelrod announced a computerized Prisoner's Dilemma tournament. Participants were invited to submit any strategy they wished, no matter how complicated, as long as it could be written as a (Fortran) program. Submissions for the tournament came in from game theorists in economics, psychology, sociology, political science, and mathematics.

In Axelrod's tournament each strategy was pitted against every other in a 'round robin'—each player played every player, including itself—with the 'winner' being the strategy that collected the most points overall. The strategies included were only those submitted together with a player that gave random responses. The winner was the simple reactive strategy TFT.[22]

Even more surprising was the result of a second tournament, run after announcing and publicly analyzing the results of the first. Participants were once again invited to submit any programmable strategy, however complex. The result of this second and significantly larger tournament was again a victory for TFT.[23]

Axelrod and Hamilton went on to develop an 'ecological' model in which strategies "reproduce" in any round as a function of their success. In such a model a strategy competes in the next round in a percentage proportionate to its success on the previous round. Using the same strategies as in the second tournament above, TFT eventually displaced all competitors.[24]

TFT was the clear victor in all of Axelrod's competitions, despite the fact that it is by no means guaranteed to win in every situation. It can in fact be easily shown that no strategy will triumph in every situation. Suppose, for example, that the opposing player is playing AllD. The best one can do in such a situation is follow a strategy that always defects. TFT will do worse in any finite number of rounds simply because it will lose on the first round. Suppose, on the other hand, that one's opponent is playing a strategy called GRIM (no relation to one of the authors), which starts off cooperating but which given any defection against it constantly defects from that point on. In that case the best possible strategy is one that *never* defects.

TFT triumphed in Axelrod's tournaments, then, despite the fact that neither it nor any other strategy is guaranteed to win in every situation. TFT triumphed, in fact, despite the fact that it *never* does better in direct competition with any single opponent. TFT will never get a higher score than its opponent; at best it will match it. Against Quaker (AllC), for example, it will get an identical score. In any finite series against AllD it will do slightly worse. The key to TFT's success in Axelrod's tournaments was thus not crushing victories against all or even any competing strategies. TFT's success lies rather in the fact that it does consistently well against other strategies in general, including doing very well against itself, thereby racking up a higher total score than its competitors overall.

Another way of considering strategies is to ask under what conditions a strategy S_1 might successfully invade a uniform population of strategy S_2 in the ecological model outlined above. TFT, it turns out, is collectively stable in the sense that no single mutation can invade it by strategic advantage. It isn't alone in this regard: AllD is collectively stable as well.[25] Although single mutations of TFT cannot invade AllD, however, Axelrod showed that a 'cluster' of TFT can, where 'cluster' is defined in terms of a higher probability of interactions between members of the cluster. This last fact will offer an intriguing comparison with some of our later results.

Axelrod's classic results are unanimous in awarding high marks to TFT. This result is perfectly in accord with Hobbes, whose second Rule of

Reason is very much in the spirit of TFT: "This is that Law of the Gospell; *Whatsoever you require that others should do to you, that do ye to them.* And that Law of all men, *Quod tibi fieri non vis, alteri ne feceris*" (*Leviathan*, XIV). More recent work, however, suggests that both Hobbes's conclusion and Axelrod's model may fail to do justice to the level of cooperation and generosity to be expected from a society of egoists. This work suggests that within more realistic constraints it is not TFT but another family of strategies that should be regarded as the ultimate winners.

4.3 GENEROSITY IN AN IMPERFECT WORLD

The world of the Axelrod tournaments is a world of perfect information and flawless action, clinically free of either communicative noise or executive error. Cooperation or defection on the other side are seen in all cases for precisely what they are. When a strategy dictates defection or cooperation, the defection or cooperation is executed without any possibility of error. The model that Martin Nowak and Karl Sigmund envisage, by contrast, is one designed to model a world much more like ours: a world of imperfect communication and/or possible mistakes in action, in which the transition from interpretation of an opponent's move to a reaction to it is always open to some possibility of error.

Nowak and Sigmund concentrate on *stochastic* reactive strategies, which respond to a single previous move by an opponent but which assign mere probabilities for cooperation or defection. Here again different strategies can be envisaged in terms of ordered triples $\langle i, c, d \rangle$, though i will be taken as the *probability* of cooperation in the initial round, c as the probability of cooperation following a cooperative move by an opponent, and d the probability of cooperation following an opponent's defection. Classical TFT would remain $\langle 1, 1, 0 \rangle$ as before, since the probabilities it dictates are entirely deterministic probabilities of 1 or 0. AllD would be represented as $\langle 0, 0, 0 \rangle$. But given a continuum of stochastic possibilities we might also introduce other strategies, including various degrees of more generous TFT (GTFT) such as $\langle 1, 1, 0.1 \rangle$ and $\langle 1, 1, 1/3 \rangle$.[26] Each of these begins with cooperation and rewards cooperation with full cooperation, but each is 'generous' in the sense of forgiving defection against it with a probability of 0.1 and 1/3 respectively.

Nowak and Sigmund envisage competitions between probabilistic strategies in terms of the convenient mathematical fiction of infinite games. In an iterated game between two simple deterministic strategies— TFT and AllD, for example—a periodic pattern of play will inevitably be established. The value for an 'infinite' game for one of these players is simply the average gain per play across that repeated period, and thus represents the value that the average score per round on games of increasing finite length will approach. Although the play of genuinely stochastic strategies cannot be expected to be periodic, scores for an 'infinite' game here too represent merely the limits of average scores that games of increasing length will approach. One simplification that this affords is that for strategies with nondeterministic stochastic values for c and d—values other than either 0 or 1—the role of the initial value i can be ignored: the influence of any initial value i will be outweighed in the long run by the stochastic values envisaged for c and d. For their purposes Nowak and Sigmund are thus able to tag strategies by values $\langle c, d \rangle$ alone.

Using Axelrod and Hamilton's technique for updating strategy proportions in a population on the basis of relative success in the previous round, Nowak and Sigmund report an evolution in which TFT plays a pivotal role but in which the ultimate winner is not TFT but 'Generous Tit for Tat' (GTFT)—the stochastic strategy $\langle 1, 1/3 \rangle$, returning cooperation with cooperation but forgiving defection with cooperation a third of the time.[27]

With n = 100 different reactive strategies uniformly distributed on the unit square, evolution proceeds in most cases towards AllD: those $\langle c, d \rangle$-strategies from the sample which are closest to $\langle 0, 0 \rangle$ increase in frequency, while all others vanish.... The outcome alters dramatically if one of the initial strategies (added by hand or by chance), is TFT, or very close to it.... The first phase is practically indistinguishable from the previous run. The strategies near AllD grow rapidly. TFT and all other reciprocating strategies (near $\langle 1, 0 \rangle$) seem to have disappeared. But an embattled minority remains and fights back. The tide turns when 'suckers' are so decimated that exploiters can no longer feed on them. Slowly at first, but gathering momentum, the reciprocators come back, and the exploiters now wane. But the TFT-like strategy that caused this reversal of fortune is not going to profit from it: having eliminated the exploiters, it is robbed of its mission and superseded by the strategy closest to GTFT [with $\langle c, d \rangle = \langle 1, 1/3 \rangle$]. Evolution then stops.[28]

Their general characterization is as follows:

We find that a small fraction of TFT players is essential for the emergence of reciprocation in a heterogeneous population, but only paves the way for a more generous strategy. TFT is the pivot, rather than the aim, of an evolution towards cooperation.[29]

Here it is important to stress, however, that Nowak and Sigmund's is a pool of strategies envisaged as interacting in a world of inevitable error and imperfect communication. For that reason, none of the triplets $\langle i, c, d \rangle$ used involves a full probability of 0 or 1 in any position: references to TFT and AllD in the quotes above, for example, must be read as references to their instantiation in an imperfect world, in which they appear only in the guise of stochastically imperfect variations such as $\langle 0.99, 0.01 \rangle$ and $\langle 0.01, 0.01 \rangle$. As noted, Nowak and Sigmund assume games between strategies of infinite length in which initial values can be ignored. Formally, these are calculated in terms of a payoff formula for strategies $s_1 = \langle c_1, d_1 \rangle$ and $s_2 = \langle c_2, d_2 \rangle$ as follows:

$$V(s_1 \text{ vs } s_2) = 1 + 4t' - t - tt'$$

where

$$t = [d_1 + (c_1 - d_1)d_2]/[1 - (c_1 - d_1)(c_2 - d_2)]$$
$$t' = [d_2 + (c_2 - d_2)d_1]/[1 - (c_2 - d_2)(c_1 - d_1)].$$

The assumption that initial values can be ignored, however, makes sense only if full values of 0 and 1 are disallowed in accord with the assumption of a world of imperfect information.[30] The payoff formula above is in fact mathematically undefined for crucial values of 0 and 1.

What if a pure TFT, without communication or executive error, were somehow included in Nowak and Sigmund's sample? A pure TFT would quite predictably block the evolution that Nowak and Sigmund trace toward more generous forms. No more generous strategy $\langle 1, 1, X \rangle$ for $X > 0$ would grow strategically in an environment occupied by $\langle 1, 1, 0 \rangle$ because payoffs for any such GTFT against TFT would be precisely the same as those for TFT against itself. Were a genuinely errorless TFT included in the sample, then, it could be expected not only to take possession but to stubbornly maintain it.

Nowak and Sigmund's work should therefore not be read as in any way contradicting the classic Axelrod's results. The world of Nowak and Sigmund's model is simply a different world from that of earlier models. It's a gritty world of ubiquitous and inevitable stochastic noise, and the failure for TFT reported for such a world is simply a failure for a stochastically imperfect instantiation of the classic strategy. That failure alone should perhaps not be too surprising. Part of TFT's success is due to the fact that it does so well in competition with itself; in a world of pure information, two TFT players simply rack up an uninterrupted series of mutual cooperations:

C C C C C C C C C...

C C C C C C C C C...

Given any chance of error on either side, however, a spontaneous defection will occur. The opponent will react to that with a further defection, prompting another from the other side, prompting another from his side.... Any error will therefore produce an echo effect, reducing TFT's play to alternating defections against cooperation and lowering its average score from 3.0 to 2.5:

C C C D C D C D C...

C C C C D C D C D...

The echo effect will continue until a spontaneous defection either reduces it further to mutual defection or restores it to mutual cooperation. As Per

Molander showed in earlier work, the presence of any amount of stochastic noise is sufficient in the long run to reduce the payoff for two TFT players to precisely that of two random players.[31]

In figure 1 we reproduce the Nowak and Sigmund result using a population of 121 purely stochastic strategies $\langle c, d \rangle$ at 0.1 intervals with full values of 0 and 1 replaced with 0.01 and 0.99, giving us a pool of strategies $\langle 0.01, 0.01 \rangle$, $\langle 0.01, 0.1 \rangle$, $\langle 0.01, 0.2 \rangle$, ... $\langle 0.99, 0.9 \rangle$, $\langle 0.99, 0.99 \rangle$. Each strategy plays all others represented in an infinitely iterated Prisoner's Dilemma in accordance with the payoff formula outlined above. At each generation $n + 1$ the proportion $p_{n+1}(s)$ of a strategy s is computed as a function of its previous proportion $p_n(s)$ and its success $V(s, m)$ against represented strategies m weighted by their proportions $p_n(m)$: $p_{n+1}(s) = f_{n+1}(s) / \sum f_{n+1}(m)$ for all strategies m, where for any strategy s $f_{n+1}(s) = p_n(s) \cdot \sum (V(s, m) \cdot p_n(m))$ for all strategies m.

Twelve thousand generations are shown. As is clear from the chart, stochastically imperfect AllD and its relatives are early winners, but are

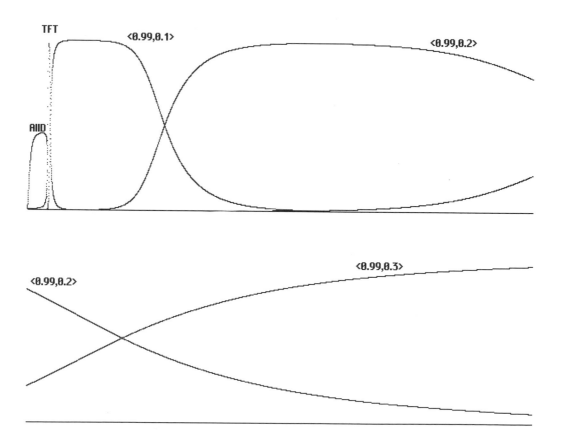

Figure 1 The Nowak and Sigmund result: evolution toward GTFT in a world of imperfect information. Population proportions for labeled strategies shown over 12,000 generations for an initial pool of 121 stochastic strategies $\langle c, d \rangle$ at 0.1 intervals, full value of 0 and 1 replaced with 0.01 and 0.99.

effectively eliminated by stochastically imperfect TFT, $\langle 0.99, 0.01 \rangle$, by the 250th generation. This stochastic approximation to TFT is unable to sustain its victory, however—it peaks and falls immediately, supplanted by the more generous strategy $\langle 0.99, 0.1 \rangle$. This strategy's tenure is longer, but in due course it too is supplanted, by strategy $\langle 0.99, 0.2 \rangle$, which is more generous still in the face of defection on the other side. $\langle 0.99, 0.2 \rangle$ is eventually conquered by $\langle 0.99, 0.3 \rangle$, the closest approximation in this run to a GTFT of $\langle 1 - \varepsilon, 1/3 \rangle$. From this point on there will be no further changes: $\langle 0.99, 0.3 \rangle$ remains in possession.

Most remarkable, perhaps, is the fact that evolution not only proceeds beyond stochastically imperfect TFT but proceeds in such clear steps, with $\langle 0.99, 0.1 \rangle$ achieving clear dominance before $\langle 0.99, 0.2 \rangle$ even begins its rise, for example. Nowak and Sigmund speak of TFT in such a model as performing a 'policing' function, clearing the field of the 'vicious' defecting strategies in order to pave the way for greater generosity. Each more generous strategy up to $\langle 0.99, 0.3 \rangle$ can in fact be seen in this role—it is only against a dominant background of TFT that $\langle 0.99, 0.1 \rangle$ can prove successful, only against a dominant background of $\langle 0.99, 0.1 \rangle$ that $\langle 0.99, 0.2 \rangle$ can rise to prominence, and only against dominant background of $\langle 0.99, 0.2 \rangle$ that our approximation to GTFT can ultimately prove triumphant.

4.4 SPATIALIZATION OF THE PRISONER'S DILEMMA

An argument can clearly be made that the stochastic imperfection of Nowak and Sigmund's model is an aspect of realism: that both biological and sociological worlds *are* gritty worlds of error and imperfect information, and that this is quite properly reflected in a model in which stochastic noise is unavoidable. Though technically unchallenged, the success of a pure TFT in Axelrod's model, classically free of error, becomes less interesting from an applicational standpoint—including the applicational standpoint of social and political philosophy.

In this section we want to add just one further aspect of realism to the stochastic model. Talk of clustering in previous work suggests a *spatial* model for the Prisoner's Dilemma, in which we envisage an array of players with different strategies interacting with their immediate neighbors. This is precisely the kind of model obtained if competing game-theoretic strategies are instantiated as a two-dimensional array of cellular automata.

The most familiar example of cellular automata is undoubtedly the Game of Life, developed by John H. Conway. The game is envisaged as beginning with a configuration of cells, which evolves through continuing generations on an infinite chess board. In the initial configuration and at each succeeding generation each cell or square of the array is either alive or dead. The neighbors of a cell are simply those that border it, and a cell's life or death on each generation is contingent on the life and death that surround it:

Birth Rule: A cell dead at generation t will come alive at generation $t+1$ if exactly three neighbors are alive at t.

Survival Rule: A cell that is alive at generation t will remain alive at $t+1$ if it is surrounded at t by precisely two or three live neighbors.

From these as the only conditions for birth and survival follows a death rule:

Death Rule: A cell will be dead at generation $t+1$ if it has fewer than two live neighbors or more than three live neighbors at time t.

A cell in Conway's Game of Life is therefore born from precisely three parents. It can die either from loneliness, when it has less than two neighbors, or from overcrowding, when it has more than three.

An initial configuration consisting of either a single live cell or two live cells side by side will disappear in the second generation by the death rule: both cells die of loneliness. Consider however the case of a line of three cells, as shown in the first frame of figure 2. On a second generation the middle cell will survive, since it has two neighbors. Cells on each end will disappear, since they each have only one live immediate neighbor. Consider also, however, the cells immediately above and below the center at our initial generation t. At t they touch three cells, and thus will come alive on generation $t+1$.

The result is that the horizontal line of three cells shown in the first frame of figure 2 will become the vertical line of three cells shown in the second frame. By reasoning symmetrical to that just given, the vertical line will revert to a horizontal line of three in the third generation, and so forth. The configuration is called the Blinker because of its clear periodicity of two generations.

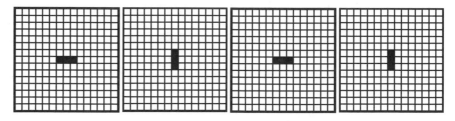

Figure 2 The Blinker configuration in Conway's Game of Life.

The Game of Life abounds with simple shapes that demonstrate startling ranges of behavior. A simple arrangement of five cells called the r-Pentomino, for example, shown in figure 3, explodes into a prodigious variety of patterns that stabilize only after 1103 generations. A pattern crucial for theoretical reasons is the Glider, an alternating configuration of five cells that travels across the array in the manner illustrated in figure 4. It is the Glider and crucially the Glider gun, a configuration that shoots out a stream of these shapes, which Conway used as the core of his demonstration of universal computation in the Game of Life. In chapter 5 we will return briefly to other configurations in Conway's Game of Life; we will return to issues of universal computation and undecidability in chapter 6.

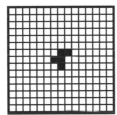

Figure 3   r-Pentomino in Conway's Game of Life.

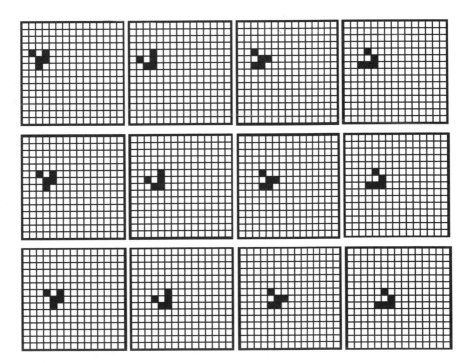

Figure 4   Movement of the Glider in Conway's Game of Life.

The Evolution of Generosity in a Hobbesian Model

The Game of Life is merely the most familiar example, however, of a wider class of cellular automata. What these have in common is simultaneous parallel processing: cells in an array can take on any of some number of states, with the state of a cell at generation $t + 1$ dictated by the states of cells in its neighborhood at generation t. The states possible for cells, the rules for state change, and the size and shape of the relevant neighborhood will dictate different forms of cellular automata. In each case, however, the evolution of an array is the result not of some master 'top-down' plan but of simultaneous local and independent computations at the level of individual cells.

In what follows we want to use cellular automata to add a further dimension of realism, the dimension of space to the Hobbesian models introduced in the previous sections. We envisage each cell within a two-dimensional array as playing against each of its neighbors and obtaining a local score as its total in these competitions. Each cell then surveys its neighbors. If no neighboring cell has a higher score, it retains its original strategy. If a cell has a neighbor or neighbors with higher scores, on the other hand, it converts to that neighboring strategy with the highest score—or is replaced by that strategy, perhaps, depending on one's perspective. In the case of two neighbors with equal scores higher than that of the central cell, the strategy of one is chosen randomly. The result is a Spatialized Prisoner's Dilemma, in which success is computed in all cases against local competitors. Reproduction—the spread of a strategy—proceeds locally as well. Both features, we think, constitute a further measure of realism with an eye to either biological or social application.

As a first example, consider an array composed of our eight simple reactive strategies, limited to a convenient 64×64 cell array. The array wraps around—cells on the bottom row have 'neighbors' on the top and those on the extreme left have 'neighbors' on the right—so the topology of our space is technically that of a torus.

We begin by assigning to each cell one of our eight simple strategies for the Prisoner's Dilemma, chosen at random. The idea is then to let each cell play against each of its neighbors in, say, two hundred rounds of the Prisoner's Dilemma (the length used in Axelrod's original tournament). At that stage each cell compares its total score with that of each of its immediate neighbors, defecting to (or being absorbed by) a neighbor with a superior total score.

For programming purposes the procedure can be simplified by proceeding in two steps. The first is to draw up a matrix of results of our eight strategies in competition with each other in two hundred games. With strategies represented on the axes in terms of their binary representations, this gives us the following matrix:

	⟨0, 0, 0⟩	⟨0, 0, 1⟩	⟨0, 1, 0⟩	⟨0, 1, 1⟩	⟨1, 0, 0⟩	⟨1, 0, 1⟩	⟨1, 1, 0⟩	⟨1, 1, 1⟩
⟨0, 0, 0⟩	200	996	200	996	204	1000	204	1000
⟨0, 0, 1⟩	1	400	450	994	6	1000	450	1000
⟨0, 1, 0⟩	200	450	200	600	203	450	500	602
⟨0, 1, 1⟩	1	4	595	598	5	8	599	602
⟨1, 0, 0⟩	199	991	203	995	202	994	206	998
⟨1, 0, 1⟩	0	0	450	993	4	400	450	998
⟨1, 1, 0⟩	199	450	500	599	201	450	600	600
⟨1, 1, 1⟩	0	0	597	597	3	3	600	600

Competition between each cell in our cellular automata array over two hundred games with any neighbor can now be calculated in terms of the values shown. The total score of any cell in a particular generation will simply be the sum of matrix values corresponding to its competition with the strategies that are its immediate neighbors.

The evolution of a 64 × 64 toroidal array from a random configuration of our eight simple reactive strategies is shown in the progressive frames of figure 5. Here AllD and Deceptive Defector ⟨1, 0, 0⟩ seem to be the early winners, with AllD progressively triumphing over Deceptive Defector. As AllD threatens to take over, however, TFT thrives in its environment, with Deceptive Defector and Suspicious TFT maintaining themselves as trace elements at crucial interfaces. In the end, however, it is TFT that conquers all other strategies in order to occupy the screen alone—a very nice vindication of TFT's robustness in the spatial model.

It is clear from such an evolution that TFT does not simply conquer all other strategies from the outset. It is the 'vicious' defecting strategies AllD and Deceptive Defector that initially seem to do that, and in fact TFT only comes into its own once the vicious strategies have eliminated large numbers of 'sucker' strategies. TFT's triumph even at that stage is not due to any particularly high score it makes against the vicious strategies—a look at the matrix makes it clear that TFT scores lower against either AllD or Deceptive Defector than they do against it—but because TFT does so much better with its own kind than the deceptive strategies do with their own kind. TFT's success and ultimate triumph in a spatial environment stem from its ability to maintain at least a decent score against the early-winning defectors while gaining fully cooperative scores with itself.

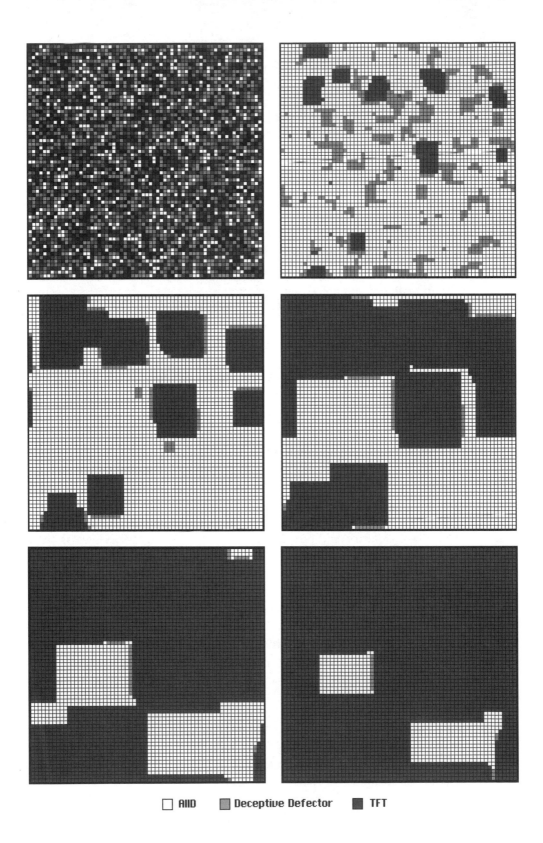

In *Morals by Agreement*, David Gauthier outlines a strategy he calls 'constrained maximization'. Though Gauthier's strategy is not simply TFT, his explanation for its success could apply perfectly to the evolution seen in figure 1:

> . . . constrained maximizers, interacting one with another, enjoy opportunities for co-operation which others lack. Of course, constrained maximizers sometimes lose by being disposed to compliance, for they may act co-operatively in the mistaken expectation of reciprocity from others who instead benefit at their expense. Nevertheless, we shall show that under plausible conditions, the net advantage that constrained maximizers reap from co-operation exceeds the exploitative benefits that others may expect. . .[32]

There is also a downside to the fact that TFT's success derives from its interaction with its own kind. Given a configuration in which, as it happens, TFT does not start with large enough clusters, it will be deprived of the benefit of cooperative scores with itself and will as a result be unable to survive and grow. In such a case—rare but not impossible in random initial configurations—defective strategies AllD and Deceptive Defector may end up in an equilibrium of mutual defection. This fact is the starting-point of the work on formal undecidability in the Spatialized Prisoner's Dilemma that appears in chapter 6.

4.5   A NOTE ON SOME DEEPER STRATEGIES

While still within Axelrod's classical constraints of perfect information, we might consider the possibility of expanding our sampling of strategies beyond the simple eight used above. One way to do so—a move to 'two-dimensional' strategies that we will consider in chapter 5—is to consider strategies calculated in terms of the last moves by players on *each* side. Another extension is to consider strategies 'two-deep', in the sense that response is calculated in terms of the last two plays by one's opponent.

'Two deep' strategies can be thought of as ordered six-tuples $\langle i1, i2, cc, cd, dc, dd \rangle$. Here $i1$ and $i2$ represent the set of initial moves by our player—00, 01, 10, or 11. The third value cc dictates the strategy's reaction to two successive cooperations by an opponent, cd a reaction to a cooperation followed by a defection, dc a reaction to a defection followed by a cooperation, and dd a reaction to two defections. We have a total of sixty-four such strategies, shown in the matrix on page 179 ($i1$ and $i2$ unseparated for clarity):

In this list strategies AllD and AllC remain unambiguous. It becomes much less clear, however, which strategy to label TFT or Suspicious TFT.

Figure 5   Progressive conquest by TFT in randomized array of eight reactive strategies, shown in three-generation intervals.

The 'purest' TFT is perhaps that strategy we have labeled TFT here: $\langle 11, 1, 0, 1, 0 \rangle$. This starts in a mode of pure cooperation, defecting only against defection by an opponent in the immediately preceding round. But we also have $\langle 11, 1, 1, 0, 0 \rangle$, which might be seen as a 'delayed' TFT, marked as DTFT above. DTFT starts fully cooperative and responds to defection with defection only after a delay of one round. For each of these strategies, moreover, we have three grades of more 'suspicious' TFT and DTFT, starting with an initial 01, 10, or 00. The four different strategies marked TF2T might be considered versions of 'Two Tits for a Tat', since they react with defection against a defection on either or both of the two previous rounds. A single defection against them thus gets counted twice, first as CD and then as DC. A double defection gets counted three times: as CD, DD, and DC. Also marked are four more tolerant versions of TFT—Tit for Either Tat, or TET—which defect only against defections by an opponent on both of the previous two rounds. Strategies labeled TF2T and TET include initially suspicious variations. One lesson of trying to label strategies in the transition from simple reactive strategies to 'two-deep' variations is that we often end up not with single unambiguous strategies—a single unambiguous TFT, for example—but classes of related strategies instead.

What happens in a randomized spatial competition between 'two-deep' strategies? In order to distinguish not eight strategies but sixty-four we have resorted to illustrations employing sixteen colors with and without central dots of contrasting colors. Started from a random distribution, one way evolution can proceed is that represented in figure 6 (only generations 1, 4, 8, 16, 24, and 32 are shown, with some simplifications for black and white reproduction). Here as before the broad family of 'vicious' strategies, variations on AllD, generally tend to be early winners, gobbling up initial territory at the expense of surrounding suckers. In the second generation of the full series, each of the top twenty-five strategies defects in the face of double cooperation. In the third generation each of the top ten strategies defects in the face of both double cooperation and double defection, with defection as well in the case of CD, DC, or both. At this point in the evolution no strategy that returns cooperation for double cooperation appears in the top seventeen.

By the sixth generation, however, pure TFT $\langle 11, 1, 0, 1, 0 \rangle$ has established itself in third place, and by the twelfth generation it occupies the bulk of the territory, maintaining that position through the twenty-fourth round. Once pure TFT is in possession, however, the possibility opens for exploitation by a slightly Suspicious Tit for Tat, $\langle 01, 1, 0, 1, 0 \rangle$, labeled simply STFT in the chart above. Since only the previous round counts for pure TFT, this more suspicious version can exploit pure TFT by means of an unpunished defection on the first play alone. In the evolution shown in figure 6 it is thus this more suspicious STFT that turns out to be the ultimate winner.

$\langle 00, 0, 0, 0, 0 \rangle$	Always Defect (AllD)	$\langle 10, 0, 0, 0, 0 \rangle$	
$\langle 00, 0, 0, 0, 1 \rangle$		$\langle 10, 0, 0, 0, 1 \rangle$	
$\langle 00, 0, 0, 1, 0 \rangle$		$\langle 10, 0, 0, 1, 0 \rangle$	
$\langle 00, 0, 0, 1, 1 \rangle$		$\langle 10, 0, 0, 1, 1 \rangle$	
$\langle 00, 0, 1, 0, 0 \rangle$		$\langle 10, 0, 1, 0, 0 \rangle$	
$\langle 00, 0, 1, 0, 1 \rangle$		$\langle 10, 0, 1, 0, 1 \rangle$	
$\langle 00, 0, 1, 1, 0 \rangle$		$\langle 10, 0, 1, 1, 0 \rangle$	
$\langle 00, 0, 1, 1, 1 \rangle$		$\langle 10, 0, 1, 1, 1 \rangle$	
$\langle 00, 1, 0, 0, 0 \rangle$	A Tit for 2 Tats (TF2T)	$\langle 10, 1, 0, 0, 0 \rangle$	a TF2T
$\langle 00, 1, 0, 0, 1 \rangle$		$\langle 10, 1, 0, 0, 1 \rangle$	
$\langle 00, 1, 0, 1, 0 \rangle$	a Suspicious TFT (STFT 2)	$\langle 10, 1, 0, 1, 0 \rangle$	STFT 3
$\langle 00, 1, 0, 1, 1 \rangle$		$\langle 10, 1, 0, 1, 1 \rangle$	
$\langle 00, 1, 1, 0, 0 \rangle$	a SDelayedTFT (SDTFT 1)	$\langle 10, 1, 1, 0, 0 \rangle$	SDTFT 2
$\langle 00, 1, 1, 0, 1 \rangle$		$\langle 10, 1, 1, 0, 1 \rangle$	
$\langle 00, 1, 1, 1, 0 \rangle$	Tit for Either Tat (TET)	$\langle 10, 1, 1, 1, 0 \rangle$	TET
$\langle 00, 1, 1, 1, 1 \rangle$		$\langle 10, 1, 1, 1, 1 \rangle$	
$\langle 01, 0, 0, 0, 0 \rangle$		$\langle 11, 0, 0, 0, 0 \rangle$	
$\langle 01, 0, 0, 0, 1 \rangle$		$\langle 11, 0, 0, 0, 1 \rangle$	
$\langle 01, 0, 0, 1, 0 \rangle$		$\langle 11, 0, 0, 1, 0 \rangle$	
$\langle 01, 0, 0, 1, 1 \rangle$		$\langle 11, 0, 0, 1, 1 \rangle$	
$\langle 01, 0, 1, 0, 0 \rangle$		$\langle 11, 0, 1, 0, 0 \rangle$	
$\langle 01, 0, 1, 0, 1 \rangle$		$\langle 11, 0, 1, 0, 1 \rangle$	
$\langle 01, 0, 1, 1, 0 \rangle$		$\langle 11, 0, 1, 1, 0 \rangle$	
$\langle 01, 0, 1, 1, 1 \rangle$		$\langle 11, 0, 1, 1, 1 \rangle$	
$\langle 01, 1, 0, 0, 0 \rangle$	a TF2T	$\langle 11, 1, 0, 0, 0 \rangle$	a TF2T
$\langle 01, 1, 0, 0, 1 \rangle$		$\langle 11, 1, 0, 0, 1 \rangle$	
$\langle 01, 1, 0, 1, 0 \rangle$	STFT	$\langle 11, 1, 0, 1, 0 \rangle$	TFT
$\langle 01, 1, 0, 1, 1 \rangle$		$\langle 11, 1, 0, 1, 1 \rangle$	
$\langle 01, 1, 1, 0, 0 \rangle$	SDTFT 3	$\langle 11, 1, 1, 0, 0 \rangle$	DTFT
$\langle 01, 1, 1, 0, 1 \rangle$		$\langle 11, 1, 1, 0, 1 \rangle$	
$\langle 01, 1, 1, 1, 0 \rangle$	TET	$\langle 11, 1, 1, 1, 0 \rangle$	TET
$\langle 01, 1, 1, 1, 1 \rangle$		$\langle 11, 1, 1, 1, 1 \rangle$	AllC

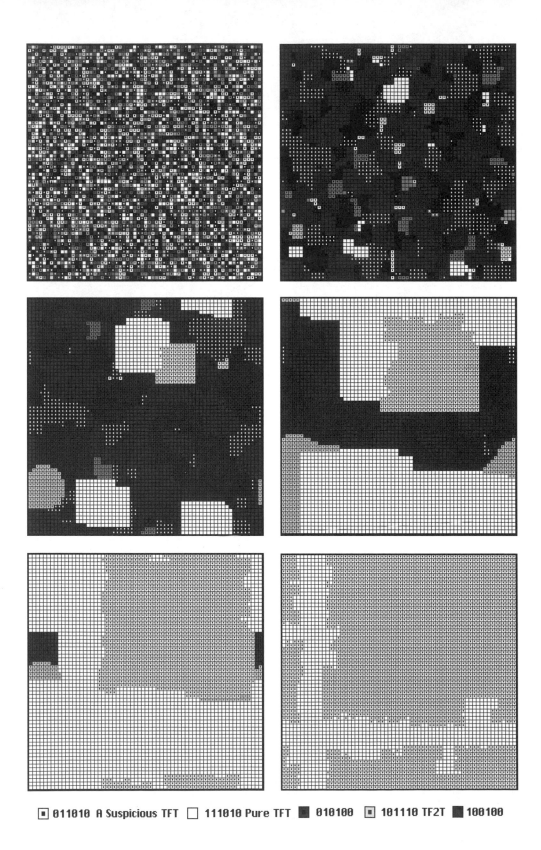

□ 011010 A Suspicious TFT   □ 111010 Pure TFT   ■ 010100   ■ 101110 TF2T   ■ 100100

Total conquest by any single strategy in a 'two-deep' competition turns out to be the exception rather than the rule, however. A much more common pattern of evolution is one toward a stable equilibrium among several strategies. A simple example is shown in figure 7 (once again with some simplifications for black and white reproduction). Relatives of AllD are once again early winners, and are once again conquered by a pure TFT, which eventually gives way to a suspicious variant. But here a Delayed Tit for Tat $\langle 1, 1, 1, 1, 0, 0 \rangle$, which rewards cooperation two rounds ago with cooperation, also shows some success both against the later defecting strategies and in the context of a pure TFT. In the end, a few generations beyond the last frame shown in figure 7, islands of this DTFT form a stable equilibrium with the dominant STFT. Small purely rectangular islands of pure TFT remain as well. From that point on nothing changes, and no single strategy conquers the entire field.

The success of DTFT in the context of TFT is easily understandable: each starts with cooperation on the first two rounds, and rewards that double cooperation with cooperation from then on. Thus DTFT and TFT are playing games of full cooperation with each other throughout.

The stability of DTFT with a suspicious STFT is a bit harder to understand. In games of two-hundred rounds, as employed in this model, the two strategies set up a pattern of periodic play in which STFT wins by a single round of defection against cooperation.[33] At the same time, however, DTFT plays a game of full cooperation with its own kind. STFT does not—its full cooperation with itself is marred by a first round of mutual defection. Here it must be remembered that in the move from one generation to the next cells adopt the strategy of the highest-scoring neighbor, and thus the fact that a cell stays with a particular strategy may indicate not that *that* cell is doing particularly well with that strategy but that a neighboring cell is. This allows for the possibility of a 'buffer situation', which appears to be what is happening here. In the right configuration a cell c of DTFT can be next to another cell c' of DTFT, which does very well from mutual cooperation. On each generation cell c 'changes' to that same strategy. Despite the deceptive appearance of stability cell c may itself not be doing very well in direct competition with a neighboring STFT cell, which may maintain *its* strategy as STFT because its total score is higher than that of its DTFT neighbor.

In other cases other strategies may play a significant role in a final equilibrium. Here a TF2T $\langle 1, 1, 1, 0, 0, 0 \rangle$ is particularly interesting. This TF2T plays against both TFT and DTFT, as well as against itself, in pure cooperation, and thus can establish an easy equilibrium with these. Games between TF2T and STFT produce a far poorer score than games between

Figure 6   One pattern of evolution in a randomized array of 64 classical '2-deep' strategies: conquest by a suspicious TFT shown for generations 1, 4, 8, 16, 24, and 32. (Some simplifications made for black and white presentation.)

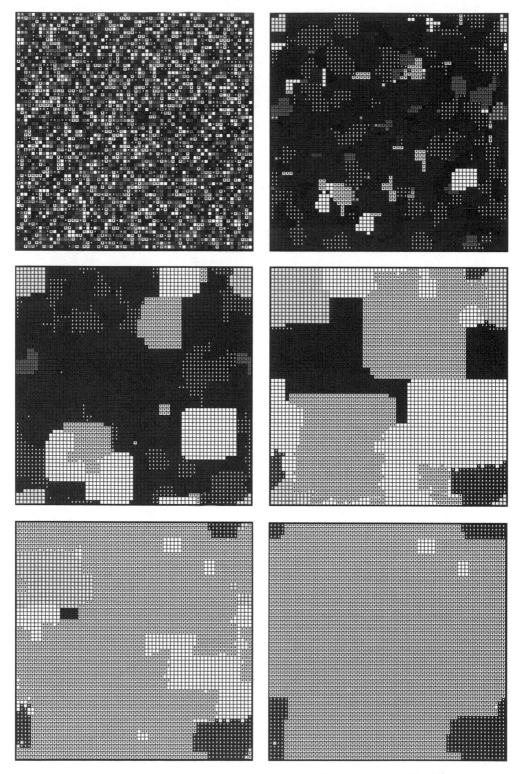

■ 011010 A Suspicious TFT   □ 111010 Pure TFT   ■ 111100 DTFT   ▨ 111110 TF2T

DTFT and STFT, but produce an identically poor score for both sides: TF2T's score against STFT is the same as STFT's score against it, and thus an equilibrium between STFT and TF2T is also possible. The possibility of a three-way equilibrium between DTFT, STFT, and TF2T appears to depend crucially on spatial arrangement, the buffer phenomenon noted above, and trace elements of pure TFT or other strategies.

With sixty-four strategies and an array as small as that shown, it turns out, the particular course of evolution is highly dependent on initial configuration.[34] Is the robustness of TFT vindicated in this more complicated spectrum of strategies? We can say that most of the successful strategies noted are cooperative on both initial rounds, and all of the successful strategies noted are cooperative on at least the second initial round. That is at least a TFT-like general feature: strategies vicious enough to start with a series of two defections do not ultimately succeed. All of the strategies noted also share the TF2T feature of responding to a series of two cooperations on the other side with cooperation. None cooperates in the face of two defections on the other side. Just as the question of what strategy counts as TFT becomes more complicated in this richer environment, however, the question of whether TFT-like strategies still prove robust becomes more complicated. What we can say is that successful strategies share at least a partial initial cooperativeness, an ability to respond with cooperation to a pattern of cooperation on the other side, and an ability to defect in the face of a pattern of defection on the other side.

The general idea of using cellular automata in a spatialization of the Prisoner's Dilemma should be clear, though to this point we have confined ourselves to the assumption of perfect communication and execution characteristic of a classic environment. What spatialization captures, and earlier models such as the Axelrod–Hamilton do not, is the fact that interaction must proceed locally, with any global evolution merely the consequence of changes at the local level.

Such a spatialization, we think, is entirely appropriate to a Hobbesian model. As originally printed, the 1651 title page of Hobbes's treatise portrays the emergent Leviathan as a giant composed of a myriad of small individuals (figure 8). Hobbes's opening passage, remarkably enough, both refers to that Leviathan as an automaton and anticipates the contemporary claim that cellular automata might be thought of as exhibiting artificial life:

Figure 7 Another pattern of evolution: to equilibrium primarily between a suspicious TFT and a DTFT, shown for generations 1, 4, 8, 16, 24, and 36. (Some simplifications made for black and white reproduction.)

Nature (the Art whereby God hath made and governes the world) is by the *Art* of man, as in many other things, so in this also imitated, that it can make an Artificial Animal. For seeing life is but a motion of Limbs, the beginning whereof is in some principall part within; why may we not say, that all *Automata* (Engines that move themselves by springs and wheels as doth a watch) have an artificiall life?... *Art* goes yet further, imitating that Rationall and most excellent worke of Nature, *Man*. For by art is created that great LEVIATHAN called a COMMON-WEALTH, or STATE, (in latine CIVITAS) which is but an Artificiall Man....[35]

Figure 8 The 1651 title page of Hobbes's *Leviathan*.

4.6 GREATER GENEROSITY IN AN IMPERFECT SPATIAL WORLD

The illustrations of the Spatialized Prisoner's Dilemma offered in the previous sections were explicitly limited to Axelrod's world of perfect information and execution: a world in which cooperations and defections are always seen for what they are and in which attempts to defect or cooperate always come off without a hitch. In the work of Nowak and Sigmund, we've noted, that assumption is replaced with the more realistic notion of a world of imperfect information and execution. One result of that move to greater realism is the apparent victory not of a stochastically imperfect TFT but of the significantly more generous GTFT, which forgives defection against it with a probability of 1/3.

What happens when we turn to a *spatialized* form of the stochastic Prisoner's Dilemma? Once the full story is in, it turns out that spatialization as an additional move toward realism favors an even *greater* level of generosity. In a first simple study, we used the same stochastic strategies introduced by Nowak and Sigmund: 121 purely stochastic strategies $\langle c, d \rangle$ at 0.1 intervals with full values of 0 and 1 replaced with 0.01 and 0.99, giving us a pool of strategies $\langle 0.01, 0.01 \rangle$, $\langle 0.01, 0.1 \rangle$, $\langle 0.01, 0.2 \rangle$, ... $\langle 0.99, 0.9 \rangle$, $\langle 0.99, 0.99 \rangle$. Following Nowak and Sigmund, competitive scores were also calculated in terms of infinite games between strategies. Here, however, strategies were randomly instantiated as cells in a 100×100 array. Cells played against immediate neighbors as outlined in the previous sections, gaining a total local score from those competitions and converting to the strategy of any neighbor with a higher local score.

With a full 121 strategies represented, such an array is highly sensitive to initial configuration: much depends on which strategies are eliminated by immediate neighbors in the first few generations. Both $\langle 0.8, 0.2 \rangle$ and $\langle 0.9, 0.1 \rangle$ can be important players in random arrays and can in fact establish an equilibrium: both compromise their probability of cooperation against cooperation to precisely the degree that they show any probability of cooperation against defection. Unless it is eliminated in early rounds, however, it is the more cooperative $\langle 0.99, 0.1 \rangle$ that tends to dominate both of these. A typical evolution to $\langle 0.99, 0.1 \rangle$ is shown in 11-generation intervals in figure 9 (with some simplifications for black and white presentation). Even $\langle 0.99, 0.1 \rangle$, of course, is just barely more generous than a stochastically impure TFT of $\langle 0.99, 0.01 \rangle$. Strategies approximating Nowak and Sigmund's GTFT did not seem to play a dominant role in these first spatialized tournaments.

It is clear that a primary factor in these first results is the limit of our spatial array, however. Such an array inevitably imposes not only a sensitivity to the precise initial configuration, but a significantly greater 'death factor' than is present in the population proportion algorithm used in both Axelrod and Hamilton's and Nowak and Sigmund's work. That

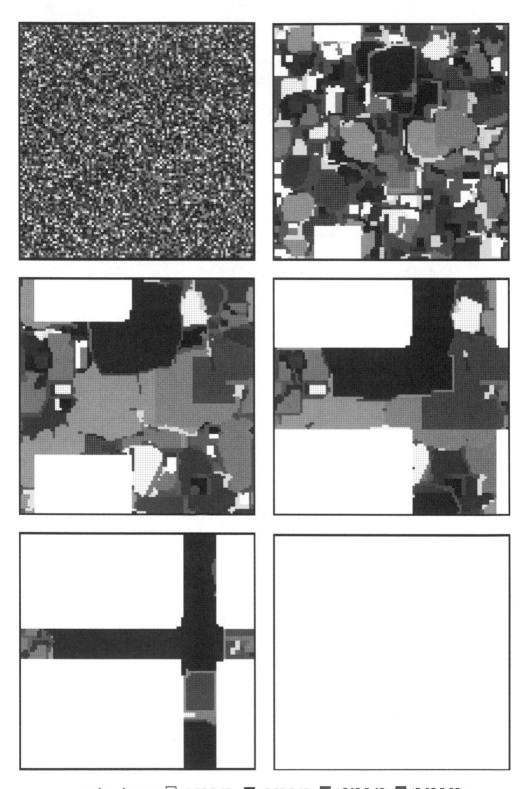

major players: □ <0.99,0.10> ■ <0.90,0.40> ▣ <.040,0.40> ▢ <0.60,0.20>

algorithm is in fact strongly biased against extinction: although a strategy's proportion in the population may diminish at each stage, it never dies completely unless it scores a full zero against all existing strategies. None of Nowak and Sigmund's stochastic strategies has a true score of zero against any other. In the evolution plotted in figure 1, the proportion of stochastically imperfect TFT falls at one point before its rise to somewhat more than half of its original representation. But the more generous $\langle 0.99, 0.2 \rangle$ falls to less than a millionth, and $\langle 0.99, 0.3 \rangle$ falls to less than a trillionth. If representation in a proportion less than that corresponding to a single individual counts as 'death', a generosity level of even $\langle 0.99, 0.1 \rangle$ would thus require a population in tens of thousands merely to survive, a generosity level of $\langle 0.99, 0.2 \rangle$ would demand a population of nearly one billion, and bare survival of a generosity level of $\langle 0.99, 0.3 \rangle$ would demand a population in the hundred trillions.

Within the limits of a finite array of automata of any manageable size, on the other hand, the death of a strategy can become very final very quickly. For this reason alone, although we can easily assume Nowak and Sigmund's pool of stochastic strategies and incorporate their payoff for infinite games in a spatial context, a tournament of this type imposes a significantly different reproductive algorithm. Given the array limits of this first attempt at spatial modeling and the very small proportions to which more generous strategies fall in the population-proportion model it is perhaps not too surprising that the upper end of the Nowak and Sigmund generosity result is cut off. $\langle 0.99, 0.3 \rangle$, our closest representation of GTFT, always seems to be extinguished much too early.

Here we should also mention another difference in the evolution of this first model. Even with a total population as small as ten thousand, we've noted, convergence is often to a strategy slightly more generous than stochastically imperfect TFT. But the evolutionary mechanism operative in this spatialization is quite different than that in the original results of Nowak and Sigmund. Within the population proportion algorithm, as indicated in figure 1, the pattern of the result is an early and almost total victory by stochastically imperfect TFT, followed step by step by successful invasions of more generous variations. Without the presence of stochastically imperfect TFT, Nowak and Sigmund indicate, evolution to more generous strategies cannot proceed. But that is not the characteristic evolution of the spatial model shown in figure 9; there it is clear that there is a direct victory by $\langle 0.99, 0.1 \rangle$ without the necessity of prior conquest by a statistically imperfect TFT $\langle 0.99, 0.01 \rangle$.

In two more sophisticated studies we used variations on this basic model to try to compensate for the effects of small arrays and small

Figure 9 The Spatialized Stochastic Prisoner's Dilemma, showing an evolution from a randomized array of 121 stochastic strategies to conquest by $\langle 0.99, 0.1 \rangle$. Frames are at eleven-generation intervals. (Some simplifications made for black and white reproduction.)

computer memories. In each case we used a randomizing procedure in which a limited sample of strategies compete in a given area, and in which losers are progressively replaced by alternatives. The idea is that in a large enough array there would be areas where significant numbers of individuals from any given handful of strategies compete, carrying the result of that competition into other areas. We simulate the larger area in bits, as it were, by progressively randomizing competing strategies into our 100×100 array. With such a procedure, the role of the death factor— the fact that all representatives of a strategy in a small randomized array may die very quickly, although that strategy might prove very successful in an environment that will evolve later on—seems properly minimized. In these more sophisticated spatial models it is not GTFT that is ultimately favored, however, with a forgiveness probability of 1/3 in the face of defection, but more generous strategies still.

In a second series of studies we began with a randomized 100×100 array of just 8 stochastic strategies chosen from the pool of 121. Each cell played against its neighbors as outlined above. When a strategy died— with no representatives left—a new competitor was sprinkled in a random eighth of the cells of the array, just as the original strategies had been sprinkled in. New competitors were chosen randomly from the pool, allowing a possibility of repetition. This procedure was introduced purely for the computational reasons outlined above, with the appearance of new strategies thought of merely as a sampling procedure across the pool of 121 strategies. Only later did we note that limitation to a fixed number of competing strategies is consistent with the broad outlines of E. O. Wilson and Robert MacArthur's 'Theory of Island Biogeography'.[36] On that theory, supported by a range of surprising data, the number of resident species on an island is proportionate to land area. It follows that the number of species in a given area will be constant over time: though different species appear and go extinct, the *number* of species over all remains the same, precisely as is true of strategies in our second formal model.[37]

Convergence to a particular strategy in the formal ecology of our second model would clearly constitute a strong argument in favor of that strategy: any such strategy must have arisen and must have maintained itself in competition with substantial distributions of large numbers of potential rivals. Given Nowak and Sigmund's work, we would not have been surprised had GTFT triumphed. As it happened, however, our results showed convergence quite standardly to significantly greater levels of generosity. Convergence was almost always to a strategy in the range of $\langle 0.99, 0.4 \rangle$ through $\langle 0.99, 0.6 \rangle$, locked in equilibrium with trace elements of other strategies in such a way as to block further incursions. Nobody fully dies and thus no further strategies are introduced. Sometimes even $\langle 0.99, 0.7 \rangle$ establishes itself as the dominant strategy, though generally with significantly more areas of incursion by other strategies in equilibrium.

Figure 10 shows typical end-states with $\langle 0.99, 0.4 \rangle$ and $\langle 0.99, 0.6 \rangle$ in final possession, locked in equilibrium with trace elements of other strategies (a 64×64 array is shown for the sake of clarity, though the work itself was generally run with the larger 100×100 array). The generosity result for this model is very resilient. Although it may take longer to develop, the basic result is the same if we start with 16 strategies rather than 8, if we introduce only 1% of an alternative strategy when one dies, or both. It also remains if we deepen approximations to 0 and 1 in our stochastic strategies to 0.000001 and 0.999999, if we sharpen approximations of GTFT in a similar way, or both.

In this second series of studies it became clear that it was the possibility of small clusters that was crucial to ecological dynamics. In a third series we therefore varied the model so as to introduce with each generation a spatial cluster of just 6 cells of a random strategy somewhere in the display. Rather than replace a full 12.5% of the display only on the death of a strategy, we replaced a clustered 0.06% of the display with a randomly chosen strategy at each generation. This allowed for a variable number of strategies to be represented at a time, rather than a constant 8 as in the model above. It also allowed us to avoid the artificial 'locking' phenomena of the second model, in which 8 strategies in equilibrium can prevent the introduction of further competitors.

In this third model an even clearer dominance by $\langle 0.99, 0.5 \rangle$ and $\langle 0.99, 0.6 \rangle$ was evident. In these studies the standard result is convergence to domination by one or the other of these strategies, in clear possession of the field but with trace elements of other strategies present in equilibrium but unable to expand. Often subdominant strategies appear in the form of periodic blinkers. Figure 11a shows $\langle 0.99, 0.6 \rangle$ in possession, with trace elements of $\langle 0.99, 0.4 \rangle$, $\langle 0.3, 0.1 \rangle$, $\langle 0.1, 0.7 \rangle$, and other strategies in equilibrium. Figure 11b shows $\langle 0.99, 0.5 \rangle$ in possession with trace elements of $\langle 0.99, 0.3 \rangle$ and other strategies.[38] As a whole, then, this series of spatialized studies indicates a victory for strategies far more generous in the face of defection than mere GTFT—strategies with generosity ranges up to and including 0.6 rather than GTFT's mere 1/3.

Within the spatial context there *is* one clear victory for pure GTFT: Nowak and Sigmund's $\langle 1 - \varepsilon, 1/3 \rangle$ emerges quite clearly as the strategy with the highest score against itself that is impervious to spatial invasion by a single unit of any other strategy. What our more generous experimental results emphasize, however, is that imperviousness to invasion by a single unit is not of ultimate importance in a spatial ecology of this kind. Though GTFT is impervious to invasion by a single unit of any other strategy, it *does* prove vulnerable to invasion by small clusters of some more generous strategies, themselves vulnerable in turn to invasion by much less generous strategies. No strategy is impervious to invasion by small clusters of all other strategies.

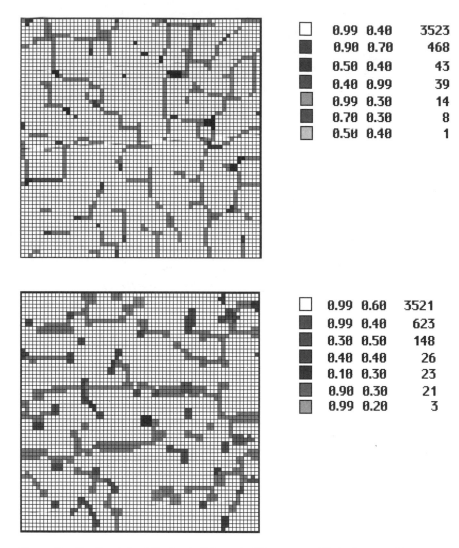

☐	0.99	0.40	3523
■	0.90	0.70	468
■	0.50	0.40	43
■	0.40	0.99	39
■	0.99	0.30	14
■	0.70	0.30	8
☐	0.50	0.40	1

☐	0.99	0.60	3521
■	0.99	0.40	623
■	0.30	0.50	148
■	0.40	0.40	26
■	0.10	0.30	23
■	0.90	0.30	21
☐	0.99	0.20	3

Figure 10 The Spatialized Stochastic Prisoner's Dilemma: equilibria dominated by greater generosity. Generated from eight initial strategies, randomly chosen and distributed, with dead strategies replaced by randomly chosen alternatives in similar 1/8 proportions.

Within a spatial model, it turns out, it becomes important to distinguish between different notions of invasion. In particular, it proves necessary at least to distinguish invasion as (a) growth, such that for some generation there is a succeeding generation in which there is a greater number of units of the invader, (b) sustained growth, such that for every generation there is some succeeding generation in which there is a greater number of units of the invader, and (c) invasion to conquest, such that for any arbitrary area, that area is eventually occupied entirely by the invader. Figure 12a shows two forms of self-limiting invasion: the unsustained periodic growth of a single unit of ⟨0.01, 0.01⟩ in a field of ⟨0.9, 0.6⟩, shown in one-generation

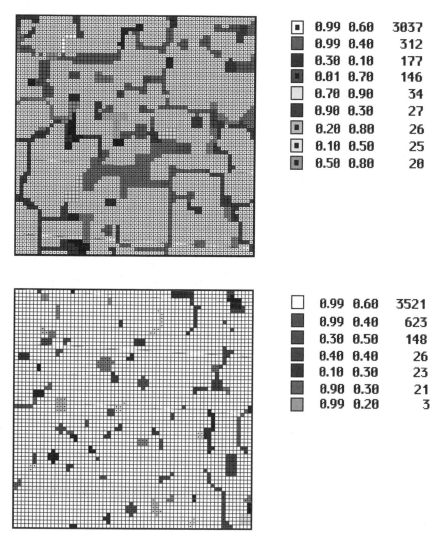

	0.99	0.60	3037
	0.99	0.40	312
	0.30	0.10	177
	0.01	0.70	146
	0.70	0.90	34
	0.90	0.30	27
	0.20	0.80	26
	0.10	0.50	25
	0.50	0.80	20

	0.99	0.60	3521
	0.99	0.40	623
	0.30	0.50	148
	0.40	0.40	26
	0.10	0.30	23
	0.90	0.30	21
	0.99	0.20	3

Figure 11 Examples of evolution to greater generosity with a variable number of random strategies, blocks of six of a randomly chosen strategy dropped in each generation.

intervals, and the sustained but self-limiting growth of ⟨0.8, 0.99⟩ in a field of ⟨0.99, 0.6⟩, shown for generations 1, 4, 7, and 12. Three common patterns of invasion to conquest appear in figure 12b, here illustrated by ⟨0.99, 0.9⟩ invaded by a single unit of ⟨0.01, 0.8⟩, ⟨0.99, 0.4⟩ invaded by a square of nine units of ⟨0.99, 0.6⟩, each shown in intervals of two generations, and ⟨0.99, 0.99⟩ invaded by a single unit of ⟨0.5, 0.6⟩, shown for generations 1, 4, 8, and 12.

Invasion patterns for GTFT provide a particularly instructive example. Although GTFT is still impervious to invasion by a single unit of any other strategy, a GTFT of ⟨0.9999999, 0.3333333⟩ is invadable to conquest by clusters as small as four units of, for example, ⟨0.9999999, 0.5⟩. It is also invadable, though not to conquest, by clusters of strategies as generous as $\langle 0.9999999, 0.9999999 \rangle$, or stochastically imperfect AllC. The complex dynamics of an invasion of stochastically imperfect GTFT by AllC is in fact quite intriguing.[39] The growth of a cluster of sixteen units of AllC in a field of GTFT, each with a stochastic imperfection of 0.0000001, is shown at intervals of six generations in figure 13. Here coding in terms of greys is used to indicate dynamics: black indicates a cell of the invading strategy that has not changed in the last round, white a cell of the invaded strategy that has not changed, vertical stripes a cell that has been invaded in the last round, and grey a cell that has reverted to the invaded strategy.[40] GTFT, then, though invulnerable to invasion by a single unit of alternative strategies, *is* vulnerable to invasion by small clusters of some more generous strategies. In this way it resembles pure non-stochastic AllD, which although *not* invadable by a single unit of pure TFT, *is* invadable by small clusters of TFT.

Strategies more generous than GTFT, up to and including $\langle 0.9999999, 0.6666666 \rangle$, prove invadable by other strategies but seem invadable *to conquest* by no others in at least standard patterns of small clusters. Here our work took the form of an empirical survey, using rectangular blocks of two and six cells, crosses of four, and square blocks of four, nine, and sixteen. In a computerized survey we dropped each of these patterns, for each of our stochastic strategies, into a background field of every other stochastic strategy. The program was written to signal whether an invasion had progressed to fill a particular border in a chosen number of generations. On the basis of this survey the region that emerged as optimal—in the sense of offering a strategy with the highest score against itself impervious to invasion to conquest from a small cluster of any other strategy—seemed to be that centered on $\langle 1 - \varepsilon, 2/3 \rangle$. That strategy we termed 'Forgiving Tit for Tat' (FTFT).[41]

Here a great deal of analytic work remains to be done. It should be possible to work out patterns of spatial invasion for clusters of particular shapes given particular ratios of Prisoner's Dilemma scores. That analytic work will require consideration of a bewildering number of cases, analyzing potential growth for cells with certain scores at particular positions in particular shapes—at corners, along straight edges, in single protuberances, and next to nicks in straight edges, for example. Our conjecture is that further analytic work will both confirm and explain the preeminence of FTFT in a stochastic spatialization.

The noteworthy feature of 'Forgiving Tit for Tat', of course, is that it displays twice the generosity of Nowak and Sigmund's 'Generous Tit for Tat' in the face of defection on the other side. This is even more remarkable in light of the fact that essentially *all* that we have added to the Nowak and Sigmund model is spatialization by way of two-dimensional cellular automata. Spatialization alone seems to favor an important increase in the level of generosity one can expect to evolve in a Hobbesian model.

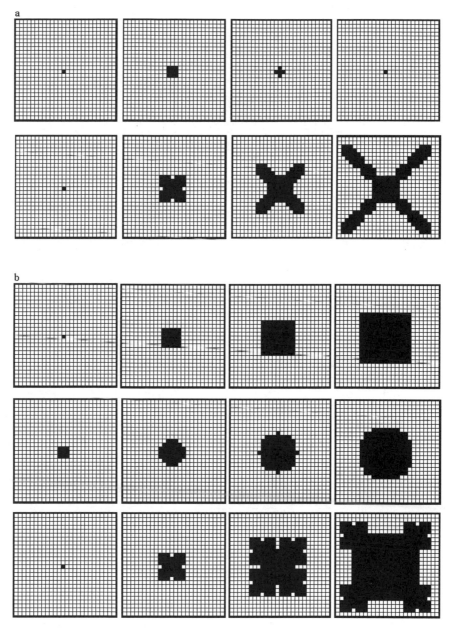

Figure 12 (a) Two common forms of self-limiting invasion; (b) three patterns of invasion to conquest.

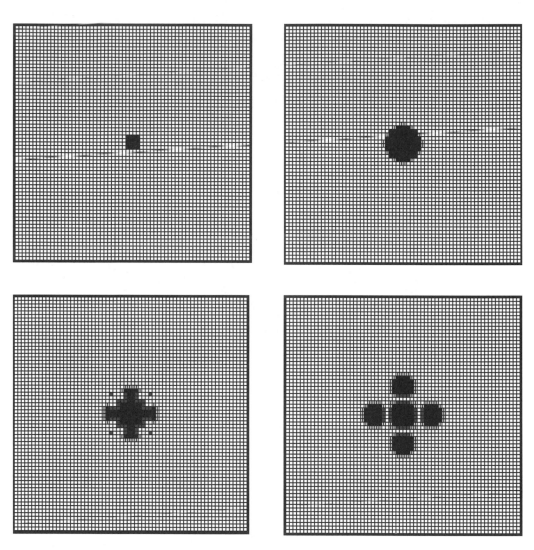

Figure 13 A field of strategy ⟨0.9999999,0.3333333⟩ invaded by a sixteen-square block of ⟨0.9999999,0.9999999⟩, shown at intervals of four generations. Vertical lines indicate cells which have been invaded in the last generation; grey indicates those that have reverted to the original strategy in the last generation.

We should also note some limitations of the above work. Building explicitly on the work of Nowak and Sigmund, it is similarly limited to one-dimensional or reactive strategies, which consider only the previous move of the opponent. Chapter 5 is devoted to work on more complex two-dimensional strategies in a continuous-valued rather than stochastic environment. Work on Hobbesian environments with the intriguing possibility of 'opting out'—of choosing not to compete at all—we leave to others or to another context.[42] Variations employing asynchronous updating—in which not all cells are updated simultaneously—are left for

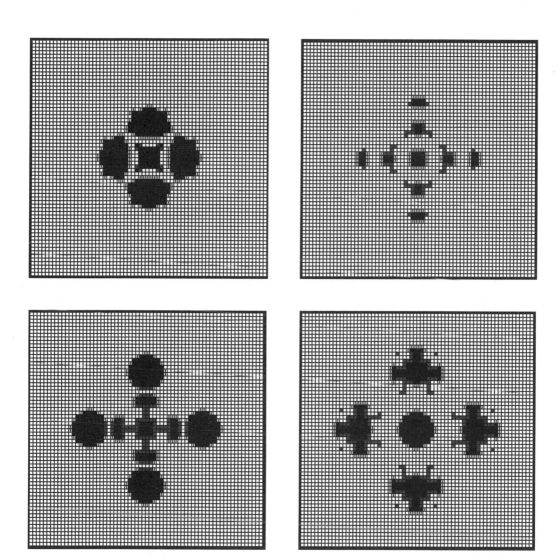

Figure 13 (*continued*).

further study as well, though on an experimental basis we have tried a limited form of asynchronous updating for results throughout by computing only a random 50% or 25% of arrays on each generation.[43] As might be expected, precise patterns of propagation dependent on the particular configuration of a group, such as those in figures 12 and 13, prove vulnerable to change from synchronous to asynchronous updating. Within the experimental limits noted, however, results regarding the greater success of generous strategies in a spatial environment seem to remain. It may also be that the stochastic character of the strategies at issue diminishes the differential effects of synchronous and asynchronous updating.[44]

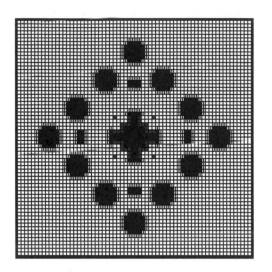

Figure 13 (*continued*).

4.7 CONCLUSION

In this chapter we have tried to approach Hobbes's question of how cooperation might arise in a community of self-seeking egoists without central control. The central question is traditional; the tools with which we've tried to explore it are not. Our attempt has been to approach Hobbes in terms of computer modeling, replacing the state of nature of Hobbes's informal imagination with arrays of players pursuing explicit strategies in an environment of competition characterized by the terms of the iterated Prisoner's Dilemma.

Within Axelrod's classical model—a world of perfect communication and errorless execution—we've seen it is TFT that is favored. That result is perfectly in accord with Hobbes, who proposes as a second "generall Rule, found out by Reason" the principle that "*Whatsoever you require that others should do to you, that do ye to them*" (*Leviathan*, Chapter XIV). What is surprising—and, we think, would have been surprising to Hobbes—is that two ways of making that model more realistic favor 'generosity' above and beyond the level of TFT. In the work of Nowak and Sigmund, the move to a world of *imperfect* information and/or execution favors not an imperfect TFT but the more generous stochastic strategy GTFT, which almost invariably rewards cooperation with cooperation but forgives defection against it with a probability of 1/3. In this chapter we have added a further measure of realism, a Spatialized Prisoner's Dilemma. In a spatialized model still more generous strategies are favored. By some measures the optimal strategy here appears to be 'Forgiving Tit for Tat' (FTFT), in which the probability of forgiving defection is a full 2/3—twice the generosity level of GTFT. What is surprising is that these generous or forgiving strategies are favored in what remains essentially a society of egoists, without the central control of Hobbes's envisaged Leviathan. All payoffs are defined explicitly in terms of the Prisoner's Dilemma matrix and the spread of strategies is governed throughout by calculation of those strategies with the highest total scores in local competition. All processing remains on the individual level and in parallel. Hobbes might well have been surprised at the high level of cooperation and generosity that evolves in even this stark a state of nature.

We've noted a number of areas in which important formal exploration needs to be done. Some of these we will take up, with an emphasis on continuous-valued rather than stochastic models, in chapter 5. There is also important philosophical work in interpretation that remains to be explored.

We have given in to the temptation throughout to speak of TFT as a 'cooperative' strategy and of GTFT and FTFT as 'generous' or 'forgiving'. In each case these informal characterizations can be cashed out in purely formal terms: TFT responds to 'C' with 'C' in the Prisoner's Dilemma, and GTFT and FTFT have significant and high probabilities, respectively, of responding to 'D' with 'C'. As emphasized in the introduction, however, the almost unavoidable tendency to think of these as literally 'generous' or 'forgiving' carries an important philosophical danger. It is hard when viewing the evolution of a cellular automata array such as those above *not* to root for TFT, GTFT, or FTFT as the 'good guys' in some moral sense. The danger is that we will misconstrue both ethics and our formal results by using a terminology borrowed from the realm of ethics but defined merely in formal terms. It is clear for example that cooperation, irrespective of group or goal, is *not* always a moral good. The formal feature referred to informally as 'generous' or 'forgiving' may in some cases amount to tolerating injustice or abetting a felony. In a full philosophical treatment it will also be important to recognize interpretation in terms of 'generosity', 'forgiveness', and a richer behavioral and moral terminology in general, as a distinct move above and beyond the formal results themselves. Here we have followed the general literature in using these informal categories to characterize formal results. As work continues and becomes more sophisticated this may well be something it becomes important to leave behind, separating the interpretation from the pure results in much the way that formal semantics is separated from syntax in standard logic.

Another remaining philosophical task will be much more difficult. We have emphasized even in the introduction that the formal strategies at issue are not themselves literally 'cooperative' or 'generous': they are at best mere models of genuinely cooperative or generous behavior. Nonetheless there is a clear intuitive motivation for categorizing strategies in this informal way: there do seem to be strong intuitive analogies between these formal behaviors and the real attitudes of real agents, including attitudes we standardly characterize in moral terms. The hard philosophical task that remains is to clarify and fill out those intuitive analogies. Precisely which characteristics of a social environment do our models capture, and which do they fail to capture? In precisely which ways do certain characteristics of our formal strategies resemble genuine cooperation and generosity, and in which ways do they not?

Any further questions of the implications of the models offered here hang on the answers to these hard interpretational questions, and not on the formal results alone. The formal models alone may show that certain analogues of some forms of moral behavior show a certain dynamics under particular constraints of interaction. What that shows us about morality, however, depends on the strength and precise character of the analogy—the hard question posed above. Certainly it does not follow from these models alone that moral behavior is to be 'justified' in terms of such dynamics, let alone that there somehow really *is* no genuine morality.

Even Hobbes, we've noted, seems to offer no unambiguous answers to questions of moral justification or reduction. It would be equally wrong, we think, to expect full answers to such questions from the contemporary Hobbesian models offered here.

5 Real-Valued Game Theory: Real Life, Cooperative Chaos, and Discrimination

The practical difficulty is not so much in knowing when to cooperate or defect but to decide what is going on. In the real world, it is not always obvious whether someone has acted cooperatively or defected.
—William Poundstone, *The Prisoner's Dilemma*[1]

Nobody, as long as he moves among the chaotic currents of life, is without trouble.
—Carl Jung

The theory of justice is a part, perhaps the most significant part, of the theory of rational choice.
—John Rawls, *A Theory of Justice*[2]

In the previous chapter, we used the Prisoner's Dilemma to introduce Hobbesian models of social interaction. There, however, we limited ourselves to a spatialized form of stochastic models, designed to capture a world of imperfect information. In this chapter we want to take spatialized models in a different direction, increasing their realism in terms not of *probabilities* of cooperation and defection but of *degrees* of cooperation and defection. In the real world it is not merely true that one sometimes doesn't *know* whether an action should be construed as cooperative or not; very often the act really *is* more or less cooperative, lying on a genuine continuum between cooperation and defection. Here we pursue such an intuition by considering a continuous-valued form of the Prisoner's Dilemma and constructing Hobbesian models of social interaction in terms of it.

Once game theory is viewed in terms of continuous values, several important connections with the material of early chapters become clear. One of these is a compelling connection between continuous-valued game theory and the infinite-valued logical connectives. Another is a clear connection between continuous-valued game theory and chaos.

In the final section of this chapter we apply some of these game-theoretic tools to a very real social problem: the issue of discrimination. This final applicational study, we think, serves to underscore both the power of this form of modeling and the importance of distinguishing carefully between work in social modeling and work in genuine social ethics.

5.1 REAL LIFE

Our ultimate goal in what follows is to provide further spatialized forms of the Prisoner's Dilemma, made more realistic by the incorporation of imperfect degrees of cooperation and defection. We begin with Conway's whimsical but suggestive Game of Life, however, to demonstrate some of the important differences that a shift to a continuum of values can make.

As outlined in the previous chapter, Conway's Game of Life is played on an infinite board of square cells. At time 0, each cell is either completely alive (1) or completely dead (0). Once a configuration is set, patterns evolve at each tick of a clock according to three rules, the Birth Rule, the Survival Rule, and the Death Rule:

Birth Rule: A cell dead at generation t will come alive at generation $t + 1$ if exactly three neighbors are alive at t.

Survival Rule: A cell that is alive at generation t will remain alive at $t + 1$ if it is surrounded at t by precisely two or three live neighbors.

Death Rule: A cell will be dead at generation $t + 1$ if it has fewer than two live neighbors or more than three live neighbors at generation t.

There are a number of intriguing denizens of Conway's Game of Life. Fundamental for Conway's universal computability result, for example, is the Glider, introduced in chapter 4. A configuration known as the Pinwheel generates four Gliders at its corners (figure 1). The Cheshire Cat disappears over several generations to a single paw print (figure 2).

Conway's Game of Life, however, makes the simplifying assumption that each cell is either completely alive or completely dead: each cell has a precise value of 1 or 0 on each generation. What happens when this simplifying restriction to bivalence is relaxed? What if we allow cells to take on a continuum of values in the real-valued internal [0,1]? This possibility is not without precedent in nature. Yeast spores, for example, come alive from a relatively dormant state when the conditions are right, and so it is natural to describe the dormant spores as neither fully alive nor fully dead.[3] Why not construct a variation of Conway's Game of Life that countenances real-valued degrees of life and death? We call this game "Real Life." It turns out that Real Life, unlike Conway's Game of Life, exhibits a sensitive dependence on initial conditions that is characteristic of chaotic systems.

We can represent the rules for Conway's Game of Life graphically. There are two cases to consider. If the center cell is dead, then, according to the

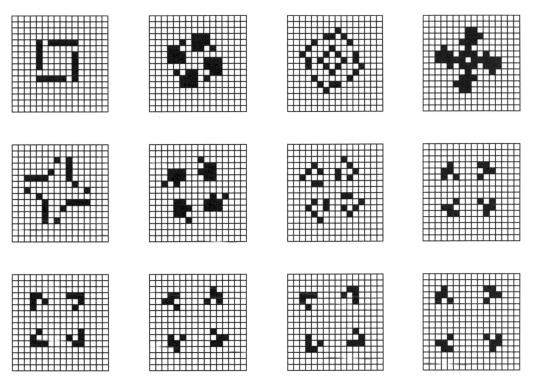

Figure 1 The Pinwheel in Conway's Game of Life generates Gliders. Generations 1 through 12 are shown.

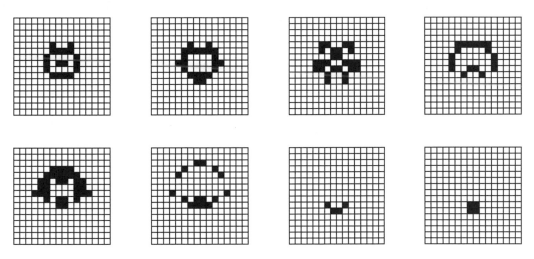

Figure 2 In Conway's Game of Life, the Cheshire Cat leaves a single paw print. Generations 1 through 8 are shown.

Real-Valued Game Theory: Real Life, Cooperative Chaos, and Discrimination

Birth Rule, it will come alive if it has exactly three live neighbors. The Birth Rule is represented by the graph on the left in figure 3. Here the x-axis represents the total amount of life in the nine-cell neighborhood at time t, and the y-axis represents the life of the center cell at time $t + 1$. The second case is when the center cell is already alive. According to the Survival Rule, the center cell will stay alive if it has no less than two and no more than three live neighbors. Counting the center cell, which is assumed to be alive, this means that the center cell will stay alive if the total amount of life in the nine neighborhood area is three or four. The Survival Rule is represented by the graph on the right in figure 3.

These graphic representations of Conway's Rules of Life suggest a natural way to generalize the bivalent rules to the real-valued case. We simply replace the vertical lines in the graphical representation of Conway's rules with tent functions whose sides have a slope of plus or minus 1. The resulting rules for Real Life are shown in figure 4. We can even formulate a single "fuzzy" rule for Real Life. We superimpose the last two graphs in figure 4 and introduce a parameter c, to range from 0 to 1, representing the life of the center cell (figure 5). In this fuzzy rule, the Birth and Survival Rules coincide on values less than 3 and on values greater than 5, and differ on the interval from 3 to 5. The Birth Rule specifies what happens in this interval when $c = 0$, and the Survival Rule specifies what happens when $c = 1$. When the value of c ranges between 0 and 1, the Survival Rule is represented by a shifting line with a slope of minus 1 and an x-intercept of $4 + c$.

Let $\sum_t$ be the sum of all the life in the nine-cell neighborhood at time t and c_{t+1} be the degree of life of the center cell at time $t + 1$. Then c_{t+1}, the degree of life of the center cell at time $t + 1$, is given by

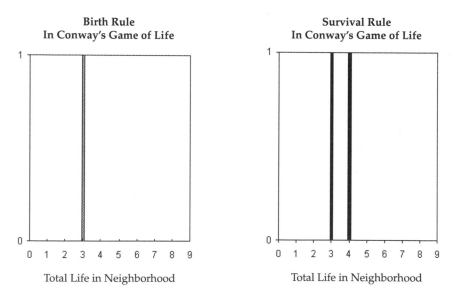

Figure 3   A graphical representation of the rules of Conway's Game of Life.

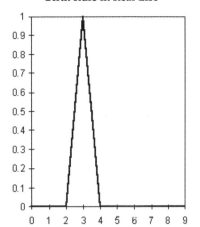

Birth Rule in Real Life

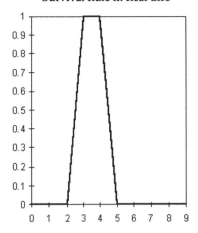

Survival Rule in Real Life

Total Degree of Life in Neighborhood · · · · · · · · Total Degree of Life in Neighborhood

Figure 4   A graphical representation of the rules of Real Life. Here vertical lines are replaced with tent functions.

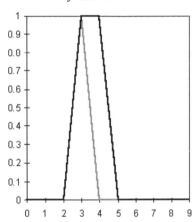

Fuzzy Rule for Real Life

Total Degree of Life in Neighborhood

Figure 5   A single "fuzzy" rule for birth and survival in Real Life.

$\text{Max}\{0, \text{Min}\{1, f(\sum_t, c_t)\}\}$, where

$$f\left(\sum_t, c_t\right) = \begin{cases} 0 & \text{if } 0 \leq \sum_t \leq 2 + c_t \text{ or } \sum_t \geq 4 + c_t \\ -\sum_t + (4 + c_t) & \text{if } 3 \leq \sum_t \leq 4 + c_t \\ \sum_t - 2 & \text{if } 2 \leq \sum_t \leq 3 \end{cases}$$

Or more simply:

$$c_{t+1} = 1 + 0.5 \cdot c_t - \text{Abs}(3 + 0.5 \cdot c_t - \sum_t),$$

where the function has a maximum of 1 and a minimum of 0.

Real Life contains Conway's Game of Life as a special case. When the initial values of the cells in Real Life are restricted to the values 0 and 1, the outcome is identical to Conway's Game of Life. Yet Real Life exhibits intriguing behavior in the interval between 0 and 1 that is not realized in Conway's Game of Life. Here we have found it convenient to represent different degrees of life with different color codes by dividing the [0, 1] interval into 16ths (figure 6). Here numerical values in particular intervals—values from 0 up to 1/16th, for example, or from 1/16th up to 2/16th—are assigned particular shades for purposes of illustration.

Gliders are perhaps the most famous of the self-perpetuating patterns in Conway's Game of Life. As outlined in chapter 4, the existence of Gliders enabled Conway to prove that the Game of Life can be used to instantiate a Universal Turing Machine.[4] In figure 1 above, we saw that the Pinwheel evolves into four Gliders. In Real Life, alternatively, we have the freedom to vary the initial values of the live cells. If the initial value of the live cells had been set at 0.992, the Pinwheels would evolve into glider-like patterns, which instead of reproducing themselves eternally, quickly disappear (figure 7). If, on the other hand, the initial value had been 0.994, the pattern would have evolved into four static glider-like shapes. If the initial value had been the intermediate value 0.993, the pattern would quickly grow and eventually cover the entire cellular automaton playing field. In Real Life, therefore, the Pinwheel exhibits an intuitively sensitive dependence on the initial conditions regarding degrees of life. A formal demonstration of sensitive dependence in a strict sense, a characteristic feature of chaotic functions is offered below.

Intuitively sensitive dependence in Real Life can also be illustrated with the pattern whimsically dubbed the Cheshire Cat.[5] In Conway's Game of Life, the Cheshire Cat pattern evolves into a single paw print (see figure 2). In Real Life, with an initial value of 0.666, the Cheshire Cat evolves into two such paw prints instead of one. Increasing the initial value by 0.001, however, leads to a pair of multicolored paw prints (figure 8a). Decreasing the initial value by 0.001, on the other hand, appears to give the Cheshire Cat more than the proverbial 9 lives. With an initial value of 0.75, the cells of the Cheshire Cat take on the cyclical values 1/4, 1/2, 3/4, and 1. This Cheshire Cat, faithful to its namesake, eventually vanishes altogether.[6]

[0,1)	[4,5)	[8,9)	[12,13)
[1,2)	[5,6)	[9,10)	[13,14)
[2,3)	[6,7)	[10,11)	[14,15)
[3,4)	[7,8)	[11,12)	[15,16]

Figure 6 Shading key for Real Life.

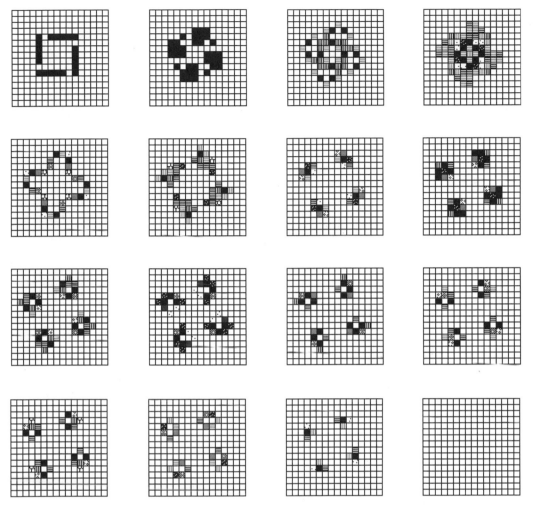

Figure 7 In Real Life, the Pinwheel can evolve into disappearing Gliders. Generations 1 through 16 are shown.

It is clear, then, that Real Life offers a range of behavior that a merely stochastic Life could not. Replacing Conway's rules with ones that afforded merely a probability of life or death in certain circumstances only removes the determinacy of the patterns. The move to continuous values of life and death retains determinacy but opens a range of more complex phenomena.

5.2 CHAOTIC CURRENTS IN REAL LIFE

Interestingly, the rules for even Conway's binary Game of Life contain a *self-referential* element: whether a cell is alive or dead depends on the

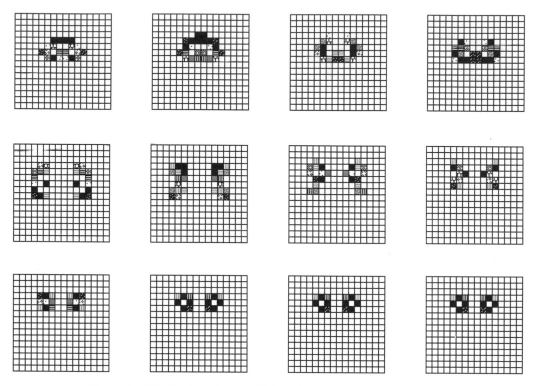

Figure 8a The Cheshire Cat in Real Life with an initial value of 0.667, generations 45 through 56 shown.

number of its *own* live neighbors. The rules for Conway's Game of Life can be stated in a way that makes this self-referential element explicit:

I will be alive at time t_{n+1} if, and only if, either *I* am not alive and exactly three of *my* neighbors are alive at time t_n or *I* am already alive and either three or four cells in *my* neighborhood (*including myself*) are alive at time t_n.

In this respect, the logic of Life is similar to the logic of self-referential sentences. One of the most intriguing self-referential sentences considered in chapter 1 was the Chaotic Liar, a natural infinite-valued generalization of the classical Liar. Recall that in contrast to the classical Liar, which is true if it is false, the Chaotic Liar asserts that it is true to the extent that it is estimated to be false:

> This statement is as true as it is estimated to be false.

The Chaotic Liar is perhaps the simplest generalization of the classical Liar in our infinite-valued self-referential logic.

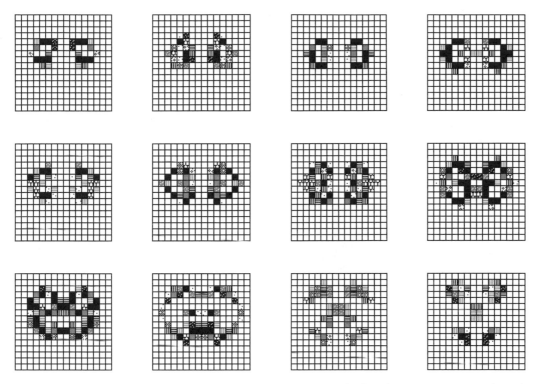

Figure 8b The Cheshire Cat in Real Life with an initial value of 0.665, generations 25 through 36 shown.

The Birth and Survival Rules for Real Life can also be stated as infinite-valued self-referential sentences. Let's call the number of cells required for birth the 'Genesis Constant.' The Birth Rule then states that the center cell is alive to the extent that the sum total of life in the neighborhood does not differ from the Genesis Constant $g = 3$. The corresponding algorithm is:

$$c_{t+1} = 1 - \text{Abs}(3 - \textstyle\sum_t),$$

where $\sum_t$ is the sum total of life in the neighborhood at time t and c_{t+1} is the life of the center cell at time $t + 1$ and the function is assumed to have a maximum of 1 and a minimum of 0. The Survival Rule states that the center cell stays alive if and only if the total degree of life in the neighborhood is 3 or 4 (including the center cell) at time t_n. The corresponding algorithm is:

$$c_{t+1} = 1.5 - \text{Abs}(4 - \textstyle\sum_t),$$

where the function again is assumed to have a maximum of 1 and a minimum of 0.

We have already illustrated the fact that Real Life exhibits an intuitively sensitive dependence on initial values, characteristic of chaotic functions.

How can we establish the relationship between the rules of Real Life and chaotic functions more formally? Recall that we obtained a single fuzzy rule that incorporates the Birth and Survival Rules by introducing a constant c for the degree of life ranging from 0 to 1 of the center cell:

$$c_{t+1} = 1 + 0.5 \cdot c_t - \text{Abs}(3 + 0.5 \cdot c_t - \textstyle\sum_t),$$

where the function is assumed to have a maximum of 1 and a minimum of 0. Let's introduce some additional parameters into the fuzzy rule and simplify the initial configuration to a single cell. Consider the dynamical function (again with a maximum of 1 and a minimum of 0):

$$c_{t+1} = 1 + h - \text{Abs}(g + h - c_t/m),$$

where g is the Genesis Constant, h is the height of the peak of the tent above 1, and m is a factor that varies the slope of the tent function. The parameter g determines the center line of the peak of the graph of the fuzzy rule. The parameter h determines how wide the interval is in which there is neither too little nor too much life to sustain the life of the center cell. The parameter m determines the rate at which the center cell makes the transition from death to life, or conversely. Now if we set $g = 1$, $m = 1/2$ and set $h = 0$, we obtain the standard chaotic tent function for the [0, 1] interval.

Depending on the value of the initial center cell, successive generations will appear as nested series of variously evolving square patterns. Consider now the cells along a diagonal extending from the center cell. Notice that the corner of the outermost evolved square will be the only live cell in the neighborhood of the next cell along that diagonal. The cells propagating from the diagonals of the original center cell will therefore assume the iterated values of a chaotic tent function. Figure 9, for example, shows the diverging patterns evolving from center cells having the initial seed values of 0.918 and 0.919, respectively. In the accompanying chart one can verify that the values of the cells propagating along the diagonals are precisely those of the iterated tent function for the initial seed values.

Real Life, therefore, demonstrates all the complexities of chaos. Though it contains Conway's Game of Life as a special case, Real Life exhibits a wider range of dynamical phenomena. It is interesting to note that our use of the chaotic tent function in Real Life follows a precedent set by Robert May, who used the chaotic logistic function to model ecological growth and decline.[7] The self-referential rules of Real Life can be formulated naturally within the context of a self-referential infinite-valued logic, and the patterns of Real Life exhibit the sensitive dependence on initial conditions characteristic of chaotic systems. With regard to matters of life and death, therefore, patterns in Real Life are more subject than are Conway's to the turbulence of the "chaotic currents of life."

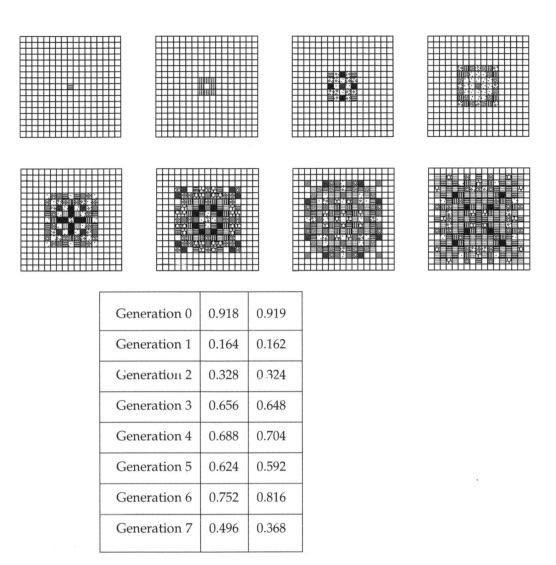

Generation 0	0.918	0.919
Generation 1	0.164	0.162
Generation 2	0.328	0.324
Generation 3	0.656	0.648
Generation 4	0.688	0.704
Generation 5	0.624	0.592
Generation 6	0.752	0.816
Generation 7	0.496	0.368

Figure 9 Cells propagating along the diagonals of the original center cell assume the iterated values of the chaotic tent function.

5.3 REAL-VALUED PRISONER'S DILEMMAS

Real Life has its fascinations, but for our purposes here it is merely an example: an example of the subtle and major differences that can appear—importantly, a sign of chaos—when we open our consideration to include a full continuum of values. In what follows we want to apply that same lesson to spatialized game theory by considering cellular automata instantiations of a continuous-valued Prisoner's Dilemma.

Recall that in the original Prisoner's Dilemma, two suspects are imprisoned separately. The District Attorney does not have enough evidence to convict the pair for their suspected crime. He does, however, have enough to imprison each on a lesser charge. Wishing to obtain a conviction for a more serious charge, the District Attorney offers to be lenient in sentencing the prisoner who will 'squeal' on his accomplice. If one prisoner squeals (i.e., defects on his accomplice) while the other 'sits tight' (i.e., cooperates with his accomplice), the prisoner who defects will get off scot-free while the one who cooperates will be sentenced to 5 years. If both prisoners independently reject the District Attorney's offer (i.e., they cooperate with each other), each prisoner will be sentenced to 2 years. However, if both prisoners squeal (i.e., defect) on each other, both will be sentenced to 4 years. Assuming a year in prison has a utility of -1, we obtain the following payoff matrix, with values shown for the row player:

	Cooperate	Defect
Cooperate	-2	-5
Defect	0	-4

If we represent not negative years in prison but positive years of freedom out of the next 5 years, we obtain the standard payoff matrix for the Prisoner's Dilemma:

	Cooperate	Defect
Cooperate	$R=3$	$S=0$
Defect	$T=5$	$P=1$

Here, as before, T is the *temptation* to defect, R is the *reward* for cooperation, P is the *punishment* for defection, and S is the *sucker's payoff*. Technically, a Prisoner's Dilemma matrix requires that $T > R > P > S$ and $2 \cdot R > T + S$.

No matter how convincingly one spins the standard Prisoner's Dilemma story, however, it remains artificial in a number of respects. 'Confession' is treated as an all-or-nothing affair, for example, with distinct punishments allotted in terms of it. But surely the normal case is one in which there are *degrees* of cooperation with the authorities as well as *degrees* to which each prisoner can 'keep the faith' with the other. Each prisoner may be *more or less* open about the details of the crime, and in return the authorities can be *more or less* generous in their treatment. In real life, cooperation (or defection) is rarely an all-or-nothing affair. Our choices are often a matter of cooperating and defecting to a certain degree, rather than of cooperating or defecting completely, and our rewards often depend on the relative levels of cooperation or defection.

Suppose, for example, that the prisoners can choose various levels of cooperation with the District Attorney. Let us say that the first prisoner neither wants to play the 'stool pigeon' nor be taken for the 'sucker'. He compromises and divulges only half the information the District Attorney requests. The second prisoner independently arrives at the same compromise. What happens when both the prisoners cooperate only 50%? We might expect the penalty for each to be somewhere between 2 to 4 years (the sentences for mutual cooperation and mutual defection, respectively). What would the payoffs be if one prisoner cooperates 75%, say, while the other cooperates only 25%? How can we generalize the above bivalent payoff matrix for continuously varying levels of cooperation between the prisoners?

One way would be to generalize the payoff matrix to the payoff plane shown in figure 10. This plane is the union of two triangular planes, one determined by the triple of points $\{(0, 0, P), (1, 1, R), (0, 1, T)\}$ and the other determined by $\{(0, 0, P), (1, 1, R), (1, 0, S)\}$. Given an ordered pair (x, y) specifying the first and second player's respective levels of cooperation, we can calculate the first player's payoff $f(x, y)$ as:

$$f(x, y) = \begin{cases} (R - T) \cdot x + (T - P) + P, & \text{if } x \geq y \\ (S - P) + (R - S) + P, & \text{if } y > x. \end{cases}$$

Notice that the corner values of the payoff plane are precisely the values—T, R, P, S—of the standard bivalent Prisoner's Dilemma payoff matrix. The payoff plane is symmetrical along the $x = y$ line, so the second player's payoff is given by $f(y, x)$.

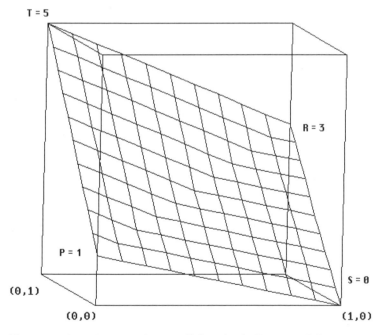

Figure 10 A continuous-value payoff plane for the Prisoner's Dilemma.

In what follows we want to return to a spatialized Hobbesian model, but with this new continuous-valued Prisoner's Dilemma at its base. One question will be whether continuous-valued forms of generosity evolve here as well. Here we will want to examine not only one-dimensional or reactive continuous-valued strategies, which respond to the last move by the opponent, but deeper forms of two-dimensional strategies, which respond to the configuration of play by both players on the previous round. In a further section we will also show a connection between some of these deeper strategies modeling and the nonlinear dynamics of self-referential sentences explored in chapter 1.

In chapter 4 we outlined Nowak and Sigmund's work regarding stochastic strategies, which cooperate or defect according to some probability other than 0 or 1. Nowak and Sigmund found Generous Tit for Tat (GTFT), which responds to defection with cooperation with a probability of 1/3, to be superior to TFT. By not responding to defection with defection 100% of the time, in particular, GTFT was able to avoid destructive bouts of backbiting exhibited by stochastically imperfect TFT. But Nowak and Sigmund's strategies, though stochastic, are still bivalent: though governed by probabilities, their cooperation and defection on any round are still all-or-nothing affairs. Does their generosity result carry over to genuinely continuous-valued Prisoner's Dilemmas?

The one-dimensional strategies can be generalized to continuous-valued ones by allowing fractional values in the ordered triple $\langle i, c, d \rangle$ specification of a strategy, where i, c, and d represent degrees of cooperation. The continuous-valued counterpart to Nowak and Sigmund's stochastic GTFT, for example, would be $\langle 1, 1, 1/3 \rangle$. What this means is perhaps clearest when represented graphically (figure 11). AllD, in a continuous-valued context, will always defect no matter what the other player's level of cooperation. It can thus be represented by the line $y = 0$. TFT, on the other hand, defects in response to defection $(0, 0)$ and cooperates in response to cooperation $(1, 1)$. One continuous-valued generalization of TFT is a strategy that mirrors its opponent's previous level of cooperation. This continuous-valued TFT is graphically represented by the line $y = x$ connecting the endpoints $(0, 0)$ and $(1, 1)$. In general, a linear continuous-valued generalization of a strategy $\langle i, c, d \rangle$ is given by $y = (c - d) \cdot x + d$ and represented by a line whose endpoints are $(0, d)$ and $(0, c)$.

Here it is helpful to introduce some descriptive terminology. A strategy will be called *friendly* to the extent it cooperates on the first move, and *suspicious* to the extent it defects. A *cooperative* strategy responds to cooperation with cooperation, whereas a *defective* strategy responds to cooperation with defection. Finally, a strategy will be called *exploitable* if it responds to defection with cooperation, and *unexploitable* if it responds to defection with defection.

Consider a tournament between two continuous-valued strategies, Generous TFT = $\langle 1, 1, 0.3 \rangle$ (GTFT), which is initially friendly, fully

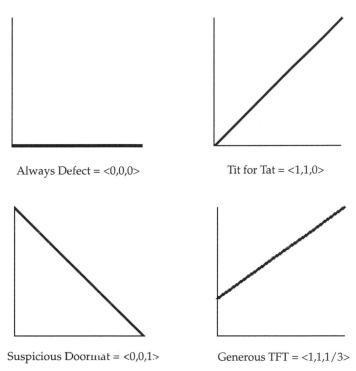

Always Defect = <0,0,0>

Tit for Tat = <1,1,0>

Suspicious Doormat = <0,0,1>

Generous TFT = <1,1,1/3>

Figure 11 Graphical representations of continuous-valued one-dimensional strategies.

cooperative in the face of cooperation, but mildly exploitable by defecting strategies, and a strategy we'll call Skeptical Reserved TFT = $\langle 0.2, 0.7, 0 \rangle$ (SRTFT), which is mildly unfriendly ('skeptical'), not fully cooperative ('reserved'), and completely unexploitable. In round one, GTFT plays 1 and SRTFT plays 0.2. Play in round 1 can then be represented as (1, 0.2). We then use the graphs of the strategies to obtain their next pair of moves. The graph for GTFT is specified by $y = (1 - 0.3) \cdot x + 0.3$, and the graph for SRTFT is specified by $y = 0.7 \cdot x$. Hence we have that GTFT's next move is $y = (1 - 0.3) \cdot 0.2 + 0.3 = 0.44$. SRTFT's next move is $y = 0.7 \cdot 1 = 0.7$. Play in round 2 is thus (0.44, 0.7). This can be represented graphically in the manner of figure 12. We then use the payoff plane to obtain the respective payoffs. Here are the results for the first 20 rounds, listed with cooperation levels and payoffs for GTFT first in each pair, shown in the following matrix.

The total score after twenty rounds is 3.32 for GTFT and 5.27 for SRTFT.

At the Fourth Summer Institute on Game Theory and Economics at the State University of New York at Stony Brook, July 1993, participants at the conference were invited to submit infinite-valued one-dimensional strategies to compete in a *spatialized* tournament of continuous-valued strategies. In this tournament each cell of an array played each of its eight neighbors in a competition of 200 games. At that point each cell surveyed its neighbors. If any did better in local competition, the cell adopted the

Real-Valued Game Theory: Real Life, Cooperative Chaos, and Discrimination

Round	Cooperation Levels	Payoffs
1	(1.00, 0.20)	(0.06, 0.46)
2	(0.44, 0.70)	(0.29, 0.16)
3	(0.79, 0.30)	(0.11, 0.35)
4	(0.51, 0.55)	(0.21, 0.19)
5	(0.68, 0.36)	(0.14, 0.30)
6	(0.55, 0.48)	(0.18, 0.22)
7	(0.63, 0.38)	(0.15, 0.27)
8	(0.57, 0.44)	(0.17, 0.23)
9	(0.61, 0.40)	(0.15, 0.26)
10	(0.58, 0.42)	(0.17, 0.24)
11	(0.60, 0.40)	(0.16, 0.25)
12	(0.58, 0.42)	(0.16, 0.25)
13	(0.59, 0.40)	(0.16, 0.25)
14	(0.58, 0.41)	(0.16, 0.25)
15	(0.59, 0.41)	(0.16, 0.25)
16	(0.58, 0.41)	(0.16, 0.25)
17	(0.59, 0.41)	(0.16, 0.25)
18	(0.58, 0.41)	(0.16, 0.25)
19	(0.58, 0.41)	(0.16, 0.25)
20	(0.58, 0.41)	(0.16, 0.25)

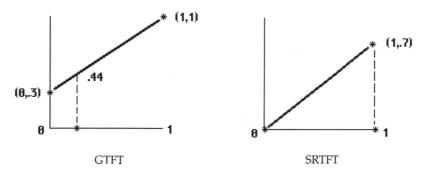

Figure 12 A graphical computation of payoffs in a game between GTFT $\langle 1, 1, 0.3 \rangle$ and SRFT $\langle 0.2, 0.7, 0 \rangle$.

strategy of a neighbor with a maximal score. The results after 1000 generations, expressed in terms of the percentage of the field occupied by particular strategies, were the following:

Strategy	Population %
$\langle 1.0, 1.00, 0.20 \rangle$	18.43%
$\langle 0.0, 0.80, 0.10 \rangle$	0.22%
$\langle 0.8, 0.80, 0.10 \rangle$	0.00%
$\langle 0.0, 0.50, 0.00 \rangle$	0.00%
$\langle 1.0, 1.00, 0.50 \rangle$	18.65%
$\langle 1.0, 1.00, 0.40 \rangle$	18.48%
$\langle 0.0, 0.00, 1.00 \rangle$	0.22%
$\langle 1.0, 0.51, 0.49 \rangle$	0.00%
$\langle 1.0, 0.9754, 0.0001 \rangle$	0.00%
$\langle 0.0, 0.90, 0.00 \rangle$	22.00%
$\langle 0.9, 1.00, 0.40 \rangle$	1.03%
$\langle 1.0, 1.00, 0.80 \rangle$	6.88%
$\langle 1.0, 1.00, 0.00 \rangle$	4.57%
$\langle 1.0, 0.90, 0.00 \rangle$	0.00%

Continues overleaf

Real-Valued Game Theory: Real Life, Cooperative Chaos, and Discrimination

Strategy	Population %
⟨0.9, 1.00, 0.10⟩	0.20%
⟨1.0, 1.00, 1.00⟩	1.56%
⟨0.0, 1.00, 0.00⟩	0.22%
⟨1.0, 1.00, 0.00⟩	6.10%
⟨0.5, 1.00, 0.00⟩	0.22%
⟨1.0, 1.00, 0.66⟩	10.21%
⟨1.0, 1.00, 0.33⟩	12.79%

In a spatial tournament with 27 trivalent strategies, using only the values 1, 0.3, and 0, we found that TFT and GTFT eventually take over, with TFT occupying about 75% of the field. In a similar tournament limited to suspicious strategies, the suspicious version of GTFT ⟨0, 1, 0.3⟩ completely takes over the field. In a spatial tournament among the friendly strategies of this sort, we obtained similar results to the trivalent tournament mentioned above.

By increasing the pool of strategies that cooperated fully in the face of cooperation but were less than completely friendly on the initial play, we were able to increase significantly the final percentage of GTFTs. In one tournament, for example, we obtained the following results:

Strategy	Coding	Round 0	Round 1	Round 2
Generous TFT	⟨1.0, 1.0, 0.3⟩	33.03%	91.72%	92.07%
TFT	⟨1.0, 1.0, 0.0⟩	33.67%	7.86%	7.91%
Reserved TFT	⟨0.7, 1.0, 0.0⟩	33.30%	0.42%	0.02%
Skeptical TFT	⟨0.3, 1.0, 0.0⟩	33.08%	0.00%	0.00%

In general, we took our results to confirm a Nowak and Sigmund-like result for the spatial and continuous-valued Prisoner's Dilemma. In the spatial setting, moreover, we found that strategies even more generous than GTFT (for example, ⟨1.0, 1.0, 0.4⟩) do even better. In chapter 4 it became clear that spatialization favors stochastic generosity. What these studies indicate is that local spatial modeling favors continuous-valued generosity as well.

GTFT's superiority to TFT in these competitions, it is important to note, is due to its 'generosity'—its willingness to risk exploitability for the sake of breaking a vicious cycle of mutual defection. TFT is completely unexploitable, and therefore it is constrained to rigidly pay back defection with defection. GTFT's weakness, on the other hand, is that its generosity is indiscriminate. This weakness is exposed when the competition is expanded to two-dimensional strategies, which we turn to next.

5.4 PAVLOV AND OTHER TWO-DIMENSIONAL STRATEGIES

A reactive or *one-dimensional* strategy is one for which each move, after the first, is strictly determined by the opponent's previous move. A *two-dimensional* strategy is one for which each move, after the first, is strictly determined not by merely by its opponent's previous move but by the previous *pair* of moves by both players.[8] In later work Nowak and Sigmund report that in the case of stochastic strategies the two-dimensional strategy known as PAVLOV is superior to GTFT.[9]

GTFT responds to defection with an indiscriminate generosity $1/3$ of the time. PAVLOV, on the other hand, can be more discriminating with its generosity. If its opponent defected while it cooperated, PAVLOV will defect. But PAVLOV will respond generously by cooperating after mutual defection. PAVLOV's strategy, which Nowak and Sigmund characterize as 'win-stay lose-shift', can be summarized in a matrix. PAVLOV cooperates only after mutual cooperation or mutual defection; that is, it cooperates after ⬜ but defects after ⬜:

		Opponent	
		Cooperate	Defect
PAVLOV	Cooperate	$R = 3$	$S = 0$
	Defect	$T = 5$	$P = 1$

Two-dimensional strategies can be represented as ordered five-tuples $\langle i, c_1, c_2, d_1, d_2 \rangle$. Here i is the strategy's initial response. The values c_1 and c_2 represent the strategy's responses to cooperation on the part of its opponent. The strategy's response to mutual cooperation in the previous round (i.e., [1, 1]) is designated as c_1; the strategy's response when it defected while its opponent cooperated (i.e., [1, 0]) is designated c_2. The values d_1 and d_2 represent the strategy's response to defection on the part of its opponent. Here d_1 is the strategy's response to being taken advantage of in the previous round (i.e., its opponent defected while it cooperated,

[0, 1]), and d_2 is the strategy's response to mutual defection (i.e., [0, 0]). There will be thirty-two two-dimensional bivalent strategies:

1	$\langle 1, 1, 1, 1, 1 \rangle$	17	$\langle 0, 1, 1, 1, 1 \rangle$
2	$\langle 1, 1, 1, 1, 0 \rangle$	18	$\langle 0, 1, 1, 1, 0 \rangle$
3	$\langle 1, 1, 1, 0, 1 \rangle$	19	$\langle 0, 1, 1, 0, 1 \rangle$
4	$\langle 1, 1, 1, 0, 0 \rangle$	20	$\langle 0, 1, 1, 0, 0 \rangle$
5	$\langle 1, 1, 0, 1, 1 \rangle$	21	$\langle 0, 1, 0, 1, 1 \rangle$
6	$\langle 1, 1, 0, 1, 0 \rangle$	22	$\langle 0, 1, 0, 1, 0 \rangle$
7	$\langle 1, 1, 0, 0, 1 \rangle$	23	$\langle 0, 1, 0, 0, 1 \rangle$
8	$\langle 1, 1, 0, 0, 0 \rangle$	24	$\langle 0, 1, 0, 0, 0 \rangle$
9	$\langle 1, 0, 1, 1, 1 \rangle$	25	$\langle 0, 0, 1, 1, 1 \rangle$
10	$\langle 1, 0, 1, 1, 0 \rangle$	26	$\langle 0, 0, 1, 1, 0 \rangle$
11	$\langle 1, 0, 1, 0, 1 \rangle$	27	$\langle 0, 0, 1, 0, 1 \rangle$
12	$\langle 1, 0, 1, 0, 0 \rangle$	28	$\langle 0, 0, 1, 0, 0 \rangle$
13	$\langle 1, 0, 0, 1, 1 \rangle$	29	$\langle 0, 0, 0, 1, 1 \rangle$
14	$\langle 1, 0, 0, 1, 0 \rangle$	30	$\langle 0, 0, 0, 1, 0 \rangle$
15	$\langle 1, 0, 0, 0, 1 \rangle$	31	$\langle 0, 0, 0, 0, 1 \rangle$
16	$\langle 1, 0, 0, 0, 0 \rangle$	32	$\langle 0, 0, 0, 0, 0 \rangle$

PAVLOV cooperates if and only if the previous pair of moves were the same. So PAVLOV is specified by $\langle 1, 1, 0, 0, 1 \rangle$. One-dimensional strategies are special cases of two-dimensional strategies in which $c_1 = c_2$ and $d_1 = d_2$; for example, TFT $= \langle 1, 1, 1, 0, 0 \rangle$.

Here again it is useful to introduce some descriptive terminology. Let us say that the value c_1 is a measure of a strategy's *constructiveness* or *destructiveness*. A constructive strategy will tend to continue to cooperate after there has been mutual cooperation, whereas a destructive strategy will give in to the temptation to defect. The value c_2 is a measure of a strategy's being *merciful* or *exploitative*. A merciful strategy will cooperate after successfully defecting on a cooperating opponent, whereas an exploitative strategy will continue to press its advantage by continuing to defect. The value d_1 measures the strategy's tendency to be *forgiving* or *vengeful*. A forgiving strategy will continue to cooperate even after its opponent has defected when it cooperated; a vengeful strategy will defect after its has been 'burned' when its opponent defected while it cooperated. Finally, the value d_2 measures the strategy's *dovish* or *hawkish* tendencies. A dove will attempt to turn the tide of mutual defection by giving cooperation a chance. A hawk will insist on defection after a previous round of mutual defection.

Using this terminology, TFT can be characterized as completely friendly on initial play, constructive, and merciful, but also completely vengeful and hawkish. PAVLOV, on the other hand, is completely friendly on initial play, constructive, and dovish, but also completely exploitative and vengeful.

Nowak and Sigmund show PAVLOV to be superior to GTFT in a nonspatial competition. Is PAVLOV still superior to GTFT once we spatialize the Prisoner's Dilemma? Is there another a two-dimensional strategy that is superior even to PAVLOV in a spatial context? The answer to both questions is 'yes'. PAVLOV is consistently beaten in spatial competition by strategy 8 above, the continuous-valued counterpart to a GRIM strategy.[10] GRIM is initially completely friendly and constructive, but it is also completely exploitative, vengeful, and hawkish. Here, for example, is a typical tournament ranking after twenty generations of a two-dimensional bivalent spatial tournament:

Strategy	Coding	Population Percentage
GRIM	$\langle 1, 1, 0, 0, 0 \rangle$	91.2%
PAVLOV	$\langle 1, 1, 0, 0, 1 \rangle$	7.0%
Tit for Tat	$\langle 1, 1, 1, 0, 0 \rangle$	1.4%
Converse	$\langle 1, 1, 1, 0, 1 \rangle$	0.4%

GRIM cooperates if you cooperate with it, but any defection on your part leads to unrelenting defection, no matter how many times you cooperate. This rigid lack of generosity is reminiscent of TFT, and suggests that we look to more generously continuous-valued two-dimensional strategies. Are there continuous-valued strategies that are superior to GRIM in same way that GTFT is superior to TFT?[11]

Continuous-valued two-dimensional strategies can be represented graphically as the union of two triangular planes, each determined by one of the triples $\{\langle 1, 1, c_1 \rangle, \langle 0, 0, d_2 \rangle, \langle 1, 0, c_2 \rangle\}$ and $\{\langle 1, 1, c_1 \rangle, \langle 0, 0, d_2 \rangle, \langle 0, 1, d_1 \rangle\}$. These continuous-valued two-dimensional strategies are specified by:

$$s(x, y) = \begin{cases} (c_1 - d_1) \cdot x + (d_1 - d_2) \cdot y + d_2, & \text{if } x \geq y \\ (c_2 - d_2) \cdot x + (c_1 - c_2) \cdot y + d_2, & \text{if } y > x \end{cases}$$

The number of possible strategies is now fairly large compared to the size of our playing field. Tournament outcomes are therefore fairly sensitive to the initial distribution of strategies. We can simulate some of the effects of a larger playing field, however, by introducing clustering. In a larger playing field, there would tend to be more and larger clusters of similar strategies. Such clusters could model the effects, for example, of families or other groupings with similar strategies.

Restricting ourselves to a 64×64 playing field, we decided to simulate the effect of a larger playing field by clustering instead of making the initial distribution completely random. Here we assigned a *cluster value* to the distribution as a whole. The cluster value is a probability assigned that a cell will match one of the four adjacent cells generated before it—three cells to the left and one directly above it—rather than the strategy it would otherwise be assigned randomly. If a cell does cluster, each of those previous cells is given an equal chance of its strategy being copied by the new cell.[12] A cluster value of 0 thus gives us a completely random distribution—a probability of 0 that an otherwise random strategy assignment will be superseded by clustering. At the beginning of the series of strategy assignments we read 'probability of matching one of four preceding cells' to mean 'probability of matching preceding cells up to four'. A cluster value of 1 would thus mean that whichever strategy appeared first would occupy the whole playing field. Practically speaking, with a 64×64 field, we found 85% was the highest cluster value we could use without biasing the initial percentages of each strategy too much. Higher values tended to result in so much clustering that some strategies had drastically higher initial percentages than others, thus giving an unnatural bias to certain random strategies.

Spatial tournaments run with clustering suggest that being friendly and constructive has significant survival value. Recall that TFT, which dominated the one-dimensional bivalent tournament, exhibited these qualities. In the continuous-valued case, however, GTFT's generosity gave it an advantage over TFT by breaking destructive cycles of mutual defection. In the spatial setting, moreover, PAVLOV remains superior to GTFT since PAVLOV's two-dimensionality allows its generosity to be more discriminate.[13] PAVLOV, however, is indiscriminately dovish and loses to the completely hawkish GRIM.

Our continuous-valued two-dimensional spatial tournaments appear to favor strategies that are less bivalent—strategies more hawkish than PAVLOV, but more dovish than GRIM. The addition of variations of PAVLOV with a range of hawkish/dovish values ranging from 0.1 to 0.9 strongly favored merciful and non-exploitative strategies like TFT. Clustering, in fact, hinders domination by GRIM and improves the chances of constructive and merciful strategies like TFT. Here for example is the result of one of the spatial two-dimensional *bivalent* tournaments after 20 generations:

Strategies	Coding	Cluster $=0\%$	Cluster $=20\%$	Cluster $=50\%$	Cluster $=85\%$
GRIM	$\langle 1, 1, 0, 0, 0 \rangle$	91.2%	88.2%	77.9%	65.6%
PAVLOV	$\langle 1, 1, 0, 0, 1 \rangle$	7.0%	9.0%	12.9%	24.7%
TFT	$\langle 1, 1, 1, 0, 0 \rangle$	1.4%	2.2%	7.3%	6.0%
Converse	$\langle 1, 1, 1, 0, 1 \rangle$	0.4%	0.6%	1.9%	3.7%

Here in contrast are results of a tournament including hawkish to dovish variations of PAVLOV ranging from 0.1 to 0.9, with a clustering value of 85%. The chart shows results after 60 generations:

Strategy	Coding	Population %
TFT	$\langle 1, 1, 1, 0, 0 \rangle$	61.4%
GRIM	$\langle 1, 1, 0, 0, 0 \rangle$	19.5%
PAVLOV	$\langle 1, 1, 0, 0, 1 \rangle$	15.0%
Converse	$\langle 1, 1, 1, 0, 1 \rangle$	2.9%
Skeptical PAVLOV	$\langle 0, 1, 0, 0, 1 \rangle$	0.8%
Dovish Skeptical PAVLOV	$\langle 0, 1, 0, 0, 0.6 \rangle$	0.4%

Clustering appears to benefit TFT by the formation of cooperatives in which TFT's mercifulness facilitates mutual cooperation.

We shall now turn our attention to a natural embedding of our continuous-valued two-dimensional strategies in an infinite-valued logic. In this context PAVLOV leads quite naturally to chaotic cooperative dynamics.

5.5 COOPERATIVE CHAOS IN INFINITE-VALUED LOGIC

The infinite-valued logic we shall use here is that outlined in chapters 1 and 3. Our basic connectives are:

$$/\sim \mathbf{p}/ = 1 - /\mathbf{p}/$$
$$/(\mathbf{p} \wedge \mathbf{q})/ = \text{Min}\{/\mathbf{p}/, /\mathbf{q}/\}$$
$$/(\mathbf{p} \vee \mathbf{q})/ = \text{Max}\{/\mathbf{p}/, /\mathbf{q}/\},$$

where $/\mathbf{p}/$ stands for the value of the proposition $\mathbf{p}$. Here we shall insist on the Łukasiewiczian conditional:

$$/(\mathbf{p} \rightarrow \mathbf{q})/ = \text{Min}\{1, 1 - /\mathbf{p}/ + /\mathbf{q}/\}.$$

Given the standard definition of the biconditional as the conjunction of a conditional and its converse, the value of a biconditional will be the extent to which the values of its constituents do not differ, that is,

$$/(\mathbf{p} \leftrightarrow \mathbf{q})/ = 1 - \text{Abs}(/\mathbf{p}/ - /\mathbf{q}/).$$

The naturalness of this embedding is confirmed by the fact that the two-dimensional strategies that emerged as dominant in our two-dimensional bivalent tournament correspond to standard logical connectives. Ignoring the initial move, the remaining four values in the specification of a two-dimensional strategy correspond to the final column of a truth table for standard binary logical connectives:

Strategy	Coding	Symbol	Connective
GRIM	$\langle 1, 1, 0, 0, 0 \rangle$	$(\mathbf{p} \wedge \mathbf{q})$	Conjunction
PAVLOV	$\langle 1, 1, 0, 0, 1 \rangle$	$(\mathbf{p} \leftrightarrow \mathbf{q})$	Biconditional
Tit for Tat	$\langle 1, 1, 1, 0, 0 \rangle$	$\mathbf{p}$	Left Projection
Converse	$\langle 1, 1, 1, 0, 1 \rangle$	$(\mathbf{p} \leftarrow \mathbf{q})$	Converse Conditional

The winning strategies of the bivalent two-dimensional spatial tournament can, in fact, all be expressed in sentences using standard logical connectives:

GRIM: I will cooperate if, and only if, both my opponent cooperated *and* I cooperated.

PAVLOV: I will cooperate if, and only if, my opponent cooperated *if and only if* I cooperated.

TFT: I will cooperate if and only if my opponent cooperated.

CONVERSE: I will cooperate if, and only if, my opponent cooperated *if* I cooperated.

Our basic strategies can thus also be exhibited in terms of the Łukasiewicizian truth solids introduced in chapter 3. This surprising graphical correspondence is illustrated in figure 13.

Having embedded our two-dimensional strategies within an infinite-valued logic, we can now take advantage of 'dynamical semantics', outlined in chapter 1 as an application of dynamical systems theory to study the semantic paradoxes. We will present PAVLOV in our infinite-valued logic using the following scheme of abbreviation:

$\mathbf{p}_n$: I cooperated in game n

$\mathbf{q}_n$: My opponent cooperated in game n

$\mathbf{p}_{n+1}$: I will cooperate in game $n+1$.

PAVLOV can then be expressed as a nested biconditional:

$\mathbf{p}_{n+1} \leftrightarrow (\mathbf{q}_n \leftrightarrow \mathbf{p}_n)$

It seems natural to interpret the truth-value of the proposition $\mathbf{p}_{n+1}$ as PAVLOV's level of cooperation in game $n+1$. The self-referential component in the above strategies can then be modeled by iteration. Using the infinite-valued Łukasiewiczian rule for the biconditional, we obtain the following dynamical system for PAVLOV:

$x_{n+1} = 1 - \text{Abs}(y_n - x_n),$

where $/\mathbf{p}_{n+1}/ = x_{n+1}$, $/\mathbf{p}_n/ = x_n$, and $/\mathbf{q}_n/ = y_n$.

Let us further assume that the opponent's level of cooperation can be expressed as a function $\text{OP}(x_n)$ of PAVLOV's level of cooperation x_n. PAVLOV's successive levels of cooperation can then be computed using the algorithm

$x_{n+1} = 1 - \text{Abs}(\text{OP}(x_n) - x_n).$

If, for example, PAVLOV is playing Quaker, which always cooperates completely, then PAVLOV will continue to cooperate at its initial level of cooperation. A completely suspicious PAVLOV $\langle 0, 1, 0, 0, 1 \rangle$ will continue to defect completely, a completely friendly PAVLOV $\langle 1, 1, 0, 0, 1 \rangle$ will continue to cooperate completely, and a moderately suspicious PAVLOV $\langle 1/3, 1, 0, 0, 1 \rangle$ will continue to cooperate at a level of $1/3$.

Suppose PAVLOV is playing a strategy that cooperates at 50% of PAVLOV's current level of cooperation. PAVLOV's successive levels of cooperation is then given by

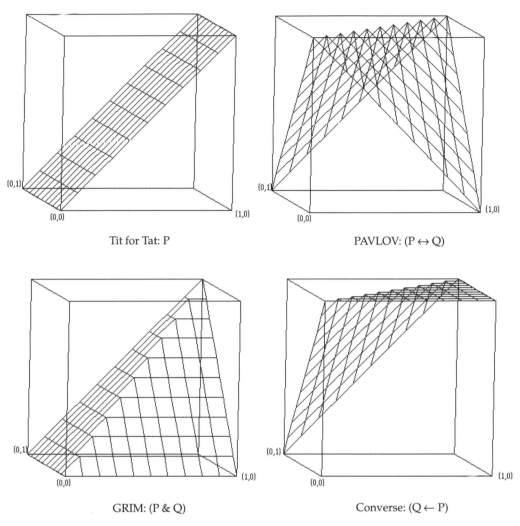

Tit for Tat: P

PAVLOV: $(P \leftrightarrow Q)$

GRIM: $(P \& Q)$

Converse: $(Q \leftarrow P)$

Figure 13 Continuous-valued two-dimensional strategies correspond to infinite-valued Łukasiewicz connectives.

$$x_{n+1} = 1 - \mathrm{Abs}(0.5 \cdot x_n - x_n).$$

We can graphically represent the evolution of cooperation in this dynamical system using a web diagram. In this case, the web diagram exhibits the fixed-point attractor characteristic of the Half-Sayer, outlined in chapter 1. No matter what the initial levels of cooperation, both players are inevitably drawn toward a level of 2/3 mutual cooperation (figure 14).

Or consider the perverse case of an opponent who *defects* to the extent that PAVLOV *cooperates*. In that case PAVLOV's successive levels of cooperation is given by

$$x_{n+1} = 1 - \mathrm{Abs}((1 - x_n) - x_n).$$

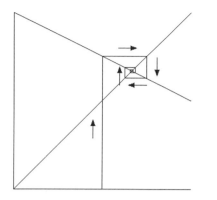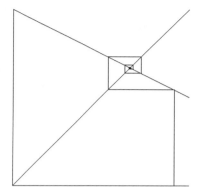

Figure 14 Cooperation with PAVLOV to a level of 50% of PAVLOV's level of cooperation yields a fixed-point attractor at 2/3, corresponding to the Half-Sayer of chapter 1.

Alternatively, we may suppose PAVLOV is playing an opponent who cooperates to the extent that their previous levels of cooperation differed. The two components of the dynamical system are then given by:

$$y_{n+1} = \text{Abs}(y_n - x_n)$$

and

$$x_{n+1} = 1 - \text{Abs}(y_n - x_n).$$

If PAVLOV's opponent initially defects to the extent PAVLOV initially cooperates, we would again obtain

$$x_{n+1} = 1 - \text{Abs}((1 - x_n) - x_n)$$

as a description of PAVLOV's successive levels of cooperation. This dynamical system is the now familiar Chaotic Liar (figure 15).

We can also go on to model 'very' and 'fairly' in terms of squares and square roots, in the tradition of fuzzy logic outlined in chapter 1. This would allow a fuzzy variation of PAVLOV, whose strategy can be expressed as follows:

I will cooperate in game $n+1$ if, and only if, my opponent's level of cooperative was not *very* different from my level of cooperation in game n.

Given an opponent's previous level of cooperation is y_n, PAVLOV's successive moves are then given by:

$$x_{n+1} = 1 - (y_n - x_n)^2.$$

Considering again the perverse case in which PAVLOV's opponent defects to the extent that PAVLOV cooperates, we find that PAVLOV's responses are given by the famous logistic map (figure 16):

$$x_{n+1} = 1 - ((1 - x_n) - x_n)^2 = 4x_n(1 - x_n).$$

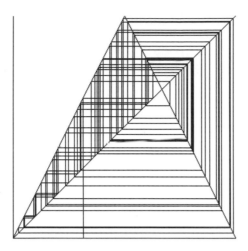

Figure 15 Defection to the extent that a continuous-valued PAVLOV cooperates yields the chaotic tent function, corresponding to the Chaotic Liar of chapter 1.

Another fuzzy variation of PAVLOV that also yields the logistic map is:

I will cooperate in game $n+1$ if, and only if, the value of my opponent's being *very* cooperative was not *very* different from the value of my being *very* cooperative in game n.

Here as in previous chapters, the emergence of chaos suggests the presence of fractal images. One way to investigate the cooperative dynamics between our continuous-valued PAVLOV

$$x_{n+1} = 1 - \mathrm{Abs}(y_n - x_n)$$

and a continuous-valued ANTI-PAVLOV

$$y_{n+1} = 1 - \mathrm{Abs}((1 - x_n) - y_n),$$

which cooperates to the extent PAVLOV defects, would be to use an escape-time diagram of the form outlined in chapter 1. In our escape-time diagram, we assign each point in the coordinate plane a different color depending on the number of iterations it takes the point to move under iteration across some chosen threshold. A natural threshold would be a specified vector distance $d = \sqrt{x^2 + y^2}$ from $(0, 0)$ or complete mutual defection. Here we have chosen a threshold to be slightly over 1, or a vector distance of combined cooperation levels equal to complete cooperation. In figure 17 the four corners of the unit square are the tangent points of the four circles. Figure 17 as a whole, however, exhibits a familiar fractal image in which the cooperation levels for x and y are extended a unit in each direction.

The Prisoner's Dilemma has become a paradigm of game theory, often used to illustrate the evolution of cooperation. In this chapter we have tried to make it more realistic, not only by developing it in the spatial context of a cellular automata playing field, but by replacing the standard

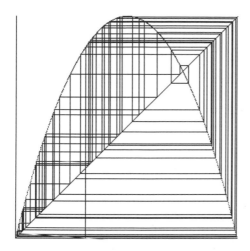

Figure 16 PAVLOV's opponent defects to the extent that PAVLOV cooperates: the Logistic map.

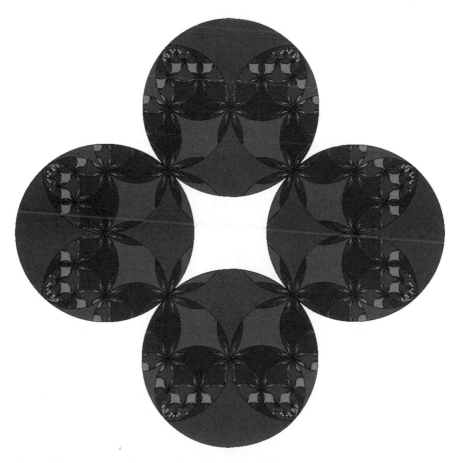

Figure 17 An escape-time diagram with a threshold of mutual cooperation between a continuous-valued PAVLOV and ANTI-PAVLOV: the Chaotic Dualist of chapter 1.

Real-Valued Game Theory: Real Life, Cooperative Chaos, and Discrimination

assumption of bivalence with degrees of cooperation and defection. Spatialization brings about the emergence of continuous-valued strategies more successful than TFT, more generous that GTFT, and less dovish than PAVLOV. It turns out we can embed the continuous-valued Prisoner's Dilemma within an infinite-valued logic, allowing us to build on earlier results in proving that the cooperative dynamics between continuous-valued strategies are paradigmatically chaotic. The presence of chaos signals a practical unpredictability that is characteristic of many real life choice situations.

5.6   THE PROBLEM OF DISCRIMINATION

A number of philosophers and social scientists have tried to extract profound conclusions about the evolution of cooperation and the nature of ethics from simplified Prisoner's Dilemma tournaments. We have noted previously how tempting it is to think of strategies such as TFT and GTFT as themselves genuinely 'cooperative' or 'generous' in an ethical sense, rather than simply as mathematical models of certain formal dynamics. From there some have treated it as a short step to the conclusion that these models show how genuine ethics evolves as an epiphenomenon of social dynamics, or even show that ethics is nothing more than that strategy of social interaction that has proven evolutionarily dominant. Philosopher of biology Michael Ruse has expressed this Darwinian position in particularly blunt terms:

Once we see that our moral beliefs are simply an adaptation put in place by natural selection, in order to further our reproductive ends, that is an end to it. Morality is no more than a collective illusion fobbed off on us by our genes for reproductive ends.[14]

Ruse candidly admits that his Darwinian naturalism, rather than *explaining* the biological basis of morality, ends up *explaining away* any reason we have for believing in morality at all. However, rather than attempting to justify his claims Ruse assumes its correctness to answer charges of its implausibility:

Morality remains without foundation. Yet, to ask one final question, Why does such a thesis as is being argued for here seem so intuitively implausible? Why does it seem—or so it appears to many people—so ridiculous to argue that morality is not more than an illusion of genes? Why does it seem so silly to suggest that moral claims are on par with the rule in cricket law that there should be six balls to an over? . . . . There is a simple answer and when seen it adds to the evolutionist's case rather than detracts from it. The simple fact is that if we recognized morality to be no more than an epiphenomenon of our biology, we would cease to believe in it and stop acting upon it. At once, therefore, the powerful forces which make us co-operators would collapse. Unfortunately, from a biological point of view, although some of us might get an immediate gain, most of us would be losers.[15]

We have said before that we are deeply suspicious of any such leap: at the very least, any such position demands a great deal of argument above and beyond what mere formal modeling can provide.

A clear—and formal—indication of how wrong-headed it can be to identify morality with successful strategies can be found in a range of strategies that haven't yet been discussed in the literature. One point of interest about these strategies is that they show a clear pattern of evolutionary dominance in a wide range of environments, and yet are clearly *not* strategies we are tempted to characterize as genuinely ethical. Another point of interest is that these strategies offer quite clear analogues to a very real social problem: race, class, gender discrimination. In these final few sections we want to consider an issue that is quite seriously a real life issue, though we will approach it in terms of formal game theory.

We call a strategy *discriminatory* if it adopts one strategy against players of another color and a different strategy against strategies of its own color. Discriminatory TFT (DTFT), in particular, adopts the strategy of TFT with strategies of its own color but adopts the strategy of Always Defect (AllD) when playing strategies of other colors. In the classical bivalent Prisoner's Dilemmas of the Axelrod studies, we've seen, it is TFT that is given the highest marks. But TFT fares poorly in competition against DTFT. DTFT punishes individual efforts to establish an impartial, color-blind TFT, and DTFT, once entrenched, is stable.[16]

In a first tournament we pitted the eight possible bivalent one-dimensional or reactive strategies against two forms of DTFT. The two DTFTs quickly eliminated all the first-order strategies with the possible exception of clusters of TFT. This clustering result is somewhat surprising, since TFT individually always has a lower individual score against a neighboring DTFT. In a spatial model, small clusters of TFT could survive in spite of the fact that a TFT on the 'front lines' always loses to DTFT. The reason why a cooperative community of TFT can survive is that a TFT from within the TFT community achieves an even higher score than the opposing DTFT and so steps in to replace the TFT on the 'front lines'. Spatialization, therefore, models the survival value of cooperative communities (figure 18).

The surviving communities of TFT, however, are quite marginalized and static. It is interesting to note that an initial distribution with an even higher percentage of Quakers (AllC) is detrimental to TFT. Quakers, while peacefully co-existing with TFT, are easily exploited by DTFT. The Quakers, in effect, occupy regions that will be eventually occupied by exploitative strategies such as AllD and DTFT. We mention this phenomenon now since we later investigate conditions that contribute to the survival of strategies more generous or forgiving than regular TFT but less exploitable than Quaker.

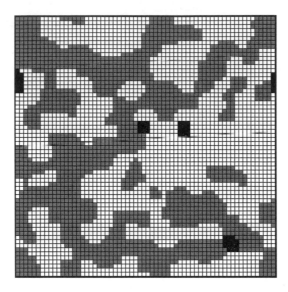

Figure 18 The eight simple reactive strategies are readily eliminated by the two DTFTs (shown in white and grey), with the possible exception of clusters of TFT (shown in black). Here after 12 generations TFT survives in stable but marginalized communities.

What if we include all discriminatory strategies in such a tournament—all reactive strategies that may treat others differently than they treat themselves? Since there are eight reactive or one-dimensional strategies, there will be sixty-four such discriminatory strategies. In a second tournament, we explored whether DTFT would still emerge as the dominant strategy from an evolutionary tournament involving competition with all possible discriminatory strategies. In our model we coded the sixty-four possible discriminatory strategies as a pair of triples or a six-tuple. The first triple of the code represents what strategy is adopted with its own color; the second triple represents the strategy adopted against all others. Thus, for example, we have

Discriminatory TFT	DTFT	$\langle 110, 000 \rangle$
Discriminatory Quaker	DQ	$\langle 111, 000 \rangle$
(Color-Blind) Tit for Tat	TFT	$\langle 110, 110 \rangle$

Rather than simple displacement by the winner in the center cell, we decided to use a *genetic algorithm* to preserve some diversity and variability within the population. The basic idea of genetic algorithms is to hybridize coded characterizations—in this case, coded characterizations of strategies—much as chromosomes are crossed in sexual reproduction. In general, genetic algorithms proceed on two lines of code by randomly choosing a break point in each line and by combining code before that break point from one element with code after that break point from the other.[17] Here we used a genetic algorithm to cross the strategy of a center cell with that strategy obtaining a maximal score in the nine-cell neighborhood. To implement genetic crossing, we rolled a six-sided die and flipped a coin as randomizing devices. We can explain the method with a simple example. Suppose the die roll is four and the flip is heads. The genetic crossing is the result of taking the first four elements of the winning strategy and concatenating it with the last two elements of the strategy in the center. If, on the other hand, the result is tails, we reverse the order of which segment is first in the crossing: we take the first four elements of the center strategy and concatenate it with the last two elements of the winning strategy. The strategy that is the result of the genetic crossing replaces the center cell at each generation.

Genetic algorithms allow for a measure of elegance. Seeding the field with a random distribution of all sixty-four discriminatory strategies would lead to overcrowding. Using a genetic algorithm, however, we found that we could simulate a random distribution by seeding the field initially with just the two pure strategies—AllD and AllC ('Adam and Eve')—as shown in the first frame of figure 19. By the third generation, the genetic algorithm results in an explosion of diversity, simulating a field with a random distribution of discriminatory strategies (figure 19b). The use of genetic algorithms also allows for the possibility that a strategy eliminated at an earlier stage could be reintroduced by genetic crossing at a later stage. In this way, cooperative strategies that are not well suited to an early competitive environment may be reintroduced to prove themselves successful at a later stage.

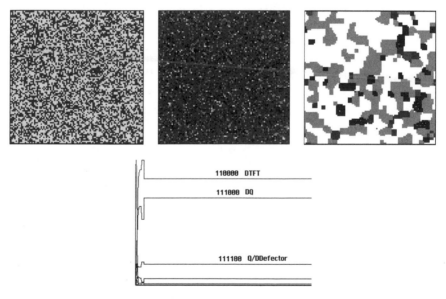

Figure 19 Evolution of a genetic algorithm-evolved field of discriminatory strategies. Generation 1, seeded with just AllD and AllC, explodes into a wide range of diversity by generation 3. By generation 21 an equilibrium is established between DTFT (white), DQ (light grey), and Quaker/Deceptive Defector (black).

In our second tournament we used a genetic algorithm with bivalent discriminatory strategies to see whether DTFT and DQ would still emerge as dominant in competition with a fuller range of strategies. Figure 19 shows such a tournament at generations 1, 3, and 21. We found it is typical for an array to reach equilibrium by generation 21 or so, with a clear dominance by the discriminatory strategies DTFT (here 52%), DQ (35%), and a discriminatory combination of Quaker with Deceptive Defector (8%). In a field of discriminatory strategies, TFT is no longer the optimal strategy: discrimination is more successful than impartial fairness.

It is clear from even these simple examples that discriminatory strategies play an important and domineering role in the simple game theoretic environments at issue. This comes as close as a formal argument can, we think, to making the philosophical point that socially dominant strategies need not in any way be genuinely ethical ones.

5.7 CONTINUITY IN COOPERATION, THE 'VEIL OF IGNORANCE', AND FORGIVENESS

In the previous section, we limited our discussion of models of discrimination to classically bivalent strategies, which cooperate or defect fully and determinately on any given round. What happens if we once again open our modeling to encompass a range of degrees of cooperation and defection?

With an eye to the problem of discrimination, we also want to add another continuous value to our model: that of a 'veil of ignorance'. One thing that a formal model of race, class, or gender discrimination can give us is a way of investigating how one might disarm discrimination. One influential philosophical model in this regard is of course that of John Rawls, whose *Theory of Justice* uses a 'veil of ignorance' regarding information such as one's social standing or ethnic background's to cancel out the effects of partiality. In a political context, the veil of ignorance could correspond to limiting access to a job applicant's sex, race, or ethnicity. More recently, in "Darwin Meets *The Logic of Decision*," Brian Skyrms has argued that the precondition for normal cooperation in the strongly shared fate of somatic-line cells is analogous to the cooperation Rawls tried to engineer behind the 'veil of ignorance'.[18] Skyrms dubs this the 'Darwinian Veil of Ignorance'.

We modeled the idea of a veil of ignorance in our tournaments by limiting the extent to which a strategy could correctly identify the color of its opponent. The intuitive idea is that we could undermine the advantage of discriminatory strategies by 'dimming the lights.' Clearly such a limitation would affect only discriminatory strategies like DTFT, since the simple reactive strategies are too unsophisticated to take advantage of such information.

Let us define an *impartial* strategy as a discriminatory strategy in which the first triple is identical to the second. We modeled a *veil of ignorance* by introducing a stochastic parameter v as a measure of the extent to which a strategy is able to correctly identify the color of its opponent. If the random number generator gives us a value less than v, then the discriminatory strategy will choose the *wrong* strategy—it plays against its own color what it normally plays against its opponent, and vice versa.

The imposition of a veil of ignorance does, we found, make some important differences in the evolution of arrays of strategies. But in a field of standard strategies, either bivalent or continuous-valued, a veil of ignorance below a level of mere randomness does not simply defeat discriminatory strategies or restore the dominance of impartiality.

In a third series of computer tournaments, we investigated the effect of small imperfections in the degrees of cooperation and defection among the eight reactive strategies and two dominating discriminatory strategies DTFT and DQ. Here we simply replaced values of full cooperation for such strategies with a cooperation of 99%, values of full defection with values of cooperation of 1%. In such an environment, a veil of ignorance set at 0.4 typically led to an intriguing symbiotic relationship between imperfect versions of DQ and Suspicious TFT (010, 010). This is represented by the zig-zag graph in figure 20. STFT is of course an impartial strategy, but DQ is not. The third major strategy on the graph, which makes a comeback and subsists at a subsidiary level, is AllD.

A full tournament incorporating all multivalent discriminatory strategies would require strategy coding strings of length twelve, quickly exceeding the speed and memory limitations of our computers. To increase the generality of our results, therefore, we decided to combine discriminatory strategies with multivalent reactive strategies.

To model multivalent strategies, we used two binary bits each to code i, c, and d in the standard three-tuple representations of reactive strategies. We chose to represent the valences 1, 2/3, 1/3, and 0 by the codes (1, 1), (0, 1), (1, 0), and (0, 0), respectively. Thus, Generous TFT = $\langle 1, 1, 1/3 \rangle$ would be coded by the binary string $\langle 11, 11, 10 \rangle$, while Forgiving TFT = $\langle 1, 1, 2/3 \rangle$ would be coded by the binary string $\langle 11, 11, 01 \rangle$.

To combine multivalence with discrimination we adopted a method that allowed us to read the binary code for a strategy in two ways. In this dual coding system each six-tuple is alternatively read as a multivalent reactive strategy as above, as well as a bivalent discriminatory strategy. Rather than simply concatenating two triples, we interweave them. The odd numbered elements of the six-tuple code the bivalent reactive strategy played with the strategy's own color; the even numbered elements code the strategy adopted against all other strategies. The two i values for the discriminatory strategies are then combined to determine the i value for the multivalent strategy, and similarly for c and d. This method of interweaving allows the alternate values for i, c, and d to be adjacent to one another and to be

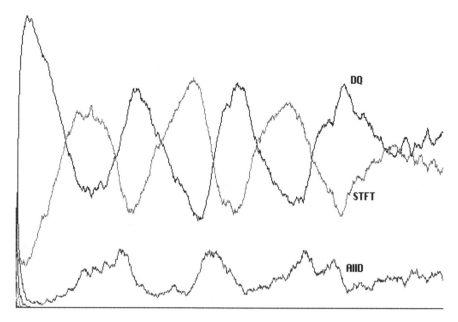

Figure 20 Symbiosis between DQ and STFT in a field of slightly imperfect versions of the eight reactive strategies together with DTFT and DQ, shown over 1000 generations. Here the veil of ignorance is set at 0.4.

combined into the multivalent strategy. This method also makes it less likely that the genetic algorithm would separate information that is relevant to the strategy's initial response, its response to cooperativeness, or its response to defection.

In this final tournament, we used the dual coding for strategies, which therefore played alternately as discriminatory strategies and multivalent strategies. Here veil levels of 1/3 and 2/3 were significant points of instability. Above a veil level of 1/3, generous strategies such as 111110, alternatively read as Quaker/TFT and GTFT $\langle 1, 1, 1/3 \rangle$, play an important role. Above a veil level of 2/3, strategy 111101, alternatively read as Quaker/Doormat and FTFT, is clearly dominant. Runs of 1000 generations are shown in figure 21.

We began with the perhaps disturbing result that discriminatory strategies DTFT and DQ have a decisive advantage over color-blind, impartial TFT. Such a result seems to provide both a prediction of success and a strategic rationale for discriminatory practices and separatist movements that violate our intuitive conceptions of justice as fairness or impartiality.

The optimistic side of the tournaments offered here is that there are prospects for environmental changes, worthy of further investigation, that can restore a major role for impartiality, generosity, and forgiveness. Dual-coding a model intended to capture a full spread of impartial and

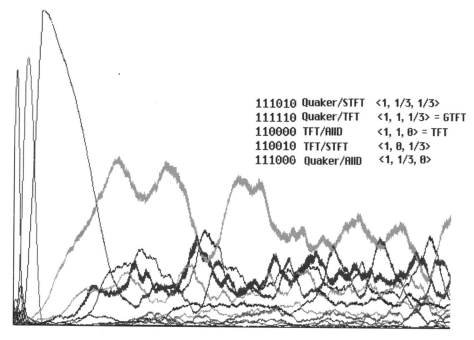

111010	Quaker/STFT	⟨1, 1/3, 1/3⟩
111110	Quaker/TFT	⟨1, 1, 1/3⟩ = GTFT
110000	TFT/AllD	⟨1, 1, 0⟩ = TFT
110010	TFT/STFT	⟨1, 0, 1/3⟩
111000	Quaker/AllD	⟨1, 1/3, 0⟩

$v = 0.33$

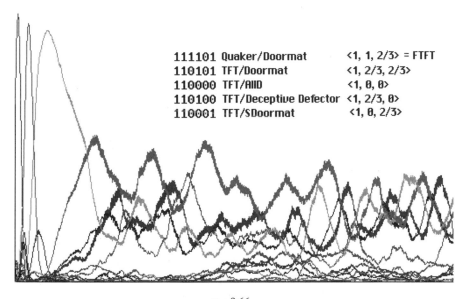

111101	Quaker/Doormat	⟨1, 1, 2/3⟩ = FTFT
110101	TFT/Doormat	⟨1, 2/3, 2/3⟩
110000	TFT/AllD	⟨1, 0, 0⟩
110100	TFT/Deceptive Defector	⟨1, 2/3, 0⟩
110001	TFT/SDoormat	⟨1, 0, 2/3⟩

$v = 0.66$

Figure 21 The final tournament, with dual coding and different levels of veil of ignorance. $v = 1/3$ and $v = 2/3$, shown in the first two graphs, are important instability points (strategies are listed in the order they appear at the extreme right of the screen). Above $v = 1/3$ generous strategies play a major role. Above $v = 2/3$ FTFT clearly dominates.

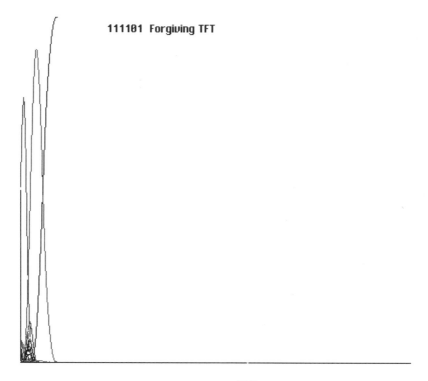

111101 Forgiving TFT

$v = 0.75$

Figure 21   (*continued*).

discriminatory strategies, for example, drawn in terms of a range of degrees of cooperation and defection, suggests that a high enough veil of ignorance may allow even Forgiving TFT to prevail over discrimination.

5.8   CONCLUSION

What we've attempted in this chapter is a series of explorations in continuous-valued game theory. From the initial example of Conway's Game of Life it is clear that the move to continuous values introduces important differences. It also introduces, interestingly enough, all the elements of classical chaos. More important for social application, perhaps, is the fact that such a result is evident in a field of two-dimensional strategies within a continuous-valued and spatialized Prisoner's Dilemma. In the final sections of the chapter we tried to take the idea of social application seriously enough to examine the particular phenomenon of discrimination, with the intent of introducing modeling tools suggestive for further formal investigation of both possible causes and potential cures.

6 Computation and Undecidability in the Spatialized Prisoner's Dilemma

In the *Scienza nuova* of 1744, Vico assures us that social interactions, because made by us, will therefore be understandable by us:

But in the night of thick darkness enveloping the earliest antiquity, so remote from ourselves, there shines the eternal and never failing light of a truth beyond all question: that the world of civil society has certainly been made by men, and that its principles are therefore to be found within the modifications of our own human mind. Whoever reflects on this cannot but marvel that the philosophers should have bent all their energies to the study of the world of nature, which, since God made it, He alone knows; and that they should have neglected the study of the world of nations, or civil world, which, since men had made it, men could come to know.[1]

Karl Marx, though in pursuit of scientific history in a spirit inspired by Vico, came to take a significantly less optimistic view of full intelligibility. If Vico's 'modifications of our own human mind' are ideas or aspects of consciousness, the principles of history are to be found *not* within modifications of mind but rather in the conditions of our material existence. Thus Marx abandons Vico's assurance that the civil world is one which 'since men made it, men could come to know'. He concludes instead that any science of history must fall short of the philosophical intelligibility of a complete abstract recipe:

Where speculation ends—in real life—there real, positive science begins.... Empty talk about consciousness ceases, and real knowledge has to take its place. When reality is depicted, philosophy as an independent branch of knowledge loses its medium of existence. At the best its place can only be taken up by a summing-up of the most general results, abstractions which arise from the observation of the historical development of men. Viewed apart from real history, these abstractions have in themselves no value whatsoever. They can only serve to facilitate the arrangement of historical material, to indicate the sequence of its separate strata. But they by no means afford a recipe or schema, as does philosophy, for neatly trimming the epochs of history. (Marx and Engels, *The German Ideology*, Part One)[2]

At least at first glance, the formal model we offer here seems to support Marx's side of the debate. What it shows is that there are formal computational limits to the predictability of social evolution even in a model that *is* constructed in terms of the simplest of principles 'within the modifications of our own human mind'. Read in this spirit, what we have to offer is a vindication of Marx against Vico by way of—of all people—Turing and Gödel.

The related limitative results of Gödel, Turing, Rice, and Chaitin carry well-deserved reputations as solid metamathematical theorems. But for most purposes such results seem safely distant from immediate concerns. These are, after all, results regarding axiomatic arithmetic, abstract machine theory, recursion theory, and algorithmic information theory. None of these is the stuff of everyday applied mathematics or mathematical modeling in the 'real' worlds of working physics, engineering, economics, or theoretical biology. Certainly such metamathematical results seem very far from the concerns regarding social intelligibility quoted above in Vico and Marx.

In this chapter, however, we want to bring formal undecidability a little bit closer to such concerns. More precisely, we want to bring undecidability as close as the Prisoner's Dilemma, explored in previous chapters as a standard paradigm of game theory. Although still abstract (and abstract in respects essential for the results that follow), the model of the Prisoner's Dilemma has carved itself a central applicational role within theoretical biology and economics over the past thirty years. It has been referred to as the *e. coli* of social psychology.[3] If undecidability shows up here, it shows up even in some of our simplest attempts to understand ourselves as biological and social organisms.

Whether such a result would really refute Vico, of course, is another matter. What we do show is that the simplest of social principles, far from guaranteeing a simple social science, may explode in computational complexity to full formal undecidability. But in fairness to Vico it must be admitted that complexity and undecidability are familiar aspects of contemporary mathematics. One way Vico makes his central claim in the *Scienza nuova* is by assuring us that social science, constructed also from human concepts, should prove as intelligible as mathematics.

6.1 UNDECIDABILITY AND THE PRISONER'S DILEMMA

In the preceding chapters we have explored a range of Hobbesian models, constructed on the basis of a range of variations on the Prisoner's Dilemma. In the later sections of chapter 4, for example, the stochastic representation of a world of imperfect information played a major role. In chapter 5 we shifted to a full continuum of values for cooperation and defection. Here, with an eye to the issue of undecidability, we want to return to a simpler model much like that with which we began. The spatialized model we will use to explore undecidability is one based on a simple and classical Prisoner's Dilemma.

On each round Players A and B each choose one of two options, to 'cooperate' (C) or 'defect' (D). The standard payoffs, listed with gains for player B to the left and for player A to the right, are as follows:

Player A

		Cooperate	Defect
Player B	Cooperate	3, 3	0, 5
	Defect	5, 0	1, 1

This simple model, as we've noted, seems to capture in miniature something of the tension between individual acquisitiveness and the goals of collective cooperation, which is of course precisely why it has been so widely used in economics and theoretical biology. Indeed it captures that tension in a particularly pointed way: each player's apparently rational pursuit of his or her own advantage leads predictably to an inferior outcome for all. Defection is dominant: given either choice by the other player, I will do better if I defect. My rational choice in a single round, then, seems to be defection. Knowing that the other player is equally rational, I know that he or she will follow the same course of action. In an attempt to maximize our gains, then, we will choose a course of action which we know will get us each a score of only 1—this despite the fact that we also know we could each achieve a far superior score of 3 by the simple option of joint cooperation.

In an iterated Prisoner's Dilemma, competing strategies emerge for extended play over time. The simplest of these are reactive strategies, which respond only to the opponent's last play, including Quaker (AllC), Always Defect (AllD), Deceptive Defector, Tit for Tat (TFT) and Suspicious Tit for Tat (STFT).[4] Due primarily to the work of Robert Axelrod, it will be remembered, TFT has established a reputation as a particularly robust strategy in the classical iterated Prisoner's Dilemma.[5]

For present purposes we will once again use the convenient mathematical fiction of infinitely iterated games, applied here to a classical rather than stochastic Prisoner's Dilemma.[6] Often it is easy to predict that strategies pitted against each other in an iterated game are bound to settle down into some monotonously repeated pattern of play. From their specifications, for example, we might be able to tell that a pair of Strategies S1 and S2 will establish and then simply repeat a pattern such as the following:

Strategy 1:   DDCDCDCDCDCDCDCDCDCDCDCD...

Strategy 2:   CD CDDCCCDC CDDCCCDC CDDCCCDC...
                 repeated unit of play

The longer a finite iterated game we play, the more the relative scores in this repeated unit will matter and the less will matter any differences in score before that period was established or in any fragmentary period played at the very end. Average scores within the repeated unit of play alone can thus be taken as a limit toward which average scores will tend over finite games of increasing length. What we take as the score of Strategy 1 versus Strategy 2 in an infinitely iterated game is simply that limit.

In this example the scores for each strategy over the repeated unit of play stack up as follows:

1's points: 3 1 0 5 3 5 0 5

Strategy 1:   C D C D C D C D

Strategy 2:   C D D C C C D C

2's points: 3 1 5 0 3 0 5 0

Strategy 1's average over the repeated period is 22/8 or 2.75. This is the limit toward which its average score will converge in games of increasing length and is thus what we take as its pure score in a game of infinite length. Strategy 2's average score is 2.125.[7] Though scores for infinitely iterated games are used throughout this chapter, the basic results will also hold for finite games of sufficient length.

In the Spatialized Prisoner's Dilemma, of course, we add a further dimension: that of space. Players with different strategies are envisaged as competing against immediate neighbors in a two-dimensional field in the manner outlined in previous chapters. In the model used here each player competes with its neighbors in an infinitely iterated Prisoner's Dilemma and converts to the strategy of any neighbor with a higher score.[8]

Terrell Carver's gloss on Marxist theory in the *Cambridge Companion to Marx* might almost have been written with such a model in mind:

Human agents are rational actors who are defined by their class relations and who *choose among possible strategies* in order to realize their interests under circumstances of material and social constraint characteristic of a specific period of historical development. [our italics][9]

As should now be familiar, fields of strategies in the spatialized Prisoner's Dilemma evolve in the manner of cellular automata. Figure 1 starts from a randomized field of the eight reactive strategies, including AllC, AllD, TFT, STFT, Suspicious Quaker, and three others.[10] Each cell plays its neighbors in an infinitely iterated Prisoner's Dilemma, resulting in the evolution shown here for generations 1, 3, 5, and 10. AllD and Deceptive Defector, shown using gray and white respectively, seem the early winners. As these threaten to take over, however, black clusters of TFT grow and thrive in the new environment they've established. In the end it is TFT that conquers all other strategies, ultimately occupying the

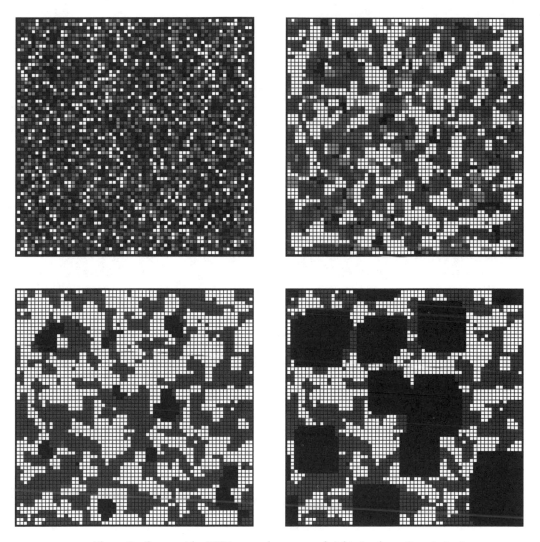

Figure 1 Conquest by TFT in a random array of eight simple reactive strategies.

field alone; by the twenty-sixth generation the screen is entirely black. Figure 1 thus shows once again a nice vindication of the robustness of TFT in a spatial context.[11]

Although this is a standard result for a random configuration of these eight strategies, it should be noted that conquest by TFT is *not* inevitable. Figure 2 shows the evolution of an array with the same eight strategies in the same proportions but in which TFT does not invade to conquest. In the evolution of this second array AllD and Deceptive Defector retain their dominance, quickly establishing an equilibrium with each other, and with occasional individual hold-outs by TFT and STFT. Figure 2 shows generations 1, 2, 3, and 5; from this point on the array is frozen in static equilibrium with no further change.

Computation and Undecidability in the Spatialized Prisoner's Dilemma

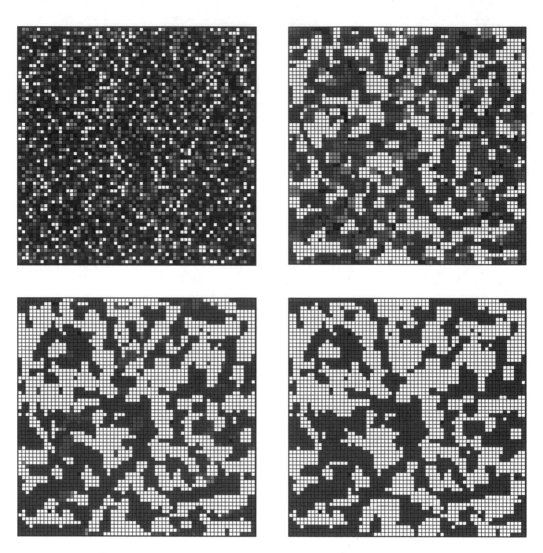

Figure 2 Evolution to equilibrium dominated by AllD and Deceptive Defector in an array of the same strategies in the same proportions.

A question often arises with regard to arrays of strategies in the spatialized Prisoner's Dilemma whether one or another strategy will grow to conquest (TFT or AllD, say) or whether some equilibrium will be established among different strategies. With genuinely infinite arrays in mind, rather than computer-limited finite displays, the question might be posed as follows. Given a particular initial configuration, will a single strategy S eventually grow to dominate any arbitrarily chosen finite area of the array? It is clear from the simple examples above that the answer to such a question in a particular case may depend not merely on the strategies represented, and not merely on their proportions, but on details of their initial spatial configuration as well.

Let us suppose a standard infinite background. In the simplest case this will consist of an infinite plane of cells all of which are occupied by a single strategy—a sea of some strategy B stretching unbroken in every direction. In the midst of this background we insert a smaller finite configuration composed of various strategies—an island patchwork of cells with different strategies, dropped in the midst of the infinite sea of B (figure 3). The result of such an insertion may be different in different cases. Some finite configurations dropped into our infinite sea may result in progressive conquest by a single strategy, dominating its neighbors and expanding ever outward. Some configurations may do something entirely different—they might disappear completely, for example, or remain static and unchanged. They might churn forever internally without expansion, or periodically pulse through cycles of expansion and contraction.

For any chosen background, is there a step-by-step procedure—an algorithm—that will tell us in each case the result of embedding a certain finite configuration? Is there an algorithm that will tell us, say, whether or not an embedded finite array will result in progressive conquest by a single strategy S? Given a computer big enough or fast enough, a mind without limits of attention span or memory or attention to detail, is there some systematic computation that will tell us in each case whether an embedded finite array will result in progressive conquest or not?

The work outlined below answers this question firmly in the negative. There is no effective procedure that will in each case tell us whether or not a given configuration of Prisoner's Dilemma strategies embedded in a uniform background results in progressive conquest.[12] Despite the fact that

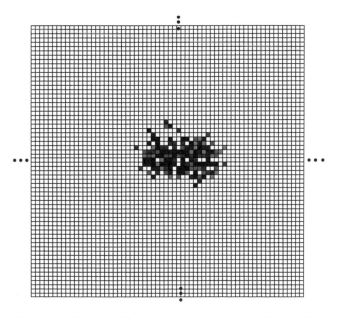

Figure 3 A finite configuration of strategies dropped in an infinite sea.

it is one of the simplest models available for basic elements of biological and social interaction, the spatialized Prisoner's Dilemma proves formally undecidable in the full classical sense.

The proof introduces undecidability into game theory in three steps. In section 6.2, two classes of abstract machines are introduced: close relatives of Turing machines, on the one hand, and forms of Minsky register machines, on the other.[13] These abstract machines arc outlined in just enough detail to indicate their computational universality and to sketch some fairly standard undecidability results for them, patterned on the familiar Halting Problem. Section 6.3 indicates how such machines, wired to auxiliary 'strategy bombs', can be instantiated within a particular species of cellular automata. The evolutionary behavior of such cellular automata directly simulates the behavior of the relevant machines.

From these first two steps we will be able to conclude that the classical undecidability of the abstract machines at issue also appears within the class of cellular automata constructed to model them. The last piece of legerdemain appears in section 6.4, in which it is shown that there is a set of describable Prisoner's Dilemma strategies, spatial arrangements of which will constitute cellular automata of precisely the type outlined in section 6.3. Undecidability thus carries over to the Spatialized Prisoner's Dilemma as well.

The strategy of the argument as a whole parallels J. H. Conway's proof of universal computation and undecidability in the Game of Life.[14] Here as there the trick is to show that a particular species of cellular automata is capable of instantiating logical mechanisms adequate for arbitrary computation and that are thus sufficient to raise the Halting Problem. The rules for the Game of Life, however, were quite deliberately selected in the hopes of producing such a result; the appearance of a related result within the familiar and widely applied decision-theoretic model at issue here is by no means trivial. In the work that follows, on the other hand, the complexities of two components are in something of a balance: the complexities of (a) instantiating a Turing- or Minsky-like machine within a cellular automata, and (b) defining essential components of that cellular automata in terms of spatial competitions between Prisoner's Dilemma strategies. We have accepted significant complications in (b), obvious from a glance at the appendix, in order to keep (a) as simple as possible. Complications deferred to computations regarding competing strategies allow us to use a cellular automata instantiation of abstract machines in terms of wires and gates much simpler than Conway's.

We would not want to claim that the basic result at issue could be demonstrated only by means of computer-instantiated models. Quite the contrary. Undecidability for the Spatialized Prisoner's Dilemma is in a clear tradition of limitative results extending from Turing and Gödel to Rice and Chaitin, and it might in principle be demonstrated without the computer simulations used here. As a matter of practice rather than a matter of principle, however, our development of the argument was in fact heavily dependent on computer experimentation. A great deal of tinkering with arrays and alternative strategies was necessary in order to construct Prisoner's Dilemma instantiations for basic Boolean gates, for example. Though the final result itself is thus not in principle tied to computers, we find it difficult to imagine what it would have been like to work out the crucial details without the constant aid of computer modeling.

6.2 TWO ABSTRACT MACHINES

Turing machines are undoubtedly the most familiar abstract model of mechanical computation. Operating in terms of a specified machine table governing a finite number of internal states, a standard Turing machine moves back and forth over a finite number of symbols on a tape infinite in both directions. All processing is in terms of discrete steps. At each step the machine is able to read only the symbol in the square on which it stands; given that information and the rules of its machine table it either leaves that symbol or substitutes another, and then moves left, right, or halts. The beauty of Turing's conception of an abstract machine, of course, is not just its simplicity but its power: anything computable by any device, computable in any sense, it appears will be computable by a standard Turing machine.[15]

Somewhat less familiar in philosophical circles are other abstract machines, provably equivalent to Turing's. To any Turing machine will correspond a machine of any of these alternative classes, which performs precisely the same computation. There is no loss of power in Turing machine variations that are limited to a single symbol beyond the blanks on their infinite tape, for example. There is no loss of power in variations in which the tape is infinite only in one direction ('semi-infinite'), or in which the machine is limited both to a single symbol and a semi-infinite tape. There is no loss in power even in Turing machines that have lost the ability to erase symbols entirely, and which can therefore never change a once-written symbol.[16] If we allow a machine two semi-infinite tapes, any computation can in fact be done by a machine that has lost the ability to either erase *or* write on its tapes, and is able only to detect when one of its tapes has come to an end.[17]

In this section we want to outline two classes of abstract machines. The first can be thought of as a variant on standard Turing machines, which uses a tape expandable on one end as needed—the equivalent of a 'semi-infinite' tape. Rather than moving back and forth on its tape, however, this variant sits perfectly still: a non-touring Turing machine. Its tape comes to it in the form of an ever-circling loop, marching its parade of symbols in a single direction past the reading and writing head of the machine. At each pass the machine may change a symbol and may add spaces to enlarge the loop. It then waits patiently for the parade of symbols on its tape to pass again. We'll show below that any computational task performable by a standard Turing machine will be performable by this close cousin as well.

Such a machine appears in somewhat more detail in figure 4. Here block A represents a finite computational unit; all else in the diagram represents the mechanism of the tape loop, which in the manner of Turing machines everywhere serves both as input device and as an infinitely expandable external memory. Among standard Turing machines, differences from particular machine to particular machine consist in their internal states and the machine table that governs them. In the present class of machines, differences from machine to machine consist entirely in the contents of their computational unit A. Because the structure of the tape loop is a constant from machine to machine, we will be able to enumerate machines of this type in terms of the contents of their computational units alone.

We will assume that a close-up of unit A for any machine would reveal a finite tangle of wires. All we really need to demand of such 'wires', however, is that they be paths along which something called 'electrons' travel at a standard rate. If we think of wires as marked off in units, we can think of electrons as traveling at the rate of one unit per 'tick' of time, uniform for the machine as a whole. No electrical properties in any richer sense are required.[18] Within a computational unit wires will turn corners and cross each other either with interaction or without. Some wire configurations can be expected to function as diodes, allowing electron motion in one direction but not another along a wire. These in turn may form part of the construction of 'or' and 'not' gates. It has long been clear that this handful of elements offers a complete base for Boolean functions in any number of variables; with any form of wires capable of forming these basic elements we can rest assured that some configuration will serve the nonmemory functions of any computational unit we might desire.[19]

For present purposes we want the tape loop to be instantiated in a pattern of wires as well. What will 'loop', in fact, won't be a paper tape but

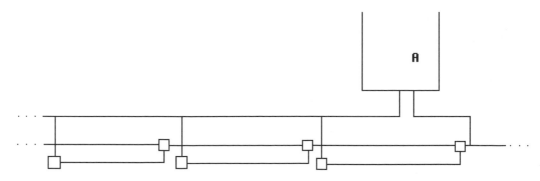

Figure 4 Abstract machine with tape loop.

a series of electron impulses along a wire. In a simple model, one might envisage a closed loop of wire around which our signal circulates, running through the read and write head of our computational unit each time around. Were our tape or memory of a limited size, in fact, that is all that we would need. In order to model an infinitely expandable memory, on the other hand, we need to model an infinitely expandable wire loop. Figure 4 shows one way of doing so. Here a series of linked loops extend infinitely to the left, to be tapped into as needed. We can think of our signal as running initially around the smallest loop at the right. If and when the signal length requires, we create a longer course to accommodate it by closing and opening gates so that it runs around the equivalent of two loops. Should additional signal length eventually require a further addition we tap into the third loop to the left, and so forth.

Those who wish to skip the morbid details of the tape loop are invited to pass over the next eleven paragraphs or so. For those who want the details, the construction of one version of this type of tape loop is shown in figure 5. Here an encoded input, marked with some coding α for its beginning and ω for its end, enters from the right as a finite series of spaced electron pulses along the wire. At the first branch the coded series moves straight ahead, with a diode blocking similar travel northward. It passes through a counter unit marked C1 which is triggered by the beginning code α to start a 100-tick 'clock'. If the end ω of the encoded message arrives before the clock has ticked off its 100 pulses, C1 returns to its starting position. If not, a single pulse is sent by a southerly route to signal block S1 and C1 then returns to its starting position.

After triggering C1, the signal moves left into a labyrinth of twists and turns. The labyrinth is 150 tick-units long, let us say, designed so that an impulse sent south from C1 can arrive at S1 before the beginning of the message series arrives at the juncture above S1. On receiving an impulse

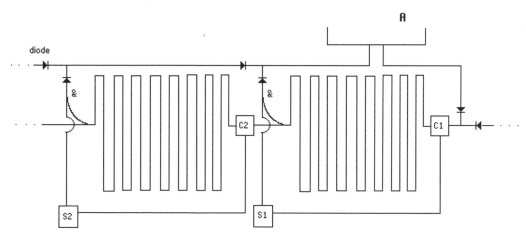

Figure 5 Tape loop details.

Computation and Undecidability in the Spatialized Prisoner's Dilemma

from C1, S1 starts a constant pulse of 150 electrons at the standard clocked interval and then resets. Above it in the diagram, marked with an ampersand, is an 'and' gate. Thus if the series of signals is less than 100 units, the series will travel through the labyrinth and branch up to the 'and' gate, where it will meet a steady series of positive pulses from S1. Wherever an electron appears in the signal series, the 'and' together with the positive pulse from S1 will transfer an electron through the gate; wherever an electron fails to appear in the signal, the 'and' will fail to be satisfied and no electron will go through. If it is less than 100 units long, then, the signal series will effectively travel up through the 'and' gate to the upper wire and to the right, on to the computational unit at A. Our working loop will be complete. Because of branching just before the 'and' gate a doppelgänger of the signal series will also continue to the left, into C2 and beyond, but in that direction the signal travels harmlessly into an infinite limbo of unused coils of wire.

What if the signal series is more than 100 units long? In that case S1 will not be triggered. S1 will send no series of pulses, the 'and' gate will never be satisfied, and the signal will fail to cycle north. It will however travel left to a second counter C2, which at the beginning signal α starts a clock of 200 tick-units. If the end signal ω arrives before the clock reaches 200, a signal is sent to S2, which begins a regular series of 250 pulses. All else operates as before. If the signal series is longer than 100 units but less than 200, then, it will cycle north not at the first juncture but the second.

The structure of linked loops continues infinitely to the left, with labyrinth units increasing by any regular interval and the clocked units of C and S components increasing accordingly. For illustration additive units of 100 have been used, but increasing powers of 10 could do as well. The purpose of the whole should be clear: any finite message will trigger a recycling loop large enough to accommodate it. Because C and S units are reset each time they are triggered, the loop is ready for a new message of any finite length leaving the computational unit and circling around again. The infinite loop structure as a whole opens up or closes off in accord with the current length of the signal.

Here the important point is simply that a tape loop can be conceived of entirely in terms of wires and basic gates. In the form outlined, the tape loop consists only of lengths of wire (including infinite wires) linked with diodes, 'and' gates, and devices C and S. C and S devices can be thought of as simple finite computational devices in their own right, easily constructed from wires and standard gates. In each case the crucial timing element can be simply a loop of wire of a certain length.

Improvements on this tape loop mechanism are clearly possible. Figure 6 shows a simpler variation in that it operates with a few factory-identical units instead of ever-larger clocks and signal-generators. Here the only requirements are required are a beginning-detector B (triggered by α), an

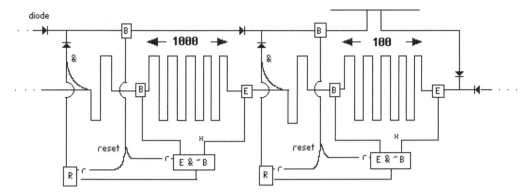

Figure 6 Tape loop with simpler components.

end-detector E (triggered by ω), a 'repeater' R, and a signal box. The repeater simply generates a stream of pulses when triggered, and continues to do so until reset. The signal box outputs a single pulse if an input from an end-detector E has been received at x and one from a beginning detector B has not, resetting on a signal at r. Given these elements the function of progressively longer clock devices in the version above can be replaced simply by increasing wire lengths between beginning- and end-detectors as the structure extends infinitely to the left.

To this point messages carried on the tape loop have been specified as series of clocked electron pulses along a wire, marked with a coding for beginning and end. This is again a matter of mere detail, and here again there is a wide range of alternatives. For the sake of concreteness, however, it may be useful to specify encoding in a particular form. The beginning signal α, we might suppose, consists of two contiguous 1s; the ending signal ω consists of three. These are what our beginning- and end-detectors can detect. Between beginning and end is a series of spaces to be treated as registers, separated by dividers which double as addresses. The first register space appears immediately following the beginning signal, and requires no further address. The second register space is marked by an initial address of 1111 (using one more 1 than our ending signal), the third by 11111, and so forth. As a whole the message then takes the following form, with ellipses to indicate register spaces:

11...1111...11111... 111

Register contents can be envisaged in monadic notation, suitably disambiguated from their addresses. One simple way to do this is to begin and end register contents with 0s, inserting 0s between any digits within them as well.[20] A content register of '5' would thus become 01010101010. '0' would become 000. A complete message with beginning and end markers but using only three registers, containing numbers 5, 0, and 1, respectively, would then appear as follows:

110101010101011110001111111010111

Given some appropriate convention for message encoding, a tape loop of the form outlined constitutes an infinitely expandable external memory for the computation center at A. The tape might be thought of as containing an infinitely expandable number of memory registers, each of which is capable of holding an arbitrarily large integer. It has long been known that such a memory, together with the arbitrary Boolean power of a finite computation center composed of wires, 'or', and 'not' gates, is sufficient for the computational universality familiar in standard Turing machines.[21]

An alternative conception of register contents offers a still more direct link with Turing machines. On this alternative conception the first two registers of the signal might be envisaged as containing 'position' and 'state' numbers, with all other registers arbitrarily limited to simple contents of either 0 or 1. Operations on the looped signal can now be thought of as corresponding directly to those of a Turing machine on a single semi-infinite tape. The Turing machine's semi-infinite tape contents will correspond digit by digit to the register contents of our looped signal beyond the second register. Changes in position and state in the Turing machine, on the other hand, will correspond to changes in the position- and state-*numbers* in the first two registers of the looped signal. Given these conventions the quintuplets of any Turing machine table can be rewritten directly as programmed instructions within the wired computational unit of our looped machine.

Corresponding to any Turing machine, then, will be an abstract machine of the sort outlined. Any Turing-computable function—given Church's thesis, any computable function at all—will be computable by a wired computation center attached to an empty tape loop itself instantiated in a pattern of wires.

Here we also want to outline a second type of abstract machine, one that uses no tape at all. Little differs at its core: here again we find a computational unit composed of a tangle of 'wires'. In place of the familiar Turing tape, however, we find two registers, which can be thought of as storage pits, each capable of holding a single arbitrarily large integer. In place of tape reading- and writing-abilities, we insist only that the computational core of the machine be capable of adding a single unit to a register, of subtracting a unit, and of checking whether there is anything in a register at all—whether its contents are zero. These abstract devices we'll refer to as Minsky register machines. The proof that they are equivalent to Turing machines—that they can simulate any Turing machine and can be simulated by Turing machines in return—appears in classic work by Minsky.[22]

In the paragraphs above we took some pains to show that all components of looped Turing machines could be instantiated in a network of wires. Here computational units are essentially the same, and comments on wiring for computational units can thus be expected to carry over. The new elements at issue are the Minsky registers. Can *these* be wired?

The answer is 'yes', although details quickly become complex. A complete outline of register wiring is left to a later section. For the moment we ask you to trust us: in the sense we will require, Minsky register machines can indeed be wired. We thus have two forms of abstract machines, differing essentially only in the form of their external memory, each of which can be instantiated as a pattern of electrons traveling along wires.

The reason for introducing two forms of abstract machines rather than one is to offer two forms of the basic proof at issue. In the discussion above it may be the looped Turing machine that appears more complex. In later sections that more complex machine allows for a much simpler model in terms of cellular automata and the Prisoner's Dilemma, however, and thus for a conceptually simpler form of the basic undecidability argument. The Minsky register machine will require a more complicated modeling. But in the end it will also allow a more elegant formulation of undecidability.[23] The two machines thus offer something of a trade-off. By having both on hand we hope to be able to introduce certain steps of the argument in a conceptually simple form and yet be able to finish them off with a bit more generality and elegance.

Each of our two forms of abstract machines, we've said, is equivalent to a standard Turing machine: any systematic computation or step-by-step procedure whatsoever can be performed by some form of either machine. Along with such a parallel to standard Turing machines comes a parallel to the standard Halting Problem. A slight variation on the Halting Problem will be at the core of the results below.

A simple presentation of the problem can be borrowed from John Conway:[24] We know that a Turing machine, and thus an abstract machine of either sort at issue here, can be constructed for the express purpose of investigating any explicitly specified, and arbitrarily hard, arithmetical question. We might construct a looped Turing machine to search for counterexamples to Goldbach's conjecture, for example—that every even number greater than 2 is the sum of two primes. Programmed to proceed even integer by even integer, checking alternative sums of lesser primes one by one, our machine could be designed to indicate that it has found a counterexample either by printing a particular message on its tape or by some convenient auxiliary signal—a single pulse sent down a designated signal wire, for example. A Minsky register machine could of course be constructed to the same effect.

We can then envisage a range of machines, for a range of purposes, built with convenient signal wires. Our Goldbach machine, a carefully designed pattern of wires, is to send a pulse down its signal wire when a counterexample to Goldbach's conjecture is found. Our Fermat register machine, itself merely a different pattern of wires, is to send a pulse down its signal wire if and when it reaches a set of integer values satisfying $(x + 1)^{w+3} + (y + 1)^{w+3} = (z + 1)^{w+3}$.

Because both looped Turing machines and Minsky register machines are distinguished from each other by the finite contents of their computational units, all machines of either set can be listed, or enumerated, in terms of those contents. They can, in effect, be 'coded' by their central wiring diagrams, and we can compile a list of machines in terms of those wiring codes alone. Those machines with auxiliary signal wires will simply form a partial list.

The crucial question, however, is this: Is there an algorithm that will tell us, for any machine on the list, whether it will or will not eventually send a pulse down its signal wire? The answer is 'no'. If there were such an algorithm, it would effectively tell us whether arbitrary difficult arithmetical problems have solutions. But as Conway notes, "mathematical logicians have proved that there's no technique which guarantees to tell when arbitrary arithmetical problems have solutions."[25] There can thus be no algorithm that predicts in each case the behavior of our abstract machines.

In somewhat deeper detail, and without unnecessary appeal to the authority of mathematical logicians, classical undecidability for either family of abstract machines might be outlined as follows. Let us conceive of all machines at issue as starting on inputs and rigged with a uniform output signal. In the case of looped Turing machines, the input will be an initial finite configuration of symbols on the feed wire shown to the right of the tape loop in figures 4 and 5. In the case of Minsky register machines the input can be thought of as a similar signal series fed directly into the computation center. Output for our chosen class of machines we specify in terms of a special signal wire, located at some conveniently uniform corner in each machine, and down which an electron may or may not eventually be sent. That signal wire might be thought of as the lead to a light bulb, for example, flashing 'on' just in case a Goldbach machine has found a counterexample.

Our different machines can be fed different inputs. Some machines, started on some inputs, will eventually send a pulse down their signal wire. Others, started on other inputs, will not. Within a given class, we've said, machines at issue differ only in the finite contents of their computation centers and can be indexed accordingly. Some machines, started on an input that happens to correspond to their own index,[26] will eventually send an 'on' signal. Some will not.

Is there a machine that will send an 'on' signal just for a particular class of inputs: the index numbers of machines that don't send a signal when fed their own numbers? No. For suppose there were such a machine, and suppose it were fed its *own* number. It would then flash an 'on' signal just in case it would never flash an 'on' signal. The supposition boxes us in contradiction: there can be no such machine.

We can also ask a more general question. Is there a machine that will signal whether or not a numbered machine, started on a given input, will eventually send an 'on' signal? No. For given *that* machine, we could construct the machine we've just proven impossible simply by fiddling with signal wires and attaching an initial message duplicator.[27]

Given Church's thesis, any algorithm whatsoever can be instantiated by either a looped Turing or Minsky register machine. If so, the signaling problem is formally undecidable. There is no effective decision procedure, no step-by-step computation, and no systematic chain of thought that will predict in all cases the signaling behavior of the abstract machines at issue.

None of this should be too surprising: the familiar undecidability of the Halting Problem has simply been carried over to two slightly different species of abstract machines. The details are interesting, perhaps, but the general result is uncontroversial. In the following sections, however, we want to put these results to work in a new way—first in the context of a particular type of cellular automata, and then in application to the Spatialized Prisoner's Dilemma.

6.3 COMPUTATION AND UNDECIDABILITY IN COMPETITIVE CELLULAR AUTOMATA

In this section we want to change the subject, leaving abstract machines and classical undecidability results behind for a moment to sketch a species of cellular automata. The particular species with which we will be concerned is in fact a slightly unusual one, most easily outlined for example in terms of a two-step rather than the usual one-step pattern of computation. We'll begin with a simpler one-step relative, however, in order to outline some basic ideas.

This simpler cellular automaton, dubbed 'wireworld' by A. K. Dewdney, first appeared in a programming environment called the Phantom Fish Tank, created by Brian Silverman of Logo Computer Systems.[28] Two-dimensional cellular automata consist of regular spatial arrays of cells, each of which is in a particular state at any given time. Each cell operates as a simple finite-state automaton that it follows rules for state change written in terms of its current state and the states of its proximate neighbors. Within Silverman's wireworld the rules of state change are written in such a way that certain configurations of cells end up mimicking the behavior of electrons moving along wires. Silverman's wires can turn and cross, with further configurations that function as diodes, 'and', 'or', and 'not' gates. With these we can construct cellular automata equivalent to any finite computer.

Wireworld operates in terms of just four cellular states: at any given time a cell might be of a background state **b**, might be a wire cell **w**, an electron head **e** or electron tail **t**. The rules are simple. With each tick of the automata clock, or within each generation of the array's development, electron heads **e** become electron tails **t** and electron tails **t** become wire cells **w**. Wire cells become electron heads just in case they are bordered by one or two electron heads. Background cells never change. Figure 7 shows a sample: a simple 'or' gate for Silverman's wireworld, incorporating two diodes. In black and white, the background **b** is coded white, wire cells **w** appear as grey, and electron heads and tails **e** and **t** appear as black and dotted cells respectively. One can work through the rules by hand in order to watch the electron head and tail as they move right through the first diode and then branch at the junction, with one copy traveling south and the other extinguishing at the diode on the right.

Because wireworld can be used to simulate the operation of arbitrary finite computers, and because the looped tape mechanism of section 6.2 can itself be simulated using (infinite) Silverman wires, we are able to carry over a simple undecidability result regarding wireworld. Consider any enumeration of finite wireworld arrays that might serve as our computational units for looped Turing machines. Consider further those finite cellular automata arrays composed of particular computational units together with particular inputs, including perhaps their own enumerations as inputs. We can think of all such machines as rigged with a designated signal wire and embedded in a standard tape loop background.

Is there any algorithm or effective procedure that will tell us whether or not an arbitrary finite array of cells, following Silverman's rules and embedded in a background corresponding to an infinite tape loop, will generate a positive signal? By a slight variation on the argument of section 6.2 the answer is 'no'. Were there such an algorithm, we would in effect have an algorithm that would decide for any machine whether or not it would generate a positive signal if started on its own encoding. Since we know there can be no algorithm of the latter sort, we know there can be

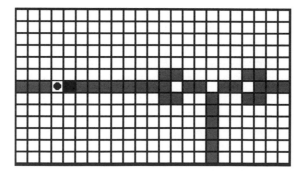

Figure 7 Silverman 'or' with diodes.

none of the former sort either: the evolution of wireworld displays proves formally undecidable.[29]

The work that follows uses this same basic idea: the abstract machines at issue are simulated within certain types of cellular automata in order to carry over the result of abstract undecidability. Here as in Silverman's wireworld, moreover, the strategy will be to model within cellular automata the movement of electrons along wires, allowing the construction of basic components adequate as a complete base for Boolean operations.

Beyond these points of common strategy, however, things become significantly more complex. Silverman's rules require a simple one-step computation for each cell: any cell can calculate state change merely by noting its own state and, if it is a wire cell, how many electron heads adjoin it. The cellular automata we want to consider here, in contrast, are 'competitive' automata, most naturally envisaged in terms of a more elaborate two-step computation. Here cells will be thought of as gaining particular scores in competition with their immediate neighbors, thereby amassing a total score in their immediate neighborhood. In a second step they then compare their score with that of their immediate neighbors. Should a neighbor have a higher local score, they convert to that neighbor's strategy or state. If thought of as a form of rules for cellular automata in general, of course, these may seem peculiarly complicated. Conceived of as a prospective link with a Spatialized Prisoner's Dilemma, on the other hand, they should seem exactly right.

The basic rule set for our competitive automata might be thought of as follows. At each evolutionary generation, or tick of the automata clock, each cell of an array is playing one of four strategies against all of its neighbors. These strategies can be thought of in terms of functions: background **b**, wire **w**, electron head **e**, and electron tail **t**. In black and white they are represented as white, gray, black, and dotted cells. Standard game scores can be determined in advance for each two-color competition: wires **w** get a standard score of 3 in competition with electron tails **t**, let us say. A background cell **b** achieves only a score of 0.868 against any nonbackground competitor.

At each tick of the clock each cell competes in this way against its eight neighbors and totals its score. It then stands back to survey its neighbors, converting to the strategy of a neighboring cell should there be one that achieved a higher local score. A wire cell might thus become an electron head because of the higher local score of a neighboring **e** cell. An electron tail might become a wire cell because the **t** cell's local score was lower than that of its **w** neighbor.

Can the behavior of electron movement along wires, configurations for wire crossings and Boolean gates be modeled in this more competitive wireworld? The short answer is 'yes', although computation and gate configurations are necessarily more complicated than those of the original wireworld.

The following game scores, arrived at by the simple expedient of excruciating and laborious experimentation, give us an operating wire-like simulation. Here 'ww' represents the score of strategy **w** in competition against itself, '**we**' the score of wire against electron head, etc.:

ww 2.412	**ew** 2.485
we 2.534	**ee** 2.412
wt 3.000	**et** 2.542
wb 2.472	**eb** 2.472
tw 2.583	**bw** 0.868
te 2.567	**be** 0.868
tp 2.412	**bt** 0.868
tb 2.472	**bb** 2.667

How all this works can be illustrated by considering the not-so-simple phenomenon of a single wire consisting of strategy **w** maintained on a background field of **b**. At each tick of the automata clock, each cell of an array competes against its eight immediate neighbors. In order for a **w** cell to remain **w**, therefore, no non-**w** neighbor can have a higher score. For its **b** neighbors to remain background **b**, on the other hand, they must be in contact with a **b** cell the total score of which is greater than the score of their **w** neighbor. With the scores listed above, a **w** wire cell in contact with two other **w**s (the continuation of its 'wire' left and right) and 6 background **b**s receives a total score of 19.656, higher than that of a background **b** in contact with 5 **b**s and 3 **w**s (15.939), but less than the score of a background **b** cell surrounded by 8 **b**s (21.336). In each competitive round the **w** cells of the wire thus dominate their neighboring **b**s, but are counterbalanced by the proximity and higher score of background cells in competition with 8 background cells. The **w** wire remains tenuously balanced between extinction and explosion within a surrounding field of background **b**. Given the scores above, a similar balance keeps electron **e** and tail **t** cells from either vanishing or exploding when placed on an otherwise blue wire.

The simulation of electron travel along a wire—an **e** and **t** pair moving on a strip of **w** against a background of **b**—is achieved by awarding an **e** cell bordering a wire cell **w** a higher total score in context, a **t** cell bordering an **e** a higher score than its **e** neighbor, and a **w** cell bordering a **t** a higher score still. The result is the one-cell-per-clock-tick simulation of movement illustrated in figure 8. Black and white coding is as before: white for the background, grey for wires, and black and dotted cells for electron heads and tails respectively. The reality of the computation, of course, is that of a field of static cells, which merely change strategies as the result of perpetual competition with their neighbors. No cell literally

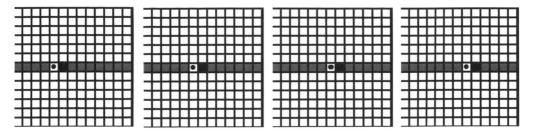

Figure 8 Electron moving along wire in competitive automata.

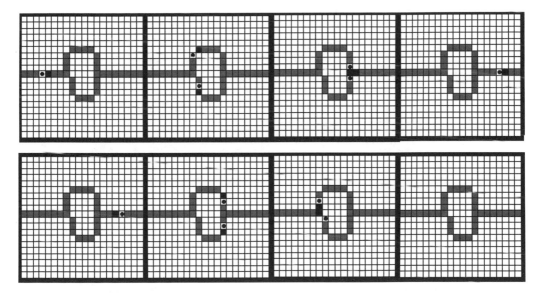

Figure 9 Diode in operation: electrons pass left to right but self-extinguish right to left.

moves. In familiar cinematic fashion, however, the inescapable impression given by an evolving array is one of electron pairs moving along thin wires.

It is clear that a wire-like simulation adequate for computation will call for more than merely electron movement along straight wires. The scores above have in fact been carefully selected to allow for electron movement around what turn out to be two importantly different types of corners— solid and nicked. They have also been selected to satisfy a crucial sensitivity of wire **w** cells to electron heads **e**, fine-tuned enough to allow both for electron branching and for a 'kill' function used as a basic element in diodes and fundamental operators. All of these details can be seen in the operation of a diode, illustrated by selected frames in figure 9. Here electron travel is allowed left to right but blocked by self-extinction right to left.

The complications of wire-crossing are illustrated in figure 10. Here an electron can travel south to north without propagating to cause

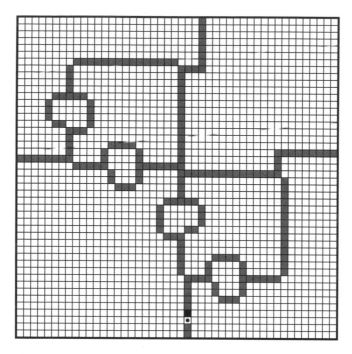

Figure 10 Wire crossing, allowing electron travel either south to north or west to east.

interference east or west, or can travel west to east without propagating
north or south. Traveling north, as illustrated, the electron will divide
at the first branch with copies proceeding unharmed through each of
two diodes. At the central cross it will propagate in all three forward
directions. The copy moving west, however, will be killed at the first
diode. The one moving right will be extinguished by a kill from the
doppelgänger that split off earlier. The one moving north will continue
through. A late twin generated to the left, at a kill site needed for travel
west to east, will be harmlessly extinguished at a diode down its left
passageway.

'Or' and 'not' gates are shown in figure 11. The 'or' gate is ascetically
simple and self-evident. The operation of the negation loop, however, calls
for some explanation. Here a timing convention is assumed for signals
within the constructed machine; for purposes of illustration we've
assumed a convention of 34 spaces between consecutive signal units sent
along a wire. A signal series ... 11111 ... will thus actually consist of a
string of pulses sent 34 spaces apart on a wire, or arriving each 34 ticks of
the automata clock. We can represent the zeros of a signal series
... 10101 ... by leaving out electrons at the relevant intervals. What
negation requires is an invertor designed to convert a series of spaced
signals—1011001100, say—to its negative image: 0100110011. The 'not'
gate illustrated in figure 11 achieves this by generating impulses in its
lower loop in synch with our standard signal rate, sending these out to a

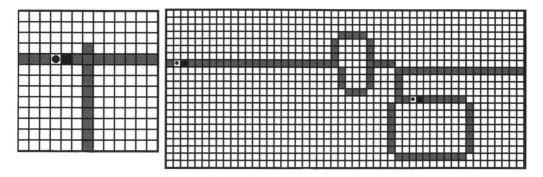

Figure 11 'Or' and 'not' gates.

point vulnerable at a 'kill' gate. A signal series is thought of as arriving through a diode from the left. If at the 34-space interval a timed electron representing a '1' arrives at the kill gate, it and the electron generated by the lower loop mutually annihilate and no pulse is sent out to the right. If at the 34-space interval no electron arrives, on the other hand—signaling a '0'—the pulse generated by the lower loop travels out undisturbed to the right. An electron copy to the left is extinguished by the diode. A signaled '1' from the left therefore gives us a '0' to the right and a '0' gives us a '1', exactly as required.

With these basic elements we can simulate, within a competitive cellular automata array, any finite arrangement of wires and standard gates. There will therefore be finite configurations of cells within two-dimensional arrays that correspond to the computational units of looped Turing machines, and also configurations that correspond to computational units together with chosen inputs. Using infinite wires, these same basic elements suffice for the construction of the standard tape loop. The undecidability results shown for looped Turing machines, therefore, carry over to competitive cellular automata as well: there is no algorithm that will tell us, for arbitrary finite configurations of our four strategies dropped into the field of an infinite loop, whether the evolution of that configuration will result in behavior corresponding to a positive signal.

Can a Minsky register machine be similarly embedded within competitive cellular automata? The computation center of such a machine will consist of wires and standard gates much like that of the looped Turing machine. Since such a machine requires not an infinite tape but merely two registers with finite contents, however, it will be significantly more compact.[30] Instantiated within a cellular automata array, in fact, such a machine could be thought of as a finite configuration dropped into the simple infinite field of a single background strategy. In the end this will allow us a simpler and more elegant formulation of the basic un-decidability at issue. The technical aspects of the simulation we have to offer for Minsky registers, on the other hand, are somewhat more complex. As outlined below, for example, it uses not four basic strategies but twelve.[31]

What is required of a Minsky register, it will be remembered, is that the computation center be able to add one to the register's contents, to subtract one, and to check whether the register has anything in it at all—whether its contents are zero. We will continue to think of the computation center as 'wired' using four basic strategies: wire **w**, background **b**, electron head **e**, and electron tail **t**. Messages from the computation center to memory registers will thus be envisaged in the form of standard electrons composed of electron head-electron tail **et** pairs, although particular messages may require carefully timed sequences of such pairs down particular wires. In the simulation design of the memory register itself, on the other hand, we have chosen to use a handful of different electrons with relative scores tuned to perform different tasks. In addition to the familiar **et** electron pair we will use **et2** as a 'special electron', in which the standard tail **t** is replaced by a variant strategy **t2**. We will also use two further electron pairs, **e2t** and **e3t**, in which the standard electron head **e** is replaced by variants **e2** and **e3**, and a final electron **e2t3**, in which **e2** replaces **e** and **t3** replaces **t**.[32]

The relative scores of these strategies, together with four more, are listed in Table 1.[33] Here we add strategy **m** for a memory tip, **c** for a collar, **d** for a diode collar, and **b2** as a variation on our standard background. The function of each of these will be explained in due course. An asterisk in place of a competitive score indicates that for present purposes any score will do in that place.

A complete schematic for a competitive automata memory register appears in figure 12. Its operation becomes more comprehensible when outlined bit by bit. The core of the memory register appears in the upper right hand corner: a 'fat wire' three **w** cells wide, tipped with a column of memory tip **m**. This is the memory site itself, where an integer is stored and where the fundamental operations of addition, subtraction, and zero-checking are accomplished. All else that appears in figure 12 is simply management machinery—the circuitry required in order for a computation center to control these functions within the fat wire by sending timed combinations of standard electrons down standard wires.

A larger or smaller integer is stored in memory in terms of the length of the fat wire segment itself: a longer triple segment corresponds to a larger integer, a shorter segment to a smaller one. Although the fat segment is never reduced to a true length of zero, we can think of a given initial length as representing our '0'. By convention we might for example represent our zero as the sixth cell to the right of the collar of strategy **c** (represented in black and white using horizontal stripes). A positive integer can then be represented in terms of cells to the right beyond that point, perhaps using two cells for each unit: a segment longer by two cells represents an integer

Table 1 Competitive strategy scores for a Minsky register.

ww = 2.412	ew = 2.485	tw = 2.583	bw = 0.868
we = 2.534	ee = 2.412	te = 2.567	be = 0.868
wt = 3.000	et = 2.542	tt = 2.412	bt = 0.868
wb = 2.472	eb = 2.472	tb = 2.472	bb = 2.612
wm = 2.495	em = 2.341	tm = 2.485	bm = 1.216
we2 = 2.534	ee2 = 1.000	te2 = 2.567	be2 = 0.868
wb2 = 2.502	eb2 = 2.526	tb2 = 2.526	bb2 = 2.615
wt2 = 3.000	et2 = 2.542	tt2 = 2.412	bt2 = 1.841
wd = 2.472	ed = 2.472	td = 2.472	bd = 2.615
we3 = 2.534	ee3 = 2.412	te3 = 2.567	be3 = 0.868
wc = 2.472	ec = 2.472	tc = 2.472	bc = 2.615
wt3 = 3.000	et3 = 2.542	tt3 = 2.412	bt3 = 0.868
mw = 2.485	e2w = 2.485	b2w = 0.859	t2w = 2.583
me = 2.419	e2e = 1.000	b2e = 0.867	t2e = 2.567
mt = 2.999^{47}	e2t = 2.542	b2t = 0.867	t2t = 2.412
mb = 2.469	e2b = 2.472	b2b = 0.849	t2b = 2.470
mm $-$ 2.412	e2m = 2.759	b2m = 0.929	t2m = 2.180
me2 = 2.886	e2e2 = 2.412	b2e2 = 0.867	t2e2 = *
mb2 = 2.476	e2b2 = 2.472	b2b2 = 2.667	t2b2 = 2.472
mt2 = 2.189	e2t2 = *	b2t2 = 0.867	t2t2 = 2.412
md = 2.472	e2d = 2.472	b2d = *	t2d = 2.472
me3 = 0.692	e2e3 = 1.000	b2e3 = *	t2e3 = *
mc = 2.472	e2c = 2.472	b2c = *	t2c = 2.472
mt3 = 2.999	e2t3 = 2.542	b2t3 = 0.867	t2t3 = 2.412
dw = 0.868	e3w = 2.485	cw = 0.868	t3w = 2.583
de = 0.868	e3e = 2.412	ce = 0.868	t3e = 2.567
dt = 0.868	e3t = 2.542	ct = 0.868	t3t = 2.412
db = 0.849	e3b = 2.472	cb = 0.849	t3b = 2.472
dm = 0.868	e3m = 2.340	cm = 0.868	t3m = 2.485
de2 = 0.868	e3e2 = 2.458	ce2 = 0.868	t3e2 = 2.567
db2 = *	e3b2 = *	cb2 = *	t3b2 = 2.526
dt2 = 0.868	e3t2 = *	ct2 = 0.868	t3t2 = 2.412
dd = 2.667	e3d = 2.472	cd = *	t3d = 2.472
de3 = 0.868	e3e3 = 2.412	ce3 = 0.868	t3e3 = 2.567
dc = *	e3c = 2.472	cc = 2.667	t3c = 2.000
dt3 = 0.868	e3t3 = 2.542	ct3 = 0.750	t3t3 = 2.412

Computation and Undecidability in the Spatialized Prisoner's Dilemma

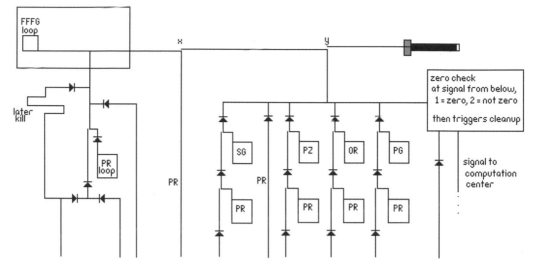

Figure 12   Schematic for a Minsky register.

larger by one.[34] What is required for Minsky memory is thus the ability to make the fat segment grow to the right in order to represent addition, to make it shrink to the left in order to represent subtraction, and the ability to check whether its length at any point corresponds to our specified zero mark.

Figures 13 and 14 illustrate how addition and subtraction are accomplished within the memory core itself. A crucial part of the process in each case is played by the memory tip of the core, composed of strategy **m** and shown as dark grey in black and white. This memory tip flashes from a single to a double column every second generation as an effect of our competitive scores. The total scores generated for a single row of **m** are such that they overpower the **w** neighbors to their left. **m**'s score against itself is then insufficient to maintain the advantage, however, and the core returns to a single rather than a double **m** tip.

Selected steps in the process of addition are shown in figure 13.[35] Here we send a carefully timed **et** pair—our standard electron—into the memory core. On encountering the triple rows of the fat segment the electron itself expands to a tripled form, continuing its movement to the right. Once the **e** head of the electron reaches the **m** tip of the memory core, however, the high scores of **m** against **e** cause an explosion of the **m** tip both to the left and to the right, forming a triple block of nine cells. In the next generation the wire strategy **w** eliminates the electron tail **t**, and from there eats away at the memory tip until it is again down to a single column of three. In the process, however, the memory tip of **m** is eaten down to its extreme right position, which now is one unit further to the right than where it started. By sending a standard electron into the memory core

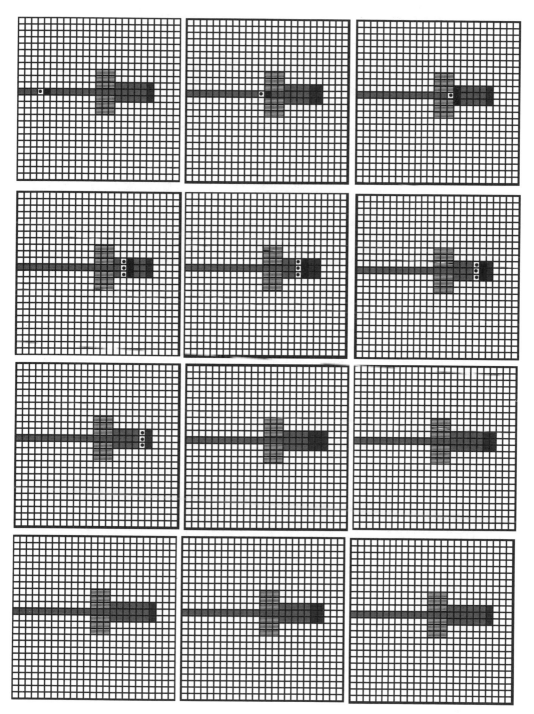

Figure 13 Addition.

Computation and Undecidability in the Spatialized Prisoner's Dilemma

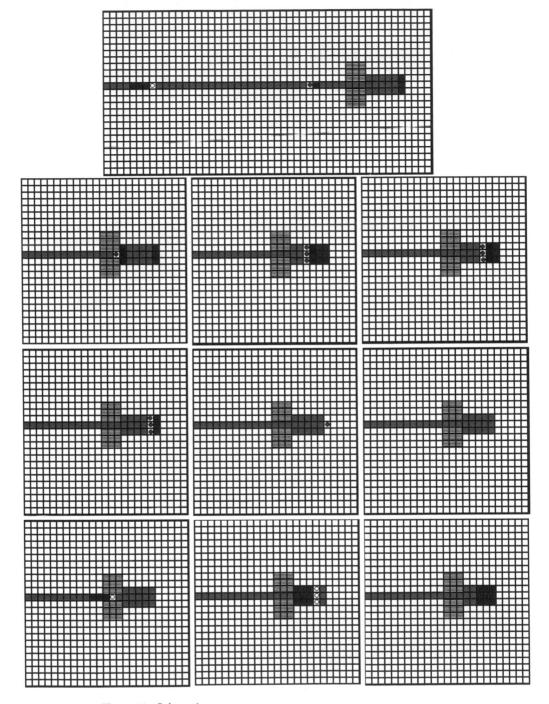

Figure 14   Subtraction.

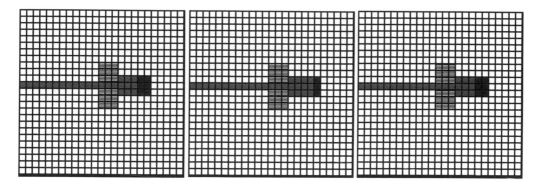

Figure 14 (*continued*).

we have thus expanded it to the right by one cell. If we repeat the process we will have lengthened it by two cells—the equivalent of adding by one.

The process of subtraction, shown in figure 14, is more complicated in several regards: it uses a special electron with a different timing and also requires a supplementary second step. Here the electron sent into our memory core is of the form **et2**, with a standard electron head **e** but a variant tail of strategy **t2**. In black and white, **t2** is marked by a grey dot. Scores for strategies **t2** and **e** have been chosen so that this special electron will travel down both a single and triple wire precisely as did its standard **et** predecessor. In the case of subtraction, however, timing differs by a single tick—enough to keep electron head **e** and memory tip **m** from coming into direct contact. What happens instead is that our electron effectively drives the memory tip off the end, ultimately leaving only a **t2** tip in its place as the special electron's payload. Strategy **t2**, however, has a set of scores much more vulnerable in competition with background **b** than those of **m**. In two generations the **t2** tip has been eliminated, leaving a memory core composed entirely of wire strategy **w**—without any tip at all—one unit shorter than the original.

A second step is required to restore the memory tip. Here again we use a special electron, though in this case our electron is composed of a head of strategy **e2** and three tails of strategy **m**. In black and white coding a hollow dot is used for **e2**, with **m** portrayed as dark grey. Despite its size, a four-cell **e2mmm** electron travels down our standard wire and into the memory core just as would a standard **et** electron. At the end of the register the **e2** head disappears, but the **m** tails remain. Eventually these shrink to a single flashing row. That new row, however, sits at the tip of our *shortened* memory segment; in two steps we have successfully shortened our memory core by a single cell. On repeating our two-step process we will have shortened our memory core by two cells—the equivalent of subtracting by one.[36]

What of the zero-check? Here the basic trick is to send a special electron, designed to bounce back, into the memory core. We carefully note when it is sent, and wait expectantly for its return. If our memory core is in fact of the length corresponding to our chosen 'zero', the electron will bounce back in a predictable number of generations. If our memory core is longer, the bouncing electron will not have returned by the appointed time and we will know that our contents are not zero. The role of the control mechanism in all of this, of course, is timing and registering the return of the prodigal electron. The crucial phenomenon required within the memory core itself is the bouncing electron.

In this case the electron used is a carefully timed **te2** pair. Sent down the single wire, it travels into the triple core precisely as did its predecessors. The **e2** head is timed to meet a double column of strategy **m** at the tip, with relevant scores chosen to give **e2** with an **m** backing an advantage over its own **t** tail. The result, shown in figure 15, is that our electron loses its tail and the **e2** head starts to move left trailed by cells of strategy **m** extending from the end of the memory core. Our original **te2** electron is thus transformed into something peculiarly different—a trail of **m**s with an **e2** at the head growing in the opposite direction—but it does give us the basic mechanism of an electron 'bounce'. That, at any rate, is the theory; things become messier in practice. Were our returning **e2** head to travel left through the collar of strategy **c**, moving smoothly from a triple wire to a single, its return could be used for the zero-mark timing check precisely as outlined above. Here we face a complication, however: the strategies outlined, carefully chosen to satisfy other desiderata, are such that the returning **e2** ends up stuck at the bottleneck transition from three wires to one. There it remains in the form of the flashing unit of strategy **e2** shown in the final frames of figure 15.

The flashing unit at the bottleneck can still be exploited as part of the timing strategy of our zero check, however. Given a memory core precisely as long as our chosen 'zero mark', our special electron will bounce back to establish a bottleneck in a predictable number of generations. If the memory core is longer than zero, on the other hand, a bottleneck will not have been established by the appointed time. Our timing check can still be completed from the left, therefore, if we perform a secondary bounce off the bottleneck. This secondary bounce can be accomplished by sending down an **e2mmm** series at the proper time followed by a special electron composed of an electron head **e2** and a tail of strategy of **t3**. Our **e2t3** pair is shown in black and white using a hollow-dotted **e2** and a white dot on black for **t3**.[37]

As a whole, then, the zero-check proceeds by sending a carefully timed **e2t** down the lead wire of the memory core, followed by a synchronized **e2mmm** and **e2t3**. The entire process is illustrated in figures 15 and 16 taken together. If our memory is at 'zero', the **e2t** electron will bounce back to establish a bottleneck at precisely the time that the later **e2mmm** is

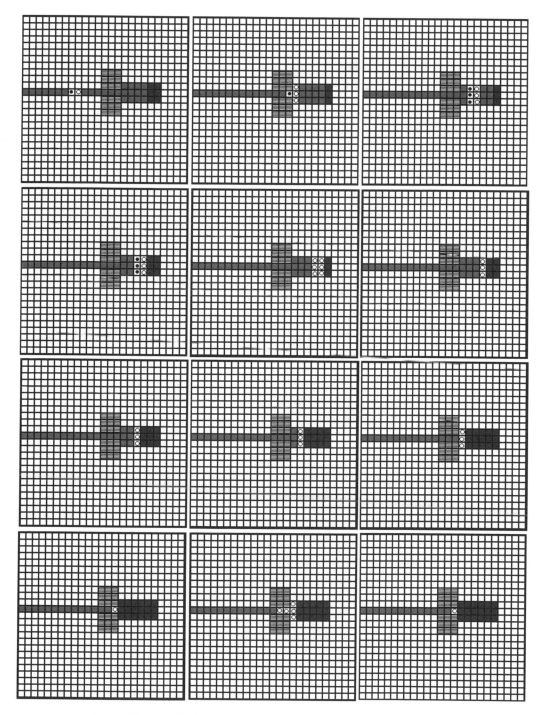

Figure 15 Zero-check electron 'bounce' in the memory core.

Computation and Undecidability in the Spatialized Prisoner's Dilemma

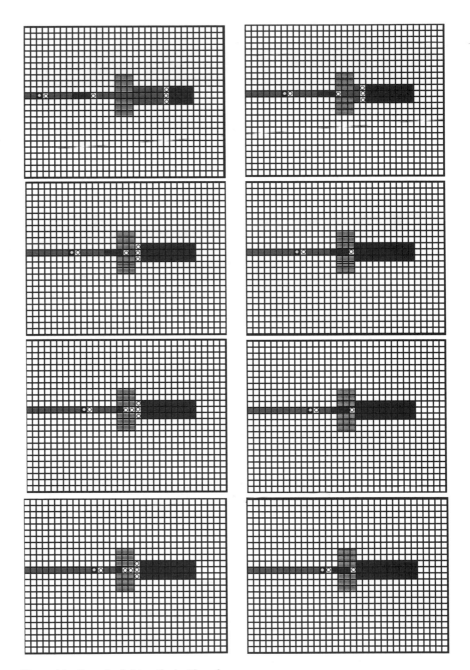

Figure 16 Zero-check from the bottleneck on.

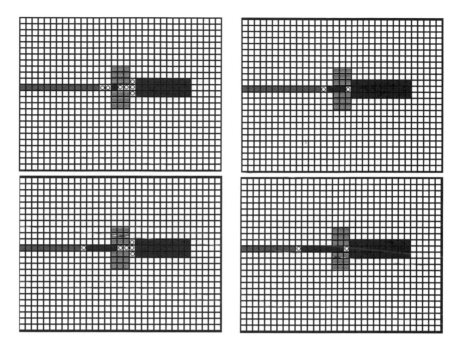

Figure 16 (*continued*).

scheduled to hit it. That will extend the bottleneck left in such a way that our special **e2t3** electron will reverse itself left in the form of an **e2** trailed by **m**s, returning along the single wire by an appointed time to tell us that our memory was indeed at the zero mark. If our memory is longer than 'zero', on the other hand, and a bottleneck has not yet been established, our **e2mmm** will travel into the memory core and the **e2t3** electron will simply be extinguished at the **c** collar of the memory register.[38] Our bouncing electron **e2t** will eventually return down the memory core in the form of a **e2mmm** trail, meeting the incoming **e2mmm** head-on and establishing a stationary flashing 'block'. By that time our **e2t3** electron will have vanished. If memory is greater than zero, then, there will be no message sent back down the single wire.

All of this accomplishes the desired result: a memory register at 'zero' will bounce back a special electron, whereas a memory register containing some greater integer will not. The process does leave us with a very untidy memory unit, however. If the process of our double bounce registers a 'zero', we are left with a solid memory core of strategy **m** and a **e2mmm** trail extending left from a bottleneck of strategy **e2**. If our memory is longer than zero we have a flashing block stuck deep in the memory core. A supplementary clean-up process is thus required, triggered by the appropriate response received in our check. In the nonzero case, two special **e3t** electrons are sufficient for clean-up duty; our memory register is returned to a solid band of wire strategy **w** with an alternating memory tip

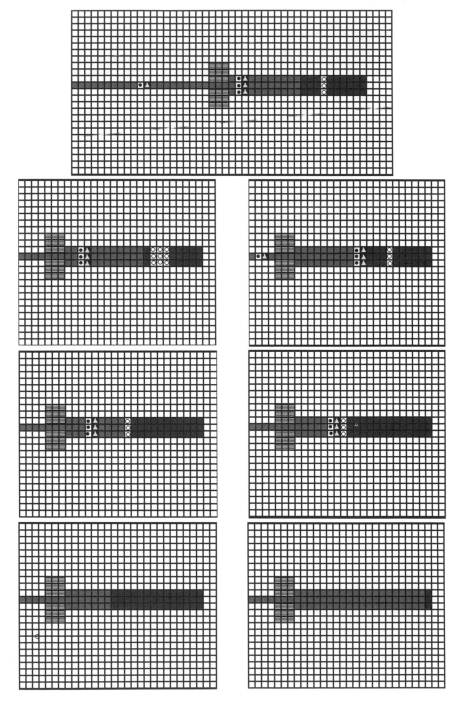

Figure 17 Clean-up in the non-zero case.

of **m**. The process is illustrated in figure 17, coding **e3** with a white triangle against black and **t** with a black dot. In the zero case our final return detector can be built so as extinguish the **e2** head of the single-wire **e2mmm** trail when it is encountered. The headless string of **m**s will shrink back to the bottleneck, where two **e3t** pairs again suffice to restore the original memory core.

All basic functions of Minsky register memory, then, can be accomplished in the context of our competitive cellular automata: addition by one, subtraction by one, and zerocheck. The rest of the register schematic in figure 12 portrays the management mechanism, which in effect converts messages received in terms of normal electrons from the computation center into pulses of special electrons sent into the memory core.

For those interested in the details we provide close-ups of a few of the essential management components.

One component used repeatedly in the schematic is a two-loop conversion mechanism, which takes a normal electron as input and sends some special electron out the other side. A simplified illustration of the basic principle appears in figures 18a and 18b. Essential to the process is the fact that strategy scores have been chosen so that a standard electron **et** pair can extinguish any other special electron pair at a kill site. Without an electron input from the left, therefore, the two loops shown generate electrons that mutually annihilate at the last kill site, much in the manner of negation (figure 18a). An electron input, however, kills off an **et** pair from the first loop and therefore allows a special electron to escape from the second; we have effectively converted a normal electron to a special electron (figure 18b). Any particular synchronization for particular electrons with respect to other parts of the register mechanism can be set by the length of the output wire.

The one special electron that consists of more than a pair, the **e2mmm** quadruplet used in the zero-check procedure and required for memory replacement within the subtraction procedure, turns out to be the hardest to control. Because such an electron refuses to turn a standard wire corner within a standard background field, for example, a different background strategy **b2** is used for the **e2mmm** breeding loop in the upper left hand corner of the schematic. In other regards the double-loop mechanism is similar to others in the schematic: loop-generated **e2mmm**s and standard **et**s mutually annihilate at an upper kill site, unless an electron signal is sent in on the first input line from the left. When an **e2mmm** is released to the right, however, a copy also travels south, calling for the later head-on kill provided by a delayed electron on the western loop.

In its passage to the memory core, the **e2mmm** quadruplet still needs to pass through two kill gates at x and y in figure 12, required for other purposes. Transfer at each point is choreographed using one timed electron from the rear and one from the south, as illustrated in figure 19. For this

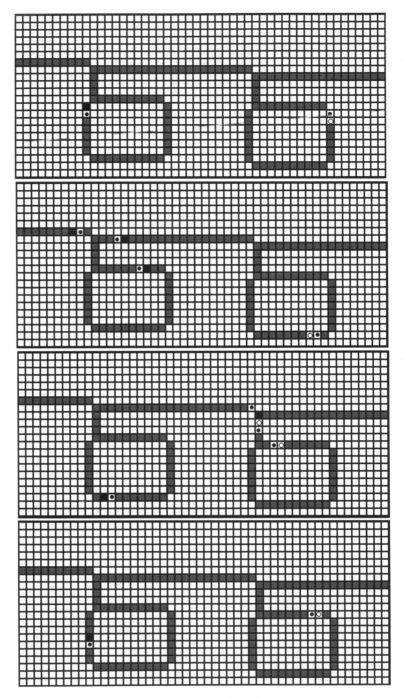

Figure 18a The principle of the double-loop transfer: given no input from the left, mutual kill and no output to the right. (For purposes of illustration, a diode left of each loop is omitted and loops are shortened accordingly.)

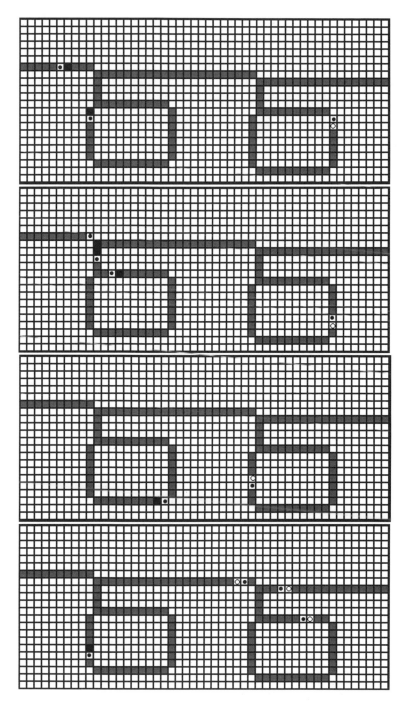

Figure 18b The principle of the double-loop transfer: **et** input from the left resulting in **e2t** output from the right. (For purposes of illustration a diode left of each loop is omitted and loops are shortened accordingly.)

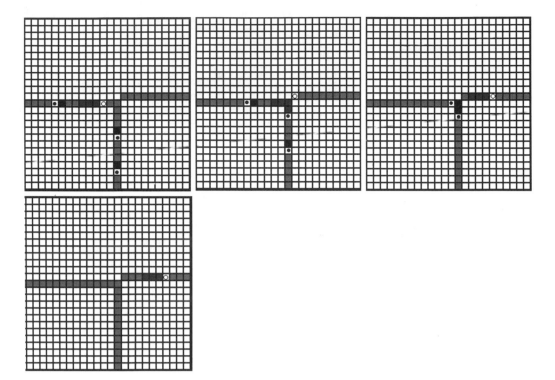

Figure 19 **e2mmm** transfer.

reason provision was also made near the **e2mmm** loop for sending independent **et** pairs down the feed wire and out to the right.[39]

The one management mechanism left to be described is the component of the zero-check that registers whether or not a **e2mmm** trail has bounced back from the memory core in the time required to signal a memory contents of zero. Here two standard electrons are used at gate y in the manner illustrated in figure 20. If an **e2mmm** series has arrived at the proper time, only one of these will travel south to a final detector (as shown). If an **e2mmm** has not arrived, indicating a memory contents greater than zero, both electrons will travel south to be registered. The signal required at the final detector is thus simply '2 = not zero, 1 = zero'.[40]

We note one final complication. In tweaking strategies to achieve the basic mechanisms of a Minsky register, a slight change in scores has been required for strategy **b** against itself. In the initial outline of strategy scores for basic wires in section 6.3, **bb** appears as 2.667; in Table 1, for the full Minsky register, it appears as 2.612. The only basic mechanism this affects is the T-branch, of for example the original diode, which now requires the protective collar of strategy **d** (for 'diode collar') shown in figure 21.

Although details are somewhat complicated, then, a Minsky register machine can effectively be wired within our cellular automata. Unlike a

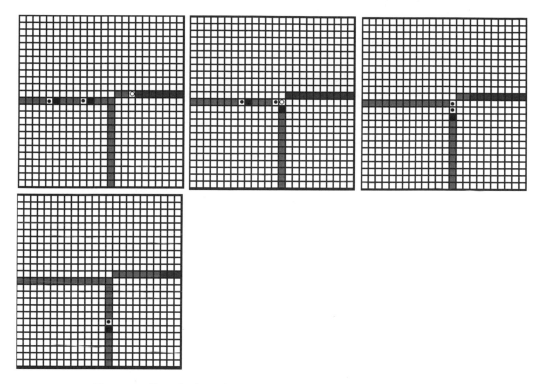

Figure 20 Zero-check mechanism.

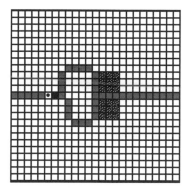

Figure 21 Diode variant.

looped Turing machine, moreover, which requires the complex background of an infinite tape loop, a Minsky register machine is elegantly self-contained. Because register contents are always finite, the initial state of any Minsky register machine can be instantiated as a finite configuration of strategies dropped into an unbroken infinite sea of a uniform background **b**, shown in black and white as an unbroken sea of white.

This allows us, finally, a more elegant statement of formal undecidability for the competitive automata at issue. Is there any algorithm that will tell us in each case what the result of embedding a finite configuration of strategies in a sea of strategy **b** will be? Because those finite configurations will include the instantiations of arbitrary Minsky register machines, equivalent to Turing machines, the answer must be 'no'.

Here we can also make undecidability a bit more graphic.

Let us add two additional strategies to those outlined above—**f** and **a**, for 'flask' and 'acid'. These are shown in black and white using square dots and vertical stripes. A short set of scores for **f** and **a**, in competition with our four basic strategies, is as follows:[41]

wf	= 2.412	**ef**	= 2.485
wa	= 0.857	**ea**	= 0.857
tf	= 2.583	**bf**	= 0.868
ta	= 0.857	**ba**	= 0.857
fw	= 2.412	**aw**	= 4.428
fe	= 2.534	**ae**	= 4.428
ft	= 3.000	**at**	= 4.428
fb	= 2.472	**ab**	= 4.428
ff	= 2.412	**af**	= 0.868
fa	= 2.472	**aa**	= 2.667

Beyond these scores the crucial requirement is simply that acid **a** will get a very high score against any other strategy, which will get very low score against it. We can stipulate that all other strategies score 0.857 in such a competition, with **a**s score an overpowering 4.428. Scores ϕ**f** and **f**ϕ for strategies ϕ other than those shown won't matter and can be listed as *.

What these two additional strategies allow is the construction of a 'strategy bomb': a device that will keep hostage and harmless a small patch of acid—strategy **a**—unless a pulse is sent down a particular wire. Given a pulse down that wire, on the other hand, our acid strategy will be released to expand without obstacle ever outward, progressively conquering all strategies in its path. Such a bomb is shown in figure 22 using a central block of nine **a** cells surrounded by a protective border of **f**. Left alone it remains harmless. Send a single pulse down its feed wire, however, and an all-invading cloud of acid will be released.

Consider now arbitrary finite arrangements of six basic strategies, our original four plus **f** and **a**, embedded in a standard infinite field that contains the cellular equivalent of a tape loop. Is there any algorithm or step-by-step procedure that will tell us in each case whether the result will be a progressive conquest by strategy **a** or not?

Consider, alternatively, arbitrary finite arrangements of all fourteen strategies, embedded in a uniform infinite field of background strategy **b**. Given a computer large enough or fast enough, a mind without limits on attention span or memory or attention to detail, is there any systematic

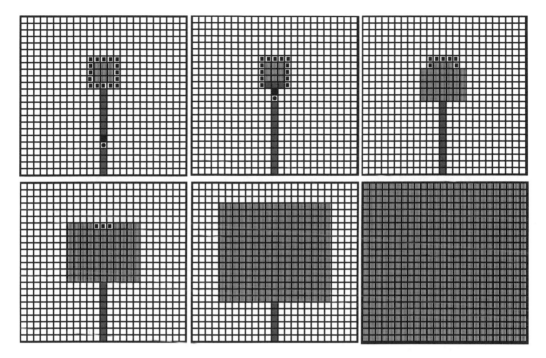

Figure 22 Explosion of strategy bomb.

mental or mechanical calculation that will tell us in each case whether or not the result will be progressive conquest by strategy **a**?

In each case the answer is 'no'.

Abstract machines of either looped Turing or Minsky register configuration can be constructed to look for solutions to arbitrarily hard arithmetical problems. Either type of abstract machine, suitably wired to a strategy bomb, can further be instantiated as an array of competitive cellular automata. Thus to arbitrarily difficult arithmetical problems will correspond arrays of the relevant set of strategies that will or will not result in a progressive conquest by acid strategy **a** depending on whether there is a solution to the problem at issue. Were there an algorithm that sorted the relevant arrangements into those that would result in conquest and those that would not, it would give us as well an algorithm suitable for deciding whether arbitrarily difficult arithmetical problems have solutions. Since there can be no algorithm of the latter sort, there can be no algorithm of the former sort either.

This is the Conway form of the proof. In somewhat more complete and traditional detail the argument can be presented in three steps: Minsky register machines, as outlined, can be instantiated as competitive cellular automata arrays. Those arrays can themselves be thought of as encoded, either directly or in terms of the abstract machine they instantiate. The first question is whether there can be any algorithm that decides, for arbitrary machine-configuration encodings of this type, whether the larger array composed of that machine-configuration started on its own encoding as input will result in conquest by strategy **a** or not.

The answer is no. If there were such an algorithm, it could be computed by a Minsky register machine, and that machine could in turn be instantiated as a cellular array with a strategy bomb fixed to the relevant signal wire in such a way that a positive answer would prevent, and a negative answer would produce, a progressive conquest by strategy **a**. That machine-configuration would itself be assigned an encoding.

Consider the array composed of that machine-configuration begun on its own encoding as input. Were that array not to result in conquest by **a**, the core machine would give a negative answer, exploding the strategy bomb, which would result in precisely the conquest at issue. Were the array to result in conquest, on the other hand, the instantiated machine would never send a signal, and the array has been constructed so that no conquest by acid will in that case take place. The array at issue would thus result in conquest by strategy **a** just in case it would not. The contradiction shows us that there can be no such array, and thus there can be no machine and no algorithm of this first type.

As a second step, we can ask whether there can be an algorithm that decides, for any machine-configuration and any input, whether the result will be an unlimited conquest by acid strategy **a**. Again, the answer is no. If there were, that algorithm would be computable by an abstract machine from which the machine above could be obtained simply by adding an initial input duplicator (for the machine-arrays at issue here, achievable simply by a branching wire). We've seen that there can be no machine and thus no algorithm of that first type, and thus there can be no algorithm of this more general second type either.

Consider finally just finite configurations of our fourteen strategies, dropped into unlimited seas of a uniform background. Will any algorithm decide for each case whether the result will be unlimited conquest by strategy **a** or not? Again, no. Since the possible configurations at issue include those corresponding to Minsky register machines started on any input, an algorithm of this final type would give us an algorithm that told us, for any machine-configuration and any input, whether it would result in unlimited conquest by **a**. By the second step above there can be no such algorithm, and thus there can be no algorithm of this final sort either. There is no algorithm adequate to decide the general question of conquest for arbitrary, finite configurations of competitive strategies.

At this point we've moved from the classic undecidability of abstract machines, via their instantiation within competitive cellular automata, to the undecidability of competitive cellular arrays. The structure of these results thus parallels the basic strategy of Conway's proof for universal computation and undecidability in the Game of Life, though here the automata at issue are of an importantly different and more complex kind.[42]

It is the particular characteristics built into these automata that allow for the final application outlined in the next section.

6.4 COMPUTATION AND UNDECIDABILITY IN THE SPATIALIZED PRISONER'S DILEMMA

The final step is to show that the undecidability discussed for abstract machines in section 6.2 and carried over to competitive automata in section 6.3 is ultimately an undecidability that appears within game theory as well: the undecidability of the Spatialized Prisoner's Dilemma.

This is in fact the easiest step of all. The requirements are simply the specifications for a set of Prisoner's Dilemma strategies that will generate payoffs in infinite games, which correspond to the scores used in constructing the competitive cellular automata of section 6.3 above. A set of strategies satisfying that requirement is exhibited in Appendix A.

Although other approaches are surely possible, the general idea of the particular construction used here is to have each strategy—**w, e, t, b**, etc.— begin its infinite series of play with a short signature set of cooperations and defections. Strategy **w** always begins with four defections, strategy **e** with three defections and a cooperation, and so forth. The strategies at issue are thus designed to begin play with what amounts to an identifying code. Given that convenient self-labeling, the behavior of each strategy on our list can be specified in terms of the codes of its opponents, which affords a great deal of flexibility in the fine-tuning of desired scores. Strategy **b** can be written as a series of individual clauses: 'If opponent started DDDD, play . . . , if opponent started DDDC, play . . . ,' and so forth. What is at issue are infinite games, as noted in the introduction, and the strategies listed in Appendix A are in all cases designed to set up periodic competitive play. Their scores thus depend in the end only on average scores over the infinitely repeated period of play; scoring within the initial signature set can simply be ignored. Because finite games of increasingly length will progressively swamp any initial scoring in precisely the same way, the basic results at issue could also be shown for finite games of sufficient length.[43]

Evidence that configurations of Prisoner's Dilemma strategies in fact constitute competitive automata arrays adequate to model either of our basic abstract machines—and therefore inherit their undecidability—need go no further than such a list of particular strategies. Though clumsy, perhaps, the proof could hardly be more constructive. It is also possible to take a more general approach. Using the basic techniques indicated above, we can in fact design Prisoner's Dilemma strategies that will give us essentially any desired competitive scores between 1 and 3 for each strategy. This suffices to specify the overwhelming majority of scores required in the present case. Where one of a pair of strategies is below 1 or above 3 we can also pinpoint a highest and lowest possible score for an opposing strategy, and can design a strategy to give us any chosen score between those points. Algebraic details for this more general approach are outlined in Appendix B.

Cooperative behavior is a basic fact of both economics and biology. Accounting for that fact is a theoretical challenge, and both theoretical economics and theoretical biology have imported resources from game theory in the attempt to do so. The primary model appealed to in both disciplines has been the Prisoner's Dilemma, which in iterated and spatialized forms offers a compelling picture of surprising but intelligible ways in which cooperation can arise from and serve the needs of self-interest. These game-theoretic models thus constitute some of our simplest attempts at understanding this aspect of ourselves as both biological and social organisms.

What the work above indicates is that formal undecidability shows up even in these simple models. In that sense classic limitative results refuse to keep their intellectual distance, safely locked away in the higher reaches of axiomatic arithmetic, abstract machine or algorithmic information theory. The phenomenon of undecidability, it turns out, characterizes even some of our simplest models of ourselves. To the extent that Vico represents a thesis of transparent intelligibility in the social sciences, with Marx arguing the contrary, such a result offers formal support for Marx's side of the debate.

An important qualification should also be noted, however. One clearly unrealistic aspect of the models used throughout is that they employ an infinite two-dimensional field. That feature is in fact crucial for our undecidability results—the modeling of arbitrary Minsky Register machines, for example, requires an infinite background sea in order to allow memory cores to expand as needed. The core undecidability result can therefore only be said to apply to our models in an abstract form, rather than immediately to the non-abstract phenomena that they model.[44]

None of this, moreover, should be taken as indicating that game-theoretic modeling is somehow conceptually doomed or hopeless, any more than standard Gödel results indicate that arithmetical programming is doomed or hopeless. None of it indicates that there is anything wrong with our attempts to use the Spatialized Prisoner's Dilemma as a model within either biology or economics. If anything, the work above is rather a reflection on the surprising depth of even the simple models we now use. Simple as they are, these abstract models are sufficient for the classical phenomena of universal computation and formal undecidability. Thus even if biological or economic phenomena were themselves as simple as some of our simplest existing models for them, the basic abstract principles of those phenomena would afford a complexity comparable to some of our richest mathematics.

APPENDIX A: COMPETITIVE STRATEGIES ADEQUATE FOR A MINSKY REGISTER MACHINE

In the specifications that follow, please note that

$$\underbrace{010101\ldots01}_{100\text{ plays}}$$

indicates 100 Prisoner's Dilemma competitions, in the first of which the player defects, in the second of which he cooperates, and so on. The notation above thus specifies a block of 100 plays. The notation below, in contrast:

$$\underbrace{01010101010}_{100\text{ times}}$$

indicates that a block of 11 set moves is to be repeated 100 times. It thus specifies a sequence of 1100 plays.

Strategy **w**: Start with 0000. Then:

If opponent started 0000, play 11111111111100000, repeat.	(gives **ww** = 2.412)
If opponent started 0001, play $\underbrace{010101\ldots01}_{100\text{ plays}}$ followed by 011, repeat.	(gives **we** = 2.534)
If opponent started 0010, play 1111111111100, repeat.	(gives **wt** = 3.000)
If opponent started 0011, play $\underbrace{1000000000}_{10\text{ times}}$ followed by 000000, repeat.	(gives **wh** = 2.472)
If opponent started 0100, play $\underbrace{01010101\ldots01}_{500\text{ plays}}$, followed by 11111000001	(gives **wm** = 2.495)
If opponent started 0101, play $\underbrace{010101\ldots01}_{100\text{ plays}}$ followed by 011, repeat.	(gives **we2** = 2.534)
If opponent started 0110, play $\underbrace{1000000000}_{20\text{ times}}$ followed by 0000000000000, repeat.	(gives **wb2** = 2.502)
If opponent started 0111, play 111111111100, repeat.	(gives **wt2** = 3.000)
If opponent started 1000, play $\underbrace{1000000000}_{10\text{ times}}$ followed by 000000, repeat.	(gives **wd** = 2.472)
If opponent started 1001, play $\underbrace{010101\ldots01}_{100\text{ plays}}$ followed by 011, repeat.	(gives **we3** = 2.534)
If opponent started 1010, play $\underbrace{1000000000}_{10\text{ times}}$ followed by 000000, repeat.	(gives **wc** = 2.472)
If opponent started 1011, play 111111111100, repeat.	(gives **wt3** = 3.000)

Strategy **e**: Start with 0001. Then:

If opponent started 0000, play $\underbrace{101010\ldots10}_{100\text{ plays}}$ followed by 111, repeat.	(gives **ew** = 2.485)
If opponent started 0001, play 11111111111100000, repeat.	(gives **ee** = 2.412)
If opponent started 0010, play $\underbrace{010101\ldots01}_{180\text{ plays}}$ followed by $\underbrace{111\ldots111}_{20\text{ plays}}$ and 111, repeat.	(gives **et** = 2.542)
If opponent started 0011, play $\underbrace{1000000000}_{10\text{ times}}$ followed by 000000, repeat.	(gives **eb** = 2.472)
If opponent started 0100, play $\underbrace{11111111111111000000}_{31\text{ times}}$, followed by $\underbrace{11111\ldots11}_{20\text{ plays}}$, repeat.	(gives **em** = 2.341)

If opponent started 0101, play repeated 0. (gives **ee2** $= 1$)

If opponent started 0110, play $\underbrace{1000000000}$ followed by 00000000001, repeat. (gives **eb2** $= 2.526$)
  20 times

If opponent started 0111, play $\underbrace{010101\ldots01}_{180\text{ plays}}$ followed by $\underbrace{111\ldots111}_{20\text{ plays}}$ and 111, repeat. (gives **et2** $= 2.542$)

If opponent started 1000, play $\underbrace{1000000000}$ followed by 000000, repeat. (gives **ed** $= 2.472$)
  10 times

If opponent started 1001, play 11111111111100000, repeat. (gives **cc3** $= 2.412$)

If opponent started 1010, play $\underbrace{1000000000}$ followed by 000000, repeat. (gives **ec** $= 2.472$)
  10 times

If opponent started 1011, play $\underbrace{010101\ldots01}_{180\text{ plays}}$ followed by $\underbrace{111\ldots111}_{20\text{ plays}}$ and 111, repeat. (gives **et3** $= 2.542$)

Strategy **t**: Start with 0010. Then:

If opponent started 0000, play 111111111101, repeat. (gives **tw** $= 2.583$)

If opponent started 0001, play $\underbrace{101010\ldots10}_{180\text{ plays}}$, followed by $\underbrace{111\ldots111}_{20\text{ plays}}$ and 011, repeat. (gives **te** $= 2.567$)

If opponent started 0010, play 11111111111100000, repeat. (gives **tt** $= 2.412$)

If opponent started 0011, play $\underbrace{1000000000}$ followed by 000000, repeat. (gives **tb** $= 2.472$)
  10 times

If opponent started 0100, play $\underbrace{111111\ldots111}_{19,854\text{ plays}}$, followed by $\underbrace{000\ldots000}_{5146\text{ plays}}$, followed by 0, repeat. (gives **tm** $= 2.485$)

If opponent started 0101, play $\underbrace{101010\ldots10}_{180\text{ plays}}$, followed by $\underbrace{111\ldots111}_{20\text{ plays}}$ and 011, repeat. (gives **te2** $= 2.567$)

If opponent started 0110, play $\underbrace{1000000000}$ followed by 00000000001, repeat. (gives **tb2** $= 2.526$)
  20 times

If opponent started 0111, play 11111111111100000, repeat. (gives **tt2** $= 2.412$)

If opponent started 1000, play $\underbrace{1000000000}$ followed by 000000, repeat. (gives **td** $= 2.472$)
  10 times

If opponent started 1001, play $\underbrace{101010\ldots10}_{180\text{ plays}}$, followed by $\underbrace{111\ldots111}_{20\text{ plays}}$ and 011, repeat. (gives **te3** $= 2.567$)

If opponent started 1010, play $\underbrace{1000000000}$ followed by 000000, repeat. (gives **tc** $= 2.472$)
  10 times

If opponent started 1011, play 11111111111100000, repeat. (gives **tt3** $= 2.412$)

Strategy **b**: Start with 0011. Then:

If opponent started 0000 play $\underbrace{1111000000}$, followed by 111100, repeat. (gives **bw** $= 0.868$)
  10 times

If opponent started 0001 play $\underbrace{1111000000}$, followed by 111100, repeat. (gives **be** $= 0.868$)
  10 times

If opponent started 0010 play $\underbrace{1111000000}$, followed by 111100, repeat. (gives **bt** $= 0.868$)
  10 times

If opponent started 0011, play $\underbrace{111\ldots111}_{1612\text{ plays}}$ followed by $\underbrace{000\ldots000}_{180\text{ plays}}$, repeat. (gives **bb** $= 2.612$)

(For **bb** $= 2.667$, as outlined earlier in the paper: If opponent started 011, play 111111111100, repeat.)

If opponent started 0100, play $\underbrace{111\ldots111}_{187\text{ plays}}$ followed by $\underbrace{000\ldots000}_{213\text{ plays}}$ followed by (gives **bm** $= 1.216$)

$\underbrace{1010\ldots10}_{402\text{ plays}}$, repeat.

If opponent started 0101, play $\underbrace{1111000000}$ followed by 111100, repeat. (gives **be2** $= 0.868$)
  10 times

If opponent started 0110, play $\underbrace{1000000000}_{\text{20 times}}$ followed by $\underbrace{000000}_{\text{3 times}}$, repeat.   (gives **bb2** $= 2.615$)

If opponent started 0111, play $\underbrace{1111\ldots111}_{\text{1292 plays}}$ followed by $\underbrace{000\ldots000}_{\text{708 plays}}$, repeat 1871 times, (gives **bt2** $= 1.841$)

followed by $\underbrace{1010\ldots1010}_{\text{2000 plays}}$, repeat 629 times, repeat whole.

If opponent started 1000, play $\underbrace{1000000000}_{\text{20 times}}$ followed by 000000, repeat.   (gives **bd** $= 2.615$)

If opponent started 1001, play $\underbrace{1111000000}_{\text{10 times}}$ followed by 111100, repeat.   (gives **be3** $= 0.868$)

If opponent started 1010, play $\underbrace{1000000000}_{\text{20 times}}$ followed by $\underbrace{000000}_{\text{3 times}}$, repeat.   (gives **bc** $= 2.615$)

If opponent started 1011, play $\underbrace{1111000000}_{\text{10 times}}$ followed by 111100, repeat.   (gives **bt3** $= 0.868$)

Strategy **m**: Start with 0100. Then:

If opponent started 0000, play $\underbrace{01010101\ldots01}_{\text{500 plays}}$, followed by 11111000000   (gives **mw** $= 2.485$)

If opponent started 0001, play $\underbrace{11111111111111000000}_{\text{31 times}}$, followed by $\underbrace{1010\ldots10}_{\text{20 plays}}$, repeat.   (gives **me** $= 2.419$)

If opponent started 0010, play $\underbrace{111111\ldots111}_{\text{19,854 plays}}$, followed by $\underbrace{010101\ldots01}_{\text{5146 plays}}$, followed by 0, (gives **mt** $= 2.99992$)
repeat.

If opponent started 0011, play $\underbrace{111\ldots111}_{\text{187 plays}}$ followed by $\underbrace{000\ldots000}_{\text{213 plays}}$ followed by (gives **mb** $= 2.469$)
$\underbrace{0000\ldots00}_{\text{402 plays}}$, repeat.

If opponent started 0100, play 11111111111100000, repeat.   (gives **mm** $= 2.412$)

If opponent started 0101, play $\underbrace{111\ldots111}_{\text{100 plays}}$ followed by 000000000000, repeat 2373 (gives **me2** $= 2.886$)

times, followed by $\underbrace{0000\ldots00}_{\text{200 plays}}$, repeat 127 times, repeat whole.

If opponent started 0110, play $\underbrace{1000000000}_{\text{12 times}}$ followed by 000111, repeat.   (gives **mb2** $= 2.476$)

If opponent started 0111, play $\underbrace{111\ldots1111}_{\text{1184 plays}}$ followed by $\underbrace{000\ldots000}_{\text{816 plays}}$, repeat 55 times, (gives **mt2** $= 2.819$)

followed by $\underbrace{000\ldots000}_{\text{200 plays}}$, repeat whole.

If opponent started 1000, play $\underbrace{1000000000}_{\text{10 times}}$ followed by 000000, repeat.   (gives **md** $= 2.472$)

If opponent started 1001, play $\underbrace{101010000010}_{\text{90 times}}$ followed by 11111111111, repeat.   (gives **me3** $= 0.692$)

If opponent started 1010, play $\underbrace{1000000000}_{\text{10 times}}$ followed by 0000 repeat.   (gives **mc** $= 2.472$)

If opponent started 1011, play $\underbrace{111111\ldots111}_{\text{19,854 plays}}$, followed by $\underbrace{010101\ldots01}_{\text{5146 plays}}$, followed by 0, (gives **mt3** $= 2.99992$)
repeat.

Strategy **e2**: Start with 0101. Then:

If opponent started 0000, play $\underbrace{101010\ldots10}_{\text{100 plays}}$ followed by 111, repeat.   (gives **e2w** $= 2.485$)

If opponent started 0001, play repeated 0.   (gives **e2e** $= 1$)

If opponent started 0010, play $\underbrace{010101\ldots01}_{\text{180 plays}}$ followed by $\underbrace{111\ldots111}_{\text{20 plays}}$ and 111, repeat.   (gives **e2t** $= 2.542$)

If opponent started 0011, play $\underbrace{1000000000}_{\text{10 times}}$ followed by 000000, repeat. (gives **e2b** $= 2.472$)

If opponent started 0100, play $\underbrace{111\ldots111}_{\text{188 plays}}$ followed by 000000000000, repeat 2373 (gives **e2m** $= 2.759$)

times, followed by $\underbrace{0101\ldots01,}_{\text{200 plays}}$ repeat 127 times, repeat whole.

If opponent started 0101, play 11111111111100000, repeat. (gives **e2e2** $= 2.412$)

If opponent started 0110, play $\underbrace{1000000000}_{\text{10 times}}$ followed by 000000, repeat. (gives **e2b2** $= 2.472$)

If opponent started 0111, * (any strategy will do. gives **e2t2**)

If opponent started 1000, play $\underbrace{1000000000}_{\text{10 times}}$ followed by 000000, repeat. (gives **e2d** $= 2.472$)

If opponent started 1001, play $\underbrace{111\ldots1111}_{\text{6996 plays}}$ followed by $\underbrace{000\ldots0000,}_{\text{1304 plays}}$ repeat 521 times, (gives **e2e3** $= 0.9999$)

521 times, followed by $\underbrace{101010\ldots10,}_{\text{20000 plays}}$ repeat 729 times, repeat whole.

If opponent started 1010, play $\underbrace{1000000000}_{\text{10 times}}$ followed by 000000, repeat. (gives **e2c** $= 2.472$)

If opponent started 1011, play $\underbrace{010101\ldots01}_{\text{180 plays}}$ followed by $\underbrace{111\ldots111}_{\text{20 plays}}$ and 111, repeat. (gives **e2t3** $= 2.542$)

Strategy **b2**: start with 0110. Then:

If opponent started 0000, play $\underbrace{1111000000}_{\text{20 times}}$ followed by 1111101111100, repeat. (gives **b2w** $= 0.859$)

If opponent started 0001, play $\underbrace{1111000000}_{\text{20 times}}$ followed by 11111111111, repeat. (gives **b2e** $= 0.867$)

If opponent started 0010, play $\underbrace{1111000000}_{\text{20 times}}$ followed by 11111111111, repeat. (gives **b2t** $= 0.867$)

If opponent started 0011, play $\underbrace{1111000000}_{\text{20 times}}$ followed by $\underbrace{111111,}_{\text{3 times}}$ repeat. (gives **b2b** $= 0.849$)

If opponent started 0100, play $\underbrace{1111000000}_{\text{12 times}}$ followed by 111111, repeat. (gives **b2m** $= 0.9285$)

If opponent started 0101, play $\underbrace{1111000000}_{\text{10 times}}$ followed by 111100, repeat. (gives **b2e2** $= 0.868$)

If opponent started 0110, play $\underbrace{111\ldots1111}_{\text{1667 plays}}$ followed by $\underbrace{000\ldots000,}_{\text{333 plays}}$ repeat. (gives **b2b2** $= 2.667$)

If opponent started 0111, play $\underbrace{1111000000}_{\text{10 times}}$ followed by 111100, repeat. (gives **b2t2** $= 0.868$)

If opponent started 1000, * (any strategy. gives **b2d**)

If opponent started 1001, * (any strategy. gives **b2e3**)

If opponent started 1010, * (any strategy. gives **b2c**)

If opponent started 1011, play $\underbrace{1111000000}_{\text{20 times}}$ followed by 11111111111, repeat. (gives **b2t3** $= 0.867$)

Strategy **t2**: Start with 0111. Then:

If opponent started 0000, play 111111111101, repeat. (gives **t2w** $= 2.583$)

If opponent started 0001, play $\underbrace{101010\ldots10}_{\text{180 plays}}$ followed by $\underbrace{111\ldots111}_{\text{20 plays}}$ and 011, repeat. (gives **t2e** $= 2.567$)

If opponent started 0010, play 11111111111100000, repeat. (gives **t2t** $= 2.412$)

If opponent started 0011, play $\underbrace{1111\ldots111}_{1292 \text{ plays}}$ followed by $\underbrace{000\ldots000}_{708 \text{ plays}}$, repeat 1871 times,   (gives **t2b** = 2.470)

followed by $\underbrace{0000\ldots0000}_{2000 \text{ plays}}$, repeat 629 times, repeat whole.

If opponent started 0100, play $\underbrace{111\ldots1111}_{1184 \text{ plays}}$ followed by $\underbrace{000\,000}_{816 \text{ plays}}$, repeat 55 times,   (gives **t2m** = 2.180)

followed by $\underbrace{111\ldots111}_{200 \text{ plays}}$, repeat whole.

If opponent started 0101, *   (any strategy will do. gives **t2e2**)

If opponent started 0110, play $\underbrace{1000000000}_{10 \text{ times}}$ followed by 000000, repeat.   (gives **t2b2** = 2.472)

If opponent started 0111, play 11111111111100000, repeat.   (gives **t2t2** = 2.412)

If opponent started 1000, play $\underbrace{1000000000}_{10 \text{ times}}$ followed by 000000, repeat.   (gives **t2d** = 2.472)

If opponent started 1001, *   (any strategy. Gives **t2e3**)

If opponent started 1010, play $\underbrace{1000000000}_{10 \text{ times}}$ followed by 000000, repeat.   (gives **t2c** = 2.472)

If opponent started 1011, play 11111111111100000, repeat.   (gives **t2t3** = 2.412)

Strategy **d**: Start with 1000. Then:

If opponent started 0000, play $\underbrace{1111000000}_{10 \text{ times}}$ followed by 111100, repeat.   (gives **dw** = 0.868)

If opponent started 0001, play $\underbrace{1111000000}_{10 \text{ times}}$ followed by 111100, repeat.   (gives **de** = 0.868)

If opponent started 0010, play $\underbrace{1111000000}_{10 \text{ times}}$ followed by 111100, repeat.   (gives **dt** = 0.868)

If opponent started 0011, play $\underbrace{1111000000}_{20 \text{ times}}$ followed by $\underbrace{111111}_{3 \text{ times}}$, repeat.   (gives **db** = 0.849)

If opponent started 0100, play $\underbrace{1111000000}_{10 \text{ times}}$ followed by 111100, repeat.   (gives **dm** = 0.868)

If opponent started 0101, play $\underbrace{1111000000}_{10 \text{ times}}$ followed by 111100, repeat.   (gives **de2** = 0.868)

If opponent started 0110, *   (any strategy. Gives **db2**)

If opponent started 0111, play $\underbrace{1111000000}_{10 \text{ times}}$ followed by 111100, repeat.   (gives **dt2** = 0.868)

If opponent started 1000, play $\underbrace{111\ldots1111}_{1667 \text{ plays}}$ followed by $\underbrace{000\ldots000}_{333 \text{ plays}}$, repeat.   (gives **dd** = 2.667)

If opponent started 1001, play $\underbrace{1111000000}_{10 \text{ times}}$ followed by 111100, repeat.   (gives **de3** = 0.868)

If opponent started 1010, *   (any strategy. gives **dc**)

If opponent started 1011, play $\underbrace{1111000000}_{10 \text{ times}}$ followed by 111100, repeat.   (gives **dt3** = 0.868)

Strategy **e3**: Start with 1001. Then:

If opponent started 0000, play $\underbrace{101010\ldots10}_{100 \text{ plays}}$ followed by 111, repeat.   (gives **e3w** = 2.485)

If opponent started 0001, play 11111111111100000, repeat.   (gives **e3e** = 2.412)

If opponent started 0010, play $\underbrace{010101\ldots01}_{180 \text{ plays}}$ followed by $\underbrace{111\ldots111}_{20 \text{ plays}}$ and 111, repeat.   (gives **e3t** = 2.542)

If opponent started 0011, play $\underbrace{1000000000}_{\text{10 times}}$ followed by 000000, repeat. (gives **e3b** $= 2.472$)

If opponent started 0100, play $\underbrace{000000000000}_{\text{90 times}}$ followed by 111111111111, repeat. (gives **e3m** $= 2.340$)

If opponent started 0101, play $\underbrace{111\ldots1111}_{\text{6996 plays}}$ followed by $\underbrace{000\ldots0000}_{\text{13004 plays}}$, repeat 521 times, (gives **e3e2** $= 2.458$)

followed by $\underbrace{000000\ldots00}_{\text{20000 plays}}$, repeat 729 times, repeat whole.

If opponent started 0110, * (any strategy. Gives **e3b2**)

If opponent started 0111, * (any strategy. Gives **e3t2**)

If opponent started 1000, play $\underbrace{1000000000}_{\text{10 times}}$ followed by 000000, repeat. (gives **e3d** $= 2.472$)

If opponent started 1001, play 11111111111100000, repeat. (gives **e3e3** $= 2.412$)

If opponent started 1010, play $\underbrace{1000000000}_{\text{10 times}}$ followed by 000000, repeat. (gives **e3c** $= 2.472$)

If opponent started 1011, play $\underbrace{010101\ldots01}_{\text{180 plays}}$ followed by $\underbrace{111\ldots111}_{\text{20 plays}}$ and 111, repeat. (gives **e3t3** $= 2.542$)

Strategy **c**: Start with 1010. Then:

If opponent started 0000, play $\underbrace{1111000000}_{\text{10 times}}$ followed by 111100, repeat. (gives **cw** $= 0.868$)

If opponent started 0001, play $\underbrace{1111000000}_{\text{10 times}}$ followed by 111100, repeat. (gives **ce** $= 0.868$)

If opponent started 0010, play $\underbrace{1111000000}_{\text{10 times}}$ followed by 111100, repeat. (gives **ct** $= 0.868$)

If opponent started 0011, play $\underbrace{1111000000}_{\text{20 times}}$ followed by $\underbrace{111111}_{\text{3 times}}$, repeat. (gives **cb** $= 0.849$)

If opponent started 0100, play $\underbrace{1111000000}_{\text{10 times}}$ followed by 111100, repeat. (gives **cm** $= 0.868$)

If opponent started 0101, play $\underbrace{1111000000}_{\text{10 times}}$ followed by 111100, repeat. (gives **ce2** $= 0.868$)

If opponent started 0110, * (any strategy. gives **cb2**)

If opponent started 0111, play $\underbrace{1111000000}_{\text{10 times}}$ followed by 111100, repeat. (gives **ct2** $= 0.868$)

If opponent started 1000, * (any strategy. gives **cd**)

If opponent started 1001, play $\underbrace{1111000000}_{\text{10 times}}$ followed by 111100, repeat. (gives **ce3** $= 0.868$)

If opponent started 1010, play $\underbrace{111\ldots1111}_{\text{1667 plays}}$ followed by $\underbrace{000\ldots000}_{\text{333 plays}}$, repeat. (gives **cc** $= 2.667$)

If opponent started 1011, play 1000, repeat. (gives **ct3** $= 0.75$)

Strategy **t3**: Start with 1011. Then:

If opponent started 0000, play 111111111101, repeat. (gives **t3w** $= 2.583$)

If opponent started 0001, play $\underbrace{101010\ldots10}_{\text{180 plays}}$, followed by $\underbrace{111\ldots111}_{\text{20 plays}}$ and 011, repeat. (gives **t3e** $= 2.567$)

If opponent started 0010, play 11111111111100000, repeat. (gives **t3t** $= 2.412$)

If opponent started 0011, play $\underbrace{1000000000}_{\text{10 times}}$ followed by 000000, repeat. (gives **t3b** $= 2.472$)

If opponent started 0100, play $\underbrace{111111\dots111}_{19,854 \text{ plays}}$, followed by $\underbrace{000\dots000}_{5146 \text{ plays}}$, followed by 0, (gives **t3m** = 2.485)
repeat.

If opponent started 0101, play $\underbrace{101010\dots10}_{180 \text{ plays}}$, followed by $\underbrace{111\dots111}_{20 \text{ plays}}$ and 011, repeat. (gives **t3e2** = 2.567)

If opponent started 0110, play $\underbrace{1000000000}_{20 \text{ times}}$ followed by 00000000001, repeat. (gives **t3b2** = 2.526)

If opponent started 0111, play 11111111111100000, repeat. (gives **t3t2** = 2.412)

If opponent started 1000, play $\underbrace{1000000000}_{10 \text{ times}}$ followed by 000000, repeat. (gives **t3d** = 2.472)

If opponent started 1001, play $\underbrace{101010\dots10}_{180 \text{ plays}}$, followed by $\underbrace{111\dots111}_{20 \text{ plays}}$ and 011, repeat. (gives **t3e3** = 2.567)

If opponent started 1010, play 0000, repeat. (gives **t3c** = 2.000)

If opponent started 1011, play 11111111111100000, repeat. (gives **t3t3** = 2.412)

APPENDIX B: AN ALGEBRAIC TREATMENT FOR COMPETITIVE STRATEGIES

Using the basic techniques outlined in section 6.4, it is possible to design Prisoner's Dilemma strategies that will give us essentially any desired competitive score between 1 and 3 for each strategy. Where one of a pair of strategies scores below 1 or above 3 we can also pinpoint the highest and lowest possible score for an opposing strategy, and design a strategy to give us any chosen score between those points.

Let us begin with an intuitive algebraic recipe for competitive strategies with desired scores between 1 and 3. In each round of a Prisoner's Dilemma there are just four scoring possibilities:

$$1 \ 3 \ 5 \ 0$$
Player A $\quad$ D C D C
Player B $\quad$ D C C D
$$1 \ 3 \ 0 \ 5$$

For periodic infinite games between any players A and B, therefore, averages for each player over the repeated period of play will consist of some combination of these score pairs, summed for each player and divided by the length of the repeated period of play.[45]

Consider first the special case where we wish A and B to have identical strategies generating the same score x between 1 and 3. What is required is simply the right relative number of 3s and 1s on each side: the right relative numbers p and q of joint cooperations and defections, respectively. Algebraically, since each p generates 3 points on each side, each q nets 1, and the length of our period can simply be of length $p + q$, what we want is:

$$\frac{3p + 1q}{p + q} = x$$

which we can transform as

$$3p + q = x(p + q)$$

$$3p + q = xp + xq$$

and finally

$$(3 - x)p = (x - 1)q.$$

Given a particular choice for x, $(3 - x)$ and $(x - 1)$ will be numbers between 1 and 3. If x is a terminating decimal of d decimal places, we can do justice to our equation above and obtain integer values for p and q by setting p at $(x - 1) \cdot 10^d$ and q at $(3 - x) \cdot 10^d$.[46] Among those strategies that will give us a score of x against each other in infinite play will then be the following:

A: Play p Cs followed by q Ds, repeat.

B: Play p Cs followed by q Ds, repeat.

A slightly more complex recipe will give us strategies which generate any chosen *unequal* scores between 1 and 3. Here an intuitive way to build on the previous result is to think of our desired scores y and z as resulting from some pattern of regular divergence tacked on to a previous pattern establishing a 'middle point' of equal score. A strategy designed in such a way will consist of two parts: a first pattern that establishes an appropriate 'middle point', followed by a second pattern that adds the right amount of divergence to reach our desired y and z.

By convention we specify y as our higher score and A as our higher-scoring player. The desired divergence in scores can be produced simply by repetitions of an unequal round:

	5
Player A	D
Player B	C
	0

What we want then is some 'middle point' x and two series of plays of length r and s such that

$$\frac{(x \cdot r) + 5s}{r + s} = y$$

and

$$\frac{(x \cdot r) + 0s}{r + s} = z.$$

Algebraically, these give us:

$$(x \cdot r) + 5s = yr + ys$$

and

$$(x \cdot r) = zr + zs.$$

Subtracting each side of the lower equation from the corresponding side of the upper equation,

$$5s = (y - z)r + (y - z)s$$

$$(5 - (y - z))s = (y - z)r.$$

Given specific choices for y and z, then, we will be able to solve for s and r. If y and z are terminating decimals with d the greater number of decimal places, we can obtain integer values for r and s by setting s at $(y - z) \cdot 10^d$ and r at $(5 - (y - z)) \cdot 10^d$.

With values established for r, s, y and z, we can return to either of our initial equations in r and s above to obtain the necessary value for our middle point x. A series of plays that will produce that middle point as an average score can then be constructed using a subroutine of p mutual cooperations and q mutual defections following our first recipe above.

To obtain our desired pair of unequally scoring strategies A and B, we can then construct a period of repeated play consisting of two parts: one in which the average score is x for each player, the other in which A scores 5 points on every round to B's 0. The length ratio of the first component of play to the second will be r/s. Since $p + q$ plays of mutual cooperation and mutual defection have been calculated to give us an average score of x, the following strategy specifications will always give us our desired y and z:

Strategy A: Play p Cs, followed by q Ds, repeat r times, then play $s \cdot (p + q)$ Ds, repeat whole.

Strategy B: Play p Cs, followed by q Ds, repeat r times, then play $s \cdot (p + q)$ Cs, repeat whole.

Such a recipe assures us of Prisoner's Dilemma strategies which when in competition with each other will give us any chosen scores between 1 and 3.

Two strategies cannot both score lower than 1, of course, nor can two both score greater than 3. Nonetheless for a score x lower than 1, or a score y greater than 3, there is generally a considerable latitude for the score on the other side.

For a score x, $0 < x \leq 1$, what is the highest score y possible for an opponent? Here let us return to our four possibilities on each play, coding them conveniently as K, L, M, and N:

	K	**L**	**M**	**N**
	1	3	5	0
Player A (score y)	D	C	D	C
Player B (score x)	D	C	C	D
	1	3	0	5

With player A and score y as the higher by convention, we can eliminate pattern N from consideration; any relative scores for $y \geq x$ obtained using

N can also be obtained, in a shorter period, without it. Note also that any $0 < x \le 1$ can be obtained using only combinations of L and M, and that the highest y for any given value of x will be that with the highest proportion of Ms to all plays. Because the score for K is so low, that proportion will be highest when there are no plays of type K. Alternately put: For any scores x and y, under our assumptions, obtained using a combination of scores K, L, and M, there is pair of scores with the same x and a higher y obtained using only Ls and Ms.[47]

Under the present assumptions, then, Ks can be eliminated from consideration as well. For $0 < x \le 1$ and using L, and M for the numbers of each type of play in a repeated period, this gives us:

$$x = \frac{3L + 0M}{L + M} \qquad y = \frac{3L + 5M}{L + M}$$

or

$$x = \frac{3L}{L + M} \qquad y = \frac{3L + 5M}{L + M}.$$

From the left equation we have:

$$3L = x(L + M)$$

$$L = \frac{x}{3}(L + M).$$

We are of course concerned only with ratios between types of play L and M. Let us thus 'normalize' L at 1. We then have:

$$1 = \frac{x}{3}(1 + M)$$

$$\frac{3}{x} = M + 1$$

$$M = \frac{3}{x} - 1$$

and our proportions between play types M and L will be

$$\frac{M}{L} = \frac{\frac{3}{x} - 1}{1}.$$

Substituting these proportions in our right-hand equation for y above,

$$y = \frac{3 + 5\left(\frac{3}{x} - 1\right)}{1 + \left(\frac{3}{x} - 1\right)}$$

$$y = \frac{\frac{15}{x} - 2}{\frac{3}{x}} = \frac{15 - 2x}{3} = 5 - 2/3x.$$

For $0 < x \leq 1$, therefore, our highest possible y is $5 - 2/3x$. As $x \rightarrow 0$, max $y \rightarrow 5$. Similar calculations show that for $0 < x \leq 1$, y's lowest possible value is $5 - 4x$. As $x \rightarrow 1$, min $y \rightarrow 1$. For a given $y \geq 3$, on the other hand, the lowest possible x is $5 - y/4$ and the highest possible is $7.5 - 1.5y$. As $y \rightarrow 5$, min $x \rightarrow 0$; as $y \rightarrow 3$, max $x \rightarrow 3$. For any chosen pair of values in those ranges it is possible to construct a recipe for appropriate strategies in the spirit of the simpler cases above.[48]

All of this assures us of strategies A and B which in competition with each other will give us chosen values x and y in a considerable range—a range within which all pairs of scores listed in Table 1 comfortably lie. With the coding trick for initial sequences outlined above the result can be extended from pairs of strategies to a recipe for constructing a finite set of strategies in competition with each other. The strategies used in Appendix A do not in fact all follow the computational pattern outlined above, though it is clear that equivalent strategies could be generated that would.

Afterword

Represent them then, as it were, by a line divided into two unequal sections and cut each section again in the same ratio—the section, that is, of the visible and that of the intelligible order—and then as an expression of the ratio of their comparative clearness and obscurity you will have, as one of the sections of the visible world, images. . . . As the second section assume that of which this is a likeness or an image. . . . Would you be willing to say, said I, that the division in respect of reality and truth or the opposite is expressed by the proportion—as is the opinable to the knowable so is the likeness to that of which it is a likeness?
—Plato, *Republic*[1]

"Would you tell me, please, which way I ought to go from here?"
"That depends a good deal on where you want to get to," said the Cat.
—Lewis Carroll, *Alice's Adventures in Wonderland*

Our attempt here has been to offer a sample, rather than a survey, of explorations in philosophical computer modeling. Surveys are possible in retrospect, only when a full terrain has become visible. What we have tried to offer here are merely the first glimpses of a new territory.

The work of the preceding chapters has focused on models for semantic paradox, for varieties of epistemic chaos, for formal systems, and for a variety of Hobbesian models of social interaction simply because these are the areas of exploration to which our curiosities have happened to lead us. Continuous values, the different perspectives afforded by richer dimensions, and formal undecidability have been recurring themes throughout. These happen simply to be *our* first areas of exploration, however, with unifying themes dictated by our own philosophical interests.

Our hope is to have offered a suggestive first word in philosophical computer modeling—a set of examples indicating some of the surprising applications and intriguing results that are possible when the computer is employed as a tool of philosophical imagination. In the long run we expect others will develop radically different forms of computer modeling, applied to radically different questions in radically different philosophical areas. Given the processing power of the contemporary computer, we expect those further explorations to offer a technological sophistication extending the ancient tradition of conceptual modeling in deep and important ways. We also expect, given its power, that the philosophical computer will extend the ancient tradition of conceptual modeling in unpredictable ways.

Patrick Grim
Gary Mar
Paul St. Denis

Notes

INTRODUCTION

1. Redwood City, California: Addison-Wesley, 1992; p. 15.

2. Quoted in Clifford A. Pickover, *Computers, Pattern, Chaos, and Beauty*, New York: St. Martin's Press, 1990, p. 10.

3. *Autobiography*, vol. 1, New York: Bantam Books, 1968, pp. 200–201.

4. Here it is of course only the alternation between True and False at discrete points of deliberation that is graphed. 'Bounce' lines between points of deliberation are not meant to indicate that deliberation passes through intermediate truth values.

5. In *Z zaganień logiki i filozofii*, Warsaw: Paustwowe Wydawnictwo Naukowe, 1961, tr. by Peter Geach in *A Wittgenstein Workbook*, Berkeley: University of California Press, 1970, p. 22.

6. See for example W. V. Quine, *Methods of Logic*, New York: Holt, Rinehart, and Winston, 1959.

7. See for example Manfred Schroeder, *Fractals, Chaos, Power Laws*, New York: W. H. Freeman, 1991.

8. Hobbes, *Leviathan*, Part I, ch. 13. All quotations from the Norton Critical Edition. New York: W. W. Norton, 1997.

9. Hobbes, *Leviathan*, Part I, ch. 14.

10. John Horton Conway's 'Game of Life' itself plays an important role in a later chapter including 'Real Life' and in the background motivation for the undecidability result of chapter 6. Hobbes himself, interestingly, begins the *Leviathan* by asking "may not we say, that all *Automata* have . . . an artificiall life?"

11. Hobbes, *Leviathan*, Part I, ch. 14.

12. Joseph Weizenbaum, quoted in *Time*, *The Merriam-Webster Dictionary of Quotations*, 1996.

CHAPTER 1

1. Jon Barwise and John Etchemendy, *The Liar: An Essay on Truth and Circularity*, New York: Oxford University Press, 1987.

2. Diogenes Laertes notes that Eubulides "kept up a controversy with Aristotle and said much to discredit him." Diogenes Laertes, *Lives of the Eminent Philosophers*, II. 108, tr. by R. D. Hicks. Cambridge, Mass.: Loeb Classical Library, Harvard University Press, 1972.

3. Kurt Gödel, "Über formal unentscheidbare Sätze der *Principia Mathematica* und verwandter Systeme I," *Monatschefte für Mathematik und Physik* 38, 173–198, tr. as "On formally

undecidable propositions of *Principia Mathematica* and related systems I" by Jean van Heijenoort in *From Frege to Gödel: A Source Book in Mathematical Logic, 1879–1931*, Cambridge, Mass.: Harvard Univ. Press, 1967, pp. 596–617, p. 598.

4. Alfred Tarski, "Der Wahrheitsbegriff in den formalisierten sprachen," *Studien Philosophica* I (1935), 261–405, tr. as "The Concept of Truth in Formalized Languages" by J. H. Woodger in John Corcoran, ed., *Logic, Semantics, Meta-mathematics*, second edition, Indianapolis: Hackett Pub. Co., 1983, pp. 152–278; Alan Turing, "On computable numbers, with an application to the entscheidungsproblem," reprinted in Martin Davis, ed., *The Undecidable*, Hewlett, New York: Raven Press, 1965, pp. 116–303; Alonzo, Church, 1936, "A note on the Entscheidungsproblem," *Journal of Symbolic Logic* 1 (1936), 40–41, 101–102.

5. Gregory Chaitin, 1990, *Information, Randomness and Incompleteness—Papers on Algorithmic Information Theory*, second edition, World Scientific, Singapore. Gödel's comment appears in a footnote to "Über formal unentscheidbare Sätze der *Principia Mathematica* und verwandter Systeme I," op. cit., p. 598.

6. Bas van Fraassen, "Presupposition, Implication, and Self-Reference," *Journal of Philosophy* 65 (1968), 136–152; Robert L. Martin, "A Category Solution to the Liar," in R. L. Martin, ed., *The Paradox of the Liar*, Reseda, Calif.: Ridgeview, 1970; Saul Kripke, "Outline of a Theory of Truth," *Journal of Philosophy* 72 (1975), 690–716, reprinted in Robert L. Martin, ed., *Recent Essays on Truth and the Liar Paradox*, New York: Oxford University Press, 1984, 53–81.

7. Hans Herzberger, "Notes on Naive Semantics," *Journal of Philosophical Logic* 11 (1982), 61–102, reprinted in Robert L. Martin (ed.) *Recent Essays on Truth and the Liar Paradox*, New York: Oxford Univ. Press, 1984; Anil Gupta, "Truth and Paradox," *Journal of Philosophical Logic* 11 (1982), 1–60, reprinted in Martin, op. cit., 175–235.

8. Barwise and Etchemendy, *The Liar*, op. cit.; Peter Aczel, *Lecture Notes on Non-Well-Founded Sets*, Center for the Study of Language and Information, Stanford, 1987; Haim Gaifman, "Pointers to Truth," *Journal of Philosophy* LXXXIX (1992), 223–261, reprinted in Grim, Mar, and Williams, eds., *The Philosopher's Annual*, vol. XV, Atascadero, Calif.: Ridgeview Press, 1994.

9. Pierre Simon de Laplace, *Essai philosophique sur les probabilités*, 1814, tr. as *A Philosophical Essay on Probabilities* by F. W. Truscott and F. L. Emory, New York: Dover, 1951.

10. Douglas Hofstadter, "Mathematical Chaos and Strange Attractors," *Scientific American*, November 1981, reprinted in Hofstadter, *Metamagical Themas*, New York: Basic Books, 1985.

11. For a critical survey, see for example Grim, *The Incomplete Universe*, Cambridge: MIT Press/Bradford Books, 1991, chapter 1.

12. Herzberger outlines his approach as follows: "Rather than attempting to resolve the paradoxes by rendering critical statements truth-valueless or otherwise neutralizing them, naive semantics undertakes to exhibit and characterize their specific patterns and degrees of instability." (Herzberger, "Notes on Naive Semantics," op. cit., p. 135). Gupta says "I . . . am suggesting that underlying our use of 'true' there is not an application procedure but a revision procedure instead. When we learn the meaning of 'true' what we learn is a rule that enables us to improve on a proposed candidate for the extension of truth. It is the existence of such a rule, I wish to argue, that explains the characteristic features of the concept of truth" (Gupta, "Truth and Paradox," op. cit., p. 212). See also Anil Gupta and Nuel Belnap, *The Revision Theory of Truth*, Cambridge, Mass.: MIT Press/Bradford Books, 1993.

13. Jean Buridan, *Sophisms on Meaning and Truth*, tr. by T. K. Scott, New York: Appleton-Century-Crofts, 1966, p. 203.

14. For ease of exposition we speak of sentences as being true or false, though at present we see no need to commit ourselves to any particular philosophical position regarding the bearers of truth values.

15. Tarski credits Łukasiewicz with this formulation of the paradox of the Liar. See Tarski, "The semantic conception of truth and the foundations of semantics," *Philosophy and Phenomenological Research*, IV (1944), 341–376, p. 347, footnote 10.

16. Tarski himself regarded his schema as formalizing the classical Aristotelian notion of a correspondence theory of truth (Tarski, "The semantic conception of truth and the foundations of semantics," op. cit., pp. 342–343).

17. J. L. Austin, "Truth," *Proceedings of the Aristotelian Society*, Supplement 24 (1950), reprinted in J. O. Urmson and G. J. Warnock, eds., *Philosophical Papers of J. L Austin*, Oxford: Clarendon Press, 1979, pp. 117–133, pp. 129–130.

18. George Lakoff, "Hedges: A Study of Meaning Criteria and the Logic of Fuzzy Concepts," *Journal of Philosophical Logic* 2 (1973), 458–508, p. 458.

19. Here we restrict ourselves to persuasive examples, without attempting any knock-down argument for infinite-valued logics in general. For an interesting argument for infinite-valued logics as a treatment for Sorites paradoxes, however, see Graeme Forbes, *Modern Logic*, New York: Oxford Univ. Press, 1994.

Although we want to be explicit about the features of the philosophical model we are building, moreover, we won't pretend that every aspect of that model will be philosophically uncontentious. At even this early stage there are in fact two assumptions that may be open to philosophical dispute. The first is of course the quite basic intuition that truth and falsity *can* be treated as matters of degree. A second assumption, important but perhaps not so obvious, is that the [0,1] continuum is an appropriate model for degrees of truth.

One philosophical objection is that a modeling in terms of such values imposes an artificial precision above and beyond any intuitive notion of degrees of truth. Susan Haack makes the charge as follows: "In the basic logic, though one isn't obliged to insist that (say) Jack must be either definitely tall or definitely not tall, nor that he must be either definitely tall or definitely not tall or definitely borderline, one will be obliged to insist that he is tall to degree 0.7 or to degree 0.8 or ... is not this an artificial imposition of precision?" (*Philosophy of Logics*, Cambridge: Cambridge University Press, 1978, pp. 167–168). The proper response to this charge, we think, is to emphasize that what infinite-valued logics are intended to offer is a *model* of intuitive degrees of truth. It is a commonplace that models will differ in some regard from that which they are intended to model: that is what makes them models. One approach, then, is to treat the artificial precision of infinite-valued logics as nothing more than a modeling artifact, harmless when recognized as such. On such an approach we can concede that it sounds artificial to speak of 'Bill is tall' as having a truth value of precisely 0.7, while still insisting that the model as a whole does offer a simple and powerful way of capturing important aspects of 'matters of degree' familiar from ordinary discourse.

20. See for example W. V. Quine, "What Price Bivalence?" *Journal of Philosophy* LXXVII (1981), 90–105.

21. On this critical point I am obliged to Leon Porter for helpful correspondence.—PG.

22. See Nicholas Rescher, *Many-valued Logic*, New York: McGraw-Hill, 1969, reprinted Hampshire, England: Gregg Revivals, 1993. The infinite-valued Kleene generalization Rescher labels '$S_{\aleph}^{?}$'.

23. An accuracy interpretation for this form of negation is outlined in chapter 2. In terms of something like a compass model we can think of predicates as coming in matched pairs of opposites: 'north' and 'south', 'noon' and 'midnight', 'parallel' and 'perpendicular'. In an accuracy interpretation negation can then be treated as an 'opposite-operator': to add a negation to a sentence is to change its basic predicate to its paired opposite. 'The enemy approaches from the south' will be the negation of 'The enemy approaches from the north'; if the first sentence has accuracy $/\mathbf{p}/$ the second will have accuracy $1 - /\mathbf{p}/$.

24. See R. E. Bellman and M. Gietz, "On the analytic formalism of the theory of fuzzy sets," *Information Sciences*, 5 (1973), 149–156.

A further option for the basic connectives would be to follow probabilistic renderings. Where $(q^e \backslash p^e)$ represents the conditional probability of the event described by **p** given the event described by **q**:

$$/\mathbf{p}/ = 1 - /\mathbf{p}/$$

$$/(\mathbf{p} \,\&\, \mathbf{q})/ = /\mathbf{p}/ \cdot (q^e/p^e)$$

$$/(\mathbf{p} \vee \mathbf{q})/ = /\mathbf{p}/ + /\mathbf{q}/ - /(\mathbf{p} \,\&\, \mathbf{q})/$$

25. On senses of 'fuzzy logic' see B. R. Gaines, "Foundations of fuzzy reasoning," *International Journal of Man-Machine Studies*, 8 (1976), 623–336.

Although he doesn't express it in this way, several of Lotfi Zadeh's early pieces can be read as insisting that the only truth predicates within the language itself are the denumerable set of "linguistic" truth values: 'true', 'false', 'very true', 'not very false', etc. Numerical truth values, we might stipulate—'0.75 true', '0.2 false'—appear only in the semantics for that language. Such an approach would offer a second response to the charge of artificial precision considered in note 19. The language itself can be treated as containing no 'artificially precise' numerical truth predicates. All the language itself contains, on such an approach, are predicates such as 'very true'; numerical values are only features of our semantic model. For a treatment of some of the issues of this chapter purely in terms of fuzzy logic see P. Grim, "Self-Reference and Chaos in Fuzzy Logic," *IEEE Transactions on Fuzzy Systems*, 1 (1993), 237–253.

26. See for example L. A. Zadeh, "A fuzzy-set-theoretic interpretation of linguistic hedges," *Journal of Cybernetics*, 2 (1972), 4–34; R. E. Bellman and L. A. Zadeh, "Local and fuzzy logics," in J. Michael Dunn and George Epstein, eds., *Modern Uses of Multiple-Valued Logic*, Dordrecht: D. Reidel, 1977; J. F. Baldwin, "A new approach to approximate reasoning using a fuzzy logic," *Fuzzy Sets and Systems*, 2 (1979), 309–325; H.-J. Zimmerman, *Fuzzy Set Theory and Its Applications*, Dordrecht: Kluwer-Nijhoff, 1985.

27. A simple illustration of functional iteration would be entering an initial value on a scientific calculator and then repeatedly pressing one of the function keys. If, for example, you input the value of 0.54321 and repeatedly press the COS function key (set for radians) you'll reach the fixed number 0.739085133; using the same initial input and the $1/x$ function key, you'll get a repeating cycle between two numbers (1.80908673 and 0.54321); and using the TAN function key, you'll get a seemingly patternless cycle of new numbers.

28. As noted in the discussion of time series graphs in the introduction, it is of course only the alternation between True and False at discrete points of deliberation that is graphed. 'Bounce' lines between points are not meant to indicate that deliberation passes through intermediate truth values.

29. Reference in each case to a sentence's 'estimated value', of course, serves as an indexical element: given a revised estimate, what such sentences assert effectively changes. Similar indexicals appear in a number of the sentences we consider.

30. A more complete algebraic derivation of fixed points is left for development in chapter 2.

31. These are in fact forms of the 'Bionic Liar,' introduced in P. Grim, *The Incomplete Universe*, Cambridge, MA: MIT Press/Bradford Books, 1991, p. 16 ff.

32. The solution to $x = \sqrt{1-x}$ is $(-1 \pm \sqrt{5})/2$. Only $(-1 + \sqrt{5})/2$ appears within our semantic interval [0, 1], however. Similar comments apply with respect to $x = (1-x)^2$ and the semantic fixed point $(3 - \sqrt{5})/2$ for the Emphatic Liar. In an entertaining knights-and-knaves exploration of some of these ideas, Nathaniel Hellerstein refers to the Modest Liar as the 'Golden Liar', pointing out that its attractor fixed point is $1/\phi$, where ϕ is the golden ratio (*Isle of Paradox and Other Logic Adventures*, unpublished, 1992). The repeller fixed point for the

Emphatic Liar is $1 - 1/\phi$. The golden ratio itself turns up in a number of surprising places: ϕ is the limit of the Fibonacci series $1/1, 2/1, 3/2, 5/3, 8/5, \ldots$; $\phi - 1 = 1/\phi$; $\phi = \sqrt{1 + \sqrt{1 + \sqrt{1 + \ldots}}}$, etc. On the golden ratio see Clifford Pickover, *Computers and the Imagination*, New York: St. Martin's, 1991.

33. This definition is taken directly from Robert L. Devaney, *An Introduction to Chaotic Dynamical Systems*, second edition, Menlo Park: Addison-Wesley, 1989.

34. The metaphor comes from Edward Lorenz's "Predictability: Does the Flap of a Butterfly's Wings in Brazil Set Off a Tornado in Texas?" address to the Annual Meeting of the Association for Sciences, Washington D.C., 1979.

35. Henri Poincaré, "Chance," in James R. Newman, ed., *The World of Mathematics*, New York: Tempus Press, 1988.

36. Initial values 0.314 and 0.3141 for the Chaotic Liar give us quickly divergent iterations:

Iteration	0.314	0.3141
1	0.626	0.6282
2	0.744	0.7436
3	0.512	0.5128
4	0.976	0.9744
5	0.048	0.0512
6	0.096	0.1024
7	0.192	0.2048
8	0.384	0.4096
9	0.768	0.8192
10	0.464	0.3616
11	0.928	0.7232
12	0.144	0.5536
13	0.288	0.8928
14	0.576	0.2144
15	0.848	0.4288
16	0.304	0.8576
17	0.608	0.2848
18	0.784	0.5696
19	0.432	0.8608
20	0.864	0.2784

37. See K. Falconer, *Fractal Geometry: Mathematical Foundations and Applications*, New York: Wiley, 1990, pp. 171 ff.

38. Robert May, "Simple mathematical models with very complicated dynamics," *Nature* 261 (1976), 459–467.

39. We are indebted to Nathaniel Shawn Hellerstein for suggesting the 'variance' transition from the Chaotic to the Logistic Liar.

40. A. N. Sarkovskii, "Coexistence of cycles of a continuous map of a line into itself," *Ukranian Mathematics Journal* 16 (1964), p. 61.

41. See for example Manfred Schroeder, *Fractals, Chaos, and Power Laws*, New York: W. H. Freeman, 1991, chapter 2. The period-doubling route to chaos is further discussed in section 2.4.

42. Jean Buridan, *Sophisms on Meaning and Truth*, op. cit., p. 200.

43. Fractal images of linked algorithms of this general type, though in a logically uninterpreted form, have been explored extensively by Roger Bagula in his marvelous

Fractal Translight Newsletter (11759 Waterhill Rd., Lakeside, CA 92040). I am grateful to Bagula for extensive correspondence—PG.

44. A more complete outline of Hausdorff dimension is offered in section 3.4.

45. These images are actually in pseudo-3D, created by taking slices across the solid in the *z* dimension and spreading those slices so as to give the illusion of different perspectives in three dimensions. Programming for these images is due to Matt Neiger.

46. See Alfred Tarski, *A Decision Method for Elementary Algebra and Geometry*, second edition, Berkeley and Los Angeles: Univ. of Calif. Press, 1951; Hartley Rogers, *Theory of Recursive Functions and Effective Computability*, New York: McGraw-Hill, 1967; Donald Kalish, Richard Montague, and Gary Mar, *Logic: Techniques of Formal Reasoning*, second edition, New York: Harcourt Brace Jovanovich, 1980.

47. It is also because such systems contain only denumerably many expressions, of course, that they will be Gödel numberable using only the natural numbers.

48. See George Boolos and Richard Jeffrey, *Computability and Logic*, second edition, Cambridge University Press, 1980.

49. Alfred Tarski, "Sur les ensembles définissables des nombres réels. I," *Fundamenta Mathematicae* 17, 210–239, tr. As "On Definable Sets of Real Numbers" by J. H. Woodger in John Corcoran, ed., *Logic, Semantics, Meta-mathematics*, second edition, Indianapolis: Hackett, 1983, pp. 110–151, p. 118.

50. The precise form of the diagonal lemma required is that for any formula $F(x, y)$ of our language there will be a formula $G(y)$ such that

$$\vdash_T G(y) \leftrightarrow F(\#G(y), y).$$

Here Boolos and Jeffrey's proof for the diagonal lemma can simply be extended, given appropriate restrictions, to formulae with one additional variable. The generalized diagonal lemma also appears in George Boolos, *The Unprovability of Consistency*, New York: Cambridge University Press, 1979, pp. 49–50.

51. See H. Gordon Rice, "Classes of recursively enumerable sets and their decision problems," *Transactions of the American Mathematical Society* 95, 1953, 341–360, and Hartley Rogers, Jr., *Theory of Recursive Functions and Effective Computability*, New York: McGraw-Hill, 1967.

CHAPTER 2

1. Michel de Montaigne, *An Apology for Raymond Sebond*, translated by M. A. Screech. New York: Penguin Books, 1987, p. 173.

2. Book II, Chapter IX, "Of Perception," *An Essay Concerning Human Understanding*.

3. See for example Patricia Smith Churchland, *Neurophysiology: Toward a Unified Science of the Mind/Brain*, Cambridge, Mass.: MIT Press/Bradford Books, 1986.

4. See esp. Michael S. Gazzaniga and Joseph E. LeDoux, *The Integrated Mind*, New York: Plenum, 1978.

5. Montaigne, *An Apology for Raymond Sebond*, op. cit., pp. 84–85.

6. Hume, *Treatise of Human Nature*, ed. L. A. Selby-Bigge (London: Oxford Univ. Press, 1941), Bk. I, iv, vii, pp. 267–269.

7. Alasdair MacIntyre, "Epistemological Crises, Dramatic Narrative and the Philosophy of Science," *Monist* 60 (1977), 453–472; p. 453.

8. See for example C. Alchourrón, P. Gärdenfors, and D. Makinson, "On the logic of theory change: partial meet contraction and revision functions," *Journal of Symbolic Logic* 50 (1985), 510–530; Peter Gärdenfors, *Knowledge in Flux: Modeling the Dynamics of Epistemic States*, Cambridge, Mass.: MIT Press/Bradford Books, 1988; Johan van Benthem, "Logic and the flow of information," in D. Prawitz et. al., eds., *Proceedings of the 9th International Congress of Logic, Methodology, and Philosophy of Science*, Amsterdam: North-Holland, 1991; and the various pieces in Jan van Eijck and Albert Visser, *Logic and Information Flow*, Cambridge, Mass.: MIT Press, 1994.

9. F. Veltman, "Defaults in Update Semantics," in Hans Kamp, ed., *Conditionals, Defaults, and Belief Revision*. Edinburgh: CCS, 1990. See also Jeroen Groenendijk, Martin Stokhof, and Frank Veltman, "This Might Be It," in J. Seligman and D. Westerst-Estl, eds., *The Moraga Proceedings*, CSLI Publications, 1995.

10. There are actually two ways to reason to the falsity of this statement. One, reliant on a principle of non-contradiction, is as follows:

If the statement is true, then it is both true and false. That is a contradiction, which cannot be true. Thus the statement must be false. (No similar contradiction follows from an assumption of falsity).

An importantly different form of reasoning, to the same conclusion, is as follows:

If the statement is false, then clearly it is false. If it is true, it is both true and false and therefore false. In either case, therefore, we can conclude that the statement is false.

11. Here again there are two possible lines of reasoning:

If the statement is false, then it is false that it is not both true and false. If it is false that it is not both true and false, it must be true that it is both true and false. But that is a contradiction, and thus cannot be true. Thus the statement cannot be false; it must be true. (No similar contradiction follows from an assumption of truth). If the statement is true, then clearly it is true. If it is false, then it is false that it is not both true and false. It must then be true that it is both true and false. Thus if it is false it is also true: assumption of either truth or falsity leads to the conclusion that it is true.

12. We remark later on the possibility of empirically disguised self- and mutual-reference.

13. W. V. Quine, "Two Dogmas of Empiricism," in *From a Logical Point of View*, Cambridge, Mass.: Harvard University Press, 1961. See also Quine and J. S. Ulian, *The Web of Belief*, New York: Random House, 1978. Note we need not deny the philosophical possibility of points of epistemic foundation, what Quine elsewhere calls the "fancifully fancyless medium of unvarnished news." The dream of epistemic foundationalism has always been that there are pieces of information the truth or falsity of which is not a matter of internal content and yet which are themselves free of the complications painted for epistemic predicaments discussed here: the incorrigible epistemic atoms from which all else is constructed. Even if such a view is true, however—even if some species of sense-data acquaintances or observation sentences are free of the general epistemic predicament sketched above—it is clear that the evaluation of most middle-sized empirical claims *is* embedded within such a predicament, subject to evaluation only within a tangle of claims regarding the acceptability of other claims and information regarding the reliability of general sources of information. If epistemic foundationalism is false, on the other hand, *all* empirical claims are of this type.

14. Anil Gupta, "Truth and Paradox," *Journal of Philosophical Logic* 22 (1982) 1–60, reprinted in Robert L. Martin, *Recent Essays on Truth and the Liar Paradox*, Oxford University Press, 1984, pp. 175–235; see p. 210. The version of Gupta's puzzle offered here is in fact closer to that presented by Barwise and Etchemendy in *The Liar* (Oxford Univ. Press, 1987, pp. 23–24),

simplified from Gupta's original by the elimination of several claims established on external grounds. If we eliminate all such claims we get a purer example, still decidable within mutual reference:

A1:   All of the claims made by B are true.

A2:   At least one of the claims made by B is false.

B1:   At most one of the claims made by A is true.

The contradiction between A1 and A2 shows us the truth of B1, which in turn shows us the truth of A1.

Cases similar to Gupta's, interestingly enough, are offered by Louis Sachar in a children's puzzle book entitled *Sideways Arithmetic from Wayside School* (New York: Scholastic, Inc., 1989). One of Sachar's simpler examples is the following:

C.   The answer to this statement is the same as the answer to statement D.

T   F

D.   The answer to this statement is different from the answer to statement C.

T   F

If we answer 'T' to (C), we are obliged to answer 'T' to (D). But then (D) is false, and thus at least one of our answers is wrong. The alternative is to answer 'F' to (C), which allows us to answer 'T' to (D), without internal inconsistency.

15. On these critical points I am obliged to Leon Porter for helpful correspondence.—PG

16. A somewhat similar case is:

A.   This statement is fairly accurate.

Using the representation of the hedge 'fairly' outlined above, the value of (A) will be the square root of the value of 'This statement is accurate' simpliciter. Revised values for (A) can thus be represented by putting the right hand side of such **Vvp** schema under the radical

$$x_{n+1} = \sqrt{1 - \text{Abs}(1 - x_n)}.$$

For positive x_n less than 1 this can be simplified to

$$x_{n+1} = \sqrt{x_n}.$$

'This statement is fairly accurate' has two fixed points; it can consistently be assigned an accuracy of either 0 or 1. Those two fixed points have a very different status, however. 0 is a repeller fixed point: values arbitrarily close to 0 are driven, through revision, farther away. 1 is an attractor fixed point, drawing non-zero values to it like a magnet. The dynamics for (A) is shown in a web diagram on the left below.

Sentence (B) is emphatic where (A) was modest, using a boastful 'very accurate' in place of 'fairly accurate':

B.   This statement is very accurate.

Using the squaring function to model 'very', revised values for (B) will be given by

$$x_{n+1} = x_n{}^2.$$

The fixed points, interestingly enough, are precisely the same: 0 and 1 are again the only consistent accuracies assignable. Here, however, it is 1 that is the repeller point and 0 that is the attractor point. The dynamics for (A) and (B) are shown in the illustrations.

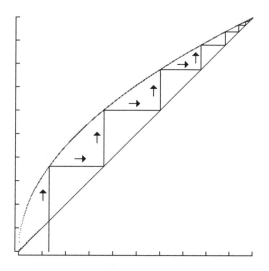

A   'This statement is fairly accurate' with initial value of 0.13.

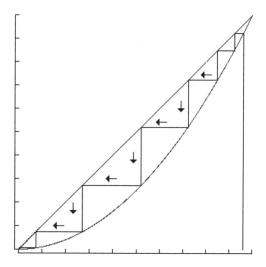

B   'This statement is very accurate' with initial value of 0.96.

17. J. B. Gunn has done significant work in solving various self-referential sentences in this sense. See for example "Notes on an Algebraic Logic of Self-Reference," unpublished. I am obliged to Gunn for extensive and very helpful correspondence.—PG

18. The claim that the basic epistemic question is "Who do you trust?" is one Alasdair MacIntyre made informally years ago. Like many of MacIntyre's dictums, it has taken me a long time to fully appreciate its truth.

19. A point emphasized in Kripke, "Outline of a theory of Truth," *Journal of Philosophy* 72 (1975), 690–715.

20. Heinz Pagels, *The Dreams of Reason*, New York: Simon and Schuster, 1988, p. 145.

21. John le Carré, *Smiley's People*, New York: Knopf, 1980.

22. For some purposes it might also be important to have a reliability estimate that hedges against over-confidence. In such a case it might be the square of the formula above that is more appropriate:

$$R_{n+1} = (((2 \cdot R_n) + /\mathbf{p}/)/3)^2$$

In cases where we worry about underestimating reliability the square root of the formula might be used instead:

$$R_{n+1} = \sqrt{(((2 \cdot R_n) + /\mathbf{p}/)/3)}.$$

Moreover, no provision has been made here for different types of information counting differentially in a reputational formula. For a more realistic model of reputation as applied to secret agents, for example, we might also want to incorporate a measure of informational importance. On that more complex model it would be accurate and *important* information which creates a positive reputation and *important* inaccuracy which can damage it.

23. 1/2 is the only initial estimate for (40) that will not force us to an oscillation between 0 and 1. In that case, of course, we escape an oscillation in the background reliability estimate as well.

24. This is a feature of the current modeling for reliability updating which would not hold for a simple averaging formula.

25. George J. Klir and Tina A. Folger, *Fuzzy Sets, Uncertainty, and Information*, Englewood Cliffs, New Jersey: Prentice Hall, 1988. Note also that the familiar debates over interpretation of probability theory might be viewed as debates over whether it should be construed as a theory of level-one or level-two phenomena.

26. Standard examples of computational complexity involve problems with complete information and exact solutions. A class of problems involving partial information instead—thereby combining some aspects of this rung with that beneath it—has been introduced as displaying 'information-based complexity' by Edward W. Packel and J. F. Traub ("Information-based complexity," *Nature* 328 (July 1987), 29–33).

27. The *locus classicus* for Dualist forms of the Liar is the *Sophismata* of Jean Buridan (c. 1295–1356). Buridan's own treatment of the problem, however, extends beyond simple truth and falsity to cases more closely related to those at issue here, including cases of coordinated action and even deontic questions of promise-keeping. See John Buridan, *Sophisms on Meaning and Truth*, tr. by Theodore Kermit Scott, New York: Appleton-Century Crofts, 1966, pp. 219–221.

28. Take a line segment and remove the middle third. For each of the remaining segments remove the third, and so on. Cantor dust is the set of points that remains after an infinite number of iterations: an infinite set of points with no length.

Interestingly, Aristotle comes very close to the notion of Cantor dust in *On Generation and Corruption*. Aristotle has us imagine a body "divisible through and through, whether by bisection [i.e., by progressive bisection *ad infinitum*], or generally by any method whatever";

Since, therefore, the body is divisible through and through, let it have been divided. What, then, will remain? A magnitude? No: that is impossible, since then there will be something not divided, whereas *ex hypothesi* the body was divisible *through and through*. But if it be admitted that neither a body nor a magnitude will remain, and yet division is to take place, the constituents of the body will *either* be points (i.e., without magnitude) *or* absolutely nothing. If its constituents are nothings, then it might both come-to-be out of nothings and exist as a composite of nothings: and thus presumably the whole body will be nothing but an appearance. But if it consists of points, a similar absurdity will result: it will not possess any magnitude. (I.2, 316a 15–30, tr. by H. H. Joachim)

29. David Lewis, "Immodest Inductive Methods," *Philosophy of Science* 38 (1971), 54–63; p. 55.

30. The notion of rigid designators is of course taken from the work of Saul Kripke. See for example "Naming and Necessity" in Donald Davidson and Gilbert Harman, eds., *Semantics of Natural Language*, Dordrecht: D. Reidel, 1972, pp. 253–355.

31. Indefinite repetition of such messages gives an even more stable result: regardless of either initial accuracy estimates or initial background reputation we get a unique fixed point for each of the messages. Under unlimited repetition (17) converges on both an accuracy and reputation value of 2/3, precisely like its Half-Sayer relative. (18), claiming a reliability twice its agent's reputation, converges to final values of 1/2 for both accuracy and reputation. Dynamic behavior is not parallel to accuracy analogues throughout, however: (19), corresponding to the Chaotic Liar, converges to a value of 2/3 precisely as does (17). (21) *converges* to 1/2, rather than oscillating periodically for other values. For (22), the correlate to the Minimalist, 2/3 forms an attractor rather than a repellor fixed point.

32. See for example Manfred Schroeder, *Fractals, Chaos, and Power Laws*, op. cit., chapter 12.

33. In Ernest Nagel, ed., *John Stuart Mill's Philosophy of Scientific Method*, New York: Hafner Publishing Company, 1950; p. 11.

CHAPTER 3

1. *Autobiography*, vol. 2, New York: Bantam Books, 1968, pp. 326–327.

2. Hao Wang, *Reflections on Kurt Gödel*, Cambridge, Mass.: MIT Press/Bradford Books, 1987, p. 112.

3. Arend Heyting, "The Intuitionist Foundations of Mathematics," in Rudolf Carnap, Arend Heyting, and Johann von Neumann, "Symposium on the Foundations of Mathematics," *Erkenntnis* (1931), 19–121, reprinted in Paul Benacerraf and Hilary Putnam, *Philosophy of Mathematics*, second edition, New York: Cambridge University Press, 1983, pp. 52–61, p. 53.

4. Paul Bernays, "L'enseignement mathématique," 1st ser. Vol. 34 (1935), pp. 52–69, translated by C. D. Parsons as "On Platonism in Mathematics," in Paul Benacerraf and Hilary Putnam, *Philosophy of Mathematics*, second edition, New York: Cambridge University Press, 1983, pp. 258–271, pp. 258–259.

5. The game fractal outlined here can be thought of as a fractally embedded form of the familiar game tree. See for example A. K. Dewdney, *The New Turing Omnibus*, New York: Computer Science Press, 1993, esp. ch. 6, and A. L. Samuel, "Some studies in machine learning using the game of checkers," in *Computers and Thought*, eds. E. A. Feigenbaum and J. Feldman, New York: McGraw-Hill, 1968, pp. 71–108.

6. Because of color manipulations, the shades on the axes in these illustrations are no longer reliable.

7. Mere propositional formulae might either be assigned a special 'formula value', representing the fact that they fall short of full formal sentences, or be treated as carrying the truth-values of their universally quantified forms.

8. Here we've purposely limited the scheme to monadic predicates applied to variables. Constants a, b, c . . . could also be interwoven with variables in the plan above, but at the cost of serious complications. The difficulty for a map including both Fa and ∀xFx, for example, is that these are not easily linked in ways reflected in the Sheffer stroke, the core connective of the map. It would be easy to assign each of these formulae an independent contingency color, but the map would then fail to reflect the fact that ~ Fa →~ ∀xFx, for example, is a tautology: such a map would exhibit not all tautologies of monadic propositional calculus but merely those dependent on the connective NAND alone. A complete map of tautologies for the full propositional calculus would thus require a structure beyond the one proposed here.

9. Another intriguing representation is possible in terms of Conway numbers. In Conway's system, a '1' can be taken to represent a unit forward and a '0' a unit backward; however, whenever there is a change from '1' to '0' or from '0' to '1' in the sequence, units are halved. Below, for example, is a binary tree representing some of the finite Conway numbers.

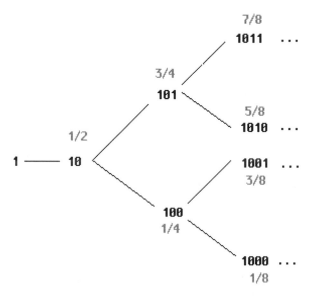

A binary tree representing some Conway numbers

In terms of Conway numbers, the progressive and regressive Achilles series are as follows:

Fraction	Conway Representation
1/2	10
3/4	101
7/8	1011
9/16	10111
⋮	

Fraction	Conway Representation
1/2	10
1/4	100
1/8	1000
1/16	10000
⋮	

10. Michael Barnsley, *Fractals Everywhere*, San Diego: Academic Press, 1988. On the Sierpinski triangle or gasket in general see for example Robert L. Devaney, *Chaos, Fractals, and Dynamics*, Menlo Park: Addison-Wesley, 1990; Heinz-Otto Peitgen, Hartman Jürgens, and Dietmar Saupe, *Fractals for the Classroom*, New York: Springer-Verlag, 1992; and A. J. Crilly, R. A. Earnshaw, and H. Jones, eds., *Fractals and Chaos*, New York: Springer-Verlag, 1991.

11. See Manfred Schroeder, *Fractals, Chaos, Power Laws*, New York: W. H. Freeman, 1991, p. 21 ff.

12. Tyler Burge, "The Liar Paradox: Tangles and Chains," *Philosophical Studies* 41 (1982), 353–366; Brian Skyrms, "Intensional Aspects of Semantical Self-Reference," in Robert L. Martin,

Recent Essays on Truth and the Liar Paradox, New York: Oxford University Press, 1984, pp. 119–131.

13. Manfred Schroeder, loc. cit.

14. Here there is a strong affinity to August Stern's matrix logic, outlined in brilliant detail in his *Matrix Logic* (Amsterdam: Elsevier Science Publishers, 1988), *Matrix Logic and Mind* (Amsterdam: Elsevier, 1992) and *The Quantum Brain* (Amsterdam: Elsevier, 1994). The connections Stern draws to the logic of quantum phenomena are well worth further study.

15. It is tempting—but would be mistaken—to try to use this schema as a representation not only for the full propositional calculus, but for a full infinitary propositional calculus, allowing for infinite formulae involving infinite connectives by way of conjunction, disjunction, or Sheffer strokes. (Infinitary systems of this type appear in Leon Henkin, "Some Remarks on Infinitely Long Formulas," in International Mathematical Union and Mathematical Institute of the Polish Academy of Sciences, eds., *Infinitistic Methods*, New York: Pergamon Press, 167–183, and in Carol Karp, *Languages with Expressions of Infinite Length*, Amsterdam: North-Holland, 1964).

This is tempting for one reason because infinite disjunctions of sentence letters represented in this way might seem to offer *non-periodic* binary decimals. A simple example consists in the disjunction of all our atomic sentence letters, giving us the truth table 0111…, with no repetition of its initial zero. For a more interesting example, consider an infinite disjunction which leaves out some of the set of sentence letters. Leave out only the second sentence letter, as outlined above, and you would appear to get the disjunctive value 01011111…. Leave out only the third and you would appear to get the pattern 01110111…. In general, leaving out the nth sentence letter from an infinite disjunction of all sentence letters appears to introduce a zero in the $(2^{n-1} + 1)$th place. If every even sentence letter of the set were left out, so the reasoning goes, the result would be a classic non-periodic decimal in which 0s are separated by ever-increasing expanses of 1s.

An interpretation of infinitely-extended truth tables is also tempting given that universal quantification can be thought of as an infinite conjunction, existential quantification as an infinite disjunction. Were this scheme interpretable in such a way, then, it would offer a model not only for propositional but for predicate calculus. Restricted to finite connectives it can at best correspond only to arbitrarily large finite models for propositional calculus.

The difficulty that blocks both of these tempting moves, however, is that the infinite extension of truth tables outlined, although adequate for arbitrarily large finite complexes, cannot be thought of as adequate for genuinely infinite complexes. This becomes evident if one asks at what point in the table we will find a row which represents a '1' value for all of our sentence letters; it is clear that such a row can have no (finite) place in the scheme. A standard diagonal argument gives the same result: there will be an infinite complex of our sentence letters that has no corresponding row in the table, and thus the table is not be adequate for representation of all values in a genuinely infinitary system. For that we require truth tables somehow not merely of countably infinite but of uncountable length.

16. Here we are obliged to an anonymous reader.

17. See Manfred Schroeder, *Fractals, Chaos, and Power Laws*, New York: W. H. Freeman and Co., 1991, esp. pp. 20–25.

18. The correspondence between the Sierpinski triangle and the value space for NAND might also be understood in terms of a 'throw-out' procedure. Consider a value space structured as in figure 21, and envisaged as initially filled. A NAND compound is true just in case at least one of its components is false, and thus represents a tautology if there is no case in which both components are true. To find the entries in a NAND space that form tautologies under NAND, we can therefore proceed by repeatedly discarding any cell for which corresponding bits in both of its axis values are 1.

Starting with the entire value space, it is clear that the first (leftmost) bit in all values in the bottom half of the left axis is 1. It is also clear that the first bit in all values in the right half of the top axis is 1. Any point of intersection between these values will thus have two 1s in the first bit position, and thus will not be a tautology. We 'throw out' the lower right quadrant as a potential area for NAND tautologies.

We can now repeat the procedure with each of the three remaining quadrants, concentrating on the second digit. The lower half of each quadrant is governed by a 1 in the second bit position on the left axis. The right half of each quadrant is governed by a 1 in the second position on the top axis. These intersections will fail as tautologies, and thus we 'throw out' each of their lower right corners.

If we proceed in this manner we will end up with an image of the Sierpinski triangle. The general procedure will be the same regardless of the number of values on our axes (or their length in bits), and thus it is clear that we will get a similar Sierpinski triangle for NAND regardless of the number of values in the system. The general procedure will also carry over to other connectives, since we can in each case phrase rules similar to the principle used above—that we find where NAND is always true by discarding areas in which corresponding bits are both 1. Here we are obliged to the careful work of an anonymous reader.

19. See Gerald A. Edgar, *Measure, Topology, and Fractal Geometry*, New York: Springer-Verlag, 1990.

Other topological properties of logical interest may hold in the infinitely-grained case. It has been conjectured, for example, that any non-tautology will have a circle around it of some dimension that contains only non-tautologies, whereas any non-point circle around any tautology, however small, will also contain non-tautologies.

20. Łukasiewicz himself outlined his system in terms of implication and negation. Here we take as a Łukasiewicz 'or' the classical transform from implication: $/p \vee q/ = / \sim p \rightarrow q/$, with 'and' by a similar transformation. See Nicholas Rescher, *Many-valued Logic*, New York: McGraw-Hill, 1969.

21. Tommaso Toffoli and Norman Margolus, "Programmable Matter: Concepts and Realization," *Physica D* 47 (1991), 263–272; see also Ivan Amato, "Speculating in Precious Computronium," *Science* 253 (August 1991), 856–857.

CHAPTER 4

1. London: Macmillan, 1902, p. 163.

2. New York: Basic Books, 1984, p. 3.

3. All quotations from the Norton Critical Edition. New York: W. W. Norton, 1997.

4. "Do not do to others what you would not want done to yourself."

5. Quoted in William Poundstone, *Prisoner's Dilemma*, New York: Doubleday, 1992.

6. Edmund Wilson, *Sociobiology: the New Synthesis*. Cambridge, Mass.: Harvard University Press, 1975. For recent work on philosophical 'justifications' of morality see David Gauthier, *Morals by Agreement*, Oxford: Clarendon Press, 1986, and Peter Danielson, *Artificial Morality: Virtuous Robots for Virtual Games*, New York: Routledge, 1992.

7. Michael Oakeshott, from "Introduction to *Leviathan*" in *Hobbes on Civil Association*, Berkeley: Univ. of California Press, 1975, pp. 15–28, reprinted in Richard E. Flathman and David Johnston, *Leviathan: A Norton Critical Edition*, New York: W. W. Norton, 1997, pp. 311–320, p. 318.

8. John P. Somerville, *Thomas Hobbes: Political Ideas in Historical Context*, New York: St. Martin's Press, 1992, reprinted in Richard E. Flathman and David Johnston, *Leviathan: A Norton Critical Edition*, op. cit., pp. 334–338, p. 334.

9. Cambridge, Mass.: Harvard University Press, 1971, p. 269.

10. William Poundstone, *The Prisoner's Dilemma*, op. cit., p. 8.

11. David Gauthier, *Morals by Agreement*, op. cit., pp. 80–81. The organization of the chart has been changed slightly to afford direct comparison with the matrix above.

12. *The Complete Works of Edgar Allan Poe*, vol. 5, New York: AMS Press, 1965, pp. 6–7.

13. *The Complete Works of Edgar Allan Poe*, vol. 5, op. cit., pp. 59–60.

14. Putting the problem this way emphasizes the connection between the Prisoner's Dilemma and Newcomb's Problem. See Richard Campbell and Lanning Sowden, *Paradoxes of Rationality and Cooperation*, Vancouver: University of British Columbia Press, 1985, esp. David Lewis, "Prisoner's Dilemma is a Newcomb Problem," pp. 251–255.

15. R. Duncan Luce and Howard Raiffa, *Games and Decisions*, New York: John Wiley and Sons, 1957; Mineola, New York: Dover Publications, 1989, p. 100.

16. Robert Axelrod, *The Evolution of Cooperation*, New York: Basic Books, 1984, pp. 10–11.

17. Anatol Rapoport and Albert M. Chammah, *Prisoner's Dilemma*, Ann Arbor: University of Michigan Press, 1965, p. 29.

18. William Poundstone, *Prisoner's Dilemma*, New York: Doubleday, 1992, p. 229.

19. Poundstone, op. cit., p. 218 ff.

20. Jean-Jacques Rousseau, *Discourse on the Origin of Inequality*, trans. by Franklin Philip, New York: Oxford University Press, 1994, pp. 57–58.

21. In "Evolving cooperation: strategies as hierarchies of rules," *BioSystems* 37 (1966), pp. 67–80, P. Crowley offers an alternative way to represent basic strategies in terms of hierarchical rules. In Crowley's representation AllD appears as the single rule /:D, indicating that whatever you did on the last move (indicated before the slash), and whatever the opponent did on the last move (indicated after the slash), the move dictated after the colon is D. In such a representation AllC appears as /:C. TFT is represented as:

/:C

/D:D

using the provision that higher order rules—roughly, those which fit the situation in more specific detail—supersede lower-order rules. When conditions of two or more rules of the same order are in competition and no conditions are met in higher-order rules, Crowley specifies the rule followed is to be chosen randomly.

22. Robert Axelrod, "Effective Choice in the Prisoner's Dilemma," *Journal of Conflict Resolution* 24 (1980), 3–25.

23. Robert Axelrod, "More Effective Choice in the Prisoner's Dilemma," *Journal of Conflict Resolution* 24 (1980), 379–403, *The Evolution of Cooperation*, op. cit., and "The Emergence of Cooperation Among Egoists," in Campbell and Sowden, eds., *Paradoxes of Rationality and Cooperation*, op. cit., 320–339.

24. Robert Axelrod and William Hamilton, "The Evolution of Cooperation," *Science* 211 (1981), 1390–1396.

25. Despite some confusion in the literature, however, neither TFT nor ALLD strictly qualifies as an 'evolutionarily stable strategy' or ESS in the sense of Maynard Smith, *Evolution and the Theory of Games*, Cambridge: Cambridge Univ. Press, 1982. Representing the payoff for a player x against a player y in a given series of games as $P(x, y)$, Smith's formal definition specifies that a strategy x is evolutionarily stable just in case $P(x, x) > P(y, x)$ or both $P(x, x) = P(y, x)$ and $P(x, y) > P(y, y)$ for all strategies $y \neq x$. It is true that both TFT and AllD resist invasion in that no other strategy can get a higher score against TFT or AllD than they

get against themselves and at the same time get an equal or higher score against itself than they get against it. But there are strategies that do precisely as well against TFT and AllD as they do against themselves and that also do as well with their own kind as TFT and AllD do with them: AllC does as well in a context of TFT as TFT does, for example, and Suspicious Tit for Tat (STFT) does as well in a context of AllD as AllD does. The conditions of Smith's formal definition are thus not fulfilled for either TFT or AllD, and neither qualifies as an ESS. With an eye to natural selection, as Nowak and Sigmund note, although such strategies cannot invade by strategic advantage, they can invade by something like genetic drift (see Nowak and Sigmund, "Game-Dynamical Aspects of the Prisoner's Dilemma," *Applied Mathematics and Computation* 30, 1989, 191–213, and "Oscillations in the Evolution of Reciprocity," *Journal of Theoretical Biology* 137 (1989), 21–26).

In *The Evolution of Cooperation*, op. cit., Axelrod labels a strategy x 'collectively stable' just in case there is no alternative strategy y such that $P(y, x) > P(x, x)$, and notes that this is equivalent to x being in Nash equilibrium with itself. In "Stochastic Strategies in the Prisoner's Dilemma," *Theoretical Population Biology* 38 (1990), 93–112, Nowak labels a strategy x 'incapable of invasion by selection pressure' if $P(x, x) > P(y, x)$ or $P(x, x) = P(y, x)$ and $P(x, y) \geq P(y, y)$ for all alternative strategies y. Although they do not qualify as ESSs, it is clear that TFT and AllD are in these senses both collectively stable and incapable of invasion by selection pressure.

As all this should make clear, notions of stability against invasion call for careful handling. For further discussion see esp. Brian Skyrms's wonderfully clear exposition in "Chaos in Game Dynamics," *Journal of Logic, Language, and Information* 1 (1992), 111–130. As indicated later in the chapter, notions of stability also need to be handled carefully in extension to fully spatial models. It should finally be noted that stable strategies in any of the senses above must be distinguished from 'attractor' strategies toward which a system may be drawn. As indicated in Nowak, "An Evolutionarily Stable Strategy May Be Inaccessible," *Journal of Theoretical Biology* 142 (1990), 237–241, these are in principle distinct.

26. In the alternative hierarchical rule representation outlined in note 21, GTFT with a forgiveness rate of 1/3 would take the following form:

/:C

/D:D

/D:D

/D:C

27. In "Cooperation among unrelated individuals: reciprocal altruism, byproduct mutualism and group selection in fishes," *BioSystems* 37 (1996), 19–30, L. Dugatkin and M. Mesterton-Gibbons suggest that egg-swapping fish may use a strategy similar to GTFT.

28. Nowak and Sigmund, "Tit for tat in heterogenous populations," *Nature* 355 (1992), 250–252; p. 252. Conventions for $\langle c, d \rangle$ have been changed to match the text.

29. Nowak and Sigmund, "Tit for tat in heterogenous populations," op. cit., p. 250.

30. Consider for example strategies $\langle 0, 1, 0 \rangle$ and $\langle 1, 1, 0 \rangle$, which differ only in their initial value. Against itself the first will achieve a constant score of 0 in an infinite game; against itself the second will achieve a constant score of 1.

31. P. Molander, "The optimal level of generosity in a selfish, uncertain environment," *Journal of Conflict Resolution* 29 (1985), 611–618.

32. Gauthier, op. cit., p. 15.

33. In either a game of 201 rounds, interestingly enough, or an infinite game as outlined below and in chapter 6, the STFT and DTFT considered here would have identical scores against each

other. In a game of 201 rounds STFT would still do worse against itself than DTFT against itself, but in an infinite game their scores against themselves would be identical as well.

34. We have also found cases in which STFT is extinguished early enough to leave pure TFT as a major player, and one case in which the evolutionary dynamics allow a major island of $\langle 0, 1, 1, 0, 1, 1 \rangle$ in equilibrium with STFT and DTFT.

35. *Leviathan*, Introduction.

36. R. MacArthur and E. Wilson, *The Theory of Island Biogeography*, Princeton: Princeton Univ. Press, 1967. For a popular presentation of central ideas and personal histories see David Quammen, "Life in Equilibrium," *Discover* 17 (March 1996), pp. 66–69, 72–77.

37. The Theory of Island Biogeography is sometimes offered as support in turn for the Red Queen, Leigh Van Valen and Michael Rosenzweig's hypothesis that evolutionary change in one species is fueled in large part by competition with other species, and thus that a pattern of evolution will continue even in a constant physical environment. See L. Van Valen, "A New Evolutionary Law," *Evolutionary Theory* 1 (1973), 1–30, R. Lewin, "Red queen runs into trouble?" *Science* 227 (1985), 399–400.

38. Because a cluster of a new strategy is inserted in each generation, there is no truly 'final' stage in such a model. The generalizations and illustrations offered here reflect clear patterns of dominance in well-established arrays over a large number of generations.

39. Such an evolution exhibits in a natural context many of the features of Nowak and May's more artificial work on spatial chaos and fractals in evolutionary games. See M. Nowak and R. May, "Evolutionary games and spatial chaos," *Nature* 359 (1992), 826–829; M. Nowak and R. May, "The Spatial Dimensions of Evolution," *International Journal of Bifurcation and Chaos* 3 (1993), 35–78.

40. The intricacy of this illustration is due to the precarious balance between strategies at issue, its symmetry to the fact that all cells of the array are updated simultaneously. Use of an asynchronous updating—in which, say, a random 50% or 25% of the display updates at each step—can therefore be expected to give a much less dramatic result. See B. Huberman and N. Glance, "Evolutionary Games and Computer Simulations," *Proceedings of the National Academy of Science USA* 90 (1993), 7716–7718.

41. Our computers could not, of course, attempt a survey using a pure 2/3—they can handle only approximations such as 0.6666666. Progressive refinement in the surveys, however, kept identifying the closest approximation to 2/3 available at each stage as the optimal value in the sense at issue.

In Grim, "Spatialization and greater generosity in the stochastic Prisoner's Dilemma," *BioSystems* 37 (1996), 3–17, stochastic FTFT is also called "Bending Over Backwards" (BOB). In the hierarchical rule formulation suggested by Crowley, op. cit, it can be characterized as:

/:C

/D:D

/D:C

/D:C

Even the measure of optimality used here, it should be noted, concerns the invasion potential of a single strategy within a field of another strategy. Within more complicated spatial fields it is clear that combinations of several strategies can offer some surprising mechanisms of invasion.

42. See P. Kitcher, "The Evolution of Human Altruism," *Journal of Philosophy* 90 (1993), 497–516; J. Batali and P. Kitcher, "Evolution of Altruism in Optional and Compulsory Games," *Journal of Theoretical Biology* 175 (1995), 161–171; J. Orbell, A. Runde, T. Morikawa, "The

Robustness of cognitively simple judgements in ecologies of Prisoner's Dilemma games," *BioSystems* 37 (1996), 81–97; D. Ashlock, M. Smucker, E. Stanley, and L. Tesfatsion, "Preferential partner selection in an evolutionary study of Prisoner's Dilemma," *BioSystems* 37 (1996), 99–125.

43. See esp. B. Huberman and N. Glance, "Evolutionary games and computer simulations," op. cit. Although Huberman and Glance seem to insist on updating at most a single cell each generation, a fixed choice of one cell seems no less artificial than simultaneous updating of all cells. Some form of weighted randomization would seem far preferable, though what form remains an open question and might even depend on the type of species we are interested in modeling.

44. See U. Golze, "(A-)Synchronous (non-)deterministic cell spaces simulating each other," *Journal of Computer and Systems Science* 17 (1978), 176–193.

CHAPTER 5

1. William Poundstone, *Prisoner's Dilemma*, New York: Doubleday, 1992, p. 253.

2. John Rawls, *A Theory of Justice*, Cambridge, Mass.: Harvard University Press, 1971, p. 16.

3. We are indebted to Greg Lubicich for suggesting this example from nature.

4. Elwyn R. Berlekamp, John H. Conway, and Richard K. Guy, *Winning Ways for your Mathematical Plays*, Vol. II, London: Academic Press, 1982.

5. Manfred Schroeder, *Fractals, Chaos, Power Laws*, New York: W. H. Freeman, 1991, p. 375.

6. We warn the reader, however, that sensitive dependence and computational round-off can lead to computer artifacts in the graphics, especially in higher generations.

7. Robert May, "Simple mathematical models with very complicated dynamics," *Nature* 261 (1976), 459–467.

8. The 'two-deep' strategies of chapter 4, in contrast, reacted only to the two previous moves of the opponent.

9. M. Nowak and K. Sigmund, "Chaos and the evolution of cooperation," *Proceedings of the National Academy of Sciences* 90 (1993), 5091–5094, and "A strategy of win-stay, lose-shift that outperforms tit-for-tat in the prisoner's dilemma game," *Nature* 364 (1993), 56–58.

10. This strategy appears as GRIM in Nowak and Sigmund, "Chaos and the evolution of cooperation," op. cit. As noted in chapter 4, any resemblance between this strategy and one of the authors of this volume is entirely coincidental.

11. In Nowak and Sigmund's "A strategy of win-stay, lose-shift that outperforms tit-for-tat in the Prisoner's Dilemma game," op. cit., a stochastic rather than continuous-valued version of PAVLOV dominates in the long run and appears to be stable against both AllD and GRIM. Here differences in strategies and background conditions are worthy of further exploration.

12. If all four adjacent cells have the same strategy, that strategy will be the one chosen if it clusters.

13. Our results, studied here in a spatial context, appear to confirm some of those of Philip Kitcher in "The evolution of human altruism," *Journal of Philosophy* 90 (1993), 497–516. See also D. Kraines and V. Kraines, "Learning to Cooperative with Pavlov: An Adaptive Strategy for the Iterated Prisoner's Dilemma with Noise," *Theory and Decision* 35 (1993), 107–150.

14. Michael Ruse, "The significance of evolution," in Peter Singer, ed., *A Companion to Ethics*, Oxford: Basil Blackwell, 1991, pp. 500–510; p. 506.

15. Ibid., pp. 507–508.

16. Poundstone, *Prisoner's Dilemma*, op. cit., discussing Rytina and Morgan, "The Arithmetic of Social Relations: The Interplay of Category and Network," *American Journal of Sociology* 88 (1982), 88–113.

17. An informal outline of genetic algorithms, their history and a range of applications appears in Steven Levy, *Artificial Life*, New York: Pantheon Books, 1992.

18. Brian Skyrms, "Darwin Meets *The Logic of Decision*: Correlation in Evolutionary Game Theory," *Philosophy of Science* 61 (1994), 503–528.

CHAPTER 6

1. Thomas Goddard Bergin and Max Harold Fisch, trans., *The New Science of Giambattista Vico*, Ithaca: Cornell University Press, 1948, p. 97.

2. Karl Marx and Frederick Engels, *The German Ideology, Part One*, edited by C. J. Arthur, New York: International Publishers, 1993; p. 48.

3. Robert Axelrod, *The Evolution of Cooperation*, New York: Basic Books, 1984, p. 28.

4. Here we assume the more complete outline of the eight simple reactive strategies in section 2 of chapter 4.

5. Axelrod's work is discussed in detail in chapter 4. See esp. Robert Axelrod, *The Evolution of Cooperation*, op. cit.; "Effective Choice in the Prisoner's Dilemma," *Journal of Conflict Resolution* 24 (1980): 3–25, "More Effective Choice in the Prisoner's Dilemma," *Journal of Conflict Resolution* 24 (1980): 379–403, "The Emergence of Cooperation among Egoists," in R. Campbell and L. Sowden, eds., *Paradoxes of Rationality and Cooperation* (Vancouver: Univ. of British Columbia Press, 1985), and Robert Axelrod and William Hamilton, "The Evolution of Cooperation," *Science* 211 (1981): 1390–1396.

6. The notion of infinitely iterated games comes from Nowak and Sigmund, whose work is discussed extensively in chapter 4. See esp. Martin Nowak, "Stochastic Strategies in the Prisoner's Dilemma," *Theoretical Population Biology* 38 (1990): 93–112, and Martin Nowak and Karl Sigmund, "Game-Dynamical Aspects of the Prisoner's Dilemma," *Applied Mathematics and Computation* 30 (1989): 191–213, and "Oscillations in the Evolution of Reciprocity," *Journal of Theoretical Biology* 137 (1989): 21–26.

7. Not all conceivable strategies will so conveniently establish repeated periods or such easily calculated scores for infinite games. The results of the present chapter, however, demand only strategies of this manageable type.

8. The result is a model in which success is in all cases calculated against local competitors and in which replication proceeds locally as well—both features, we've argued in earlier chapters, which constitute a measure of realism with regard to either biological or sociological application. That measure of realism, however, is tempered by an aspect of the model that remains very abstract: the fact that we envisage an infinite two-dimensional space of play. As noted toward the end of the chapter, this characteristic of the model used is essential to the undecidability result.

9. Terrell Carver, *The Cambridge Companion to Marx*, Cambridge: Cambridge University Press, 1991, p. 115.

10. As in previous chapters, this is actually a toroidal 'wrap-around' display, in which a player on the top row is competing with players on the very bottom as his immediate neighbors and a player on the very left is competing with those on the very right.

Here we restrict ourselves to a two-dimensional Prisoner's Dilemma, though both higher and lower-dimensional spatializations are clearly possible. Although we haven't pursued it here, it seems clear that the basic undecidability results could be carried over to higher-dimensional spaces simply by constructing a strategy to fill layers above and below a two-dimensional plane that does not affect the dance of crucial strategies within that plane. Undecidability in two dimensions would thus become undecidability in higher dimensions by default. Quite generally, two-dimensional cellular automata are also translatable into some form of one-dimensional cellular automata. That too should be expected here.

11. Although very similar, this evolution is not precisely that illustrated in figure 5 of chapter 4. For simplicity of exposition that competition was in terms of an artificial limit of 200 rounds; here competition is in terms of infinitely many rounds.

12. The question used to illustrate undecidability throughout the chapter is whether a single strategy will dominate to conquest. This is only an example, however. Given the basic method of proof other properties of arrays can be shown to be undecidable in precisely the same way: whether TFT will ever be completely extinguished in an array, for example, or whether good in the guise of a certain level of generosity will eventually triumph.

13. An earlier and somewhat inelegant version of the Turing-machine form of the argument is included in Patrick Grim, "The Undecidability of the Spatialized Prisoner's Dilemma," *Theory and Decision* 42 (1997), 53–80.

14. Elwyn R. Berlekamp, John H. Conway, and Richard K. Guy, *Winning Ways for your Mathematical Plays*, Vol. II, London: Academic Press, 1982.

15. Here we explicitly assume Church's thesis. Part of what makes Church's thesis so interesting, however, is its in-principle vulnerability. For recent critical suspicions see Selmer Bringsjord, "Church's Thesis, *Contra* Mendelson, is Unprovable... And Worse: It May Be False," presented at the American Philosophical Association meetings, Eastern Division, Atlanta, 1993.

16. Hao Wang, "A variant to Turing's theory of computing machines," *Journal of the Association for Computing Machinery* 4 (1957): pp. 63–94.

17. Marvin Minsky, *Computation: Finite and Infinite Machines* (Englewood Cliffs, N.J.: Prentice-Hall, 1967), esp. pp. 255–281. See also George Boolos and Richard Jeffrey, *Computability and Logic*, third edition (Cambridge: Cambridge Univ. Press, 1989).

18. The 'wires' at issue might therefore be instantiated equally well by light bulbs flashing in sequence on a theater marquee or by human beings moving square-by-square down a sidewalk.

19. See Minsky, op. cit., and A. K. Dewdney, *The New Turing Omnibus* (New York: Computer Science Press, 1993), chapter 3.

20. Though useful for illustration, this simple encoding is far from economical. In terms of economy something like Roger Penrose's contracted binary notation would be far preferable; see *The Emperor's New Mind* (New York: Oxford University Press, 1989), p. 42 ff.

21. Minsky, op. cit.

22. Minsky, op. cit.

23. As outlined in later sections, the difference in conclusions afforded by the two machines turns on the different 'backgrounds' that seem required in the setting of cellular automata. Because of the mechanism of an infinitely expandable loop, the common background for looped Turing machines will be cluttered from the very beginning. Because memory in a Minsky Register machine is handled only by two extendible registers, on the other hand, the

proof can function in this case without the assumption of a pre-existent infinite structural background. It is therefore easy to think of the Minsky Register machine as a finite configuration dropped in a uniform field of one single strategy. This affords a simpler phrasing of the basic undecidability at issue: Is there an algorithm that will tell us whether a finite configuration of strategies dropped in a uniform field will result in progressive conquest?

24. Elwyn R. Berlekamp, John H. Conway, and Richard K. Guy, *Winning Ways for your Mathematical Plays*, Vol. II (London: Academic Press, 1982).

25. Berlekamp, Conway, and Guy, op. cit., p. 847.

26. On some assumed enumeration.

27. The second type of machine envisaged will take an input in some way effectively divided between coding for a candidate machine *m* and coding for its candidate input *i*. Consider then a new machine, the front end of which takes a single initial input and first converts it to this encoding: the new machine's original input is first converted to coding for both *m* and *i*. From that stage on this new machine operates on its now-doubled input precisely as does the second machine above; we can in fact think of constructing the new machine by directly borrowing the wiring or state diagram of the second machine. The incorporated machine also has some way of indicating that machine *m* started on input *i* will not result in a signal, and we append a bit of machinery to send an impulse down a signal wire just in that case. Despite these relatively trivial additions, the new machine so envisaged is now precisely the first type of machine shown impossible above: for any input *x* it will signal just in case machine *x* started on input *x* will not. Since additions in the new machine are mechanically trivial the impossibility must lie with the machine incorporated at its heart: there can be no machine of the second sort either.

28. A. K. Dewdney, "The cellular automata programs that create wireworld, rugworld and other diversions," Computer Recreations, *Scientific American* 262 (1990), 146–149; Brian Silverman, *The Phantom Fish Tank: An Ecology of Mind* (Montreal: Logo Computer Systems, 1987).

29. This argument hasn't been phrased in terms of Minsky register machines, and so it is still tied to an assumed background constituting an infinite tape loop. The "wires" outlined for Minsky register machines below in fact require resources that go beyond those of Silverman's "wireworld", though it remains possible that there is also a Minsky form of the undecidability argument for at least some variation on Silverman's "wireworld".

30. Just as it is possible to work under a convention that Turing machines start always on a blank tape, in fact, it would be possible to work with Minsky register machines using a convention that registers always start with contents of zero.

31. No claim is made that this is the simplest competitive simulation possible for Minsky registers. Here we have tried for functional clarity rather a minimum numbers of strategies. Our suspicions are that with ingenuity significantly fewer strategies would suffice, though we don't see how these could be as few as the four adequate for the basic competitive wireworld outlined above.

32. We will refer to electron head-tail pairs the same way throughout—as **et**, say, regardless of the direction in which they are moving in a particular illustration. The same holds for more complicated quadruplets such as **e2mmm**, introduced below.

33. In Table 1 only the score for **bb** is changed from the list offered for the looped Turing machine above. That change gives strategy **m** an important sensitivity in the context of **b**, used in the basic mechanism of the memory core. It also calls for a slight change in the design of wire T-branchings, however, used for example in diodes: T-branchings in general are now

assumed to have a collar of strategy **d** (for "diode collar") similar to that shown below at the neck of the memory core. A revised diode is shown in figure 21. If one looks at **w, t, e,** and **d** in place of **w, t, e,** and **b,** on the other hand, relative scores can be thought of as carried over without any change at all.

34. A convention of two cells per unit proves convenient because of timing. The end of the memory core consists of a tip of strategy **m** that changes from one column to two every second generation, and a number of basic functions are accomplished by special electrons timed to meet that tip in either its single or double form. By using two units (or any even number) to represent each integer increase we avoid having to change timing for special electrons depending on the number stored in our memory register.

For purposes of exposition we tend to use the sixth cell to the right of the **c** collar as our zero-mark throughout and will add and subtract integers in terms of multiples of two units. Within a fully operating machine it might prove convenient to increase unit multiples still further or to use a zero-mark somewhat further to the right. Memory cores of slightly different lengths are used for purposes of illustration in the figures.

35. Not all frames are shown, of course; the attempt is merely to make the process of addition understandable. The first two frames are separated by 8 generations, the second and third by 3 generations, the third and fourth by 2 generations, with all others in one-generation sequence. It should also be noted that the length of the memory core is chosen here and in other figures merely for the sake of illustrative convenience; the process remains the same whatever is chosen as our 'zero mark'.

36. Here as in other figures an incomplete selection of frames is shown, intended merely to illustrate the general mechanisms of the process. The length of the memory core reflects only illustrative convenience as well.

37. The distance between these in figure 16 is chosen merely for purposes of illustration, as is the length of the memory core. In actual operation the machine may require a significantly greater length between them. Timing is crucial in terms of even and odd: even at greater distance there will be an odd number of cells between the electron heads, as shown, and an odd number of cells between them and the advancing head of the **e2mmm** trail in the memory core.

38. This is in fact the reason for using the special strategy **t3**.

39. The fact that these electrons also travel left from the upper junction causes a minor complication. For this reason we envision the feed wire from the **e2mmm** loop as long enough to contain a chain of oncoming **e2mmm**s. Moving to the left, an independent **et** eventually meets an oncoming **e2mmm** head-on in mutual annihilation. This means, however, that an **e2mmm** of the chain will not be present to mutually extinguish with its standardly synchronized nemesis from the standard **et** loop. In feeding in an independent **et** in the first place we thus arrange for a timed electron to cancel the next electron output from the **et** loop as well.

40. These electrons are thought of as originating from the wire south of junction x, with copies to the left eliminated by independent **et**s from the **e2mmm** region, controlled as outlined above.

41. These can be thought of as appended either to our original list of four strategies for looped Turing machines or to the slightly revised four of Table 1.

42. Berlekamp, Conway, and Guy, op. cit.

43. These strategies are of course not as simple as TFT or AllD, of course; that would be too much to expect. It is quite possible, however, that significantly simpler strategies than constructed here could be found with the same computational capabilities.

44. Were we to impose 'practical' finite limits on arrays, formal undecidability would be avoided. 'Practical undecidability,' in the form of unmanageable complexity, would remain. For finite arrays, given certain strategy assignments to n chosen cells, the question of whether a single strategy will prove triumphant appears to be exponential in n. If we cut the question further down to size, asking whether conquest will occur by a time limit which we carefully specify using some figure polynomial in n, our problem is still NP-complete. See Patrick Grim, "An NP-Complete Question Regarding the Spatialized Prisoner's Dilemma," research report #94-03, Group for Logic and Formal Semantics, Philosophy, SUNY at Stony Brook.

45. Within a repeated period of play it will not matter if the pattern for two strategies is for example

Player A: C D C D C D C D

Player B: C D C D C D D D

or

Player A: C C C C D D D D

Player B: C C C D D D D D

Scoring remains the same as long as the pairs played remain the same, regardless of their order.

46. If x is nonterminating we can set d at the place of any desired approximation.

47. For suppose any x and y, constructed from blocks of Ks, Ls, and Ms:

1 1...3 3...5 5...

K   L   M

1 1...3 3...0 0...

Is that the highest y possible for that x? No. For the sake of simplicity we consider the case of just one K:

1   3 3...5 5...

1   3 3...5 5...

We will get the same relative scores by tripling all units:

1 1 1   3 3 3 3 3 3...5 5 5 5 5 5...

1 1 1   3 3 3 3 3 3...5 5 5 5 5 5...

But now consider replacing the initial block of 3 Ks with the following:

5   5   3

M   M   L

0   0   3

This will give the same score for x over that initial subperiod, but a significantly higher score for y. Thus for our original x there will be a higher y. The argument can be repeated for any number of Ks, and thus for any x the highest y will include no Ks. Algebraically, using K, L, and M as the number of plays of each type in the established period, it is clear that

$$\frac{K + 3L + 5M}{K + L + M} < \frac{3(L + 1) + 5(M + K - 1)}{K + L + M}$$

will hold for K > 1/2, with the case of K = 0 trivial. Because series of play with the same proportions of K, L, and M will have the same average score, we can always ensure that K is a multiple of 3 convenient for replacement by two Ms and an L.

48. I am grateful to Steve Majewicz for assistance with the algebraic treatment in this section.—PG

AFTERWORD

1. Book VI, 509d–510b. Tr. by Paul Shorey.

Index

About the CD-ROM

The CD-ROM accompanying *The Philosophical Computer* can be used in two ways, either of which can be chosen from an early 'options' screen:

1. The full text version, containing the entire book section by section, including all color illustrations and animations.
2. Illustrations and animations only, to be used when desired while reading the book in hardcopy.

The CD-ROM also includes source code for explorations in each chapter, unprotected so as to facilitate further research.